# Financing Problems of Developing Countries

The two dramatic increases in the world price of oil during the 1970s have seriously worsened the economic prospects of many developing countries. They have done so both directly – by increasing import bills for oil – and indirectly – by slowing economic growth in the developed countries, and so reducing their imports from developing countries.

The newly industrializing countries did not find it too difficult to continue quite rapid development during the 1970s, not least because they were able to borrow oil money recycled by the big international banks. In the 1980s, the newly industrializing countries have found it more difficult to borrow, not least because many of them are now heavily in debt and some – like Mexico – have been in serious financial difficulty.

Against this background, the International Economic Association decided to organize a conference in Buenos Aires at which these issues could be considered. It was attended by leading authorities on the financing problems of developing countries, drawn from both the developing and the developed world.

A distinguished program committee organized the conference under the chairmanship of Armin Gutowski, who provides a valuable introduction to the volume, summarizing the conclusions of the conference.

Together with a summary record of the discussion of the conference, the fifteen papers provide a valuable background for all who wish to understand the difficulties being met at present in financing economic development in the Third World. It does so by summarizing and interpreting the empirical evidence; by providing analyses and models which throw new light on underlying structures, institutions and behavior; and by challenging the conventional wisdom. Hence, this volume identifies new policy options which can ease, if not remove, the current constraints on economic development in the Third World.

**Armin Gutowski** is Professor of Economics of the University of Hamburg and President of the Hamburg Institute for International Economics.

**A.A. Arnaúdo** is Professor of Economics at the Universidad Nacional de Córdoba, Argentina.

**Hans-Eckart Scharrer** is Director of International Finance at the Hamburg Institute for International Economics.

# Financing Problems of Developing Countries

Proceedings of a Conference held by the
International Economic Association in
Buenos Aires, Argentina

Edited by

Armin Gutowski

A.A. Arnaúdo

and

Hans-Eckart Scharrer

St. Martin's Press     New York

© International Economic Association 1985

All rights reserved. For information, write:
St. Martin's Press, Inc., 175 Fifth Avenue, New York, NY 10010
Printed in Great Britain
Published in the United Kingdom by The Macmillan Press Ltd.
First published in the United States of America in 1985

ISBN 0–312–28983–9

Library of Congress Cataloging in Publication Data

Main entry under title:

Financing problems of developing countries.

  Includes index.
  1. Finance—Developing countries—Congresses.
I. Gutowski, Armin.   II. Arnaúdo, Aldo A. (Aldo Antonio)
III. Scharrer, Hans-Eckart.   IV. International Economic
Association.
HG195.F54   1985        336'.09172'4        84–24830
ISBN 0–312–28983–9

# Contents

# Acknowledgements

In formulating the programme of the conference and in selecting potential authors and discussants, the authors benefited greatly from the advice of the members of the Programme Committee: Mahbub ul Haq of the World Bank; Ivan Ivanov of the Institute for World Economics in Moscow; Alexandre Lamfalussy of the Bank for International Settlements; Ronald I. McKinnon of Stanford University; Justinian F. Rweyemamu of the United Nations and Leopoldo Solis of the Banco de Mexico.

It is only fair to say that without the invitation and the strong support of the Asociación Argentina de Economia Politica and its president, Rolf R. Mantel, the conference would not have taken place at all. Luisa Montuschi not only drafted a first outline of the conference upon which the Programme Committee could draw, but she and Alfredo J. Canavese were also responsible for all the local arrangements. These ranged from fund-raising to making participants feel at home in Buenos Aires, duties which they fulfilled to the admiration of their collaborators abroad as well as of their guests. They had the generous logistic and financial support of the Central Bank of Argentina – in whose premises the conference was held – and of its staff. Financial assistance was also provided by the World Bank, UNESCO, the OPEC Fund and various national institutions. Our thanks, and the thanks of the International Economic Association go to them all.

The list of supporters deserving special gratitude would be incomplete without mentioning the IEA officers and staff. Victor L. Urquidi, the President of the IEA, was heavily involved in the preparation of the conference, suggesting potential authors and participants and raising international financial assistance. We owe much to his endeavours and advice. Luc Fauvel, the Secretary-General of the IEA and his experienced and diligent staff, especially Elisabeth Boucherant, handled complex organisational matters smoothly and efficiently. At the conference secretariat in Hamburg, Rosemari Hafkesbring and Margot Hansen had to carry out extra work besides their normal duties, and did so with skill and good humour.

Finally, we are greatly indebted to Sir Douglas Hague, the General Editor of the IEA, for his professional handling of the preparation of this volume. If, despite many difficulties and obstacles, it has finally been completed, this is mainly due to his insistence and involvement.

A.G.
A.A.
H.-E.S.

# List of Participants

Professor Robert Z. Aliber, Graduate School of Business, University of Chicago, USA

Professor Aldo Arnaúdo, Faculty of Economic Science, National University of Córdoba, Argentina

Professor David Backus, Department of Economics, Queen's University, Canada

Professor Silvio Borner, Institute for Current Economic Development, University of Basle, Switzerland

Dr Jitendra G. Borpujari, International Monetary Fund, Washington DC, USA

Professor Alfredo J. Canavese, Faculty of Economic Science, University of Buenos Aires, Argentina

Dr Francis X. Colaço, World Bank, Washington DC, USA

Dr Guillermo de la Dehesa, Bank of Spain, Madrid, Spain

Professor Victor Jorge Elias, Tucumán, Argentina

Dr Raid Fahmi, Industrial Bank of Kuwait, Kuwait

Dr Helmut Führer, OECD, Paris, France

Professor Ernesto Gaba, Buenos Aires, Argentina

Professor Armin Gutowski, HWWA–Institute for Economic Development, Hamburg, Germany

Mrs Chandra Hardy, Overseas Development Council, Washington DC, USA

Professor Alexandre Kafka, International Monetary Fund, Washington DC, USA

Dr Basant K. Kapur, Department of Economics and Statistics, National University of Singapore, Singapore

Professor Egon Kemenes, Institute for World Economics of the Hungarian Academy of Sciences, Budapest, Hungary

Professor Hector Heras Leon, National Association of Economists of Cuba, Havana, Cuba

Professor David Levine, University of California, Los Angeles, USA

Professor Herman Llosas, Buenos Aires, Argentina

Professor Rolf R. Mantel, Instituto Di Tella, Buenos Aires, Argentina

Dr Carlos Massad, Economic Commission for Latin America, Santiago, Chile

Professor Geoffrey Maynard, Chase Manhattan Bank, London, England

Professor Ronald I. McKinnon, Stanford University, California, USA

Professor Luisa Montuschi, University of Buenos Aires, Argentina

Dr Ajit Mozoomdar, World Bank, Washington DC, USA

Professor Walter T. Newlyn, Stratford-upon-Avon, England

Professor Josef Pajestka, Polish Economic Association, Warsaw, Poland

Professor Amalio H. Petrei, Fundacion Mediterranea, Córdoba, Argentina

Dr Policarpio Rodriguez, Central Bank of Venezuela, Caracas, Venezuela

Dr Justinian Rweyemamu, United Nations, New York, USA

Dr T.M. Rybczynski, Lazard Brothers & Co. Ltd., London, England

Dr Hans-Eckart Scharrer, HWWA–Institute for Economic Development, Hamburg, Germany

Professor Luigi Spaventa, Chamber of Deputies, Rome, Italy

Professor Mao-tung Teng, Anhui University, Hefei, China

Professor Niels Thygesen, University of Copenhagen, Denmark

Professor Siyanbola Tomori, University of Lagos, Nigeria

Professor Victor L. Urquidi, El Colegio de Mexico, Mexico City

# Introduction

**Armin Gutowski, A.A. Arnaúdo**
and
**Hans-Eckart Scharrer**

Financing problems of developing countries were the subject of an IEA round table conference held in October 1981 in Buenos Aires at the invitation of the Argentinian Association of Economists. This volume contains the papers prepared for the conference and a report on the discussion. The meeting was convened at a critical stage in world economic development: would the process of growth in the developing countries be able to maintain its momentum in the face of the second oil price shock; high and rising levels of external indebtedness; soaring real rates of interest; and a protracted recession in the industrialised countries?

After the first oil price increase, the highly liquid sectors of the international financial markets soon became the principal source of external finance, at least for the more advanced LDCs. Easy access to cheap bank loans and credits enabled these countries to decouple themselves from the sharp fall in the rate of real GDP growth encountered by the industrialised economies and to maintain the pace of their capital investment and development. By the early eighties, however, this policy was increasingly running into difficulty. Heavy borrowing abroad had sharply raised the level of foreign indebtedness of the LDCs in nominal terms. The appreciation of the dollar on foreign exchange markets meant an even bigger increase in this indebtedness in real terms. Finally, the surge in the (real) rate of interest compounded these factors by further increasing the burden of debt – and of debt-service payments – on the economies of the LDCs.

At the same time, recession in the industrialised world was triggered off by the second oil price increase and the sharp deceleration in the growth of the money stock in the USA, Europe and Japan. This led to a deterioration in the terms of trade of the non-oil LDCs, and also slowed the rate of expansion of their exports in real terms. The proceeds from these exports therefore fell short of the projections which underlay their ambitious investment and borrowing programmes. True, only part of the money they had raised abroad had been invested in productive assets. Some had gone into outright consumption, while part of capital spending also turned out to have been misdirected into non-productive uses. Indeed, it may well be correct to interpret the high rates of inflation which prevailed in most developing countries in the early 1980s as indicating significant internal misallocation of resources and persistent bottle–necks, as well as inconsistency between ex-ante saving and investment.

Against this background, we felt that the conference should not confine itself merely to considering aspects of the external and international financing of development, topical though these issues are. Rather, it should give equal attention to problems of domestic monetary management, all the more since the net flow of financial resources to the developing world might well taper off in the future. This view was shared by the president of the International Economic Association, Victor L. Urquidi, himself a distinguished expert in the economics of development, and by the programme committee set up for this conference. As a result, the conference was organised in two parts – though these were highly interrelated. It focused on both domestic and international aspects of the financing of development. At the same time, we felt that an interdisciplinary approach to the subject was required. We needed to bring together the different expert knowledge of the theoretical economist, the empirical researcher, the bank economist and of the government (and international organisation) official. The composition of the conference in terms both of participant and of papers selected reflects these considerations.

The opening paper by Francis X. Colaço on 'Capital Requirements in Economic Development: The Decade Ahead' is designed to put the other papers and discussions into an overall empirical and future-oriented perspective. Starting from the financing and adjustment experience of the seventies, it forecasts the capital requirements of LDCs, the prospects of their being met and the methods by which this might be achieved. It does so under two broad sets of assumptions: those of a high-growth and of a low-growth scenario for the world economy. Stressing the strong interdependence between the real and the financial sides of the international economy, the author demonstrates some crucial conditions for the continued progress of developing countries. This crucially depends on their access to both the product and the financial markets (including official development assistance) of industrialised countries.

Part Two of this volume deals with domestic aspects of the financing of developing countries. It is introduced by a paper on 'The Role and Pattern of Domestic Financing in the Process of Economic Development: Empirical Evidence', by Egon Kemenes. The author shows that in the early stages of development (i.e. for low-income countries) agriculture has generally played a decisive role in generating the resources required for economic growth. Only at a later stage do developing countries become truly monetised so that financial instruments such as (money) taxes and credits become important. In Kemenes' view, the government sector has an important part to play in mobilising and allocating financial – and consequently also real – resources for development. The case of the low-income countries is taken up again in the subsequent theoretical paper, by Jitendra G. Borpujari, on 'Savings Generation and Financial Programming in a Basic Need Constrained Developing Economy'. Borpujari starts from a Kaleckian type of model of balanced development in a two-sector economy producing 'basic' ('agricultural') and 'development' ('investment') goods. He shows that, under certain assumptions, the growth in the output of basic goods also sets a limit to financially balanced development: an economy subject to such a basic needs constraint 'cannot accelerate its development without running into domestic inflationary pressures or an external payments deficit. In other words, the acceleration of development without financial imbalances in a basic need constrained economy presupposes an appropriate rise in the supply of basics. This can come through increased domestic productivity and the production of basics; improvements in the external terms of trade; or a greater availability of external finance'. Financial imbalances are thus the consequence of real imbalances.

The issue of financial programming is also addressed, from an instrumental angle, in the paper of David Backus *et al.* on 'The Financial Sector in the Planning of Economic Development'. The authors present a one-period, general equilibrium model of the Mexican economy with sixteen intermediate goods, fifteen final goods and four factors of production. The model is an improved version of one constructed by Jaime Serra-Puche, with money added as a transactions medium. It is designed *inter alia* to trace the differential effects of changes in monetary policy between sectors, an exercise which the authors were, however, not yet in a position to undertake.

The two following papers deal with more specific institutional aspects of financial and monetary management. 'The Role of the Public Sector in the Mobilisation of Financial Resources' is the subject of a paper by W.T. Newlyn. The author starts from the assumption that the government of a developing country seeks to maximise the availability of financial resources to its public sector subject to constraints, in accordance with some social objective function. He then examines, in particular, empirical evidence about the impact of monetary financing and taxation on the pace of economic development. While generally sympathetic to the view that inflation may be conducive to investment and growth, the author emphasises the impact of the external constraint, which may well make an inflation-oriented development strategy self-defeating. As regards taxation, he comes to the conclusion that raising tax rates may stimulate rather than depress private investment, through the incentives which are generated by increased government investment in the infrastructure.

Basant A. Kapur subjects 'The Role of Financial Institutions in Economic Development' to 'a theoretical analysis'. He constructs a two-sector growth model of a financially repressed developing country with a privileged sector enjoying 'liberal' access to highly subsidised bank credit and another sector representing the rest of the economy. Kapur then inquires how changes in monetary policy affect the inter-sectoral allocation of resources and the relative price structure within an economy and its rate of growth. The model 'provides strong support for policies designed to ameliorate financial dualism'.

The theme of financial repression is further pursued in the last paper of the second part. Alfredo J. Canavese and Luisa Montuschi address the issue of 'Inflation and the Financing of Alternative Development Strategies' on the basis of Argentinian experience in the post-war period. They show the effects of the inward-looking import substitution policy adopted by the Argentinian authorities since the late 1940s, coupled as it was with a highly protectionist approach to trade, exchange controls, discriminatory credit and price policies in favour of industry and negative real interest rates. This policy not only failed to bring about the desired results in terms of growth, but also led to: a misallocation of (scarce) financial and real resources, a fragmentation of financial markets, a redistribution of income from lenders to borrowers and high rates of inflation. Ronald

I. McKinnon (in Part Three, Chapter 10) discusses in more theoretical terms 'How to Manage a Repressed Economy'. He starts from the observation that repression of foreign trade and of the domestic financial system is commonplace in developing countries and that LDCs generally rely heavily on fiscal deficits financed by the Central Bank. He goes on to enquire into the 'optimal' policy mix between a (given) fiscal deficit, exchange controls, interest ceilings and reserve requirements. Such a mix must be consistent with an acceptable rate of price inflation, maintaining the competitiveness of the export sector and avoiding 'more-than-necessary' crowding out of the private capital market. This is clearly a second-best approach. However, McKinnon points out that it may be politically more realistic to think in terms of a 'steady state of financial repression' rather than of a transition to a more liberalised state. Premature liberalisation may indeed be disastrous – as the example of Argentina demonstrates – if governments prove unable to control the fiscal deficit effectively.

Part Three discusses problems of the foreign and international financing of development. The first paper of this section, by Helmut Führer, is intended to provide a broad quantitative picture of recent trends in 'The Flow of Public and Private Financial Resources to Developing Countries'. The author looks at the overall size as well as the structure of such flows. He voices particular concern over the increase in interest rates and the outlook for official development assistance. Moreover, he emphasises the need for a two-track strategy which, besides providing finance for development, would keep the markets of OECD economies open to the exports of developing countries.

The next two papers deal with the specific sources of finance. T.M. Rybczynski enquires into 'The Role of International Financial Markets in the Financing of Development', starting from a quantitative assessment of the growth of international credit and capital markets and of their role in balance-of-payments financing since 1970. He next analyses the changes in the pattern of world savings and investment associated with the emergence of OPEC. Then he deals with the observed and potential contribution of private capital flows to the financing of 'structural' external deficits and asks whether these flows are likely to be sustainable: obviously, the assessment of creditworthiness is here of overriding significance. The role of 'oil surplus funds' in the financing of development, and more particularly 'the impact of the mode of placement' is further developed in Hazem El Beblawi's paper. Using a Keynesian approach, the author considers possible effects of the increase in OPEC savings, as expressed by the financial (and current account) surplus. Will it *ex post* be matched by an increase in the real rate of investment in the world ('investment case'); by dissaving in the rest of the world ('distribution of wealth case'); or by a purely nominal increase in investment, i.e., by inflation ('placement case')? In his view, the 'placement case' applies. He believes this outcome to be related to the fact that the OPEC surpluses are placed in OECD countries, rather than invested in LDCs. Given that the oil producing countries aim at preserving the real value of their assets, the author therefore recommends that OPEC funds should be channelled directly to developing countries under a new, global 'Marshall Plan'.

The three papers which follow address issues relating to interdependence between external financing and domestic economic management. Robert Z. Aliber in his paper, 'External Financing and the Level of Development: A Conceptual Approach', develops the similarities between the development of domestic financial structures when per capita income increases: and changes in the size and financing of the current-account deficits of individual LDCs. He begins by discussing the economic consequences of distortions within domestic financial markets as well as distortions on the boundaries between domestic and external markets, and looks at possible causes of these distortions. Subsequently, he develops a typology for relating changes in the size and financing patterns of the current-account deficits of individual developing countries to the 'levels' of per capita income. The author detects a parallelism between patterns of domestic and international financial development.

'Foreign Indebtedness and Economic Growth: Is there a Limit to Foreign Financing?' is the subject of a paper by Armin Gutowski. Extending the neo-classical approach, he introduces two types of capital which together make up the total capital stock. These are: imported capital goods, and real capital produced by indigenous physical resources (labour and capital). Countries should borrow abroad until the marginal rate of return on both types is equal to the rate of interest prevailing in the international capital market. This relationship holds whether or not the country invests in the tradeable or the non-tradeable goods sector. The relationship also holds whether or not the increase in GDP generated by the primary investment stems from: increased production of export goods; import-substituting production; or (secondary) capital formation. By improving the quality of domestic factors of production, the rate of return on capital from domestic resources may be raised and the limits to borrowing expanded.

Alexandre Kafka, in his paper on 'Exchange Rate Policy, International Capital Movements and the Financing of Development', draws attention to a number of other points which appear interesting from a policy point of view. After investigating the relationship between exchange-rate changes and capital movements in the short term, he focuses mainly on the association of observed examples of exchange-rate overvaluation of LDC currencies with capital inflows. He finds that the combination of discriminatory trade barriers favouring the import of capital goods, and overvalued exchange rates is likely to have induced trade-related capital imports. This is all the more probable since investments in real capital could be expected to yield particularly high returns. He questions, however, whether this policy-mix is sustainable, given that it will cause distortions in allocation – a point referred to already by Canavese and Montuschi in their case study of Argentina.

The concluding paper by Niels Thygesen on 'New Approaches to Development Finance: A Critical Look at the Brandt Proposals' reviews current trends in international money and finance in the light of the recommendations made by the Brandt Commission in late 1979. So far as the international monetary system is concerned, the author shows that apart from the sharp rise in the rate of real interest in international markets, developments have not been too unfavourable to the LDCs. On the other hand, the Commission's recommendations on resource transfers are found to be of little relevance to increasing the flow of financial and real resources to developing countries. Indeed, Thygesen believes that international markets perform better than they are judged to do by the Brandt Commission – views that were expectedly challenged by some of the discussants.

# Part One
# The 1980s

# 1 Capital Requirements in Economic Development: The Decade Ahead

**Francis X. Colaço***

WORLD BANK, WASHINGTON DC, USA

## I INTRODUCTION

The decade of the 1970s saw major external shocks to the economies of developing countries. Oil prices increased almost threefold in real terms in 1973–4, this was followed by a 9 per cent decline in real terms in 1975–8, and an increase of over 80 per cent in 1979–80. These events in energy markets were accompanied by a marked slowing-down of the rate of growth of industrial countries – a process which had started already in 1970–71. The growth rate of industrial countries averaged 3.3 per cent a year in the 1970s, down from over 5 per cent in the 1960s; there were major variations in annual growth rates both among countries in the group and for the group as a whole. Furthermore, there was a marked acceleration in inflation in industrial countries and it became common to talk about 'double-digit' inflation, as well as about 'stagflation'.

The international financial system (the so-called Bretton Woods System) which had characterised the post-war era began to unravel in

*The views and interpretations in this paper are those of the author and should not be attributed to the World Bank, to its affiliated organisations, or to any individual acting on their behalf. The author gratefully acknowledges comments received from Helen Hughes and D. Joseph Wood.

3

1971 and 1972 with the breaking of the link between the exchange value of the US dollar and gold. By 1973, a system of floating exchange rates was in place. Oil price increases, combined with different policy responses and growth performance of individual industrial countries, accentuated instabilities in international financial markets. The income transfers occasioned by the oil price increases of 1973–4 resulted in an expansion of liquidity in international capital markets since the major recipients of these transfers had limited capacities to expand expenditures in the short term.[1] However, the period also witnessed large imbalances on current account among industrialised countries; the USA experienced substantial deficits of about $11bn a year in 1977–8, while Germany and Japan together had surpluses of some $25bn on average in those two years. This balance-of-payments pattern, combined with marked differences in inflation rates, led to instabilities in exchange markets. High inflation rates translated themselves into high nominal interest rates, as increasing portions of loans from financial market institutions were at variable interest rates.

Section II briefly examines the impact of these changes in the international economic environment on developing countries, as well as the role which external financing played in the adjustment process in the 1970s. This is a preamble to a discussion in Section III of two broad scenarios for the 1980s which contain projections of capital requirements, and (in Sections IV and V) of the role to be played by external finance.

## II ECONOMIC ADJUSTMENTS AND EXTERNAL FINANCE IN THE 1970S

How did developing countries, in particular those which were net importers of energy, fare in the mid-1970s, in the face of these major developments in the world economy? There was a marked improvement in the external accounts of oil-exporting developing countries;[2] their current accounts which were in substantial deficit in 1965 and 1970 (3.3 per cent and 2.1 per cent of GDP respectively) were in approximate balance in 1976.

The oil importers among the developing countries (and all other countries that were net importers of oil) experienced major deteriorations in their terms of trade. These were proximately reflected in significantly expanded current account deficits – deficits equivalent to

2.8 per cent and 2.4 per cent of GDP respectively in 1965 and 1970, had increased to 5.1 per cent in 1975. Deficits at such high levels are not considered sustainable over a number of years, in the sense that financing cannot be expected to be available in required volumes, and/or that if financing were available, it would tend to lead to future debt servicing difficulties.

Developing countries were, accordingly, required to undertake measures which would reduce their current account deficits to more sustainable levels. In essence, these measures had to be designed to absorb an effective reduction in real income – since a terms of trade deterioration implies a transfer of real income – within a reasonable time span. At the same time, they needed to maintain longer-term economic development objectives. In general terms, the measures available either produced an expansion of exports or a reduction in imports. Measures which led to a reduction in the level of expenditures and/or (at a given level of expenditures) caused a switching of expenditures away from tradable goods, could accomplish these objectives.[3]

A country's ability to expand exports depends on the general level of economic activity in the world economy and on the price competitiveness of the commodities which it exports. Developing countries which are exporters of manufactured goods can, even within a given level of world economic activity, expand their exports by appropriate adjustments in exchange rates[4] and by appropriate policies which generate supplies of export goods. In the case of countries which are exporters of primary products, the demand and supply of which tend to be relatively price inelastic, the possibilities for expanding exports in the short run are more limited. In the longer run, changes in demand policies and exchange rates could be designed to diversify the export base and to provide additional degrees of freedom for action.

The expenditure-reduction and expenditure-switching measures which are designed to reduce imports, must be carefully constructed if they are not to have detrimental effects on longer-term economic growth. In general terms, imports of essential consumer and investment goods must be maintained. Policies should thus be designed to reduce imports of non-essential consumer goods (in particular, luxury consumer goods), to conserve on the use and/or expand the supply of commodities whose relative prices have increased (for example, energy), and to substitute domestic production for imports to the extent that this is economically justified. The adjustment process requires that there shall be increased efficiency in the use of resources.

The capacity of individual countries to undertake these measures, and the time spans within which they can be undertaken, is variable.

External financing[5] provides a mechanism for adapting the time-phasing of the absorption of the real income loss to the economic and socio-political constraints of the country in question. If external financing is used to maintain investment levels on economically justified projects, which also generate export earnings, future economic growth is assured. So is the ability to meet required debt servicing obligations arising from the borrowings (Kruger, 1980). If, on the other hand, foreign borrowings are used to finance consumption (even if it is consumption of essential commodities such as food), then, unless the financing is on highly concessional terms, further strains on the balance of payments in future can be expected. The possibilities for adjustment vary with the level of a country's economic development. The dilemma for low income countries[6] is that, in general, the possibilities for compressing imports are limited when there is a substantial terms of trade deterioration. Additional external finance, which must necessarily be on concessional terms, is designed to maintain essential imports and to avoid jeopardising longer-term growth. If required amounts of financing on appropriate terms are not available, there are serious consequences both for growth in the near-term and for longer-term economic development.

Developing countries undertook a wide range of measures to adjust to the adverse events of the 1970s, and the results achieved by individual countries varied accordingly.[7] For oil importers as a group, although there were major differences by country and region, two important outcomes are worth noting. The first was a major reduction in growth rates of oil importers below the levels attained in the 1960s – with an average of 5.7 per cent a year in the 1960s and 5.1 per cent in the 1970s.[8] The reduction was not, however, as large as most analysts would have anticipated and this overall result disguises two separate trends. Major groups of middle-income oil importers (those in East Asia and the Pacific, Latin America and the Caribbean, and the Middle East and North Africa) saw an acceleration in their growth rates in the 1970s from the levels of the 1960s. The low-income oil importers of Africa and Asia experienced growth rates in the 1970s which were between 1.0 and 1.6 percentage points below those attained in the 1960s. As a consequence, there was almost no improvement in average living standards (measured by GDP per person) in the low-income oil-importing countries of sub-Saharan Africa. In addition, of course, the low-income countries fell even further behind, in relation not only to industrial countries but to other developing countries as well.

A second result was the fairly rapid return to earlier levels of current account deficit as a proportion of GDP (Table 1.1). From a high of 5.1 per cent of GDP in 1975, the combined current account deficit of oil importers had declined in 1977 and 1978 to about 2.3 per cent of GDP – a level similar to that of 1970. Among the middle-income countries, there was an improvement in the balance-of-payments position in almost all regions. Among the low-income countries, there was a dramatic improvement in India's external accounts which went into surplus as a result of a combination of reduced food imports (on the heels of good harvests) and major inflows of workers' remittances. On the other hand, many other low-income countries found themselves in increasingly difficult balance of payments situations.

The discussion of adjustment mechanisms above can be used to elucidate the reasons for the differences in outcomes for different groups of countries. The discussion is necessarily broad-brush, and does not deal with some interesting aspects of the domestic policies, pursued by individual countries, in seeking to absorb the effects of terms-of-trade deterioration while minimising its impact on economic growth. A loss in real income, as indicated earlier, requires that the growth of consumption be controlled. Between 1970 and 1978 there was, in fact, an increase in the savings ratio (gross domestic savings as a proportion of GDP) of all oil importers. The ratio stood at 16 per cent in 1970, and 19 per cent in 1975 and had increased to 21 per cent in 1978. The investment ratio[9] stabilised at between 23 and 24 per cent of GDP. Domestic savings in 1975–8 covered about 85 per cent of gross investment on average; the remainder was contributed by external resources.

A second set of factors which affect the adjustment process is related to foreign trade. Three general points deserve mention here. First, primary commodity prices were at high levels in 1973 and 1974 and this provided some countries with a cushion to absorb the combined shocks of petroleum price increases and recession in industrialised countries in 1974 and 1975; the relative decline in petroleum prices between 1975 and 1978 also facilitated adjustment. Second, favourable weather conditions, combined with higher food crop productivity, reduced the needs for cereals imports by Asian countries, and provided them with an additional buffer against adverse developments in the world economy. Price increases to

TABLE 1.1   RATIOS OF CURRENT ACCOUNT BALANCES[a] TO GDP FOR GROUPS OF COUNTRIES, 1965-80

*(percentages at current prices)*

| Regions | 1965 | 1970 | 1975 | 1976 | 1977 | 1978 | 1980 |
|---|---|---|---|---|---|---|---|
| Oil importers | -2.8 | -2.4 | -5.1 | -3.2 | -2.4 | -2.3 | -4.9 |
| Low-income countries | -1.9 | -1.9 | -3.9 | -1.6 | -1.0 | -2.7 | -4.6 |
| sub-Saharan Africa | -1.5 | -4.1 | -12.4 | -8.7 | -6.4 | -10.3 | -10.2 |
| Asia | -1.9 | -1.5 | -2.2 | -0.1 | -0.2 | -0.8 | -3.2 |
| Middle-income countries | -3.2 | -2.6 | -5.4 | -3.5 | -2.7 | -2.3 | -5.0 |
| sub-Saharan Africa | -0.1 | -4.2 | -7.0 | -4.7 | -1.2 | -1.6 | -0.8 |
| East Asia and Pacific | -15.3 | -4.8 | -5.2 | -1.4 | -0.8 | -2.5 | -7.1 |
| Latin America and Caribbean | -3.8 | -2.3 | -5.2 | -2.9 | -2.2 | -2.7 | -5.5 |
| Middle East and North Africa | 1.3 | -3.7 | -6.2 | -9.4 | -12.6 | -9.6 | -14.7 |
| Southern Europe | — | -1.3 | -5.2 | -4.4 | -4.0 | -1.3 | -3.8 |
| Oil exporters | -3.3 | -2.1 | -0.9 | -0.1 | -1.5 | -4.3 | -0.2 |
| All developing countries | -2.9 | -2.4 | -3.9 | -2.3 | -2.2 | -2.9 | -3.5 |

[a] Current account balances excluding official transfers.

*Source*: World Bank, *World Development Report, 1981*.

consumers, and rationing, also served to keep demand both for energy and for imports from increasing as rapidly as would otherwise have been the case. Finally, the continuing rapid growth of exports of manufactures even from middle-income countries, combined with increases in export prices, permitted the maintenance of high levels of economic activity. But, for most of the low-income oil importers, particularly those in Africa, the downward trend in primary prices combined with poor performance by their agricultural sectors, resulted in their increasing vulnerability to external shocks.

Some fortuitous factors – including good weather and declines in oil prices in real terms – thus permitted some oil importers to weather the storms in the international economy, and to emerge in better shape than would otherwise have been the case. Despite this, the costs of adjustment are clear: oil importers as a group experienced a significant reduction in potential growth rates; perhaps even more important, there were severe adverse effects on countries with the lowest levels of income per person.

The outcomes for low-income oil importers would have been much worse had there not been a remarkable response by the international community to their difficulties. There was, for example, a quadrupling in concessional financing from industrial and OPEC countries between 1970 and 1975. Loans from multilateral institutions increased fourfold. The rapid expansion of economic activity in OPEC countries, led to attendant increases in the demand for labour. This resulted in some low-income countries (including those in the Asian subcontinent), receiving large inflows in the form of workers' remittances. As can be seen in Table 1.2, there was both a large increase in the availability of finance to low-income oil importers and an increase in the grant component of income flows. The latter was reflected in the increase in non-debt creating flows (largely official transfers) from 29 per cent of the total in 1970 to 39 per cent in 1975. For these countries, with the exception of India for the reasons discussed earlier, the availability of extra finance permitted the maintenance of imports. After 1975, however, the net capital receipts of these countries did not increase in real terms.

Middle-income oil importers, as is now well documented, had available to them financial flows from private sources in unprecedented amounts. Interest rates were at best only slightly positive in real terms, though an increasing proportion of the loans made was at variable interest rates and maturities steadily lengthened until 1978. Net borrowings by these countries from private financial institutions

TABLE 1.2   OIL-IMPORTING DEVELOPING COUNTRIES: FINANCING OF CURRENT ACCOUNT DEFICITS AND RESERVE ACCUMULATIONS, 1970–80

| *All oil importers* | 1970 | 1975 | 1976 | 1977 | 1978 | 1979 | 1980 |
|---|---|---|---|---|---|---|---|
| | | | | *(US$ millions)* | | | |
| Current account deficit | 8 636 | 38 645 | 26 756 | 25 948 | 25 503 | 44 267 | 69 642 |
| Increase in official reserves | 2 507 | −4 341 | 7 748 | 10 328 | 18 270 | 10 421 | −6 831 |
| Total | 11 143 | 34 304 | 34 504 | 33 276 | 43 773 | 54 688 | 62 811 |
| Financed by | | | | | | | |
| Nondebt-creating flows, net[a] | 2 748 | 7 151 | 7 618 | 8 509 | 9 901 | 14 034 | 13 940 |
| Long-term capital from official sources, net | 3 053 | 8 078 | 8 451 | 8 064 | 10 437 | 11 687 | 13 913 |
| Long-term capital from private sources, net | 3 382 | 14 102 | 17 477 | 18 759 | 26 355 | 26 670 | 27 511 |
| Other capital flows, net | 1 961 | 4 974 | 958 | −2 057 | −2 920 | 2 297 | 7 447 |
| *Distribution of financing flows* | | | | *(per cent)* | | | |
| Nondebt-creating flows, net[a] | 24.6 | 20.8 | 22.1 | 25.6 | 22.6 | 25.6 | 22.2 |
| Official long-term capital, net | 27.4 | 23.5 | 24.5 | 24.2 | 23.8 | 21.4 | 22.2 |
| Private long-term capital, net | 30.4 | 41.2 | 50.7 | 56.4 | 60.2 | 48.8 | 43.8 |
| Other financing flows, net | 17.6 | 14.5 | 2.7 | −6.2 | −6.6 | 4.2 | 11.8 |
| *Low-income oil importers* | | | | *(US$ millions)* | | | |
| Current account deficit | 1 675 | 5 443 | 2 355 | 1 604 | 5 113 | 7 180 | 10 898 |
| Increase in official reserves | 268 | −548 | 2 145 | 3 577 | 1 496 | 642 | −1 825 |
| Total | 1 943 | 4 895 | 4 500 | 5 181 | 6 609 | 7 822 | 9 073 |
| Financed by | | | | | | | |
| Nondebt-creating flows, net[a] | 571 | 1 913 | 1 786 | 2 076 | 2 298 | 3 081 | 3 071 |
| Long-term capital from official sources, net | 1 244 | 3 711 | 3 157 | 2 778 | 3 282 | 3 405 | 4 394 |

| | | | | | | | |
|---|---|---|---|---|---|---|---|
| Long-term capital from private sources, net | −349 | 367 | 405 | 524 | 630 | 513 | 506 |
| Other capital flows net | 478 | −1 096 | −849 | −197 | 400 | 823 | 1 103 |
| *Distribution of financing flows* (per cent) | | | | | | | |
| Nondebt-creating flows, net[a] | 29.4 | 39.1 | 39.7 | 40.1 | 34.8 | 39.4 | 33.8 |
| Official long-term capital, net | 64.0 | 75.8 | 70.2 | 53.6 | 49.6 | 43.5 | 48.4 |
| Private long-term capital, net | −18.0 | 7.5 | 8.9 | 10.1 | 9.5 | 6.6 | 5.6 |
| Other financing flows, net | 24.6 | −22.4 | −18.9 | −3.8 | 6.1 | 10.5 | 12.2 |
| *Middle-income oil importers* (US$ millions) | | | | | | | |
| Current account deficit | 6 961 | 33 203 | 24 401 | 21 344 | 20 390 | 37 087 | 58 744 |
| Increase in official reserves | 2 240 | −3 793 | 5 603 | 6 750 | 16 774 | 9 779 | −5 006 |
| Total | 9 201 | 29 410 | 30 004 | 28 094 | 37 164 | 46 866 | 53 738 |
| Financed by | | | | | | | |
| Nondebt-creating flows, net[a] | 2 177 | 5 237 | 5 832 | 6 433 | 7 605 | 10 953 | 10 869 |
| Long-term capital from official sources, net | 1 809 | 4 367 | 5 294 | 5 286 | 7 155 | 8 282 | 9 521 |
| Long-term capital from private sources, net | 3 339 | 13 734 | 17 072 | 18 235 | 25 725 | 26 158 | 27 005 |
| Other capital flows, net | 1 876 | 6 070 | 1 807 | −1 860 | −3 320 | 1 473 | 6 345 |
| *Distribution of financial flows* (per cent) | | | | | | | |
| Nondebt-creating flows, net[a] | 23.7 | 17.8 | 19.4 | 22.9 | 20.5 | 23.4 | 20.2 |
| Long-term capital from official sources, net | 19.7 | 14.8 | 17.6 | 18.8 | 19.2 | 17.7 | 17.7 |
| Long-term capital from private sources, net | 36.3 | 46.7 | 56.9 | 64.9 | 69.2 | 55.8 | 50.3 |
| Other capital flows, net | 20.3 | 20.6 | 6.0 | −6.6 | −8.9 | 3.1 | 11.8 |

[a] Official transfers, net direct investment flows, and valuation adjustments.

*Source:* World Bank data base.

increased from $2.9bn in 1970 to $24.1bn in 1978 – an annual average rate of increase of over 30 per cent. The largest borrowers were Mexico, Venezuela and Algeria (all oil exporters); as well as Argentina, Brazil, Spain, Yugoslavia and South Korea among the middle-income oil importers. These eight countries accounted for 60 per cent of commercial bank debt outstanding in 1979.

The financing of these large deficits, resulted in a fivefold expansion of the outstanding debt of the oil importers as a group from $48bn in 1970 to $226bn in 1978; and for all developing countries from $68bn in 1970 to $252bn in 1978.[10] Debt service payments (principal repayments plus interest), as a proportion of the exports of goods and services of all oil importers, increased from 6.6 per cent in 1970 to 14.8 per cent in 1978; for all developing countries, the ratio increased from 8.9 per cent in 1970 to 12.4 per cent in 1978. Thirteen borrowers[11] accounted for 62 per cent of total debt and for 65 per cent of debt service in 1979. By 1978, there were eight countries – Ivory Coast, Zambia, Morocco, Philippines, Chile, Peru, Argentina and Brazil – with debt service payments in excess of 20 per cent of their total export earnings.[12] Although it is generally agreed that there is no particular level of debt-service ratio which necessarily indicates that a country will experience debt servicing difficulties, a rapidly rising ratio together with a structure of debt which leads to lumpiness in interest service and repayments, requires that a country and its creditors should pay particular attention to management of its external accounts. This was the case for some of the major borrowers.

The structure of the outstanding debt of the different groups of countries reflects the sources of finance. In the case of the low-income oil importers, about 90 per cent of debt is held by official lenders; conversely, over 70 per cent of the debt of middle-income oil importers is accounted for by private lenders. The high nominal interest rates that have prevailed in international capital markets in recent years are reflected in the increasing proportion of total debt service payments represented by interest payments. Interest payments as a percentage of exports of goods and services (the interest–service ratio) for all oil importers more than doubled – from 2.2 per cent in 1970 to 4.7 per cent in 1978; the rate of increase was even more rapid in the case of middle-income countries, where the ratio increased from 1.8 per cent in 1970 to 4.8 per cent in 1978.[13] In part as a result, debt service payments as a proportion of the GNP of all oil importers increased from 1.2 per cent in 1970 to 3.4 per cent in 1978.

The decade of the 1970s ended for the developing countries with a second set of major shocks from the international economic environment. Oil prices rose by more than 80 per cent in real terms in 1979–80. Although, smaller in percentage terms than the increase in 1973–4, payments for oil imports represented about 25 per cent of developing countries' import bills. The increase in oil prices, and the accompanying slow-down in economic activity in industrial countries in 1979–80, has again put a major strain on the external accounts of oil-importing developing countries. The total current account deficits of the oil importers reached \$70bn in 1980, representing 4.9 per cent of their combined GDP (Table 1.1). The magnitude of the external payments' difficulties was, therefore, similar to that experienced by oil importers in 1975. Unfortunately, this time round, the prompt and concerted response of the international community, which characterised 1975, is not much in evidence. At least in the short term, therefore, the process of adjustment both for low-income oil importers, and for the middle-income countries which had not quite absorbed the effects of the earlier shocks, promises to be arduous.

## III  THE 1980s: ANOTHER PERIOD OF ADJUSTMENT

Projections of capital requirements in the 1980s have to proceed from a specification of policy behaviour in various groups of countries – industrial, centrally planned, capital-surplus oil exporters,[14] and developing countries – and from the implications of these for changes in the international economic environment. There are at present considerable uncertainties about the effectiveness of policies in major industrial countries in dealing with the problems of slow economic growth, high unemployment and high inflation. Tight monetary policies, particularly in the United States, designed to deal with inflation have provoked major increases in domestic interest rates and these have been translated into markedly higher borrowing costs in international capital markets. High borrowing costs have aggravated the financing problems currently being faced by oil-importing developing countries.

In addition, current projections indicate that the growth rate of industrial countries in 1981 cannot be much higher than that attained in 1980 – a year of very slow growth. Further, although an economic recovery is projected for 1982, on current estimates it is unlikely to attain even the 3.3 per cent average growth rates of the 1970s. This slow economic growth of the major export markets for developing countries is likely to complicate the adjustment process. There is however, one positive element in the short-term outlook. The softening of the market for oil has meant that oil prices have declined in real terms.

This short-term view has been incorporated in two broad scenarios developed for the 1980s.[15] Both are based on assumptions about domestic policies and about performance in individual countries. The High Case scenario assumes that macroeconomic, and critical microeconomic policies – in both industrial and developing economies – will deal effectively with the present difficulties and that, in the second half of the 1980s, the longer-term trends in the post-war world economy will be resumed, albeit with some adjustments. In such an environment there would be possibilities for the expansion of exports from developing countries to industrial country markets, as well as for expansion of trade among developing countries. In short, latent protectionist pressures in industrial countries would continue to be held at bay, and there could be reductions in barriers to trade among developing countries. Access by middle-income developing countries to international capital markets would continue, and concessional financing would increasingly be channelled to lower-income developing countries. A combination of continuing improvements in domestic-savings performance with increases in external finance, which would vary among countries, would provide the resources required to undertake the investments required in energy production and to adjust the pattern of production to changed international factor prices.

The Low Case assumes that industrial–country policies will not be successful in dealing with present economic problems, and that industrial–country growth will be much slower than even that achieved in the 1970s. Protectionist pressures, particularly against manufactured exports from developing countries, could be expected to become accentuated, with consequent adverse consequences for exports from middle-income developing countries. Slow export growth would make more difficult the management of the external accounts, and so constrain borrowings by developing countries from market sources. As a consequence of the continuing economic difficulties of industrial countries, low-income countries would see declines in the volume of concessional financing available to them.

## 1 GLOBAL ANALYTICAL FRAMEWORK

These two scenarios are articulated through the uses of a global analytical framework. (For a more detailed description, see Cheetham, Gupta and Schwartz, 1979.) The framework is used, in particular, to study the economic growth prospects and capital requirements of developing countries in the 1980s. It consists of three principal modules: (a) fifteen 'regional' models which describe economic activity in groups of developing countries, and projections of the principal macro-economic variables for the industrial, centrally planned, and capital-surplus oil-exporting countries; (b) a module describing volumes, prices, and patterns of international trade; (c) a module for projections of the balance of payments and of debt which includes both the global supply and allocation of different forms of capital by region, and the terms on which such flows are projected to be available.

In parallel with the global analysis, projections are also undertaken of the growth and balance-of-payments prospects of about forty major developing countries. These country projections are based on the same sets of assumptions (discussed below) of the evolution of the international environment and serve as a check on the domestic-resource mobilisation and allocation possibilities. There are several iterations in the process. The major merit of the system is that it provides a globally consistent framework.

The development of the projections starts from a set of exogenous assumptions on: the GDP growth rates of industrial countries; an index denoting trends in international inflation; and petroleum price increases, in real terms. The High Case assumes that GDP growth rates of industrial countries will average 3.3 per cent in 1980–5 and 4.0 per cent in 1985–90, to give an average in the 1980s of 3.7 per cent. The Low Case assumes a 2.6 per cent growth rate in 1980–5 and 3.0 per cent in 1985–90, for an average over the decade of 2.8 per cent. The actual average growth rate of industrial countries in the 1970s was 3.3 per cent, about in the middle of the range of the two assumptions.

The base index of international inflation is a US dollar-denominated weighted average of GDP deflators for the northern tier of OECD countries. It has been assumed that this index will increase at 8.0 per cent a year in 1980–5 and 6.0 per cent a year in 1985–90, for an average in the 1980s of 7.0 per cent. It is also assumed that the prices of internationally traded manufactured goods will increase at these rates. The same price assumption is used in both the High and Low Cases.

Petroleum prices are assumed to increase at 3 per cent a year in real terms, or at 10 per cent a year in nominal terms, in the 1980s. The OPEC average price is assumed to rise (in 1980 dollar) from $30.50 a barrel in 1980 to $42 in 1990. There are considerable uncertainties about the evolution of petroleum prices. It has been assumed, for analytical convenience, that the price trajectory is a smooth one, but one should not exclude the possibility that developments similar to those of recent years will occur.

Industrial countries are the dominant factor in world trade. The assumed growth rates of industrial countries, based on historical relationships, establish the rate of growth of world trade. The High Case projects world trade growth of 5.7 per cent a year (compared to 5.5 per cent in 1970–8); the Low Case includes a 3.7 per cent annual growth rate, reflecting what is posited to be a less-favourable world trade environment in the face of continuing difficulties in the world economy. For the developing countries, the trade projections of the High Case are built up from projections for thirty-four individual non-fuel primary commodities (for more details, see Hughes and Lutz, 1981); projections of fuel production, consumption, and trade based on the analysis of major countries; an extension of the historical manufactured export performance of the various regions, with a downward adjustment for the region that includes Hong Kong, Korea, Taiwan, Singapore, Thailand and the Philippines. (This is because exports in that region have grown at a very rapid 22 per cent a year during 1970–8 so that some of these countries have now attained very high ratios of exports to GDP); and exports of non-factor services projected by using regression results from a cross-section analysis (see Sapir and Lutz, 1980). These various exercises lead to a 7.0 per cent a year average rate of growth of export volumes (compared to 4.7 in the 1970s). Export growth rates for the oil importers in the High Case would average 8.2 per cent a year in the 1980s, as compared with 3.8 per cent a year for oil importers (reflecting slow growth in petroleum trade).

Built into the projections is a continuation of the trend of the 1970s of an increase in trade among developing countries and capital-surplus oil exporters as a group (see Havrylyshyn and Wolf, 1981). This trade, which is estimated to represent 7 per cent of world trade at present, is projected to increase to 9 per cent in 1990 and to represent about one-third (up from 27 per cent in 1980) of the total trade of these countries. Trade in primary commodities would account for the bulk of this expansion.

In the Low Case, exports of the developing countries are projected to grow at only 3.9 per cent a year in the 1980s – well below the growth rate attained in the 1970s. For all primary commodities, including fuels, exports grow more slowly largely because of the slower GDP growth rate assumed for industrial countries. For manufactured goods, however, a more than proportionate reduction in export growth rates is postulated, since it is assumed that increased protectionism does not permit exports from developing countries to raise their share in the consumption of manufactured goods in industrial countries to higher levels than those of recent years. Manufactured exports are thus projected to increase at 11.1 per cent a year in the High Case – about the same rate as in the 1970s – but at only 5.1 per cent a year in the Low Case.

The projected trade outlook, combined with the performance of domestic savings, efficiency in the use of resources, and the availability of external finance, determine the paths of structural adjustment of developing countries and their future growth prospects. This is taken up in section III, 2.

## 2 THE OUTLOOK FOR THE 1980s

The projected rates of growth of groups of developing countries, for the High and Low Cases, are summarised in Table 1.3. Both scenarios show some acceleration in GDP growth rates during the 1980s. But, the High Case projects a recovery of GDP growth rates in all developing countries, and in the major groups of low- and middle-income oil importers and oil exporters, to levels similar to those of the 1960s. The Low Case outcome is, however, well below even the slower GDP growth rates attained in the 1970s. One striking implication of the projections is that for low-income, sub-Saharan African countries at best (the High Case), GDP per person could be expected to increase only slightly over the decade, while in the Low Case the declining trend in GDP per person[16] experienced by these countries in the 1970s would continue. This latter outcome would result from a combination of faltering domestic policies (inadequate to deal both with fundamental structural problems and with problems created by the international environment) and inadequate supplies of concessional finance.

At the other extreme, the countries of East Asia and the Pacific,

TABLE 1.3  GROWTH OF GDP FOR GROUPS OF COUNTRIES, 1960–90
(average annual percentages)

| Region | High | | | | | Low | | |
|---|---|---|---|---|---|---|---|---|
| | 1960–70 | 1970–80 | 1980–85 | 1985–90 | 1980–90 | 1980–85 | 1985–90 | 1980–90 |
| Oil importers | 5.7 | 5.1 | 5.0 | 5.8 | 5.4 | 3.8 | 4.4 | 4.1 |
| Low-income oil importers | 4.2 | 3.0 | 4.0 | 4.3 | 4.1 | 2.8 | 3.2 | 3.0 |
| Sub-Saharan Africa | 4.0 | 2.4 | 3.0 | 3.0 | 3.0 | 1.8 | 2.0 | 1.9 |
| Asia | 4.3 | 3.2 | 4.2 | 4.6 | 4.4 | 3.0 | 3.5 | 3.2 |
| Middle-income oil importers | 6.2 | 5.6 | 5.2 | 6.1 | 5.6 | 4.0 | 4.7 | 4.3 |
| sub-Saharan Africa[a] | 4.1 | 3.5 | 3.0 | 3.3 | 3.1 | 2.7 | 3.0 | 2.8 |
| East Asia and Pacific | 7.9 | 8.2 | 7.8 | 8.5 | 8.1 | 6.3 | 6.5 | 6.4 |
| Latin America/Caribbean | 5.3 | 6.0 | 5.1 | 6.0 | 5.6 | 4.4 | 4.8 | 4.6 |
| Middle East, North Africa | 4.1 | 4.9 | 4.1 | 4.1 | 4.1 | 3.0 | 3.3 | 3.2 |
| Southern Europe | 7.0 | 4.6 | 4.3 | 5.0 | 4.6 | 2.5 | 3.5 | 3.0 |
| Oil exporters | 6.5 | 5.2 | 6.2 | 6.8 | 6.5 | 4.9 | 5.9 | 5.4 |
| All developing countries | 5.9 | 5.1 | 5.3 | 6.1 | 5.7 | 4.1 | 4.9 | 4.5 |

[a] Excludes South Africa.

Source: World Development Report 1981.

and Latin America and the Caribbean would be projected to have in the High Case GDP growth rates which continue the rapid growth trends of the 1960s and the 1970s. This performance would reflect both their proven ability to deal with the adjustment problems arising from the greater sophistication of their economic structures and decision-making processes, and from the continuing availability of finance to them in international capital markets.

The prospect of stagnation in low-income African countries, unless they make special efforts which are complemented by larger international assistance than has been built into the projections, has important implications. It would mean that they would find themselves left further and further behind in the development process. On the other hand, the major East Asian and Latin American countries would by 1990 more closely approximate the economic structures of present industrial countries.

## IV DOMESTIC RESOURCE MOBILISATION AND CAPITAL REQUIREMENTS

The process of adjustment to the adverse international economic events will, as discussed earlier, require oil importers to take a series of measures designed to reduce imports and increase exports, in order to bring their external accounts into more approximate balance. Included are: greater domestic resource mobilisation efforts; increased efficiency in resource use; energy conservation and production; and the reallocation of investment to reflect changed factor prices.

The High Case assumes that, depending on the country, the process of adjustment could take from two to five years. The lower a country's income the more difficult will be the adjustment process, and the larger will be the external assistance required. In the High Case, domestic savings performance is projected to improve so that domestic savings reduce somewhat the need for additional foreign capital. The export projections discussed earlier imply that exports increase from 21 per cent of GDP in 1978 to 28 per cent in 1990. The policies required will vary between countries (see World Bank, 1981, ch. 3). If, in addition, measures are taken to reduce dependence on imported energy – here again, both the capacity to undertake such measures and the additional capital required will vary between countries – the overall current account deficit of oil importers could be brought down to a sustainable level. It is projected to decline from 4.9 per cent of GNP in 1980 to 3.0 per cent of GNP in 1990 (Table 1.4).

TABLE 1.4  OIL IMPORTERS: FINANCING CURRENT DEFICITS, 1970–90
(billions current dollars)

| | 1970 | 1980ᵃ | Projections 1985 High | 1985 Low | 1990 High | 1990 Low | Annual percentage growth (current prices) 1970–80 | 1980–90 High | 1980–90 Low | Annual percentage growth (constant prices) 1970–80 | 1980–90 High | 1980–90 Low |
|---|---|---|---|---|---|---|---|---|---|---|---|---|
| Current accounts | | | | | | | | | | | | |
| Resource gap | -8.8 | -65.2 | -71.6 | -58.0 | -116.5 | -83.0 | 22.2 | 6.0 | 2.4 | 11.2 | -1.0 | -4.3 |
| Workers' remittances | 2.3 | 16.7 | 25.7 | 23.8 | 36.8 | 33.5 | 21.9 | 8.2 | 7.2 | 11.0 | 1.2 | 0.2 |
| Interest payments | -1.4 | -22.5 | -41.9 | -39.8 | -65.6 | -55.5 | 32.0 | 11.3 | 9.4 | 20.0 | 4.0 | 2.3 |
| Other current transactions | -0.7 | 1.5 | 1.7 | 2.3 | 4.0 | 3.7 | | | | | | |
| Current account balance | -8.6 | -69.6 | -86.1 | -71.1 | -141.3 | -101.3 | 23.3 | 7.3 | 3.8 | 12.1 | 0.3 | -3.0 |
| Financed by | | | | | | | | | | | | |
| Net capital flows | 9.1 | 55.3 | 96.2 | 76.1 | 161.6 | 112.2 | 19.8 | 11.3 | 7.3 | 8.9 | 4.0 | 0.3 |
| ODA: | | | | | | | | | | | | |
| Grants | 1.0 | 8.3 | 16.7 | 13.7 | 27.9 | 20.9 | 23.6 | 12.9 | 9.7 | 12.6 | 5.5 | 2.5 |
| Concessional loans | 2.1 | 8.0 | 16.2 | 13.5 | 26.4 | 20.6 | 14.3 | 12.7 | 9.9 | 4.1 | 5.3 | 2.6 |
| Total | 3.1 | 16.3 | 32.9 | 27.2 | 54.3 | 41.5 | 18.1 | 12.8 | 9.8 | 7.5 | 5.4 | 2.6 |

| | | | | | | | | | | | | |
|---|---|---|---|---|---|---|---|---|---|---|---|---|
| Medium- and long-term borrowing: | | | | | | | | | | | | |
| Official export credits | 0.5 | 2.6 | 3.6 | 3.6 | 6.7 | 5.5 | 17.9 | 9.9 | 7.8 | 7.2 | 2.4 | 0.4 |
| Multilateral | 0.5 | 3.2 | 6.3 | 5.5 | 9.0 | 8.1 | 20.4 | 10.9 | 9.7 | 9.4 | 3.5 | 2.3 |
| Private | 3.4 | 27.5 | 42.8 | 30.5 | 74.6 | 43.6 | 23.3 | 10.5 | 4.7 | 12.1 | 3.3 | -2.1 |
| Total | 4.3 | 33.4 | 52.5 | 39.6 | 90.3 | 57.2 | 22.8 | 10.5 | 5.5 | 11.6 | 3.2 | -1.4 |
| Private direct investment | 1.7 | 5.6 | 10.8 | 9.3 | 17.0 | 13.5 | 12.7 | 11.7 | 9.2 | 2.7 | 4.4 | -1.9 |
| Changes in reserves[b] and short-term borrowing | -0.5 | 14.3 | -10.1 | -4.4 | -20.3 | -10.9 | | | | | | |
| Memorandum items | | | | | | | | | | | | |
| Debt outstanding (billions of dollars) | 48.0 | 301.3 | 577.3 | 539.0 | 1047.0 | 872.7 | 20.2 | 13.3 | 11.2 | 9.1 | 5.9 | 3.9 |
| Resource gap/GNP (percentage) | 2.5 | 4.6 | 2.7 | 2.3 | 2.5 | 2.0 | | | | | | |
| Current account deficit/GNP (percentage) | 2.4 | 4.9 | 3.3 | 2.9 | 3.0 | 2.4 | | | | | | |
| Net capital flows/GNP (percentage) | 2.6 | 3.9 | 3.6 | 3.1 | 3.4 | 2.7 | | | | | | |
| Debt service/GNP (percentage) | 1.2 | 3.9 | 3.8 | 3.8 | 3.8 | 3.7 | | | | | | |
| Interest payments/GNP (percentage) | 0.4 | 1.6 | 1.6 | 1.4 | 1.3 | | | | | | | |

[a] Estimate.
[b] Minus (−) equals increase.
Source: World Development Report, 1981.

Though high by historical standards, this level seems sustainable.

In the Low Case, a less favourable view is taken of all the adjustment mechanisms. In 1990 both the savings ratio[17] and exports ratio[17] remain relatively unchanged from 1978 levels. Since it is projected that measures to change the structure of the economy – including conserving and producing energy – are less successful than in the High Case, then, in order to bring current account deficits to sustainable levels, sharp declines in GDP growth rates will be required. External capital availabilities in this case are limited, both for creditworthiness reasons and because of continuing economic difficulties of industrial countries.

## V   EXTERNAL CAPITAL

The projections for external capital shown in Table 1.4 for the High and Low Cases incorporate judgements both about future availabilities of certain categories of capital, as well as about the abilities of countries to absorb additional amounts of capital on commercial terms without experiencing major creditworthiness problems. Issues of creditworthiness are best analysed at the country level with the use of the country models (discussed earlier) for the major countries.

Net capital flows are projected to increase during the 1980s at 4 per cent a year in real terms in the High Case, and 0.3 per cent a year in the Low Case, as compared with 9 per cent in the 1970s. This slowing down in the rate of growth of external finance reflects not only the factors discussed in the preceding section, but also the constraints which seem to have emerged on the availabilities of both concessional finance and finance at market terms.

The projections of Official Development Assistance (ODA)[18] flows are based on information available from governments about their aid intentions.[19] The projections reflect the 'aid-weariness' which, combined with budgetary difficulties, is causing some major donor countries to cut back on their commitments. Low-income countries can borrow only very limited amounts on commercial terms. The projected growth of ODA is 5.4 per cent a year in real terms in the High Case and 2.6 per cent in the Low Case, as compared with 7.5 per cent in the 1970s. This slow growth is an important factor accounting for the projected slow pace of development in low-income countries (despite an allocation of 50 per cent of ODA to them in the High Case as compared with 34 per cent now).

Contributions to the multilateral development banks are also subject to increasing restraint – related to budgetary pressures in industrial countries – at a time when the demand for their resources has increased. To give an example, the World Bank has launched a new type of lending (structural-adjustment lending) which is designed to assist countries in formulating and carrying out structural-adjustment programmes. Such lending, as well as lending for increased energy production in developing countries, will displace other types of lending unless additional funding is available.

Lending by multilateral development banks acts, in many cases, as a catalyst for lending by private financial institutions. Private banks engage in co-financing operations with them and also rely on the project- and country-expertise of these institutions. Significant reductions in multilateral development lending relative to the financing requirements of developing countries, could reduce this catalytic role.

There was a very rapid increase in medium- and long-term loans provided to developing countries by private financial institutions in the 1970s (23 per cent a year in nominal terms). This expansion in lending was one important element making for a less painful adjustment of the external accounts of developing countries to the shocks of the early 1970s. A combination of high levels of borrowing, high (even in real terms) and volatile interest rates, increasing shares of variable interest rate debt and shortened maturities have complicated the task of managing the external debt of some major borrowing countries. Debt service payments now represent a significantly higher proportion of the export receipts of most major borrowers than they did in 1970. On the supply side, concerns have been expressed: that banks' capital ratios have declined since 1973; that there has been increase in banks' international assets (and their claims on oil-importing developing countries) relative to domestic assets; that some developing countries have reached what banks consider to be prudential lending limits; and that all these factors in combination could slow down the rate of lending to developing countries. The evidence for 1980–1 is that lending to developing countries continues to expand at a rapid pace, and that both risk exposure and other considerations have resulted in greater differences in pricing (spreads) for loans to different countries. (See Williams, Johnson *et al.*, 1981, p. 2.)

Based principally on creditworthiness considerations and projected export and capital market prospects, finance from private markets to oil importing countries is projected to increase at a slower rate of 10.5 per cent a year in the High Case (and a much lower 4.7 per cent a year in the Low Case). These projections could be conservative. Expansion in lending from private markets could be more rapid if the economic performance of developing countries were better than projected and if new instruments for risk-dispersion were developed.

On this basis, the outstanding debt of oil importers is projected to increase from $300 billion in 1980 to $870 billion in the Low Case, and $1,050 billion in the High Case in 1990. Debt service payments will then represent about 4 per cent of GNP over the decade, of which over 40 per cent will be in the form of interest payments. Continuing high interest rates would aggravate the debt-management task.


## VI  CONCLUDING COMMENTS

The oil-importing developing countries weathered the 1973–4 shocks from the external environment better than many had expected, by improving their domestic management and using external finance effectively. But the 1979–80 external shocks have imposed a burden, which sits particularly heavily on the low-income countries and on those middle-income countries which had not completed the process of adjustment to the earlier shocks. Thus, a number of developing countries are now faced with very difficult problems of structural adjustment. For the low-income countries, particularly of Africa, an already difficult development process has become even more complicated. In the absence of major international and domestic efforts, with financing larger than has been projected and on highly concessional terms, the prospects are for continuing economic stagnation with very severe consequences for their populations.

Some low-income countries, such as India, Pakistan and Indonesia, have made rapid strides in developing agricultural production. This represents one noteworthy achievement of domestic effort and international cooperation. Even more remarkable is the transition into the group of middle-income countries of, among others, the Philippines, Thailand, and the Ivory Coast and the rapid strides made by Brazil, Mexico, Korea and Taiwan. For these and other middle-income countries, access to the export and capital markets of industrial countries is essential to their continuing advancement and to a fuller role in an increasingly interdependent world. Domestic efforts and international cooperation will determine whether the less desirable outcomes projected are avoided, and whether the world economy returns to a more healthy path of development in the 1980s.

NOTES

1. These countries are here considered to be capital-surplus oil exporters (not included in developing countries) and include Iraq.
2. Included in the category of oil exporters are: Algeria, Angola, Bahrain, Bolivia, Brunei, Congo, Ecuador, Egypt, Gabon, Indonesia, Iran, Malaysia, Mexico, Nigeria, Oman, Peru, Syria, Trinidad and Tobago, Tunisia and Venezuela.
3. For a more extended discussion of the nature of adjustment see W. M. Corden (1977) *Inflation, Exchange Rates and the World Economy* (Chicago: University of Chicago Press), chs. 7 to 9; also Edward R. Fried and Charles L. Schultze (eds) (1975) *Higher Oil Prices and the World Economy* (Washington: Brookings Institution).
4. The implications of changes in exchange rates for the transmission of international inflation to the domestic economy must, however, be considered.
5. External financing represents a transfer of foreign savings and permits the maintenance of real income levels in the face of a terms-of-trade deterioration.
6. Here defined as countries with 1979 GNP per person of $370 and below.
7. For a discussion of individual country experiences see World Bank, *World Development Report*, 1981, chapter 6.
8. The relatively good growth performance of developing countries was a positive factor in global adjustment.
9. Gross domestic investment as a proportion of GDP.
10. For an extended discussion of external debt trends and structure in the 1970s see Nicholas C. Hope (1981) *Development in and Prospects for the External Debt of the Developing Countries: 1970–80 and Beyond*, World Bank Staff Working Paper No. 483, September.
11. Countries with disbursed and outstanding medium- and long-term debt of more than $10bn in 1979 were: Algeria, Argentina, Brazil, Egypt, India, Indonesia, Israel, Republic of Korea, Mexico, Spain, Turkey, Venezuela and Yugoslavia.
12. Including merchandise, services and workers' remittances.
13. The capital-service ratio (contractual service payments on long-term debt, plus remitted profits on direct investment divided by exports of goods and services) did not rise as rapidly.
14. Capital-surplus oil exporters (not included in developing countries) comprise Iraq, Kuwait, Libya, Saudi Arabia, and the United Arab Emirates.
15. These scenarios are detailed in World Bank, 1981. They are not forecasts of the future, but projections of policy-linked outcomes.
16. An average decline of 0.4 per cent a year.
17. As proportions of GDP.
18. ODA flows as shown in Table 1.4 refer to receipts by developing countries. They differ from data reported by the OECD Development Assistance Committee which show disbursements of all types (including technical assistance) to developing countries and multilateral institutions.
19. As of January 1981.

REFERENCES

Cheetham, R., Gupta, S. and Schwartz, A. (1979) *The Global Framework,* Washington DC, World Bank Staff Working Paper, No. 355, September.

Havrylyshyn, Oli and Wolf, Martin (1981) *Trade among Developing Countries: Theory, Policy and Principal Trends*, Washington DC, World Bank Staff Working Paper, No. 479, August.

Hughes, Helen and Lutz, Ernst (1981) 'The Outlook for the 1980s with Particular Reference to Trade', mimeograph, Washington DC, World Bank, April.

Kruger, Anne (1980) 'Trade Policy as an Input to Development', *American Economic Review*, vol. 70, no. 2, pp. 228–93.

Sapir, André and Lutz, Ernst (1980) *Trade in Non-Factor Services: Past Trends and Current Issues*, Washington DC, World Bank Staff Working Paper, No. 410, August.

Williams, Richard C., Johnson, G. G., and staff team (1981) *International Capital Markets, Recent Developments and Short-Term Prospects* (Washington DC: International Monetary Fund), August.

World Bank (1981) *World Development Report* (Washington DC: World Bank).

# Part Two
# Domestic Financing

# 2 The Role and Pattern of Domestic Financing in the Process of Economic Development: Empirical Evidence

**Egon Kemenes**

INSTITUTE FOR WORLD ECONOMICS,
BUDAPEST, HUNGARY

## I INTRODUCTION

The patterns of domestic financing in developing countries are as varied as economic reality itself, one aspect of which can be expressed in terms of income difference. According to the latest data, (World Bank, 1980) the distribution of the 124 developing countries of the world in terms of the average income level was as in Table 2.1.

TABLE 2.1

| Number of countries | Population mid-1978, millions | Average GNP per capita 1978 (US$) |
|---|---|---|
| 36 | 2 008 | 210 |
| 38 | 493 | 470 |
| 50 | 571 | 1 470 |

*Source:* World Bank (1980).

29

It is obvious that where average GNP per capita is $210 or $470, savings and taxation, for example, among the main sources of domestic financing, play an entirely different role than in those developing countries where per capita income is $1470.

The difference is, evidently, not only *quantitative* but also *qualitative*. Therefore, the examination of development financing. in this paper will be made separately (1) for countries where the average income is $210 and $470 (which we consider to be on the *first level* of development) and (2) for those where the average income is $1470 (*second level* of development).

## II  SOME ASPECTS OF DEVELOPMENT FINANCING ON THE FIRST LEVEL OF DEVELOPMENT

When judging the possibilities of domestic financing, the only possible starting point is the *given economic structure*. The present economic structure of countries on the first level of development is characterised by a *preponderance of agriculture*. In the second half of the 1970s in many developing countries the percentage share of agriculture in GDP approached or exceeded 50 per cent, while agricultural population expressed as a percentage of the total population was around 60 per cent for the developing countries as a whole (FAO, 1980).

This fact is recognised in the most recent literature in the conclusion that in many developing countries the agricultural sector could be the most important area for the mobilisation of resources (Manig, 1981, p. 517).

The possibilities for accumulation arising from agriculture coincide with the unavoidable necessity of *increasing food* production in the developing countries.

In the literature dealing with economic growth, several authors (e.g., Lewis, Kuznets and Schulz) have already pointed out the accumulation possibilities hidden in agriculture.

The validity of these theoretical findings is illustrated by the *empirical evidence* of several countries. At the start of *Japan's* economic development, after the Meiji restoration, the Japanese government made use of the preponderance of agriculture when financing development. For 1882 to 1892, it was the land tax, introduced in 1873, that supplied an average of 85.6 per cent of the income of the central government, and this figure was still 80.4 per cent in 1893–7. The direct tax ratio to income produced in agriculture averaged 22.1

per cent for the years 1888–92 (see Ohkava and Rosovsky, 1964). According to Johnston (1951) the Japanese Government applied the method of intensifying agriculture, thus increasing productivity and from this, by heavy taxation, financed industry.

As a further example of the role of agriculture as a source of domestic financing, we would like to recall also that both in the *Soviet Union* and the *People's Democracies of Europe* agriculture played an important role in the accumulation that was to become a source of financing growth in the early period of socialist development. Agriculture was utilised in many forms as a source of accumulation, for example by a price and income policy realised through a state monopoly for buying agricultural products.

From among the present day developing countries, *Mexico* may be regarded as an example of accumulation realised in agriculture. The average annual rate of agrarian growth between 1940 to 1974 exceeded 4 per cent (see Kádár, 1980). In the opinion of Schulz (1965), the rapid development of Mexican agriculture was a source of modernising industrial production and of increasing the share of industry in the national income.

This conclusion by Schulz is also in line with the experiences of Hungarian economic history. The development of agriculture that unfolded in *Hungary* in the last third of the nineteenth century, through its forward and backward linkage, furthered industrialisation and thus added to the enlarging of industrial accumulation sources. In Hungary, in 1884, the most important industrial branch was the milling industry, followed by the distilling industry, which was then called 'the great protector' of agriculture; the agricultural machinery industry was also important (see Futó, 1944). It was the agrarian industries that were technically on the highest level of development and thus added to the development of the domestic machine industry.

The case of *India* is also of interest as regards agricultural production and the possibilities it creates for accumulation. As a result of a planned development policy, the index for the volume of Indian agricultural output, taking the average for 1967–70 as 100, rose to an average of 132.8 for 1976–8. (Indian Statistical Service, 1979). This development of agriculture also expanded the sources of domestic financing: in 1976–7 national savings – at 15.7 per cent of national income – represented the record level since independence (Surányi, 1979).

On the first level of development, the opening up of resources for development financing through accumulation in agriculture has some *special features*.

One such feature is that, due to the partly non-monetary environment for the implementation of development policy, a big role is played by accumulation occurring in the non-financial, *natural form* (in kind and by labour). In Japan, after the Meiji restoration, the estate owners passed on the high land taxes to the peasantry. Thus estate owners practically played the role of tax collectors: owing to the fact that very often farm rents were paid in kind, estate owners also undertook the functions of storing and transporting products. In his recently published very thorough work on the taxation of agriculture, Manig (1981) deals in a number of places with taxation in kind and in labour, as a means of non-monetary capital formation. Construction, soil improvement, the creation of irrigation works and other infrastructural facilities, for example, are forms of contributions to accumulation by labour.

Another special feature of the implementation of planned agricultural accumulation is that it has to be started under the *given social circumstances* of present day villages in the developing countries. Both possibilities and difficulties are inherent in these circumstances. I have already dealt in greater detail in an earlier work with the sociological and political aspects of implementing accumulation through rural development (Kemenes, 1970). The transformation of traditional agriculture in the developing countries also calls for training adapted to the circumstances (Mándi, 1981).

As a third special feature of accumulation through agriculture, I should like to stress the importance of its *political conception*. It is this together with its successful implementation which determine what the *social impact* of the increase in agricultural production will be. I have already written here about India's success in increasing agricultural production. However, the social consequences of the 'green revolution' are less favourable. Under the given social relations, the capitalist form of the growth of agricultural production led to social polarisation and to the impoverishment of certain village strata. According to Harrison's (1981) data, in India the proportion of landless labourers rose by about 50 per cent during the 1970s. As Surányi (1979) writes in his study on this subject, in the course of impoverishment and social polarisation around 16 million small farmers lost their land and joined the ranks of poverty-stricken agricultural labourers. As a consequence, between 1960–1 and 1969–70 (calculated at unchanged 1960–1 prices) per capita incomes in the agrarian sector fell from 189.5 rupees to 184.1 rupees, while at the national level there was an increase of 33 rupees in per capita income. The social and political dangers of this polarisation are obvious. Among the economic consequences, we refer here only to the fact that, by reducing the purchasing power of the rural masses, this process restricts the most important market for the emerging domestic industry and, even more, the possibility for selling agricultural products. Thus we are faced with the paradoxical situation that while the *growth of agricultural production* breaks down the supply barriers, at the same time the *social circumstances* of this growth narrow the *demand* barriers. This has given rise to the situation that, in certain areas of India, the sale of agricultural produce is now posing a problem.

On the first level of development, in directing agricultural accumulation towards development objectives, two subsequent stages can be distinguished.

In the *first stage* the realistic aim is to channel existing accumulation towards growth aims and to create further conditions for increasing production and accumulation in agriculture. At this first stage of mobilising agricultural accumulation, the most urgent organisational measure is to build up product marketing under central control and to widen its circle, consciously linking producers to ultimate buyers.

In the *second stage* of implementing planned agricultural accumulation, steps may be taken to return the results of the initial stage into agriculture in the form of individual or group production credits. These credits are to be utilised primarily for raising productivity by supplying agriculture with simple tools and machines. It is an obvious fact that a certain type of industrialisation is inevitable in the successful implementation of planned agricultural accumulation: this problem is analysed in detail in the excellent work of Destanne de Bernis (1967, p. 78). According to him, supplying agriculture with home-made tools and materials makes possible an important increase in agricultural surplus production.

The second stage should start financing agricultural investments with the help of *institutional credits*. When one is utilising the results of former accumulation by extending institutional credits, financial measures have to be supplemented by organisational and advisory work. Thus, the second stage of planned agricultural accumulation is characterised by a higher degree of monetarisation, which can have comprehensive multiplying effects. Among the general effects, let us mention the growing purchasing power of agriculture. Owing to the major importance of the rural population, even a modest increment in income may mean an important increase in the *amount* of the population's purchasing base. A further general effect is the widening of internal market relations and, parallel to these, the expansion of money circulation. In this way, agricultural development also furthers industrialisation and thus enlarges the source of industrial accumulation.

When all is said and done, the success of implementing planned agricultural accumulation has only one criterion: whether or not a *reproduction on an increasing scale* can be achieved successfully within agriculture and whether – by applying sources transferred from agriculture – this can also be achieved within the entire economic life.

## III    SOME ASPECTS OF DEVELOPMENT FINANCING ON THE SECOND LEVEL OF DEVELOPMENT

As was mentioned in section I, we consider those developing countries where yearly per capita GNP is around $1500 US to be on the *second level* of development. From the structural viewpoint, agriculture is still of great importance in these countries, but they already have a substantial industrial output too and actively participate in international trading and capital relations. However, from the angle of domestic financing, the difference lies mainly in the fact that in these countries financial flows now run through the whole of economic life, although remnants of the subsistence economy can still be found in the rural sector and in certain regions. Because of the fundamentally monetary nature of these economies, specific monetary and financial means of domestic financing, such as taxation, credit, income and price policies, now come to the fore.

Although the means of domestic financing thus appear similar to those of the developed countries, the objectives and means of their application are nevertheless determined by the special circumstances of the developing countries. Planned development policy calls, above all, for the centralisation of a rational proportion of financial flows; in other words, for an increase in the proportion of taxes collected compared to GDP. This is still not being achieved to the desired extent in many developing countries. According to Manig's data (1981), for the period from 1953 to 1972 in India for example, the tax-ratio rose from an annual 6.3 per cent in 1953–5 to 15.6 per cent in 1971–2. At the same time, in many other developing countries it has increased only to a much lesser extent, has remained unchanged or has even declined.

One reason for this could be that the majority of developing countries have not yet developed autonomous taxation methods, optimally adapted to their own social and economic conditions.

In connection with the special taxation methods of developing countries, it would appear correct to note that, on the second level of development, agriculture can still be an important source of development financing, but now mainly in the form of taxation in cash. Manig deals in detail with the mechanism for this also (1981). There may be forms for the taxation of agriculture in developing countries other than the land tax applied in the European countries and Japan. Thus, for example, in Mexico at a certain stage of economic development the taxation of agriculture was achieved in part through the *ejido* (Kádár, 1980). In Ethiopia, since the land reform, taxes have been collected in the rural sector by the Peasant Associations, which are entitled to retain 2 per cent of the sum collected (Manig, 1981).

The question of the proportion to be achieved between direct taxes and indirect taxes arises in selecting the form of taxation. In the case of the developing countries, an indirect tax (which is in the nature of a consumption tax as regards its effect) is more advantageous than a direct tax, because in these countries there are more consumers than persons with taxable income. The collection of indirect taxes also involves considerably less cost than the collection of income tax. In the case of India, for example, according to the data for 1974–5 (Indian Statistical Service, 1979) in the case of corporation tax the expenditure for its collection amounted to 0.55 per cent of total receipts, while in the case of income tax this proportion was 6.43 per cent.

It is worth noting here that manufacturers' excise tax is generally applied in socialist countries too; this is collected on a single occasion in the product's journey from producer to consumer, as a percentage of the producer's price.

In his book on economic policy and planning in developing countries, Bognár (1969 and 1974) also discusses taxation policy in detail. He mentions among the criteria for correct taxation that:

(i) the taxation system should be combined with the initiation of real processes and be directed at the decisive stage of transition from a subsistence economy to a market money economy;

(ii) in general it should be possible to derive newly introduced taxes or extra taxation from the additional income earned by individuals and enterprises as a result of economic growth.

We could quote India as an example of the latter: between 1965–6 and 1976–7, total income tax increased from 11.4 per cent to 15.3 per cent of total income assessed. This increase in the tax ratio was nevertheless bearable because, despite the absolute and relative growth of the tax burden, the total income assessed more than doubled over the same period (Indian Statistical Service, 1979).

Within the orientation of financial resources towards development goals, *capital transformation* arises as a special task. By this we mean the transformation of unproductive exploitative money capital into development capital. Even in semi-agricultural countries on the second level of development, rural collector-trade and credit-usury realises enormous profits. The accumulation diverted by credit-usury and collector-trade cannot be reoriented to the right channels purely by money-market means. Administrative, social, organisational and financial measures applied in a complex manner are required for this capital to be drawn into the process of domestic development financing (Bognár, 1969 and 1974).

A phenomenon related to this to a certain extent, although of an entirely different dimension is that, in the modern sector of the developing countries, domestic financing itself frequently does not serve development which is in genuine national interests either. A domestic *source* of financing does not always mean the financing of domestic *interests*. In such cases, the *reorientation of domestic financing* is necessary. If facilities created through domestic financing serve interests of multinational corporations or domestic private ventures which are not in conformity with national development goals, they cannot be considered as genuine *development* financing. The key question is in whose hands the *accumulation* resulting from domestic financing appears, and whose interests it serves. This means that not only the *source* of the financing must be *domestic*, but also its *end result*.

Where this is not the case, domestic financing serves not domestic interests but external interests, since its use is directed from *outside* the national economy and society. Kádár describes this phenomenon in Latin American countries as follows:

Owing to their greater dynamism, an ever increasing part of the internal resources of the host countries is mobilized by the foreign subsidiaries, and the resources of the national economies are channelled more and more into the development funds of the foreign sector. In the mid-sixties, for instance, 83 per cent of the capital of US corporations in Latin America were supplied by local sources, i.e. the multinationals scarcely acted as middlemen in capital import transactions (Kádár, 1980).

As regards questions of the *institutional framework* of domestic financing, we shall deal only briefly here with the role of the *state sector*. The question of the role of the state sector was raised in the framework of ideological controversies as early as the beginning of the 1960s by the Gerschenkron hypothesis. According to this, late industrialisers tend to make greater use of strong governmental apparatus in order to mobilise capital (Gerschenkron, 1962). The past two decades have proved this hypothesis to be true and the importance of the state sector has now been recognised in Western economic literature too (Manig, 1981). Recently, it has even gained historical justification (Vernon, 1980). According to Vernon's calculations, by 1980, measured by value added, state-owned enterprises accounted for nearly 15 per cent of national output in Latin-American countries. This proportion is higher in the African countries, if only because of the greater role of the marketing boards and other public organisations. The role of the state sector is also substantial in certain Asian countries; in Iraq for example, 62 per cent of industrial output comes from state-owned plants. Measured from another angle, in 1974 the share of state-owned public enterprises (excluding banks) in total invested capital was 45 per cent in India, 38 per cent in Iran and 18 per cent in Sri Lanka (Premchand, 1979). The share of the state sector is naturally even greater in the centrally planned economies; thus in the case of Hungary, the state sector produced 73.2 per cent of total national income in 1978 (Hungarian Government, 1981).

In the study quoted, Vernon believes that he can see signs of reversal in the trend of the growth of the state-owned sector in Latin America after 1979 (specifically in the case of Chile, Argentina, Peru and Brazil). It can nevertheless be concluded, for the developing countries as a whole, that at a given stage of their development the expansion of the state sector is important for the mobilisation and orientation of the economic forces. The importance of this role is not diminished if the course of subsequent development, induced by the state sector, takes place in part within the framework of other property conditions.

## IV   DOMESTIC VERSUS EXTERNAL FINANCING

When considering the role of domestic financing, one cannot avoid the comparison with external financing.

One of the elements in this comparison is an assessment of the *realistic possibilities and limits of external financing* in the present world economic situation. Between 1973 and 1980, the external indebtedness of non-OPEC developing countries increased almost threefold to US $370bn. In 1980, the developing countries paid $75bn for interest and repayments. Not taking into account price increases, indebtedness rose by 74 per cent in these countries while at the same time GDP grew by only 40 per cent (Westdeutschen Landesbank Girozentrale, 1981). The recycling of petrodollars has provided only a temporary solution for the deficit financing of these countries and has given only a breathing space, before the unavoidable real economic adjustment.

According to historical experience, this scarcity of external financing sources in itself *limits the independence of the developing countries* in their economic decisions. As Kádár (1980) pointed out, the foreign capital flowing into the Latin-American countries was determined only to a relatively small extent by the capital requirements of development. This depended more on the credit capacity and willingness of the creditor countries, whose attitude was also influenced by their evaluation of Latin America as a means in their own international political aspirations. Thus, the strategies of the leading great powers and of the big international corporations assumed primary importance in shaping the order of magnitude of external capital supply to Latin America.

It is now generally accepted that the use by developing countries of external financing, transmitted by the multinational corporations, causes substantial loss to the former in the subsequent stage of their accumulation. According to data of Victor Perlo (1981), the profits of US-based multinational corporations derived from the developing countries amounted to $30bn in 1979. (This is confirmed from the other side by the fact that the profit rate for foreign-direct investments by the USA is higher than for domestic investments.) In this light, the conclusion of the *Brandt Commission Report* that developing countries may benefit from direct investment, but that the gains have not always been fully shared, appears to be an understatement. Besides generally siphoning off economic energies, external financing in certain cases contributes to the *distortion of internal economic life.*

As the *Brandt Commission Report* concluded, transnational corporations, in particular, have often developed cash crops for exportation at the expense of local food availability and so have contributed to the problem of local food supply. This distorting influence can also be seen in the process of industrialisation of developing countries: namely, instead of achieving autonomous development serving their own interests, they become cheap suppliers to developed capitalist countries. Because wages are low in developing countries, this limits the domestic market but their exports, organised by the multinational enterprises, are thereby made competitive (Kemenes, 1977).

In economic history, empirical evidence shows that domestic financing of economic growth is *actually possible*. In Hungary after the Second World War, in the period when economic development was launched, domestic financing was the only source of growth. Despite this, Hungary's national income rose by an average of 7 per cent per annum from 1946 to 1967 (Kemenes, 1977). In Japan in the mid-1960s, only 2 per cent of capital in industry was American-owned and the share held by the other developed capitalist countries was even smaller (Guillain, 1970). We find two periods in the economic history of Latin America when the main source of growth was domestic financing. In the 1930s, the economic growth of the Latin-American countries was predominantly financed by internal savings. Later, taking the average of the twenty years from 1950 to 1970, capital imports did not reach 1.5 per cent of national product in Latin America. Only the socialist countries and Japan, in accomplishing industrialisation, relied to a smaller extent on foreign resources in the period under review (Kádár, 1980).

Moreover, it is precisely the example of Latin America which draws attention to the fact that domestic and external financing are not alternatives that exclude each other; the relative weight of domestic and external financing can vary in the consecutive stages of growth. In the case of Latin America, external financing played a bigger role before the two periods of domestic financing mentioned. An example of the reverse case is Hungary, which also drew on external financing from the early 1970s in the interest of accelerating economic development.

The choice between domestic and external financing does not depend only on economic considerations. It is also a question of the *political conception* of national development. The present indebtedness of the developing countries is to a great extent the result of the fact that, instead of dynamically mobilising internal resources in economic development, the governments of many developing countries found it easier to rely on external resources (Diaz, 1981). It is often simpler to draw on an external resource and then to force an unpopular policy on to the country under the pretext of the resulting exigency, than to follow an independent economic policy based on domestic financing and elaborated and implemented on the basis of a broad democratic consensus.

Thus, in the final analysis, the role and pattern of domestic financing are determined not only by economic considerations, but also by *political will and determination*.

REFERENCES

Bognár, Jóssef (1969) *Economic Policy and Planning in Developing Countries*, 2nd edn. (Budapest: Akadémiai Kiadó). Spanish edn. 1974 (Barcelona: Planeta).
Bernis, Gérard Destanne de (1967) *Industries industrialisantes et contenu d'une politique d'intégration régionale* (Grenoble).
———— (1981) 'The Brandt Report: Is It Not Some Search for Conquering the Crisis within the Capitalist Order?', *Development and Socio-Economic Progress* (Cairo), Special Issue, March.
Diaz, David (1981) Intervention at the Conference on Internal and External Factors of Development Strategies (Grenoble), July.
FAO (1980) *Production Yearbook 1979* (Rome: FAO), vol. 33.
Futó, Mihály (1944) *The History of Hungarian Manufacturing Industry* (Budapest: Magyar Gazdasagkutató Intazet).
Gerschenkron, Alexander (1962) *Economic Backwardness in Historical Perspective* (Cambridge, Mass: Harvard University Press).
Guillain, Robert (1970) *Der unterschätzte Cigant* (Bern: Scherz Verlag).
Harrison, Paul (1981) *Inside the Third World – The Anatomy of Poverty*, 2nd edn. (Harmondsworth: Penguin).
Hungarian Government (1981) *Statistical Pocket Book of Hungary 1980* (Budapest).
Indian Statistical Service (1979) *Statistical Abstract for India 1978* (New Delhi).
Johnston, Bruce F. (1951) 'Agricultural Productivity and Economic Development in Japan', *Journal of Political Economy* vol. 59, no. 6, December.
Kádár, Béla (1980) *Problems of Economic Growth in Latin America* (London: St. Martin's Press).
Kemenes, Egon (1970) *Agriculture as a Possible Source of Accumulation in African Developing Countries*, Studies on Developing Countries, no. 41 (Budapest: Center for Afro-Asian Research of the Hungarian Academy of Sciences).
———— (1977) 'The Development of the Hungarian Economy

1945–1969', in Denis Siniov (ed.) *Modern Hungary* (Bloomington, Indiana: Indiana University Press).

Mándi, Péter (1981) *Education and Economic Growth in Developing Countries* (Budapest: Akadémiai Kiadó).

Manig, W. (1981) *Stevern und Rurale Entwicklung* (Saarbrücken: Breitenbach).

Ohkava, Kazushi and Henry Rosovsky (1964) 'The Role of Agriculture in Modern Japanese Economic Development', in Carl Eicher and Lawrence Witt (eds) *Agriculture in Economic Development* (New York: McGraw-Hill).

Perlo, Victor (1981) Intervention at an International Symposium on the Brandt Commission Report *Development and Socio-Economic Progress*, (Cairo), Special Issue, March.

Premchand, A. (1979) 'Government and Public Enterprises – the Budget Link', *Finance and Development*, no. 4.

Schulz, Theodore W. (1965) *Transforming Traditional Agriculture* (New York: Yale University Press).

Surányi, Sándor (1979) 'Structural Changes in Indian Agriculture and the Process of Accumulation of Wealth in Certain Sectors of Peasantry in Recent Years', in András Balogh (ed.) *Studies on Contemporary Problems of the Indian Sub-Continent* (Studies on Developing Countries, no. 98.) (Budapest: Institute for World Economics of the Hungarian Academy of Sciences).

Vernon, Raymond (1980) *State-owned Enterprises in Latin America and Western Europe: A Comparative Analysis*, Development Discussion Paper, No. 111, (Cambridge, Mass: Harvard Institute for International Development).

Westdeutschen Landesbank Girozentrale (1981) 'Die lage der Entwicklungsländes nach dem Zweiten Ölschock', *Wirtschaft*, Düsseldorf, vol. 3, June.

World Bank (1980) *Atlas* (Washington DC: World Bank).

# 3 The Financial Sector in the Planning of Economic Development

**David Backus** and **Herminio Blanco**

QUEEN'S UNIVERSITY, KINGSTON, CANADA

and

**David Levine**

UNIVERSITY OF CALIFORNIA,
LOS ANGELES, USA

## I INTRODUCTION AND SUMMARY

Financial institutions play a central role in the process of economic development, channeling consumer savings into sectors where capital is most productive. How well they perform this role determines in large part the rate and distribution of economic growth.

In Mexico, financial markets take on additional importance. The Bank of Mexico and subsidiary government agencies (public trust funds and banks) actively encourage investment in particular sectors, through a complex system of loan subsidies, selective rediscounting and restrictions on portfolios of private banks.[1]

Analysis of such policy tools can be performed either by statistical methods or by simulation. In this paper we report some work in progress on both fronts.

In Sections II and III we review the literature on selective credit controls and propose some methods to evaluate such controls. In the rest of the paper, we present a general-equilibrium model based on some characteristics of the Mexican economy in 1977. Such a model can be used to simulate the effects of changes in the cost of capital in different economic sectors.

42

## II  REVIEW OF THE LITERATURE

The literature on selective credit controls in developing economies is almost non-existent. In contrast, there is a vast, though diffuse and unfinished, bibliography for the case of the United States.[2] In the case of Mexico, there have been few attempts in this field. The traditional reference for the Mexican financial system, Brothers–Solis (1966), presents an evaluation of the selective credit apparatus up to 1964. Wilford (1977) performs a descriptive analysis of this matter. It is very surprising that a costly programme, such as the Mexican financial intervention programme, has not been formally evaluated. Such an evaluation is the main objective of our work. The main issues on this topic are the definition of the goals and the efficacy of selective credit policies.[3]

Most of the literature concentrates on approximate objectives for resource allocation to different sectors. Additionally, selective credit policies have been suggested as means of offsetting differences in the credit standing of different sectors and to neutralise differential business cycle impacts on sectors.

There is a large number of studies on the efficacy issue. Rao and Kaminow (1973) present a static general-equilibrium model of financial and real assets. They developed the conditions under which different interventions in the financial market would have the desired effect on resource allocation. The main message is that the fact that investors are typically engaged in numerous activities makes it difficult to ensure that concessions for particular types of borrowing have an effect on the real activity that the government wishes to favour. Investors may simply substitute favoured-borrowing for other sources of credit, in activities far removed from those which the government wishes to influence. As an early corollary, if changes in output patterns are desired, it is much more effective to subsidise or penalise the output or inputs directly.

It would not be an exaggeration to consider Rao–Kaminow as the 'state of the arts' in the theory of selective credit control evaluation. A theoretical study carried out with the same methodology that of O'Brien (1978).

The empirical papers can be grouped according to their statistical approach: reduced form and structural model tests. A prototype of a reduced form test is the work by Cohen (1968). By using regression analysis, he finds that narrowly defined financial flows are strongly related to specific real expenditures. He then concludes that this is a reasonable case for the efficiency issue. The problem with this approach is the simultaneity between credit and expenditure, and the stability of the parameters of the estimated equations.

The structural tests are of a wide variety. Most of them consider that no resource reallocation will take place without reallocation of credit flows. The degree of substitutability between financial market instruments by borrowers and lenders is a common vein in these studies on efficacy. In the limit, controls over instruments which have perfect substitutes will have no effect.

Silber (1976) and Swamy (1970) found, in models of financial institutions, small short-run elasticities in the demand and supplies for different assets. For the long run of their partial-adjustment equations, elasticities are substantially larger. This again is presented as evidence of the potential impact of selective credit controls. Estimates of the substitutabilities among household assets is given also by O'Brien (1975) as additional evidence.

The study of substitution among assets is an incomplete test of selective control efficacy. As both Arcelus and Meltzer (1973) and Jaffee and Rosen (1978) show, it is also necessary to consider the impact of financing the selective credit measures. Arcelus and Meltzer show that for the USA no effect on constructed or purchased house can be observed if proper allowance is made for the method of financing the government's mortgage programme. Jaffee and Rosen disprove this finding, at least for the short run, using a model of the savings and loan associations to do so.

In general, 'the empirical evidence on the efficacy question leaves much to be desired. Most evidence on the efficacy is based on incomplete tests – tests that examine only some of the links between instrument and goal. Instances of complete tests of actual or hypothetical controls are extremely rare.' (See Kaminow and O'Brien, 1975). Furthermore, most of the tests are not directly designed to examine selective credit policies.

Indeed, the econometric practice in this field leaves much to be desired. The estimation of highly *ad hoc* partial equilibrium models can be criticised on two grounds at least:

(i) Tobin and Brainard (1968) analysed the pitfalls in building models with this method. Backus *et al.* (1980) estimated a general-equilibrium financial model which incorporates the criticisms of these authors. Such a model could be extended so as to test the efficacy of selective credit controls.

(ii) The dynamic structure of these models is highly inadequate.
(iii) Lucas's econometric critique (1976) shows that the parameters of such ad hoc models are very likely to be unstable to different government interventions. For example, one should consider the different effects of temporal versus permanent controls or announced versus non-announced controls. Therefore, tests of stability should be performed on such models.

## III  STATISTICAL METHODS

In the case of Mexico, the availability of data makes it unfeasible to build a model *à la* Backus *et al.* A potentially useful technique is to use the vector auto-regressive systems proposed by Sims (1980) and Litterman (1979). Vector auto-regressions have proven to be highly effective in capturing complicated dynamic systems. The variables in these auto-regressions will be production or expenditure series, controlled and uncontrolled funds, cost of credit in alternative sources, and other variables determining the rate of production and expenditures of the different sectors.

This statistical technique is based on the multivariate version of the Wold representation theorem (see Anderson, 1971). In summary, any indeterministic co-variance process which is stationary may be represented, arbitrarily but well, by a finite order auto-regression.

Let $Y_t$ and $\epsilon_t$ be vectors of $k$ elements. Then $Y_t$ can be represented as:

$$Y_t = B(L)Y_{t-1} + \epsilon_t; \quad t = 1, \ldots,$$

where $\epsilon_t$ is a vector of non-correlated errors and $B(L)$ is a $k$ by $k$ matrix of polynomials on the lag operator.

One of the advantages of this technique is that no spurious economic theory is used in imposing restrictions on the $B(L)$ matrix. However, another method of imposing restrictions is needed to overcome the problem of multicollinearity. We shall use Litterman's (1979) Bayesian method to get around this problem.

Tests on different sets of parameters of the auto-regressive system will provide information on the efficacy of different instruments in stimulating either production or expenditures in different target sectors. These tests are the multivariate version of the Granger (1969) causality tests.

One interesting hypothesis is to suggest the existence of offsetting changes in private versus publicly controlled funds, a hypothesis which is related to the message of Arcelus and Meltzer (1973).

Building a vector auto-regressive model could also shed some light on the characteristics of a well-specified structural model. We are gathering data about the amount of resources tapped by each of these instruments and about the terms of credit to each of the input-output sectors.

This data set will be used in estimating the auto-regressive system of production, investment, consumption, flows of funds (public and private) and terms of credit. It will also allow us to formulate the cost-of-capital structure for a given year and to simulate the production, consumption, investment and income distribution effects of different interventions. We shall do this with our general-equilibrium models, to be described in the following sections.

## IV   INTRODUCTION TO THE GENERAL EQUILIBRIUM MODEL

The model's two central features are the treatment of the intertemporal allocation of resources, which depends fundamentally on the way in which expectations are formed, and the introduction of money as a transactions medium.

Intertemporal allocation relies on the common theoretical device of dating capital. Firms use current capital to produce both current goods and the next period's capital. Consumers sell their stock of current capital to firms and save (dissave) by buying more (less) of next-period capital. Government bonds are equivalent to capital from consumers' points of view, but do not enter into production processes.

Rational expectation – here perfect foresight – is not a sufficiently powerful assumption for determining the time-paths of prices. We assume, in addition, that the economy is on a steady-state path. This enables us to use consol formulæ to determine present values of capital and labour. Later, in simulations, we drop the steady-state requirement but continue to use the consol formulæ. The presumption is that, near the steady state, these equations are adequate approximations to actual perfect foresight solutions. In unguarded moments, we might even argue that our quasi-rational expectations are better replicas of 'real life' than perfect foresight is.

We generate demands for money by putting real money balances into utility and production functions. We realise that some economists begin to twitch when they see the words 'money' and 'utility' or 'production function' in close proximity, but we do not find this treatment of money any more disagreeable than similar treatments of, say, bread, labour or capital. Utility and production functions have proved to be useful constructs in the study of commodity and factor demands, despite their abstract and somewhat ephemeral natures. We think the same is true with money.

With the exception of its use of money, the one-period model is identical to that of Jaime Serra-Puche (1981). Sixteen intermediate goods are produced by a fixed-coefficient, input–output technology from a single composite factor, value-added. Value-added in each sector is generated by a sector-specific Cobb-Douglas technology from four factors: rural labour, urban labour, capital and money. All four factors are in fixed supply.

The first fifteen intermediate goods are converted into fifteen final ꞟꞟꞟꞟꞟꞟꞟꞟ goods by a second fixed coefficients' activity matrix. The final intermediate good is next period's capital stock, which is 'produced' by transmitting this period's capital stock, net of depreciation, and by the capital goods sector (number 16).

The ten groups of consumers are distinguished by income class (poor, low income, low-middle income, middle income, and upper income) and location (rural and urban). Each is endowed with capital and either rural or urban labour which is in inelastic supply in factor markets. Consumers use their factor income to buy the fifteen final goods, pay income and sales taxes, and save (buy tomorrow's capital or government debt). Money is rented from the government to facilitate current consumption.

The government collects tax revenue, rents on money and interest on its capital endowment. This may be negative if the government is a net debtor. Total revenues are then spent on intermediate goods and on factors in fixed proportions.

General equilibrium in the model is computed with a global Newton algorithm. A benchmark simulation (Section VI) shows that prices are close to those of Serra-Puche for the same tax structure. Having calibrated the model to this benchmark equilibrium, we plan in our future research to examine the effect of policy experiments and monetary institutions (Section VII).

## V  THE MODEL

The structure of the model was summarised in the introduction. Here we describe in detail our specifications of production, demand and government activity, and our definition of equilibrium.

1 PRODUCTION

Following Serra-Puche (1981), our production technology is a fixed-coefficients input–output system augmented by substitutability among factors. A list of sectors (goods) is given in Table 3.1. We have found it useful to differentiate $m$ intermediate goods, $n$ final

TABLE 3.1   LIST OF GOODS AND FACTORS

*Intermediate Goods*
  1. Agriculture
  2. Mining
  3. Petroleum and petrochemicals
  4. Food products
  5. Textiles
  6. Wood products
  7. Chemical products
  8. Non-metal production
  9. Machinery and automobiles
 10. Electric energy
 11. Commerce
 12. Transportation
 13. Services
 14. Construction
 15. Imports
 16. Next-period capital

*Final Goods*
  1. Bread and cereals
  2. Milk and eggs
  3. Other groceries
  4. Fresh fruits and vegetables
  5. Meat
  6. Fish
  7. Beverages
  8. Clothing
  9. Furniture
 10. Electronic products
 11. Medical products
 12. Transportation
 13. Educational articles
 14. Articles for personal care
 15. Services

*Factors*
  1. Rural labour
  2. Urban labour
  3. Capital
  4. Money

goods, and $k$ factors. Only final goods are demanded by consumers.

The structure of the activity matrix, parts of which depend on prices of intermediate goods $(p)$ and factors $(w)$, is

$$
\begin{array}{c}
\\
m \\
n \\
k
\end{array}
\begin{array}{c}
\begin{array}{cc} m & n \end{array} \\
\begin{bmatrix}
A(p, w) & C \\
O & D \\
B(p, w) & O
\end{bmatrix}
\end{array}
\tag{1}
$$

Columns of $A$ are activities, which produce intermediate goods using factor inputs given by $B$. $C$ and $D$ form a 'black-box' activity submatrix, which converts intermediate goods into final goods. The black box, which is common to input–output models, is required to reconcile different definitions of sectors in production and consumption data.

Factor coefficients $(B)$ depend on factor prices and, through money, on intermediate-goods prices as well. We think of intermediate goods as being produced by a single, composite factor, value-added, which is produced in a particular sector $(j)$ from four factors with a Cobb–Douglas production function. This is:

$$
VA_j = c_j r_j^{\delta_{1j}} u_j^{\delta_{2j}} k_j^{\delta_{3j}} m_j^{\delta_{4j}}, \quad \sum_{i=1}^{4} \delta_{ij} = 1,
$$

where $r_j$, $u_j$, $k_j$ and $m_j$ are inputs of rural labour, urban labour, capital and money, respectively. The money input, $m_j$, is the ratio of a nominal balance rented from the government for one period of rate $s$, to gross nominal receipts of the sector. Let $A_j^+$ denote the $j$th column of a matrix containing only the positive elements of $-A$ (the inputs) but excluding imports, which presumably require foreign money. Then $m_j$ is

$$
m_j = M_j / p' A_j^+.
$$

The relevant factor price for $m_j$ is therefore $w_4 = sp' A_j^+$. Factor input coefficients (elements of $B$) are derived by minimising the cost of producing one unit of value-added:

$$
\begin{aligned}
r_j &= \lambda_j \delta_{1j} / w_1 \\
u_j &= \lambda_j \delta_{2j} / w_2 \\
k_j &= \lambda_j \delta_{3j} / w_3 \\
m_j &= \lambda_j \delta_{4j} / sp' A_j^+ \\
\lambda_j &= \prod_{i=1}^{4} W_i^{\delta_{ij}} / c_j \prod_{=1}^{4} \delta_{ij}^{\delta_{ij}}.
\end{aligned}
$$

Demand for nominal balances of money is

$$M_j = \lambda_j \delta_{4j}/s.$$

Since the supply of money is fixed in nominal terms, this version is useful for defining an equilibrium.

For the most part $A$ is a fixed-coefficients, input–output matrix, but the final row, production of next-period capital, depends on prices. Each activity produces, in addition to its sector's product, second-hand capital. That is, it produces a quantity of next-period capital equal to this period's capital input minus depreciation. Since capital input depends upon prices, so too do the future-capital coefficients in $A$.

## 2 CONSUMPTION

Ten consumers, described in Table 3.2, are endowed with capital and labour which they sell in factor markets. The resulting income is used to pay income taxes on labour income, purchase current final goods gross of sales taxes (consume), rent money from the government and purchase next-period capital (save). By postulating Cobb–Douglas intertemporal utility functions, we are able to separate the consumption-saving decision from decisions about which final goods to consume.

Let a typical infinitely-long-lived consumer (the $i$th, say) maximise the function

$$\sum_{t=1}^{\infty} \rho_i^t \left[ \sum_{j=1}^{n+1} \alpha_{ij} \ln x_{ijt} \right], \quad \sum_{j=1}^{n+1} \alpha_{ij} = 1.$$

where $\rho$ is the consumer's subjective discount factor, $n$ is still the number of final goods, and $x_{ijt}$ is consumption of final good $j$ at time $t$. By convention, let the $(n + 1)^{st}$ good be real balances of money. (The $i$ subscripts will be omitted to simplify the notation.)

Since money is used only for current transactions, and not as a store of value, the decision to hold real balances is contained entirely in the one-period problem. Consumers maximise momentary utility.

$$\sum_{j=1}^{n+1} \alpha_j \ln x_{jt},$$

subject to a fixed quantity of consumption $C_t$;

$$\sum_{j=1}^{n+1} q_{jt}^* x_{jt} = C_t.$$

The $q_{jt}^*$ are prices of final goods, including sales taxes. This yields demands of:

$$x_{jt} = \alpha_i C_t / q_{jt}^* .$$

In a manner analogous to production, the $(n + 1)^{st}$ good, money, enters the utility function as ratio of nominal balances to nominal consumption $(C_t)$. If the rental rate on money is $(s)$ then the cost per unit of real balances is $sC_t$, and the demand for nominal balances is $\alpha_{n+1}/s$.

The maximised value of one-period utility is

$$\ell n C_t + \sum_{j \, 1}^{n+1} \alpha_j \ell n (\alpha_j / q_{jt}^*).$$

So the consumer's intertemporal problem, after omitting irrelevant constants, is to maximise

$$\sum_{t=1}^{\infty} \rho^t \ell n C_t.$$

The budget constraint requires that the present value of the consumption stream should equal the value of today's capital endowment $(K)$ plus the present value of present and future labour income $(J)$. That is:

$$\sum_{t=1}^{\infty} R_t C_t = K + J,$$

where $R_t$ is the $t$-period discount factor. Current consumption is therefore:

$$C_1 = (1 - \rho)[K + J].$$

The only difficulty is in evaluating $K$ and $J$, and this is one point at which our steady-state assumptions sneak in. Consider first the present value of a permanent endowment $\ell$ of labour. At a constant real discount rate $(r)$ and a constant after-tax real wage ($w_1^*$ or $(w_1^*)$), for rural and urban labour, this is

$$J = w_i^* \ell / r \quad i = 1, 2.$$

Next, consider the value today of $k$ units of capital. Each unit earns an after-tax rental $p^*$ and, after depreciation, returns $(1 - \delta)$ units of capital next period. If the rental, depreciation, and discount rates are constant, then the price of one unit of capital today is

$$w_3 = \sum_{t=0}^{\infty} \left( \frac{1 - \delta}{1 + r} \right)^t p^*$$

$$= \left( \frac{1 + r}{r + \delta} \right) p^*.$$

The present value of a consumer's capital endowment is therefore

$$K = w_3 k.$$

Current income is given by

$$I = w_i^* \ell + p^* k, \quad i = 1, 2.$$

So, the saving rate is

$$\frac{I - C}{I} = 1 - (1 - \rho) \left[ \frac{K + J}{I} \right].$$

We calibrated the $\rho$s so as to generate Serra-Puche's savings rates at his benchmark equilibrium prices.

## 3 GOVERNMENT AND FOREIGN SECTORS

The government serves in the model as a combination of fiscal agent and financial intermediary. It collects income and sales taxes, changes rent on money and purchases intermediate goods and labour. With real-debt growth of 3 per cent per year, the government always runs a deficit. Nominal government expenditures are equal to

$$G = TAX + sM + w_3 D - p_{16} 1.03 D,$$

where

$TAX$ = income and sales taxes paid by consumers;
$M$     = nominal money supply;
$s$      = rental rate on money;
$w_3$   = price today of one unit of current capital;
$p_{16}$   = price today of next year's capital;
$D$      = government debt in capital-equivalent units.

Government debt, which is perfectly substitutable for capital in consumer portfolios, is rolled over in each period. Interest payments on debt are included implicitly in the prices $w_3$ and $p_{16}$. Total expenditures $(G)$ are allocated among intermediate goods and labour in fixed physical proportions.

Our rudimentary foreign sector consists essentially of activity 15, net exports. This activity takes other intermediate goods and uses them to 'produce' exports. There is no substitutability among intermediate goods, so that the export-mix is fixed. The equilibrium trade deficit is fixed at its 1977 value in units of imported goods.

## 4 EQUILIBRIUM

Equilibrium in the model consists of a set of prices for which excess demands for all goods and factors are zero and all activities earn zero profits. The government and trade deficits are non-zero but fixed. In addition, we impose certain steady-state conditions to simplify expectational issues concerning the price of capital

In most models with standard input–output activity structures (for example, Shoven and Whalley (1972), Feltenstein (1981), Serra-Puche (1981)), the problem of finding an equilibrium is easily reduced to the problem of finding an equilibrium-vector of factor prices. In the present model, because the price of using real balances depends on prices of intermediate goods, this is not possible.

However, prices of final goods $(q)$ are easily eliminated to reduce the dimensionality of the problem. Given a price vector $(p)$ for intermediate goods, the zero profit conditions for final goods production are

$$p'C + q'D = 0, \tag{1}$$

or

$$q' = -p'CD^{-1}. \tag{2}$$

Let aggregate demand for final goods at these prices, given factor income and taxes, be $g_2$. Then final goods activities must be run at levels $(y_2)$ given by:

$$Dy_2 = g_2.$$

Similarly, the production of intermediate goods must equal their use in production of final goods. Thus, intermediate goods activities $(A)$ must be run at levels $(y_1)$ satisfying

$$Ay_1 + Cy_2 = 0. \tag{3}$$

Derived demand for factors is therefore

$$\begin{aligned} f &= By_1 \\ &= -BA^{-1}CD^{-1}g_2. \end{aligned} \tag{4}$$

In actually computing equilibrium, we use (2) and set the factor demands given by (4) equal to aggregate endowments. There are, however, several minor modifications which must be made to the analysis. First, government debt is included in consumer endowments of capital but cannot be used in production. We treat this by having the government buy back its debt from consumers at the start of each period and resell it at the end. Second, the government purchases intermediate goods and factors so that (3) and (4) do not hold exactly. Finally, the foreign sector starts out with an endowment of imports equal to the 1977 trade deficit, so that not all imports need to be 'produce'.

## VI  COMPUTATION OF THE BENCHMARK EQUILIBRIUM

The equilibrium conditions described in the previous section reduce to the conditions that (i) profits on final goods are zero

$$f_1(w, p) = 0 \tag{5}$$

that (ii) excess demand for factors is zero

$$f_2(w, p) = 0 \tag{6}$$

and that (iii) the government budget constraint be satisfied

$$f_3(w, p) = 0 \tag{7}$$

By Walras's law one of the equations is redundant — and we chose to eliminate the excess demand for money equation. Denote the remaining equations as $\tilde{f}(w, p)$. The equilibrium is then defined by

$$\tilde{f}(w, p) = 0. \tag{8}$$

As a computational check, we verified that our solution to (8) equated excess demand for money with zero.

### 1  COMPUTATION OF EQUILIBRIUM

Frequently, equilibria are computed by using a variant of Scarf's algorithm, such as Eaves' or Merrill's method. To simplify comparative statics, we chose instead Smale's global Newton method. This like the fixed point methods, is guaranteed to converge. Global Newton is based on the observation that the solution to the differential equation

$$[D\tilde{f}_{(p,w)}] \begin{bmatrix} \dot{p} \\ \dot{w} \end{bmatrix} = \theta[sgn \ det \ D\tilde{f}_{(p,w)}]\tilde{f}(p, w), \tag{9}$$

where sgn $\theta$ is determined by a boundary condition. When $\theta = -1$ and *sgn det* $D\tilde{f} = +1$ near an equilibrium, (9) can be written as

$$\begin{bmatrix} \dot{p} \\ \dot{w} \end{bmatrix} = -[D\tilde{f}_{(p,w)}]^{-1}\tilde{f}(p, w). \tag{10}$$

This is simply continuous-time version of ordinary Newton's method. Like Eaves' or Merrill's algorithms, Scarf's algorithm converges, like Newton's method, in the neighbourhood of an equilibrium. We found that it worked quickly and effectively.

### 2 BENCHMARK EQUILIBRIUM

Table 3.2 gives the benchmark equilibrium we computed. It is not directly comparable to Mexican prices in the base period 1976–7 (which in our price normalisation are unity), since we used current value-added taxes rather than the old sales tax. For comparative purposes, we give the prices computed by Serra-Puche for the new tax system. As can be seen, the two sets of prices are quite close. Our inclusion of a financial sector does lead to minor differences in the predicted effect of the sales tax.

## VII  PROPOSED POLICY EXPERIMENTS

The major purpose of constructing a general equilibrium model is to trace the *differential* effects of policy changes between sectors. The model we have constructed is oriented largely towards analysing changes in monetary policy. Two types of monetary policy are of interest.

General monetary policies are those designed to affect overall economic activity. They include alterations in the rate of growth of the money base, changes in the tax *level* or in government spending, and changes in the composition of national debt. Our model is not the ideal one for analysing the overall effects of such policies: a smaller, more detailed model, calibrated on time-series data, would probably be better. However, general policies also have sector-specific effects. For example, changes in the composition of the national debt may displace private investment. This has two effects.

TABLE 3.2   BENCHMARK EQUILIBRIUM PRICES

| Factors | Base simulation | Serra puche | Discrepancy % |
|---|---|---|---|
| *Intermediate Goods* | | | |
| 1. Agriculture | 1.075 | 1.065 | 0.9 |
| 2. Mining | 0.993 | 1.006 | −1.3 |
| 3. Petroleum | 0.899 | 0.889 | 1.1 |
| 4. Food | 1.027 | 1.015 | 1.2 |
| 5. Textiles | 1.032 | 1.021 | 1.1 |
| 6. Wood | 1.000 | 1.000 | 0.0 |
| 7. Chemical | 0.941 | 0.947 | 0.6 |
| 8. Non-metal | 0.990 | 0.996 | 0.6 |
| 9. Machinery | 0.962 | 0.961 | 0.1 |
| 10. Electricity | 0.981 | 0.983 | 0.2 |
| 11. Commerce | 1.102 | 1.072 | 2.8 |
| 12. Transportation | 1.016 | 1.013 | 0.3 |
| 13. Services | 1.059 | 1.038 | 2.0 |
| 14. Construction | 1.022 | 1.008 | 1.4 |
| 15. Imports | 0.895 | 0.889 | 0.7 |
| 16. Next-period capital | 27.436 | 0.994 | na |
| *Final Goods* | | | |
| 1. Bread | 1.073 | 1.034 | 3.8 |
| 2. Milk | 1.096 | 1.052 | 4.2 |
| 3. Groceries | 1.005 | 0.969 | 3.7 |
| 4. Fruit | 1.114 | 1.067 | 4.4 |
| 5. Meat | 1.066 | 1.028 | 3.7 |
| 6. Fish | 1.086 | 1.044 | 4.0 |
| 7. Beverages | 0.963 | 0.925 | 4.1 |
| 8. Clothing | 1.047 | 1.020 | 2.6 |
| 9. Furniture | 0.999 | 0.979 | 2.0 |
| 10. Electronics | 0.973 | 0.952 | 2.2 |
| 11. Medical | 0.980 | 0.960 | 2.1 |
| 12. Transportation | 0.873 | 0.870 | 0.3 |
| 13. Education | 1.037 | 1.016 | 2.1 |
| 14. Personal | 1.001 | 0.981 | 2.0 |
| 15. Services | 1.017 | 1.000 | 1.7 |
| *Factors* | | | |
| 1. Rural labour | 1.000 | 1.057 | 5.7 |
| 2. Urban labour | 1.000 | 1.028 | 2.8 |
| 3. Capital | 28.259 | 1.093 | na |
| 4. Money | 0.238 | na | na |

It may change overall activity – GNP – and it can change sector proportions, depending on capital intensities and interactive income-effects. We argue that a general equilibrium model of the type we have constructed offers the best hope of understanding inter-sectoral shifts.

A second type of monetary policy, of particular importance in a country such as Mexico, consists of specific monetary policies. These attempt to influence separately the supply of funds to different sectors, and primarily take the form of selective credit controls. Whether these policies have the desired effect – increasing agricultural activity in Mexico, for example – depends on whether the effect of the implicit tax or subsidy can be shifted. This can be answered only by a general equilibrium model.

NOTES

1. Selective credit controls can be traced back to 1948. See Brothers and Solis (1966).
2. See Kaminow and O'Brien (1975) for a useful collection of papers on this subject.
3. Extensive surveys on this field are Kaminow and O'Brien (1975) and Silber (1973). A very useful summary of the state of the arts in selective credit policies is in Kaminow and O'Brien (1975).
4. See Table 3.1 for a description of the sectors.

REFERENCES

Anderson, T. (1971) *The Statistical Analysis of Time Series* (New York: John Wiley).
Arcelus, J. and Meltzer, A.H., (1973) 'The Markets for Housing and Housing Services', *Journal of Money Credit and Banking*.
Backus, D., Brainard, W.C., Smith, G. and Tobin, J. (1980) 'A Model of U.S. Financial and Non-Financial Economic Behavior', *Journal of Money Credit and Banking*.
Brothers, D.D. and Solis, Leopoldo (1966) *Mexican Financial Development* (Austin: University of Texas Press).
Cohen, J. (1968) 'Integrating the Real and Financial via the Linkage of Financial Flow', *Journal of Finance*.
Feltenstein, A. (1981) 'Money and Bonds in a Disaggregated Open Economy', unpublished paper.
Granger, C. (1969) 'Investigating Causal Relationships by Econometric Models and Cross-Spectral Methods', *Econometrica*.

Jaffee, D.M. and Rosen, K.A. (1978) 'Estimates of the Effectiveness of Stabilization Policies for the Mortgage and Housing Markets', *Journal of Finance*.

Kaminow, I. and O'Brien, J.M. (1975) 'Issues in Selective Credit Policies; An Evaluative Essay', published in Ira Kaminow and J.M. O'Brien (eds), *Studies in Selective Credit Policies* (Federal Reserve Bank of Philadelphia).

Litterman, R.L. (1979) 'Techniques of Forecasting Using Vector Auto-regressions', Working Paper (Federal Reserve Bank of Minneapolis).

Lucas, R.E. (1976) 'Econometric Policy Evaluation: A Critique', in K. Brunner and A. Meltzer (eds), *The Phillips Curve and the Labour Market* (Amsterdam: North Holland).

O'Brien, J. (1975) 'Household Asset Substitution and the Effectiveness of Selective Credit Policies', in I. Kaminow and J.M. O'Brien, *Studies in Selective Credit Policies* (Federal Reserve Bank of Philadelphia).

O'Brien, J. (1978) 'On the Incidence of Selective Credit and Related Policies in a Multi-Asset Framework', *Journal of Finance*.

Penner, R.G. and Silber, W.L. (1973) 'The Interaction between Federal Credit Programs and the Impact on the Allocation of Credit', *American Economic Review*.

Rao, D.C. and Kaminow, I. (1973) 'Selective Credit in a General Equilibrium Approach', *Journal of Finance*.

Serra-Puche, J. (1979) 'Fiscal Policies in Mexico: A General Equilibrium Approach', unpublished Ph.D. Dissertation, Yale University.

Shoven, J. and Whalley, J. (1972) 'A General Equilibrium Calculation of the Effects of Differential Taxation on Income from Capital in the U.S.', *Journal of Public Economics*.

Silber, W.L. (1976) *Portfolio Behavior of Financial Institutions: An Empirical Study with Implications for Monetary Policy, Interest Rate Determination and Financial Model Building* (New York: Holt, Rinehart and Winston).

Silber, W.L. (1973) 'Selective Credit Policies: A Survey', (Banca Nationzale del Lavoro); also published in (1975) I. Kaminow and J.M. O'Brien, *Studies in Selective Credit Policies* (Federal Reserve Bank of Philadelphia).

Sims, C.A. (1980) 'Macroeconomics and Reality', *Econometrica*.

Swamy, D.S. (1970) 'An Econometric Study of the United States Financial Markets', unpublished Ph.D. Dissertation, University of Pennsylvania.

Tobin, J. and Brainard, W. (1968) 'Pitfalls in Financial Model Building', *American Economic Review*.

Wilford, D.S. (1977) *Monetary Policy and the Open Economy: Mexico's Experience* (New York: Praeger).

# 4 Savings Generation and Financial Programming in a Basic Need Constrained Developing Economy[1]

## Jitendra G. Borpujari

INTERNATIONAL MONETARY FUND,
WASHINGTON DC, USA

## I  PURPOSE

This paper attempts to outline an approach to economic development
that aims at avoiding domestic inflationary pressures and external
payments' imbalances, while increasing the per capita consumption
of certain commodities which are treated as 'basics'. Predictably,
a prior assessment of the availability of and demand for 'basics'
emerges as the keystone of policies for balanced development. The
argument is offered, however, as no more than a tentative first step
toward strengthening the real economic content of policies for financial balance. Also, the aim is not so much to present a complete
formal system as to assemble a few operationally related ideas. As
such, the most that the paper can offer is a theoretical basis for
further reflections upon a somewhat new framework for analysing an
old problem.

## II   THE FAMILIAR APPROACH

Savings generation has customarily been studied in the same general format irrespective of whether the economy in question is classified as developing or developed. The underlying paradigm sees the consumer always and everywhere as facing the static problem of so allocating her given income upon the available consumables as to have no other allocation that is preferable in her own eyes. Representing *any* two of the available consumables along the two axes of Figure 4.1, the consumer is seen as able to choose *any* point along a budget line such as *AB*. Invoking her map of convex and homothetic preference functions, one arrives at the typical income–consumption line, *OC*, as a summary statement of consumer behaviour anywhere and at all times. Such an undifferentiated treatment of all consumables in studies of consumption is reflected in the practice of analysing savings generation universally in terms of the standard national income identity:

$$Y = C + S \tag{1}$$

where $Y$, $C$, and $S$ refer, respectively, to the aggregates of income, consumption, and savings. The key macroeconomic question then

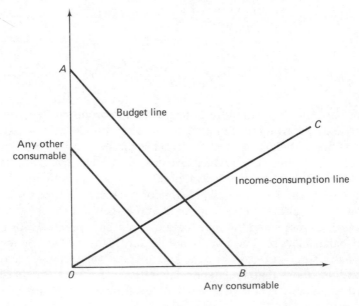

FIGURE 4.1.

becomes one simply of determining what the overall rate of savings should be. Further, identity (1) together with the equality of savings (*S*) and investment (*I*) in equilibrium imply that, given the incremental capital–output ratio (*k*), savings must grow *pari passu* with overall income, since:

$$\frac{\Delta Y}{Y} = \frac{1}{k} \frac{I}{Y} \tag{2}$$

The resulting consumption–savings dilemma has been studied for over half a century in the terms set by Ramsey (1928, p. 545):

> The more we save the sooner we shall reach bliss, but the less enjoyment we shall have now, and we have to set the one against the other. Mr. Keynes has shown me that the rules governing the amount to be saved can be determined at once from these considerations.

The growing sophistication of method notwithstanding, the subsequent optimum savings literature appears to have only repeated the original qualitative, policy implication, that is, economic development calls for a severe restraint on consumption per head in the early years, followed by relaxation in varying degrees later. Also, the promise of tomorrow that is used to justify austerity today rests wholly on the gains in productivity attributed to the adoption of modern technology. The politico-economic question of how to distribute the incidence of restraints on consumption restraint at the various income levels is simply evaded by most analysts. As Goodwin (1961, p. 764) exclaimed, in an instance of focusing usually esoteric analysis upon development policy: 'So great are the gains that we are fully justified in robbing the poor to give to the rich!.'[2]

As for financial programming, a consistent and integrated evolution of the financial and the real variables is self-evidently a crucial element in any development effort. The task is usually simplified very considerably by first taking the economy's overall growth rate (*g*) as an essentially given target. It then turns to the historical or notional link between the evolving real money stock and real output (i.e. the demand for money function) in order to determine by how much domestic liquidity is to be allowed to grow. More specifically, the consistent rate of monetary expansion equals *g* times the income-elasticity of real demand for money; as Rhomberg (1977) pointed out, at some stage the elasticity figure becomes closer to unity, and the money supply then grows approximately at the rate *g*. This happens after an economy has passed through the earlier stages of development so that the financial system can develop more rapidly than the rest of the economy. Once the permissible target for monetary expansion is determined, the core of a consistent financial policy consists of determining how that projected increase in liabilities is to be distributed on the assets side of the monetary system's balance sheet. This simple format can accommodate innumerable variations and refinements, so that one has in effect a standardised numerical framework applicable to any economy. For instance, the change in net foreign assets (i.e. the overall balance of payments) may be taken as a target, so that the ceiling on domestic credit creation turns up as a residual (cf. IMF Institute, 1981).

The rest of this paper considers mainly a framework for analysing $g$, so as to provide a basis for the financial policies described above. In so doing, a direct link is suggested between the problems of generating savings and those of designing consistent financial policies. *Inter alia*, such an integration highlights the inseparability of financial balance from meaningful economic development policies.


## III   THE PROPOSED APPROACH

In line with Engel's Law and Pasinetti (1981), the following argument sees the consumer as having certain hierarchical priorities in distributing his income among the available consumables.[3] In particular, there are now inescapable irreversibilities in the process of consumption, so that certain needs that the consumer considers to be 'basics' have to be met before non-basic, or supplementary, consumption can begin. In terms of Figure 4.2, the consumer's choice problem is qualitatively different, depending on the location of his budget line relative to $M$ – which denotes the minimum consumption of basics required for survival. The region to the left of $M$ is non-feasible, since the consumer must either die or somehow acquire the income necessary to consume $M$. Clearly, the range of feasible choices is seen as a narrower one in the basic-needs approach of Figure 4.2 than in the standard paradigm in Figure 4.1. Moreover, the customary level of the basic consumption minimum can be expected to exceed $M$ considerably. As a result, the consumer's choice can be represented by a composite linear function such as $MNC$, which shows that non-basic consumption remains nil until income has risen to a level sufficient to allow the consumer to afford the customary basic basket $N$.[4] What-

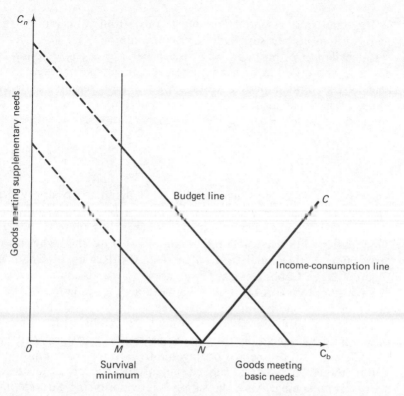

FIGURE 4.2

ever the prices, the consumer first buys his basics and then allocates any leftover income among his supplementary needs in some manner. Beyond the kink at $N$, the location of the income–consumption line can be interpreted through the standard analytical framework underlying Figure 4.1. Given such an approach, and ruling out policies that push consumers leftward along $MNC$ towards the Region of Death in Figure 4.2, the national accounting identity (1) has to be extended to allow one to analyse savings generation in a developing economy. It becomes:

$$Y = C_b + C_n + S, \tag{3}$$

where $C_b$ and $C_n$ stand, respectively, for basic and non-basic consumption. Granted that the share of basics in aggregate income $(C_b/Y)$ is not allowed to decline, (2), (3) and the equality of savings and investment in equilibrium imply that a rise in the savings ratio

($S/Y$) is not only essential, but must come from restraints on the share of non-basic or supplementary consumption ($C_n/Y$).

Kalecki's (1976) postulate of a rise in per capita consumption of basics as the criterion of economic development is consistent with Engel's Law and implies a Cobb–Douglas type relation between levels of national income ($Y$) and population ($Q$) as sources of demand for basic needs ($C_b$). The implicit relationship is simply:

$$\frac{C_b}{Q} = \left(\frac{Y}{Q}\right)^e \qquad\qquad (4)$$

where $0 < e$ is the income-elasticity of demand for basics, which depends on income-elasticities for various income classes and commodities, and on the distribution of income among these classes. In general, $e$ is a positive fraction that is closer to unity the higher is the proportion of the population on or near the Region of Death in Figure 4.2 The Cobb–Douglas formulation above, of course, treats $e$ as a constant for short-term planning, although it is admitted to be a declining function of $Y$ in the longer term.

The crucial problem of underdevelopment is obviously an economy's inability to meet the rising demand for basics as summarised in (4). Clearly, that problem is aggravated by a faster growth of population, though population may reasonably be treated as given for short-term planning. Also, the supply constraint facing a developing economy is typically the capacity to increase the availability of basics. These considerations can be made explicit by taking logarithms and rearranging the terms in (4) so that:

$$g = \frac{b}{e} - q\left(\frac{1}{e} - 1\right). \qquad\qquad (5)$$

Here, the overall growth rate ($g$) is shown as a function of the growth rate of basics ($b$), the rate of population growth ($q$), and the average income elasticity of demand ($e$) for basics. Given $q$ and $e$, the ceiling on $g$ is set by the limits on $b$.

In Figure 4.3, $BC$ represents (5) and has a positive slope determined by $e$. The economy's potential growth rate is now set at the point of intersection $P$ of $BC$ and the perpendicular to the ordinate at $b_{max}$. The ceiling $b_{max}$ has to be determined empirically as a measure of the highest rate of growth of basics that is feasible for this economy under the existing institutional and technological milieu. So long as the economy is to the left of $P$, growth of total income can be accelerated

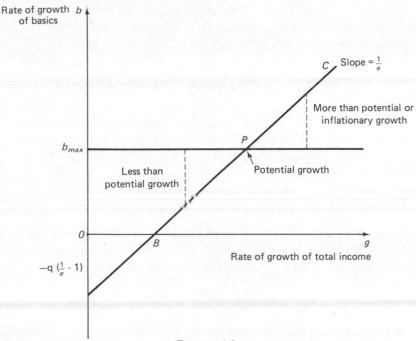

FIGURE 4.3

without necessarily creating an imbalance in the supply of and demand for basics. To the right of $P$, however, any attempt to accelerate $g$ must have inflationary consequences. In other words, except when the economy can finance an appropriate external payments deficit, there will be a leftward shift by the poorest classes along their income–consumption curves, as along $MNC$ in Figure 4.2. Thus, once the economy is at $P$, an acceleration of Kaleckian economic development requires either a relaxation of domestic production constraints on basics through technological or institutional improvements, or an increase in basic supplies through trade or aid. All such measures have the effect of shifting $b_{max}$ upwards so that the intersection point $P$ moves to the right. Notably, the underlying idea is essentially the same as the concept of an Inflation Barrier in Joan Robinson (1965, p. 356).[5]

Equation (5) both recognises the specific savings generation problem in a basic need constrained developing economy, and provides a framework for evaluating the target, $g$. Thus, the first task in designing balanced development is to determine the flexibility of basic supplies. The familiar standardised numerical framework for financial policy, mentioned in Section II, can then serve principally as the financial counterpart of the real issues.


## IV   BALANCED GROWTH CONFIGURATIONS

The balanced development argument above implies a consistency among: the growth rates for basics ($b$), total consumption ($c$), population ($q$), and overall income ($g$). This is described approximately, for $e < 1$, in Figure 4.4.

### 1   A CLOSED ECONOMY

With all axes measuring rates of growth, the right-hand quadrant of Figure 4.4. represents equation (5) by $BC$. The per capita consumption of basics remains unchanged so long as the economy is at $B$, such that:

$$b_1 = g_1 = q. \tag{6}$$

For per capita basic consumption to rise, however, production of basics must grow faster than population, with the concomitant overall income growth determined along a line such as $BC$. This lies between the 45° line and the vertical from the abscissa through $B$. In other words, the Kaleckian acceleration of $g$ beyond $g_1$ presumes an appropriate expansion of basics, following Engel's Law. The condition of rising per capita consumption of basics in a developing economy also implies, of course, that the savings generation required under (2) comes wholly from restraints on non-basic or supplementary consumption. Given the hierarchic nature of consumer behaviour outlined above, such restraints – whether voluntary or involuntary – can be expected to have no impact on the demand for basics by the higher income groups. And they would obviously represent the main source for the savings generated. Hence, the postulated link (5) between $b$ and $g$ would remain largely unaffected by the restraints on supplementary consumption required for an appropriate savings generation.

The left-hand quadrant of Figure 4.4 gives an indication of the link between $g$ and the growth rate of total consumption ($c$) which implies restraints on supplementary consumption. Under (2), to any initial overall growth rate ($g_0$), there corresponds a certain savings

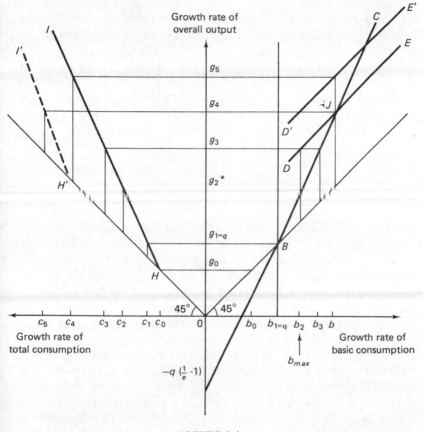

FIGURE 4.4

(= investment) proportion, which remains constant so long as the capital-output ratio ($k$) is unchanged. Any acceleration of $g$ from $g_0$ must, however, imply also a rise in the savings proportion at unchanged $k$. In other words, $g$ will exceed $c$, such that the bigger the difference ($g - c$) the greater is the average $g$ during the programme period relevant to $g_0$. Thus, the deviation of *HI* from the 45° line in Figure 4.4. gives an approximate illustration of an intuitively obvious idea. This is the growing problem of restraining supplementary consumption in order to generate the savings warranted by the need to raise the investment share in overall output in a developing economy.

Points such as $(b_0, g_0, c_0)$ and $(b_1, g_1, c_1)$ represent, approximately, the successively higher balanced-growth configurations in a developing economy. Inflation, or a decline in the real income of the population's poorer strata, is inevitable in a closed economy if an attempt is made to accelerate growth beyond the ceiling rate $g_2^*$ set by $b_{max}$, the maximum feasible expansion of basic supplies. Kaleckian development beyond $g_2^*$ presupposes either a relaxation in the domestic production constraint on basics or an appropriately structured balance of payments.

## 2  AN OPEN ECONOMY

Trade or aid can make a higher rate of balanced overall growth feasible, by easing the constraint on the supply of basics and by bringing in foreign capital to supplement domestically generated savings. Clearly, the smaller is an economy's initial volume of non-basic consumption, that is, the more underdeveloped an economy is, the greater is its dependence on the benefits of openness in order to bring about balanced development. However, trade and aid have to be appropriately structured for openness to assist rather than impede an acceleration of Kaleckian development.

In Figure 4.4, let $DE$ describe an economy's supply possibilities for basics in the presence of imports, these are assumed, for the moment, to be financed wholly by exports. The ceiling rate of autarkic balanced development is still determined by $b_{max}$ at $g_2^*$, but the economy's highest balanced growth configuration is now at $(b_{max}, g_3, c_3)$ rather than $(b_{max}, g_2^*, c_2)$, such that $g_3 > g_2^*$, and $c_3 > c_2$. The difference $(b_3 - b_{max})$ in Figure 4.4 is met by a rise in imports of basics financed *ex hypothesis* by a matching rise in non-basic exports. Such benefits of trade are indicated by the lateral distance between $BC$ and $DE$. They become increasingly difficult to achieve, however, as the export drive confronts deteriorating terms of trade and increasing trade barriers. A point is eventually reached, such that there is no further development advantage from more foreign trade. In fact, beyond $J$, the home production of basics has to rise faster, merely to finance an expanding demand for non-basic imports.

A tendency towards trade deficits is, of course, a hallmark of a typical developing economy. Since accumulated foreign exchange reserves are usually small, a trade deficit in most cases implies either borrowings or grants. The essentials of the impact of such resource flows on the balanced growth configurations of Figure 4.4 can be stated by concentrating on net receipts of grants; the conclusions will, however, apply *mutatis mutandis* to inflows that presuppose subsequent outflows in repatriated profits or payments of interest. The key impact of unrequited transfers is, of course, to expand an economy's supply of basics and non-basics at no cost to the domestic economy. Starting from the initial position at $J$, such grant inflows can be depicted as bringing about a parallel shift in the basic supply availability from $DE$, upwards to $D'E'$, and a shift in the left quadrant from $HI$ to $H'I'$. In other words, the economy can now experience higher balanced growth configurations with a greater consumption of both basics and non-basics. It will be noted that the grants received will not necessarily be absorbed in a way that accelerates Kaleckian development. They may, in fact, be spent instead wholly or partly on increased consumption of basics or of non-basics.

To sum up, the developmental benefits of opening up an economy to the rest of the world result from the opportunities that are provided (1) for adding to the domestic production of basics, and (2) for reducing the necessity to restrain growth the of non-basic consumption in order that savings maybe generated. Hence, the actual impact depends not only on whether an economy is a net recipient of external resources, but also on the precise composition and utilisation of the imports thus financed.

## V  BASICS AND DEVELOPMENT

The analysis above has indicated the consistency that a Kaleckian acceleration of economic development requires among the growth rates of basics, total consumption, population, and overall income. A more satisfactory analysis of savings generation in a developing economy in the framework of (3), requires some of the scholarly attention that the issue framed in (1) has already received. This presents us with the task of locating the consistency study above, within an overall analysis of the growth process in less-developed countries. Such an analysis, conceived independently of Kalecki but, like his, strongly reminiscent of the theory of growth in classical economics, has been developed over the years by Kaldor (1975, 1976, 1979). It is discussed in what follows.[6]

The key relationships between basics and development can most simply be presented for the special case of $e = 1$ which, from (5), implies an equality of the growth rates for overall income ($g$) and for basics (*b*). Abstracting from the external sector in the first approximation,[7] let the closed economy consist exclusively of a Basic Sector (*B*) producing only basics ($C_b$), and a Development Sector (*D*) specialising in investment goods (*I*). In a typical developing economy (cf. Section VI below), basics consist almost wholly of agricultural products – especially foodgrains. Hence, the *B* and the *D* sectors can be taken, in practice, to be agriculture and manufacturing industry respectively. We assume for simplicity that all consumption is of basic or agricultural goods.[8]

This model views economic development as a process which depends on the complementarity of *B* and *D*. In other words, *D* depends on *B* for basics, which are exchanged for the amounts of capital goods offered at the going terms of trade between the two sectors. The dependence is, however, asymmetric. First, basic needs being hierarchically prior, *D*'s dependence on *B* is irreversible, but not vice versa.[9] Second, real wages in the Development Sector have a floor, or an acceptable minimum basket of basic needs, which is set by a combination of physiology, custom, and contract. But no such downward rigidity is characteristic of the Basic Sector, which is mostly engaged in subsistence production (cf. Borpujari, 1980a). Finally, just as *D* cannot function without *B*, such as *B*'s dependence on *D* is equally complete for any *growth* in basic production which requires increased employment of the capital goods produced by *D*.

This model does *not* presuppose an inherent tendency towards equilibrium, nevertheless the attainment of inter-sectoral balance would imply an equality of the *B* and *D* sectors' 'savings' or surpluses, so that supply equals demand. In other words, the basics 'saved' by the *B* sector must equal the demand for basic consumption in *D*. Equivalently, the capital goods 'saved' and offered by *D* must equal the demand for these commodities in *B*. The fundamental prerequisite for Kaleckian balanced development is, therefore, the maintenance of an economically specified ratio between the outputs of *B* and *D*. The extra insight which Kaldor's model provides, over and above that in Sections III and IV, is that it shows the factors likely to determine the growth in *B*–output. They are explicitly considered and not simply subsumed in a fixed constraint, $b_{max}$. In particular, the focus is concentrated upon the productivity of investment in agriculture, with attention drawn also to the terms of trade between industry and agriculture. These are denoted in what follows as *p*, and are defined as the price of industrial goods in terms of agricultural goods.

Policies to maintain equilibrium over time require that the growth of the surplus of basics must match the growth of the development sector's demand for basics. Equivalently, the development sector's excess of output over its own-product absorption must grow at the same rate as the basic sector's demand for capital goods. Now, the well-known Lewis (1954) generalisation, of widespread validity for developing economies, is that agricultural output depends exclusively on the level of technology and on the amount of capital employed in production. We had ignored technological progress in order to simplify the argument. The growth in the output of basics, as of overall output in equation (2) above, depends by definition on the incremental productivity of agricultural investment and on the share of investment in agricultural output. But the investment–output ratio in the basic sector can be defined, too. It must equal the saving ratio of that sector divided by the terms of trade – the price ($p$) of investment goods in terms of agricultural goods. Thus the growth of basics is inversely related to the industrial terms of trade. This is indicated by the $bb'$ curve in Figure 4.5. Here, the ordinate measures $p$ while the abscissa measures the growth in output of basics (and, therefore, the expansion of $B$'s demand for $D$'s products). A rise in the savings ratio in basics, or in the productivity of agricultural investment, shifts $bb'$ upwards.

Similarly, the development sector's output growth depends, as in equation (2), upon the sectoral ratio of investment to output and the corresponding incremental productivity of investment. But the basic needs insight alerts one to a further fact. This is that the ratio of investment to output depends upon the amount of output which must be foregone in order that the basic needs bundle of agricultural goods may be provided for the workers who produce development goods. Given the special case $e = 1$, the agricultural goods required to satisfy these basic needs per unit output of the development sector remain unchanged. But the proportion of development–goods output which must be foregone in order to obtain these agricultural goods depends inversely on the industrial terms of trade. Thus industrial investment, and hence industrial growth, depend positively on the industrial terms of trade. This is indicated on $dd'$ in Figure 4.5. The price of development goods cannot fall below the lower limit, set at $v$, where all the development output would be devoted to purchasing the agricultural basic goods required for industrial workers. In the other direction, the growth rate approaches the productivity of investment as the amount of investment goods that has to be exchanged for basics becomes insignificant. The curve shifts up or down

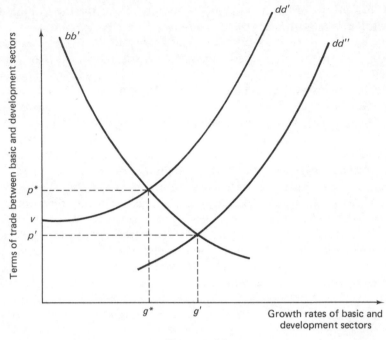

FIGURE 4.5

if these basic goods requirements rise or fall. A rise in the productivity of investment will clearly shift the $dd'$ curve outward.

Balanced growth of $B$ and $D$ is depicted in Figure 4.5 from Kaldor (1979, p. 288) as the point where the $bb'$ and $dd'$ curves intersect. Given the sectoral productivities, the economy's balanced growth path is related positively to the basic sector's propensity to save or to generate a surplus in basics; it is related negatively to the size of the minimum basket of basics (per unit of its own output) that is acceptable to labour outside the basic sector. Notably, this result holds irrespective of the economy's institutional framework. Further, this conclusion suggests a conceptual framework for thinking about economic development, and does so whether or not one considers the very short term or the distant future of an evolving economy.

This framework shows with startling clarity that economic development combined with financial balance will be impossible if the development sector attempts to press ahead and to grow faster than the growth rate that the availability of basics makes possible. Such a policy can be represented, in Figure 4.5, by an attempt to push up the growth rate to $g'$. At $g'$ there is an excess demand for basics: so there is either inflation or, *if the country is so fortunate*, a balance of payments deficit. As can be seen from the $dd'$ curve in Figure 4.5, for growth to be maintained at a rate equal to $g'$, a better terms of trade of industrial goods (i.e. a lower price of agricultural goods) is required. Such an improvement is represented formally, in Figure 4.5, by a downward shift in $dd'$ to $dd''$. Elimination of the excess demand for basics through inflation would, of course, be inconsistent both with financial balance and with the goals of the basic needs approach outline in Section III.

Kaldor's model has been extended in several policy-oriented and testable directions in Kaldor, Thirlwall, and Vines (1981). These extensions are more amenable to empirical testing than the Kaleckian formulations reviewed in Borpujari (1980b). The assumption of a closed economy can be dropped in Kaldor's model, as in the Kaleckian analysis in Section IV, by considering the external sector to represent a supplement to the Basic Sector as a source of basics, and as a supplementary market for consumables and capital goods. The role of supplementary, or luxury, consumption $(C_n)$ is formally the same as that of 'capitalist's consumption' in Kalecki (1969); an economy's balanced growth potential, under the basic needs approach, can be enhanced by reductions in the extent to which basics are allocated to produce or acquire luxuries rather than capital goods. The Kaldor model can also be reworked to accommodate the fact that, as living standards rise, workers spend a falling proportion of their wages on basics, in line with Engel's Law. In other words, although the wage-bill of the $D$-sector still rises *pari passu* with $D$-output, the proportion of that increase which is spent on basics grows by less than the rate of growth of $D$-output. Effectively, the smaller is the income-elasticity of demand for basics, then the less is the growth of $D$-output constrained by the growth in the availability of basics, and the more is it possible for the growth of $D$–output to be self-sustaining.

But, no matter how great the refinements are, the essential point about balanced development under the basic needs approach remains as in Kalecki (1970), Kaldor, (1975, 1976, 1979), Borpujari (1980b), and Kaldor, Thirlwall, and Vines (1981). An economy confronting the basic needs constraint cannot accelerate its development without running into domestic inflationary pressures or an external payments deficit. In other words, the acceleration of development without financial imbalances in a basic need constrained economy presupposes an appropriate rise in the supply of basics. This can come through increased domestic productivity in the production of basics; improvements in the external terms of trade; or a greater availability of external finance.[10]

## VI   EMPIRICAL DETERMINATION OF A BASIC NEEDS BASKET

The foregoing argument is couched entirely in concepts which are measurable in economic statistics that already exist or can be collected. Indeed, all the categories used are more or less familiar except for the term 'Basic Needs' which is still a novelty that has entered only partially into even the very comprehensive statistical lexicon of the United Nations (1980). But a Basic Needs Basket is also precisely the concept that has to be quantified and projected methodically for designing a process of balanced development as outlined above.

Once the two commodity paradigm of Figure 4.1 is given up for the basic needs format of Figure 4.2, one has to adopt a systemwide approach, where the demand for each commodity in a basket is determined simultaneously by the available income and by the prices of all commodities. Further, the equation sytem has to decompose total income so as to identify a minimum basket on which the consumer expends his income whatever the price, which the remainder of income allocated in some fashion over non-basics. A method that delivers such results is of course the Linear Expenditure System (LES) pioneered by Stone (1954) and applied extensively to developed economies as reviewed, for instance, in Phlips (1974) and Deaton and Muellbauer (1980). These have also been recent applications to developing economies by, among others, Lluch and Powell (1975), Radhakrishna (1978) and the Government of India (1979).[11]

The LES estimation which follows used the data on consumer expenditures, in rupees per person, collected in National Sample Surveys (NSS) for thirteen income categories and a number of commodities. These have been regrouped here into nine items, for rural and urban India from 1964–5 to 1970–1.[12] The price deflators are from a report by the Perspective Planning Division of India's Planning Commission and the original data were modified to match the commodity groupings in the expenditure estimates. Due adjustments were also made to normalise the per capita expenditure figures for variations in sample sizes across expenditure classes and over time. The adjusted data were then regrouped into Lower Income, Middle Income, and Upper Income categories, using the same expenditure classes, as in the 19th Round of the NSS, at 1961–2 prices. In other words, the expenditure groups were left unchanged at constant prices but varied in current prices so that, for instance, the Lower Income category covered Rs 0–11 in the first and Rs 0–18 in the last year of the experiment period. Finally, the LES was estimated by a maximum likelihood procedure, using algorithm based on a quasi-Newton method.[13]

The preliminary estimates presented in Table 4.1 are given purely as illustrations, and indicate how the basic need baskets and marginal budget shares vary across income groups. A reasonable first step in designing a Kaleckian balanced development programme would be to assume that the Middle Income category is a realistic prototype of wage-labour, and that the entire demand for basic needs induced by development is incremental. The cross-elasticities of demand have turned out to be generally negligible. Equation (5) can therefore be used, as in Table 4.1, to compute the approximate consistent growth rates of basics consistent with given growth rates of overall income and population. The task then is to evaluate the economy's capacity to satisfy these required increases in basic supplies.

A number of studies, from Mathur and Ezekiel (1961) to Isher Ahluwalia (1979), have suggested that any excess demand for basics is unlikely to be eased in the short to medium term by responses of domestic supply to a rise in basic need prices. Additionally, Table 4.1 indicates how income-elasticities of demand generally declined with a rise in income levels – except for 'other non-foods', which are mostly consumed by the richer classes. Since inflationary profits generally boost the incomes of the asset-owning classes, the rise in prices of basics is likely to have its expansionary impact mostly on the demand for non-basic consumption, as suggested, for instance, in Radhakrishna (1978). In any case, the inter-sectoral terms of trade are unlikely to shift in favour of the Basic Sector so long as organised labour in the Development Sector is able to increase its real wages proportionately. If it can, a rise in basic prices is likely to be followed by generalised inflation, as hypothesised in Kaldor (1975).

The LES is used here solely as one possible approach to the problem of quantifying the demand for basics. Table 4.1 shows that the income-elasticities exceed unity for most cases, except foodgrains. The assumption that the overall elasticity is less than unity is

TABLE 4.1 ILLUSTRATIVE BASIC BASKETS, MARGINAL BUDGET SHARES, INCOME ELASTICITIES AND REQUIRED GROWTH IN BASIC SUPPLIES FOR RURAL AND URBAN INDIA, 1964/5–1970/1[1]

| Commodity Groups | $b_i$ Basic basket | | | $m_i$ Marginal Budget Shares | | | $n_i$ Income elasticities[2] | | | Required Basic growth[3] |
| --- | --- | --- | --- | --- | --- | --- | --- | --- | --- | --- |
| | Lower income | Middle income | Upper income | Lower income | Middle income | Upper income | Lower income | Middle income | Upper income | (In per cent per year) |
| Urban | | | | | | | | | | |
| 1. Foodgrains | 2.92 | 4.61 | 8.60 | 0.26 | 0.13 | 0.08 | 0.82 | 0.46 | 0.44 | 3.38 |
| 2. Milk and milk products | 0.38 | 0.52 | 4.53 | 0.11 | 0.10 | 0.03 | 6.21 | 2.60 | 1.17 | 9.80 |
| 3. Edible oil | 0.24 | 0.30 | 0.31 | 0.01 | 0.04 | 0.04 | 0.60 | 1.34 | 1.10 | 6.02 |
| 4. Meat, eggs, and fish | 0.03 | 0.31 | 0.03 | 0.07 | 0.04 | 0.02 | 4.26 | 2.09 | 0.70 | 8.27 |
| 5. Sugar | 0.20 | 0.28 | 0.29 | 0.07 | 0.04 | 0.01 | 3.10 | 1.68 | 0.48 | 7.04 |
| 6. Other food | 0.33 | 0.47 | 0.47 | 0.21 | 0.18 | 0.10 | 2.62 | 2.17 | 0.84 | 8.51 |
| 7. Clothing | 0.16 | 0.55 | 0.56 | 0.07 | 0.12 | 0.12 | 0.15 | 0.25 | 0.26 | 2.75 |
| 8. Fuel and light | 0.37 | 0.94 | 0.93 | 0.03 | 0.05 | 0.10 | 6.94 | 4.77 | 3.22 | 16.31 |
| 9. Other non-food | 0.80 | 1.13 | 12.31 | 0.18 | 0.30 | 0.54 | 1.17 | 2.19 | 3.90 | 8.57 |
| Rural | | | | | | | | | | |
| 1. Foodgrains | 6.00 | 7.70 | 10.6 | 0.38 | 0.24 | 0.09 | 0.60 | 0.42 | 0.23 | 3.26 |
| 2. Milk and milk products | 0.39 | 0.55 | 2.79 | 0.05 | 0.05 | 0.05 | 2.58 | 0.93 | 0.45 | 4.79 |
| 3. Edible oil | 0.32 | 0.19 | 0.80 | 0.02 | 0.02 | 0.03 | 0.70 | 0.58 | 0.90 | 3.74 |
| 4. Meat, eggs, and fish | 0.06 | 0.19 | 1.00 | 0.04 | 0.07 | 0.02 | 2.15 | 2.72 | 0.78 | 10.16 |
| 5. Sugar | 0.19 | 0.30 | 1.10 | 0.06 | 0.06 | 0.02 | 2.55 | 1.79 | 0.50 | 7.37 |
| 6. Other food | 0.99 | 1.49 | 3.50 | 0.17 | 0.08 | 0.07 | 1.66 | 0.81 | 0.77 | 4.43 |
| 7. Clothing | 0.45 | 0.55 | 3.60 | 0.07 | 0.09 | 0.15 | 4.98 | 2.59 | 1.67 | 9.77 |
| 8. Fuel and light | 0.82 | 0.95 | 1.80 | 0.04 | 0.07 | 0.06 | 0.50 | 1.07 | 1.14 | 5.21 |
| 9. Other non-food | 0.80 | 0.90 | 5.59 | 0.16 | 0.33 | 0.52 | 2.33 | 3.62 | 2.99 | 12.86 |

[1] Maximum likelihood estimates of the Linear Expenditure System using a quasi-Newton method. The LES was fitted in the form: $P_{it}X_{it} = P_{it}b_i + m_i(Y_t - \Sigma_j P_{jt}b_j)$ where $P_{it}$ is the price of commodity $i$ ($i = 1, 2, \ldots, 9$), $X_{it}$ is total quantity of commodity $i$ bought at time $t$, $b_i$ is the basic part of the total purchase of $i$, $m_i$ is the marginal budget share of $i$, and $Y_t$ is the total income of the consumer; $m_i$ are proportions so that $\Sigma_i m_i = 1$.

[2] Income elasticities ($\eta_i$) are computed using the formula: $\eta_i = (m_i/W_i)$, $i = 1, 2, \ldots, 9$; where $m_i$ = marginal budget share of a group, $W_i = (P_i E_i/E_i)$ where $P_i E_i$ is the expenditure of a group on $i$ at current prices and $Y_t$ is the total expenditure at current prices.

nevertheless plausible in view of the preponderance of food-grains in total consumption, especially among the poorer classes, which account for by far the majority of a developing economy's population. The estimation of elasticities as structures rather than at individual points is essential, however, for the reliable projection of the basic need components. The disaggregated approach also makes clear the range of choices available for selecting the prototype for a basic needs basket.

The interpretative advantages of the LES are often traced to the method's consistency with the orthodox theory of consumer behaviour, as demonstrated originally by Samuelson (1947–8). However, since utility maximisation at the microlevel is no longer considered essential for deriving aggregate demand functions (cf. Sonnenschein, 1973a and 1973b; and Debreu 1973), one can as well accept the LES as a purely pragmatic statistical device.[14] The essential fact is that realistic measures seem to be within reach which provide operational significance to the distinction between basic and non-basic consumption, which is presented above as the key to a policy of financially balanced development.


## VII  A SUMMING UP

The proposal above to increase the real economic content of financial programmes in a developing economy is hinged on a definition of development as a rising satisfaction of a population's consumption needs, in a commodity sequence that follows Engel's Law. Such a definition of economic development not only appears unquestionable on grounds of common sense and physiology, but is also consistent with empirical evidence from consumption research since Ernst Engel's original essay of 1857. At the same time, acceptance of Engel's Law calls for an abandonment of the familiar aggregative approach to savings generation and development financing, in favour of another that is concerned with the commodity-mix of overall output. To say that the availability of basics is a condition of development is to imply that ceilings on the growth of basics set limits also for financially balanced development. Further, if inflation in basics is not self-correcting because of an asymmetry between the production structures of basics and non-basics, then an appropriate proportionality between basics and other products is a necessary condition of financially balanced development. Such a view makes the issues of the balance between savings and investment interchangeable with the real problems of maintaining a dynamic balance between surpluses of basics and of other commodities during the process of development.

The challenge of financially balanced development is shown as too complex and far-reaching to be contained substantively in a naive juxtaposition of the demand for money function with a monetary system's balance sheet identity. Therefore, an alternative approach is suggested, which highlights the financial analyst's preoccupations while capturing the essentials of the development process. Operationally, however, the proposed alternative is but a new anchor for the familiar financial programming framework. The analysis assigns real causes to financial imbalances without implying that such imbalances cannot be caused by monetary phenomena. The paper therefore supplements, and does not substitute, the usual policies for achieving financial balance in a developing economy.

The definition of balanced development in the proposed approach clarifies the link between financial balance and economic development, while the new perspective brings out the essential inseparability of the two problems. At the same time, the proposal recognises that there is an operationally important difference between the issues of financial balance and of economic development, comparable to the distinction between the short term and the long term in Marshall (1920, pp. 378–9). More specifically, policies for shorter-term financial balance treat as constants a number of parameters which become variable as the time-span of the argument is increased, so allowing us to consider the underlying, fundamental issues of economic development.

If the basic needs viewpoint is essentially sound, then the challenge for economists is formidable as the reconstruction must both fashion novel tools and collect new statistics. The difficulty arises partly from the lack of a familiar theoretical framework for incorporating Engel's Law into the economics of development (cf. Galbis, 1972). A more important source of the difficulty would seem to be, however, the vast commitment of resources in recent history upon the notion that a financial programme is determinable, more or less, by purely financial considerations. One is, therefore, reduced to hoping that the 53-year-old Keynes (1936, pp. 383–4) was not overly optimistic when he wrote:

> [In] the field of economic and political philosophy there are not many who are influenced by new theories after they are twenty-five

or thirty years of age, so that the ideas which civil servants and politicians and even agitators apply to current events are not likely to be the newest. But, soon or late, it is ideas, not vested interests which are dangerous for good or evil.

NOTES

1. An earlier version of the paper, entitled 'Toward a Basic Needs Approach to Economic Development with Financial Stability', was circulated as an internal document of the International Monetary Fund and discussed in seminars at the Bank of Greece, Athens, and the Nationalekonomiska Institutionen of Lund, Sweden. The present version was prepared while the author was a Visiting Associate of Clare Hall, Cambridge, and has benefited from several colleagues in the IMF, and especially from J. Borkakoti, A.S. Borpujari, R.M. Goodwin, L.K. Jha, Lord Kaldor, M. Kuman, G. Ohlin, L.L. Pasinetti, M.H. Pesaran, W.B. Reddaway, Joan Robinson, K. Velupillai, and D. Vines. The paper reflects the author's personal views which are not necessarily shared by any individual or institution he is associated with.
2. In a letter of 17 October 1981 to the author, Professor Joan Robinson noted: 'Figure 1 should emphasise that it is in terms of net saving. The assumption is that the existing stock of inputs once achieved is kept intact but if technical change is going on this is rather an awkward assumption. I think that in the early days of S = I we were a bit careless about this and it really is quite a serious blemish on the exposition of the model . . . Again emphasize that development turns on technology as well as accumulation. The average consumer is also a difficult concept. However, I don't suppose these points really matter on the level on which you are trying to get the main ideas across.'
3. A less technical but more comprehensive presentation of a similar viewpoint is in Jha (1980).
4. A method of empirically projecting growth rates for such a basket of basic needs, from household budget surveys for particular income classes at a certain time for a given economy, is suggested in Section VI.
5. The potential growth rate $P$ must not be given a standard equilibrium interpretation; there is no tendency for a typical developing economy to move sytematically towards $P$. In other words, the actual $b^{***}$ can be well below the potential $b^{***}$, reflecting an economy's institutional failure to operate at a higher level of capacity realisation.
6. The ideas sketched by Kaldor in the three papers referred to are explored more fully in a draft manuscript by Kaldor, Thirlwall, and Vines (1981) which is the basis of the following brief verbal exposition. This Section has benefited from conversations with Lord Kaldor, and with Mr David Vines of Pembroke College, Cambridge, neither of whom is responsible for any errors in the adaptation. Also, no attempt is made to relate the exercise to the large cognate literature on economic dualism in developing countries.

7. The external sector's inclusion does not change the central conclusions.
8. As shown in Kaldor, Thirlwall, and Vines (1981), this simplifying assumption in Kaldor (1979) can be relaxed without changing the central conclusions.
9. Indeed, the problem of development finance would not have arisen if labour in industry could be paid wages in industrial goods alone, just as agricultural wages are payable, in the last resort, with the products of agriculture; an agricultural labourer can manage without bicycles, but the labourer making bicycles cannot do without food.
10. The limitations of export-led development are analysed from another viewpoint in Chichilnisky (1980).
11. An interpretation of the LES inclusive of savings is provided in Lluch, Powell and Williams (1978).
12. This section is based on Borpujari (1981), a partly completed joint study with Mr M. Kumar of Trinity College, Cambridge, and helpful suggestions from Dr A.S. Borpujari of the University of Washington DC.
13. The convergence criterion for the coefficients was set at 0.001; this value was multiplied by each coefficient starting value to compute the convergence condition for each coefficient. The maximum number of iterations was specified to be 300, and the model was re-estimated with different starting values to verify that the global maximum had in fact been achieved. A large number of iterations were required in the initial runs, but convergence was much quicker in the final runs which obtained new starting values from earlier runs.
14. Dr K. Veluppillai of the European University Institute, Florence, first drew the author's attention to this literature. Use of the LES is justifiable, also, because the analysis is inherently macroeconomic and not merely an aggregation of microphenomena (cf. Pasinetti, 1974, p. 118).

REFERENCES

Ahluwalia, Isher J. (1979) 'An Analysis of Price and Output Behaviour in the Indian Economy: 1951–1973', *Journal of Development Economics*, vol. 6.
Borpujari, Jitendra G. (1980a) 'Production and Monetization in the Subsistence Sector', in W.L. Coats, and D.R. Khatkhate, (eds) *Money and Monetary Policy in Less Developed Countries* (Oxford: Pergamon).
Borpujari, Jitendra G. (1980b) 'Toward a Basic Needs Approach to Economic Development with Financial Stability', (mimeograph) International Monetary Fund.
Borpujari, Jitendra G. (1981 unpublished) 'Empirical Determination of an Economy's Basic Needs Basket.'
Chichilnisky, Graciela (1980) 'Terms of Trade and Domestic Distribution: Export-led Growth with Abundant Labour' *Journal of Development Economics*, 8.
Deaton, Angun and Muellbauer, John (1980) *Economics and Consumer Behaviour* (Cambridge: Cambridge University Press).

Debreu, G. (1973) 'Excess Demand Functions', *Journal of Mathematical Economics*, 1.

Engel, Ernst (1857) 'Die Productions- und Consumptionsverhältnisse des Königreichs Sachsen', in *Zeitschrift der Statistischen Büreaus des Königlich Sächsischen Ministerium des Inneren*, nos. 8–9, no. 22; republished in *Bulletin de l'Institut International de Statistique*, IX (1895).

Galbis, Vicente (1972) *A Contribution to the Theory of Labor Migration and Interregional Differentials*, unpublished Ph.D. dissertation, University of Wisconsin.

Goodwin, R.M. (1961) 'The Optimal Growth Path for an Underdeveloped Economy', *Economic Journal*, 71, December.

Government of India (1979) *Report of the Task Force on Projections of Minimum Needs and Effective Consumption Demand* (New Delhi: Indian Planning Commission).

IMF Institute (1981) *Financial Policy Workshops: The Case of Kenya* (Washington DC: IMF).

Jha, L.K. (1980) *Economic Strategy for the 80s* (Allied).

Kaldor, Nicholas (1975) 'What is Wrong with Economic Theory', *Quarterly Journal of Economics*, 89.

Kaldor, Nicholas (1976) 'Inflation and Recession in the World Economy', *Economic Journal*, 86, December.

Kaldor, Nicholas (1979) 'Equilibrium Theory and Growth Theory', in M. Baskia (ed.), *Economics and Human Welfare: Essays in Honour of Tibor Scitovsky* (Academic Press, 1979).

Kaldor, Nicholas, Thirlwall, A.P., and Vines, D. (1981) 'A General Model of Growth and Development', unpublished.

Kalecki, Michal (1969) 'The Marxian Equations of Reproduction and Modern Economics', in *Marx and Contemporary Scientific Thought*, International Council for Philosophy and Humanistic Studies, (Parts: UNESCO/Mouton).

Kalecki, Michal (1976) 'Problems of Financing Economic Development in a Mixed Economy', in Michat Kalecki *Essays on Developing Economies* (Harvester/Humanities).

Keynes, John M. (1936) *The General Theory of Employment, Interest and Money* (London: Macmillan).

Lewis, Arthur, (1954) 'Economic Development with Unlimited Supplies of Labour', *Manchester School of Economic and Social Studies*, 22.

Lluch, Constantino, Powell, A.A. and Williams, R.A. (1978) *Patterns in Household Demand and Saving* (Oxford: Oxford University Press).

Lluch, Constantino, and Powell, A. (1975) 'International Comparisons of Expenditure Patterns', *European Economic Review*, 5.

Marshall Alfred (1920) *Principles of Economics*, (8th edn London: Macmillan).

Mathur, P.N., and Ezekiel, H. (1961) 'Marketable Surpluses of Food and Price Fluctuations in a Developing Economy', *Kyklos*, 14.

Pasinetti, Luigi, L. (1974) *Growth and Income Distribution: Essays in Economic Theory*, (Cambridge: Cambridge University Press).

Pasinetti, Luigi, L. (1981) *Structural Change and Economic Growth; A*

*Theoretical Essay on the Dynamics of the Wealth of Nations* (Cambridge: Cambridge University Press).

Phlips, Louis (1974) *Applied Consumption Analysis* (Amsterdam: North Holland).

Radhakrishna, R. (1978) 'Demand Functions and their Development Implications in a Dual Economy: India', *The Developing Economies*, 16.

Ramsey, F.P. (1928) 'A Mathematical Theory of Savings', *Economic Journal*, 38, December.

Rhomberg, Rudolf, R. (1977) 'Money, Income, and the Foreign Balance', in *The Monetary Approach to the Balance of Payments* (Washington DC: IMF).

Robinson, Joan (1965) *The Accumulation of Capital* (London: Macmillan).

Samuelson, Paul A. (1947–8) 'Some Implications of Linearity', *Review of Economic Studies*, 15.

Sonnenschein, H. (1973a) 'Do Walras' Identity and Continuity Characterize the Class of Community Excess Demand Functions?', *Journal of Economic Theory*, 6.

Sonnenschein, H. (1973b) 'The Utility Hypothesis and Market Demand Theory', *Western Economic Journal*, 11.

Stone, Richard (1954): 'Linear Expenditure Systems and Demand Analysis: An Application to the Pattern of British Demand', *Economic Journal*, 64.

United Nations (1980) *Report of the Expert Group on Future Directions for Work on the System of National Accounts*, UN Statistical Office, E/CN.3/AC.9/5, 27 May 1980 (mimeographed).

# 5 The Role of Financial Institutions in Economic – Development a Theoretical Analysis

Basant K. Kapur

NATIONAL UNIVERSITY OF SINGAPORE

The endemic 'fragmentation' of financial markets in less-developed countries (LDCs) is by now a widely documented fact.[1] The phenomenon owes its origin primarily to governmental policies which foster the development of certain 'priority' sectors in the economy through the liberal provision of highly subsidised bank credit to them. Since a large portion of the available supply of credit is absorbed by these sectors, only a limited volume remains available for allocation to the remaining sectors of the economy, which are perforce constrained to pay much higher rates of interest on whatever loans are provided to them. The resultant wide dispersion in interest rates charged on bank loans, simply on account of differences in the sectoral allocation of these loans, constitutes the essence of the phenomenon of financial fragmentation.

Considerable progress has been made in analysing the implications of such financial policies. There are ample indications that they are inimical to allocative efficiency and to sustained rapid economic development. However, it would be of interest to investigate in detail the precise mechanisms through which such presumptively adverse effects are generated. For example, one would wish to elucidate the exact processes through which such policies as changes in bank lending rates, bank reserve ratios, and the rate of monetary expansion, affect the inter-sectoral allocation of resources, as well as relative prices within the economy, and its rate of growth.

To this end, this paper constructs and examines a two-sector growth model of a 'typical' financially repressed LDC economy. Owing to the complexity of the model, we confine ourselves to an examination of alternative steady-state growth paths, and do not attempt to characterise the dynamics of the transition from one steady-state path to another. Nonetheless, manipulation of the model yields quite a few revealing insights. In Section I the model is specified and its steady-state equilibrium identified, while in Section II we examine the effects of various financial policies upon that steady state. Finally, Section III presents some concluding observations.

## I THE MODEL

An adequate formalisation of 'financial dualism' must minimally allow for two sectors. One is the priority sector charged a low rate of interest, while the other sector (which represents the rest of the economy) pays the market-clearing rate. We shall adopt the suggestive and not excessively unrealistic convention of referring to the privileged enclave as the industrial sector, while terming the other the agricultural sector. Each sector is assumed to produce its output using capital and labour inputs, according to a linear-homogeneous production function:

$$Q_I = F_I(K_I, L_I) = L_I f_I(k_T) \tag{1}$$

$$Q_A = F_A(K_A, L_A) = L_A f_A(k_A) \tag{2}$$

Here, $Q_i$ = level of output of good $i$; $K_i$ and $L_i$ are capital and labour respectively employed in sector $i$; $k_i = K_i/L_i$; and $f_i(k_i) = F_i(k_i, 1)$ ($i$ can represent $I$ and $A$, where subscript $I$ represents the industrial, and subscript $A$ the agricultural, sector).

The agricultural sector is assumed to be purely competitive. Moreover, in accordance with the well-known Lewis (1954) model, the economy is assumed to be in labour-surplus, and to face an 'unlimited' supply of labour at a wage rate $(\bar{w})$ that is fixed in terms of the agricultural good.[2] We thus have, for agriculture:

$$\frac{\partial Q_A}{\partial L_A} = f_A(k_A) - k_A \cdot f_A'(k_A) = \bar{w}, \tag{3}$$

where the prime denotes differentiation.

It is tempting to assume competitive behaviour on the part of the industrial sector as well. However, this would not be in keeping with the 'enclave' characteristics of that sector. On the other hand, a detailed microeconomic characterisation of non-competitive behaviour would unduly complicate the analysis. We therefore adopt the following 'stylised' treatment. The industrial sector is assumed to have access to bank credit, for the purpose of purchasing units of the capital input, at a fixed, fairly 'low', nominal rate of interest of $\bar{r}_I$. Moreover, entrepreneurs in the industrial sector are assumed to comprise an oligopolistic cartel, who agree to set the price of the industrial good $p_I$ at a level that will earn a net return for them on borrowed money of, say, $s$.[3] Moreover, $s$ is not fixed, but is instead a decreasing function of the real loan rate $\bar{r}_I - \pi$, where $\pi$ is the rate of inflation.[4] The rationale for this is that, on the one hand, it may not be desirable for an increase in the borrowing cost $(\bar{r}_I - \pi)$ to be *totally* passed on in the form of a large increase in $p_I$. On the other hand, it may also be desirable for a decrease in the cost $(\bar{r}_I - \pi)$ to be partly reflected in increased profitability, rather than entirely in a reduction in $p_I$.

Algebraically, we have the following formulation. First, cost-minimising behaviour is still postulated:

$$\frac{\dfrac{\partial Q_I}{\partial L_I}}{\dfrac{\partial Q_I}{\partial K_I}} = \frac{f_I(k_I) - k_I f_I'(k_I)}{f_I'(k_I)} = \frac{\bar{w} \cdot p_A}{p_k (\bar{r}_I - \pi)}, \tag{4}$$

where $p_A$ is the price of the agricultural good; and $p_k$ the price of the capital good. Second, we have:

$$\frac{p_I Q_I - \bar{w} \, p_A L_I - p_k (\bar{r}_I - \pi) K_I}{p_k \, K_I} = s(\bar{r}_I - \pi), \quad s' < 0, \tag{5}$$

where $p_I$ is the price of the industrial good, and where the inputs $L_I$ and $K_I$ are chosen in the cost-minimising ratio, derivable from equation (4).

It is assumed that the solution to the model is such that after the industrial sector has absorbed all the bank loans it desires, additional loanable funds remain to be allocated to the agricultural sector. These funds are assumed to be provided at the highest rate that the agricultural sector is prepared to pay. We denote this as $r_A$, where $r_A$ is determined by the following condition:

$$p_A \frac{\partial F_A}{\partial K_A} = p_A f'_A (k_A) = p_k (r_A - \pi). \tag{6}$$

Here, $k_A$ is determined from equation (3), where it is assumed that the nominal interest rate $(r_A)$ adjusts whenever $\pi$, $p_A$ and $p_k$ do, to ensure that equation (6) always holds. In keeping with the dualistic characterisation of the financial market it is supposed that, in the equilibrium solution, $r_A$ initially strictly exceeds $\overline{r}_I$.[5]

Letting $M$ denote the nominal supply of money in the economy, we have:

$$M = C + L. \tag{7}$$

Here, $C$ is the stock of high-powered money (part of which comprises bank reserves and the remainder currency in active circulation), while $L$ is equal to the outstanding volume of loans. Let $C/M = 1 - q$, so that $L = q M$. (We assume for simplicity that the public's currency-deposit ratio and the banks' reserve-deposit ratio are constant, so that $q$ is also constant).

Consider now a firm which obtains a loan at a particular time and purchases a capital good with it. In the subsequent period, the price of the capital good will (as explained below) increase *pari passu* with the economy-wide rate of inflation, but the nominal loan obligation of the firm in respect of that capital good will not change. Thus, the firm enjoys a 'capital gain', and in this paper we shall assume that such gains are 'realised', in the sense that entrepreneurs actually borrow from commercial banks the equivalent of the inflation-induced increase in their net worth.[6] This assumption has, among other things, the convenient implication that at any point in time the nominal value of outstanding bank loans is equal to the *prevailing* price of capital goods multiplied by the stock of bank-financed holdings of physical capital then in existence.

In addition to funds borrowed from the banking system, the 'capitalists' in each sector are assumed to purchase capital equipment from their own savings.[7] Let $K_I^s$ be the stock of 'self-financed' capital holdings in the industrial sector, so that $(K_I - K_I^s)$ refers to loan-financed holdings. Since bank loans at a real interest charge of $(\overline{r}_I - \pi)$ are freely available to industrial capitalists, it would be reasonable to assume that they impute a rental charge of $p_k (\overline{r}_I - \pi)$ to capital goods owned by them. (All capital investment is assumed to be sector-specific.) Thus, equations (4) and (5) apply in respect of both self- and bank-financed capital holdings on the part of the industrial sector. Similarly, let $K_A^s$ denote self-financed capital hold-ings in the agricultural sector. Bank-financed holdings $(K_A - K_A^s)$ are thus determined by the condition in equation (8). We must bear in mind that, as pointed out above, $L/p_k$ is equal to the total stock of bank-financed capital in the economy). The equation is:

$$K_A - K_A^s = \frac{L}{p_k} - (K_I - K_I^s) \tag{8}$$

It is assumed that all savings are made, and all money balances held, by the capitalists. The nominal income of capitalists in the agricultural sector is $K_A^s p_A f_A(k_A) + M_A(d - \pi)$, where $M_A$ is the amount of nominal money held by them and $(d)$ is the average interest-rate on money-holdings.[8] We assume that money-holdings are directly related to income, so that:

$$M_A = f(d - \pi).[K_A^s p_A f_A(k_A) + M_A(d - \pi)]. \quad f' > 0 \tag{9}$$

Since $(M - M_A)$ would comprise nominal money-balances held by industrial capitalists, we have, analogously to equation (9) and using equation (5):

$$\begin{aligned}(M - M_A) = f(d - \pi).[&K_I^s p_k(\bar{r}_I - \pi) \\ &+ s\, p_k K_I + (M - M_A)(d - \pi)]\end{aligned} \tag{10}$$

For simplicity, function $f(d - \pi)$ is assumed to be the same across the two sectors.

Before specifying the sources of capital accumulation in the model, we shall discuss the characterisation of the capital good. We assume that both the agricultural and the industrial goods are consumer goods, and that the capital good (which is the same across the two sectors) is imported. However, in order not to complicate the focal points of our investigation, we shall treat the foreign trade sector in a rather primitive fashion. We shall assume that whenever a capitalist from either sector wishes to purchase capital goods, he is required to deposit the funds involved (which may constitute either his personal savings or monies borrowed from a bank) with a governmental agency. The latter will utilise all funds deposited with it to purchase industrial and agricultural goods domestically. It will then export these in exchange for imports of capital goods, which it will provide to capitalists who have ordered them. Moreover, we suppose that the value of industrial goods purchased by the agency for export exactly equals the value of capital goods ordered by industrial capitalists, and likewise for the agricultural capitalists.

To complete this particular aspect of the model, it is necessary to specify the prices at which trade transactions take place. For simplicity, we assume that the domestically produced industrial good and the imported capital good (the supply of which is infinitely elastic) can be exchanged on a one-to-one basis: thus, in the steady state, it is simply necessary to assume that the exchange rate depreciates at the same rate as the domestic rate of inflation. Next, we assume that *private* importing and exporting by capitalists in both sectors is prohibited. This assumption is necessary for the purpose of permitting the price ratio ($p$) between the agricultural and the industrial good to be domestically determined. Now, suppose that the domestic relative price of the agricultural good exceeds that prevailing on the world market, but that agricultural capitalists are told that, when ordering capital goods from the governmental agency, they may do so at the same price as they pay for the domestically produced industrial good. In this situation, it is evident that the amount of agricultural goods purchasable by the agency with the funds it receives from agricultural capitalists will, when sold abroad at the prevailing international price, yield too little foreign exchange to pay for the requisite imports of capital goods. We therefore suppose that the government purchases additional agricultural goods, financed through the printing of currency, in the amount necessary to meet the shortfall of foreign exchange earnings. The situation is that in which the domestic relative price of the agricultural good is below the international price, but again the price of the capital good quoted to agricultural capitalists equals the domestic price of the industrial good. Funds are now received by the government agency that are not required for the purchase of agricultural goods for export. These are simply assumed to be disbursed as transfer payments to unemployed labour.[9]

It follows that we may henceforth replace ($p_k$) by ($p_l$). We shall assume that capitalists in the agricultural and industrial sectors devote the fractions $h_A$ and $h_I$ of their incomes, respectively, to self-financed investment in capital goods. There is, however, a further source of capital funds, namely, lending by the banking system. Let us assume that the government prints currency at the rate $\mu$.[10] (This is therefore equal to $\dot{C}/C$, with dots denoting time derivatives.) Hence, the constancy of the money multiplier implies that $\dot{L} = \mu L$. Of this, the amount $\pi L$ is, as described earlier, withdrawn as capital gains by entrepreneurs and, as equations (5) and (6) indicate, this is manifested in a lowering of real loan rates. As a result, the sum $(\mu = \pi)L$ or $(\mu = \pi)qM$ is available to finance capital purchases. We thus have:

$$p_I\dot{K} = h_A[K_A^s p_A f_A'(k_A) + M_A(d - \pi)]$$
$$+ h_I[K_I^s p_I(\bar{r}_I - \pi) + s\, p_I K_I] \tag{11}$$
$$+ (M - M_A)(d - \pi)] + (\mu - \pi)qM;$$

where $K(= K_A + K_I)$ constitutes the total capital stock of the economy.

We turn now to the specification of the sectoral 'material-balance' conditions. In regard to industrial output, the sources of demand are twofold: first, the purchase of industrial goods for consumption by capitalists in both sectors; and, second, their purchase by the government for export, using funds received by it for the purpose of financing the acquisition of capital goods for use in the industrial sector. In equilibrium, therefore, we must have:

$$L_I f_I(k_I) = d_I$$
$$\left( p, \frac{K_I^s p_I(\bar{r}_I - \pi) + s\, p_I K_I + K_A^s p_A f_A'(k_A) + M(d - \pi)}{\theta p_A + (1 - \theta)p_I}, \right. \tag{12}$$
$$\left. + \frac{\dot{M} + p_I(K_I^s p_I + K_A^s)}{\theta p_A + (1 - \theta)p_I} \right) + \dot{K}_I,$$

where the function $d_I$ represents consumption demand for the industrial good, and is an increasing function of the relative price of the two goods and of the real income and the real wealth of capitalists in both sectors. (We denote the relative price, $(p_A/p_T$ by $p$.) Now $[\theta p_A + (1 - \theta)p_I]$ is the price index, with $\theta$ being the share of capitalist spending on the agricultural good. To ensure the existence of a balanced-growth equilibrium, we further assume that $d_I$ is homogeneous of degree one, in its second and third arguments jointly.

It might appear necessary to introduce formally the material-balance condition for the agricultural sector. However, this is not the case. Consistency requires that the demand for agricultural output must be obtained as the residual when all other spending and saving activities in the model have been deducted from total income, and Walras's Law then ensures that agricultural demand automatically equals agricultural supply. Consequently, the agricultural material-balance condition conveys no additional information and, from the formal stand point, may be dispensed with.

We have yet to specify the determination of $(d)$, the nominal deposit rate. In principle, it would be desirable to assume competitive behaviour on the part of the commercial banks, so that all interest-earnings from bank loans, less operating costs, would be channeled as receipts to deposit-holders. Unfortunately, in a model as complex as ours, this approach proves to be extraordinarily cumbersome, since $d$ would then depend not only upon $r_i$ and $r_A$, but also on the proportions of bank loans allocated to the two sectors. And these are themselves endogenous variables. In the interests of tractability, we merely postulate the following general function:

$$d = d(\bar{r}_I, r_A), \qquad d_1, d_2 > 0 \tag{13}$$

where subscripts denote partial differentiation. We do, however, comment upon the qualitative characteristics of this function below. Equation (13) may be rationalised by supposing that the government sets lending and deposit rates, but in doing so is cognisant of the desirability of maintaining some relationship between these.

In the steady state all real variables grow (if at all) at a common rate, which we denote as $\gamma$. Since the velocity of circulation of money ($V$) is then constant, we obtain, by logarithmically differentiating the Quantity Equation of Exchange with respect to time and setting, $\dot{V}/V = 0$,

$$\pi = \mu - \gamma. \tag{14}$$

Our specification of the model is now complete, and we proceed to express it in an analytically convenient form. From equations (4), (5) (with $p_K$ replaced by $p_I$) and (14) we have:

$$\frac{f_I(k_I) - k_I f_I'(k_I)}{f_I'(k_I)} = \frac{\bar{w}\, p}{\bar{r}_I - \mu + \gamma} \tag{4'}$$

and

$$\frac{f_I(k_I) - \bar{w}\, p - k_I(\bar{r}_I - \mu + \gamma)}{k_I} = s(\bar{r}_I - \mu + \gamma) \tag{5'}$$

Next, solving for $M_A$ from equation (9) we have:

$$M_A = \frac{f(d - \pi)\cdot K_A^s p_A f_A'(k_A)}{1 - (d - \pi)\cdot f(d - \pi)}, \tag{9'}$$

likewise, from equation (10),

$$(M - M_A) = \frac{f(d - \pi)[K_I^s p_I(\bar{r}_I - \pi) + s\, p_I K_I]}{1 - (d - \pi)\cdot f(d - \pi)} \tag{10'}$$

In the steady-state balanced-growth situation, $K_A^s$, $K_I^s$, and $L/p_I$ all grow at rate $\gamma$. Since $p_I \dot{K}_A^s$ is equal to $h_A[K_A^s p_A f_A'(k_A) + M_A(d - \pi)]$, which, from equation (9'), is equal to $h_A[K_A^s p_A f_A'(k_A)/1 - (d - \pi) f(d - \pi)]$, we have:

$$\gamma = \frac{\dot{K}_A^s}{K_A^s} = \frac{h_A p f_A'(k_A)}{1 - (d - \mu + \gamma) f(d - \mu + \gamma)} \tag{15}$$

Performing analogous manipulations with respect to $K_I^s$, we obtain

$$\gamma = \frac{\dot{K}_I^s}{K_I^s} - h_I \frac{K_I^s(\bar{r}_I - \mu + \gamma) + sL_I k_I}{[1 - (d - \mu + \gamma)f(d - \mu + \gamma)]K_I^s}$$

$$= h_I \frac{(\bar{r}_I - \mu + \gamma) + \dfrac{sL_I k_I}{K_I^s}}{[1 - (d - \mu + \gamma)f(d - \mu + \gamma)]} \tag{16}$$

where we have replaced the term $K_I$ by $L_I k_I$. We therefore require that the ratio $sL_I k_I/K_I^s$ should 'adjust' in the steady-state equilibrium, so as to ensure that the values of $\gamma$ obtained from equations (15) and (16) coincide. Moreover, it is then easily shown (using also the facts that the total capital stock $K = K_A + K_I = K_A^s + K_I^s + L/p_I$ and that $L/p_I$, which is equal to $qM/p_I$, grows at rate $\gamma$) that equation (11) can be manipulated. It will generate the same solution as equations (15) and (16) for the rate of growth of the total capital stock $(K)$.

Lastly, using equations (9') and (10') and the fact that $\dot{K}_I = \gamma K_I = \gamma L_I K_I$, we can express equation (12), after dividing it through by $L_I K_I$, as: —

$$\frac{f_I(k_I)}{k_I} = d_I$$

$$\left( p, \frac{\dfrac{K_A^s}{L_I k_I} p f_A' + s + \dfrac{K_I^s}{L_I k_I}(\bar{r}_I - \mu + \gamma)}{[\theta p + (1 - \theta)][1 - (d - \mu + \gamma)f(d - \mu + \gamma)]}, \tag{12'} \right.$$

$$\frac{K_I^s + K_A^s}{[\theta p + (1 - \theta)]L_I k_I}$$

$$\left. + \frac{f(d - \mu + \gamma)\left[\dfrac{K_A^s}{L_I k_I} p f_A' + s + \dfrac{K_I^s}{L_I k_I}(\bar{r}_I - \mu + \gamma)\right]}{[\theta p + (1 - \theta)][1 - (d - \mu + \gamma)f(d - \mu + \gamma)]} \right) + \gamma.$$

The model has now been reduced to a self-contained system of five equations – (4'), (5'), (15), (16), and (12') in five unknowns – $k_I$, $p$,

$\gamma$, $k_I^s/L_I$, and $k_A^s/L_I$. We proceed in the next section to subject the model to comparative-equilibrium analysis.

## II  EFFECTS OF VARIOUS FINANCIAL POLICIES ON THE STEADY STATE

Let us first examine the effects on the steady-state equilibrium of an increase in the rate of interest charged on loans to the industrial sector $\bar{r}_I$. Totally differentiating our five-equation system with respect to $\bar{r}_I$, it would be possible to express the resulting formulæ in matrix notation.[11] The signs of all the significant terms in the resulting Jacobian matrix would be unambiguous. Fortunately, these are of little consequence, since the first four terms in the fourth column are zero. Using the most convenient approach to obtaining the sign of the Jacobian determinant, it may be easily shown that (as sufficient conditions) if $(s)$ and $(s')$ are both fairly 'small' so long as the elasticity of substitution between $K_I$ and $L_I$ is equal to unity, or less, the determinant will be positive in sign.

Using Cramer's Rule, it readily follows that $dk_I/d\bar{r}_I$ is negative, so that an increase in $\bar{r}_I$ induces a more 'efficient' use of capital in the industrial sector. Moreover, $dp/d\bar{r}_I$ is also negative: an increase in $\bar{r}_I$ induces industrial firms to raise the price of their output *vis-à-vis* the price of agricultural output.

There are two opposing effects of an increase in $\bar{r}_I$ on $\gamma$, which may most readily be observed through an examination of equation (15). On the one hand, an increase in $\bar{r}_I$ reduces $p$, which tends to lower $\gamma$: an adverse movement in the terms of trade between agricultural and capital goods tends to depress the rate of agricultural investment. On the other hand, from equation (13), an increase in $\bar{r}_I$ increases $(d)$, which *ceteris paribus* raises $(d - \mu + \gamma)f(d - \mu + \gamma)$ and thereby tends to increase $\gamma$. The increase in bank intermediation occasioned by an increase in $(d)$, tends to stimulate growth. The net effect upon growth will thus depend upon the magnitude of $dd/d\bar{r}_I$. When $\bar{r}_I$ is below $r_A$, an increase in $\bar{r}_I$ raises $(d)$ not only directly, but also (as shown below) by inducing a relative reallocation of bank loans from the industrial sector to the higher-yielding agricultural sector.[12] Thus, $dd/d\bar{r}_I$ may be expected to be fairly high, and $d\gamma/d\bar{r}_I$ would then be positive.[13] However, once $\bar{r}_I$ rises to equality with $r_A$, further increases in $\bar{r}_I$ will induce a reallocation of loans to the now lower-yielding agricultural sector. The result will be that $dd/d\bar{r}_I$ might become zero or negative, and in this situation $d\gamma/d\bar{r}_I$ would clearly be negative.

Let us now compare the right-hand sides of equations (15) and (16). If we temporarily hold $L_I k_I / K_I^c$ (which equals $K_I / K_I^c$) fixed, and also assume that $(s')$ is not very strongly negative, the numerator of the right-hand side of equation (16) would either increase or remain approximately constant, while that of equation (15) decreases (owing to the fall in $p$). Thus, balanced growth can be maintained only if $K_I / K_I^c$ falls, which substantiates our claim above, that as a result of the increase in $(\bar{r}_I)$ the industrial sector shifts somewhat away from bank finance and towards self-finance. The effect on $K_I^c / L_I$ is, however, *a priori* indeterminate, although this appears to be a variable of limited intrinsic interest.

Our final endogenous variable is $K_A^s / L_I$, the movement of which in response to an increase in $\bar{r}_I$ is also indeterminate. However, this, too, appears to be of little intrinsic interest. Intuitively, since the function $(d_I)$ is homogeneous of degree one in income and wealth, it is unlikely that the relative shares of industrial and agricultural output will change significantly, unless consumer demand is highly sensitive to relative price changes.

On the whole, therefore, an increase in $\bar{r}_I$ towards $r_A$ has highly favourable effects. It induces a more intensive use of capital in the industrial sector, as evidenced by the reduction in $k_I$. It fosters greater bank intermediation in the investment process, since $(f)$ is an increasing function of $(d - \mu + \gamma)$. Moreover, it induces a relative reallocation of bank credit to the higher-yielding agricultural sector. As such, the economy's equilibrium growth rate is raised. This, in turn, implies a reduction in the equilibrium rate of inflation, $\pi$, which is equal to $\mu - \gamma$.

Let us turn now to an examination of the effects of manipulating other policy instruments, commencing with the rate of monetary expansion $(\mu)$. From an examination of our five-equation system, however, it is evident that the effects of a *decrease* in $\mu$ are almost identical to those of an *increase* in $\bar{r}_I$. Thus, it is not necessary to dwell in detail upon them. The only clarification that is perhaps noteworthy is in regard to the range over which reductions in $(\mu)$ lead to increases in $(\gamma)$. From equation (6), we can see that $pf'_A(k_A) = r_A - \mu + \gamma$. Since $dp/d\mu$ is positive, reductions in $\mu$ will (in the region in which $r_A$ exceeds $\bar{r}_I$) raise $(\gamma)$ and hence necessitate reductions in $r_A$. At some point, therefore, $\bar{r}_I$ will equal $r_A$. Beyond this point, further reductions in $(\mu)$ will induce a relative shift of bank loans away from the now higher-yielding industrial sector towards the lower-yielding agricultural sector. This is likely to induce severe declines in $(d)$, which may offset the favourable effect upon $(d - \mu + \gamma)$ $f(d - \mu + \gamma)$ of the reductions in $(\mu)$. So, analogously with the case of increases in $\bar{r}_I$, if the interest is in achieving high growth rates, reductions in $(\mu)$ should not be carried beyond the point at which $\bar{r}_I$ equals $r_A$.

The final policy instrument that we shall consider is an increase in the reserve-requirements ratio. McKinnon (1981, p. 376) has argued that: 'Having no recourse to organised open markets in primary securities, the government often imposes heavy "reserve" requirements against deposits in commercial and savings banks to force these institutions to buy low-interest government bonds in a noninflationary manner.' Within the context of our model, an increase in reserve requirements may be manifested in the form of an increased gap between bank lending and deposit rates.[14] Our model now generates an interesting result. The precise effects of this gap depend upon the extent to which it takes the form, primarily, of an increase in $\bar{r}_I$, as opposed to primarily a decrease in $(d)$.

Consider, first, the consequences of an increase in $\bar{r}_I$, where this is not permitted to induce an increase in $(d)$. It is easily shown that this will again generate a decrease in $k_I$ (owing to the increased cost of borrowing for purposes of industrial investment) and in $(p)$. However, from equation (15), the fall in $(p)$, with no offsetting increase in $(d)$, is seen to produce a fall in the growth rate $(\gamma)$, while the reconciliation between equations (15) and (16) is effected by having $L_I k_I / K_I^s$ decline as well.

Now let us examine instead the effects of allowing $(d)$ to decrease, holding $\bar{r}_I$ constant. *Ceteris paribus*, this generates a fall in bank intermediation and hence in $(d - \mu + \gamma)f(d - \mu + \gamma)$, which can be shown to imply a fall in $(\gamma)$. Consequently, the steady-state rate of inflation $(\pi)$ increases:[15] this reduces the real lending rate to the industrial sector $(\bar{r}_I - \pi)$. Mathematically, this can be shown to produce an *increase* in the equilibrium capital–labour ratio in industry $(k_I)$. Moreover, since industrial enterprises now have access to cheaper capital funds, they are in a position to lower their output price relative to the price of agricultural output, so that $(p)$ increases. Finally, the industrial sector's dependence upon bank lending, as measured by the ratio $L_I k_I / K_I^s$, registers an increase.

It follows that the common feature of both situations is that $\gamma$ decreases and $\pi$ increases. However, they differ in their effects upon $k_I$, $p$ and on $L_I k_I / K_I^s$. From a policy standpoint, it would be desirable for governments of LDCs to attempt to stimulate growth by instituting fiscal reforms which would permit *reductions* in high reserve-requirement ratios. Our analysis suggests that it would then be preferable to have such reductions reflected in increases in $(d)$ rather than in decreases in $\bar{r}_I$. This is because in the former situation, we should observe accompanying decreases in $k_I$, $p$ and $L_I k_I / K_I^s$. These would imply a more intensive use of capital resources and a reduced relative dependence upon subsidised bank credit on the part of the industrial sector.

### III CONCLUDING OBSERVATIONS

As the foregoing discussion indicated, the construction and analysis of a two-sector monetary growth model for an LDC economy characterised by financial imperfections is a rather complex task. Nonetheless, it has to be undertaken if we are to have at our disposal a logically self-contained and internally consistent analytical framework to serve as a 'check on our intuition' regarding the effects of financial policies. This is especially in regard to the identification not only of the direct, but also of the indirect repercussions of such policies.

Our model may also prove to be useful as a guide to empirical investigations. It identifies the strategic interactions in any economy which have to be studied in order to obtain a closer understanding of 'financial dynamics'. Such empirical studies may also indicate directions in which the model would have to be modified in order to render it more readily applicable in particular empirical contexts.

At the substantive level, the model provides strong support for policies designed to ameliorate financial dualism by increasing $(\bar{r}_I - \pi)$ towards equality with $(\bar{r}_A - \pi)$. Such policies have in the past been advocated on grounds of static allocative efficiency, but we have also provided support for them on dynamic grounds. In addition, our analysis establishes that the effects of reducing reserve requirements depend fairly critically upon whether such reductions are manifested as reductions in lending rates or as increases in deposit rates. A consideration of this issue must accompany any reduction in reserve ratios, if the favourable effects of the latter are to be maximised. The fact that our model provides sufficient analytical detail for such differential effects to be identified is important. It vividly underlines the need for closer analytical examination of the structure of the linkages between the real and the financial aspects of LDC economies.

1. See, for example, McKinnon (1973, 1981), Shaw (1973), and Fry (1980, 1981).
2. In accordance with recent empirical evidence furnished by Bertrand and Squire (1980), we do not assume the existence of a wage differential between the two sectors.
3. We abstract from the intrasectoral problem of allocating the total output to be produced among the cartel members.
4. Since we confine ourselves to an examination of steady-state growth paths, actual and expected inflation rates are assumed equal. In addition, for simplicity, capital is assumed to be non-depreciating.
5. Our model is therefore quite different from that of Galbis (1977), who assumes, rather paradoxically, that the 'enclave' is characterised by a higher rate of return to capital than the other sector, even though the former receives rationed credit at a fairly low real rate, while the latter is denied access to bank credit altogether. Other differences are that Galbis assumes that both sectors produce the same good, whereas we allow the terms of trade between the two sectors to be endogenously determined, and that his formal model does not allow for the endogenous determination of certain highly relevant variables, such as the rate of inflation and the rate of growth of real output.
6. Patinkin (1965) makes a precisely analogous assumption in his static macromodel. Discussing the effects of a once-and-for-all rise in the price level, he remarks: 'We can assume that firms immediately write up their capital equipment in accordance with its increased market value, sell additional bonds to the extent of this increased value, and pass on the implicit capital gains to their respective entrepreneurs.'
7. Labour in both sectors is assumed to spend its entire income on the agricultural good.
8. Note that competition by the agricultural sector for bank loans drives the return on bank-financed capital holdings to equality with the real rate of interest paid on bank loans, as indicated by equation (6).
9. It may appear that these ostensibly cumbersome arrangements may be obviated by the simple expedient of having agricultural capitalists face two different prices for their output, one in relation to domestically produced industrial goods, and the other in relation to imported capital goods. However, if this is permitted, while at the same time industrial consumer and capital goods exchange at a one-to-one ratio, possibilities of arbitrage through the foreign trade sector are opened up which would undermine the endogeneity of $p$. Consequently, arrangements such as those described in the text will have to be introduced, even though the institutional form they assume may vary.
10. It is assumed that such currency issue is partly devoted to the financing of any necessary purchase of agricultural output by the government for the reason indicated above (although we assume that the required purchase is fairly small as a proportion of total output), and is partly provided as transfer payments to labour.

11. Copies of the matrix can be obtained, on application, either from the author or from: The Editor General, International Economic Association, Old School, Church Hanborough, Oxon, OX7 2AB.
12. There is a slight complication here, since from equation (6) it is seen that the fall in $(p)$ will produce some reduction in $(r_A)$. However if, as is likely to be the case, the initial volume of agricultural lending is not particularly significant, the effect of this upon $(d)$ would be minimal, and can safely be ignored.
13. Note the 'cumulative causation' at work here: increases in $\gamma$ lead to increases in $(d - \mu + \gamma)f(d - \mu + \gamma)$ which occasion further increases in $\gamma$ in convergent fashion.
14. McKinnon also points out that this gap varies directly with the rate of inflation. By generating an increase in $\pi$ through an increase in $\mu$ (instead of treating $\pi$ as exogenous, as McKinnon does) and allowing $r_A$ and $(d)$ to adjust in response, our model can also be shown to yield this result.
15. This also occurs in the situation in which $\bar{r}_1$ is increased (since $(\gamma)$ declines here as well). This indicates that McKinnon's assertion – that governmental resort to reserve requirement increases is 'non-inflationary' – must be qualified.

REFERENCES

Bertrand T. and Squire, L. (1980) 'The Relevance of the Dual Economy Model: A Case Study of Thailand', *Oxford Economic Papers*, 32, no. 3, November.
Fry, M.J. (1980) 'Saving, Investment, Growth, and the Cost of Financial Repression', *World Development*, 8, no. 4. April, pp. 317–27.
Fry, M.J. (1981) 'Financial Intermediation in Small Island Developing Economies' (mimeo), Department of Economics, University of Hawaii.
Galbis, V. (1977) 'Financial Intermediation and Economic Growth in Less-developed Countries: A Theoretical Approach', *Journal of Development Studies*, 13, no. 2 January, pp. 58–72.
Lewis, W.A. (1954) 'Economic Development with Unlimited Supplies of Labour', *Manchester School of Economic and Social Studies*, May.
McKinnon, R.I. (1973) *Money and Capital in Economic Development* Washington DC: Brookings Institution.
McKinnon, R.I. (1981) 'Financial Repression and the Liberalisation Problem within Less-Developed Countries', in S. Grassman and E. Lundberg (eds), *The World Economic Order: Past and Prospects*, (London: Macmillan).
Patinkin, D. (1965) *Money, Interest, and Prices*, 2nd edn. (New York: Harper and Row).
Shaw, E.S. (1973) *Financial Deepening in Economic Development* (Oxford: Oxford University Press).

# 6 The Role of the Public Sector in the Mobilisation and Allocation of Financial Resources

**W.T. Newlyn**

LEEDS UNIVERSITY, UK

## I INTRODUCTION

Since the term 'public sector' implicitly excludes centrally planned economies, this paper deals with a market economy in which the public sector comprises all levels of government and para-statal production units.

Performance of a role implies an objective. In order to identify constraints, I propose to base the discussion in the paper on the assumption that the governments of developing countries seek to maximise the availability of financial resources to the public sector, subject to constraints, in accordance with some social objective-function.

The range of public-sector savings rates is phenomenal but the very high rates (some over 50 per cent) apply to oil and other mineral exporters, whose public sectors receive the revenue directly. The negative rates are almost all explained by deficits of para-statals.

The scope for public-sector mobilisation and for the direct allocation of resources is not, however, confined to its savings; a broader concept of the financial resources of the public sector is given by taking total government tax revenue, (including surpluses (deficits) of para-statal enterprises) and adding to it the capital of the latter. The basic constraint on the maximisation of this as a flow over time is that, if it is to be increased, the share of personal consumption (net of tax on consumption) in disposable national income has to be reduced.

The public sector's mobilisation of financial resources can be increased by: (i) borrowing from the private sector; (ii) borrowing from the domestic financial sector; (iii) an expansion of monetary credit in excess of that warranted by the demand for real money-balances; (iv) increasing the effective tax rate. Furthermore, the total flow of domestic financial resources into the public sector can be supplemented by foreign-resource inflows, comprising grants and loan proceeds.

Each of these sources will be examined, with particular emphasis on constraints on their utilisation and on the possibility that substitution effects between sources may prevent the impact being additive. Clearly, the relevance of the analysis will differ greatly over the range of developing countries, and the oil surplus countries can be explicitly excluded.

## II  BORROWING FROM THE PRIVATE NON-FINANCIAL SECTOR

The ultimate constraint on the mobilisation of financial resources from this source is the total flow of private savings. But producers are net borrowers, so that the public sector is in competition with producers for the savings of households. Because they are combined with savings of unincorporated enterprise in national accounts, the magnitude of household savings is not revealed, but it can be inferred from income surveys that in developing countries (in the lower third of the per capita income range) net savings are insignificant for all but the relatively few high incomes. For countries with higher incomes per capita, yielding substantial flows of private savings, the issue as to whether or not a capital market is necessary is central to the discussion of efficient financial systems. But it is also relevant to public-sector financing in respect of the marketing of government securities. The claim that capital markets actually increase the propensity of the private sector to save, which would also be relevant to public-sector borrowing, is dubious. (See Wai and Patrick, 1973.)

Although other papers here discuss some of these issues more fully, the relevant point for this paper is this. Capital markets can provide a market for government securities only at the stage at which the volume of private savings is sufficient to generate the demand, and provide the turnover in the market, which is a necessary condition for securing liquidity. Otherwise, the market will simply be providing indirect access to the banking system.

For countries without capital markets, direct access to private savings for public-sector finance is confined to the issue of lottery bonds and to compulsory contributions to pensions funds. The latter is an important source of funds in many developing countries, particularly in the early stages at which the inflows greatly exceed the outflows (Prest, 1969). However, the alternative of appropriate financial intermediation need not be inferior (see Shaw, 1973). Development banks and specialist finance corporations can make an important contribution to the mobilisation of financial resources, both from the private sector and from external sources. They can thereby provide capital to para-statal producers, whether or not these are themselves in the public sector, which the majority are.

## III   BORROWING FROM FINANCIAL INSTITUTIONS

With few exceptions, the government has sole access to the central bank as a source of financial resources, but it competes with the private sector for finance from other financial institutions unless, as is the case in several countries, these have been brought into the public sector. Unlike the situation in the capital market, where the flow of savings determines the availability of total finance, governments can finance public-sector expenditure by borrowing from the central bank, subject only to constraints specified in the central bank charter. In a fractional banking system, such borrowing from the central bank will create primary (high-powered) money. Part of this will be absorbed by the public, while the remainder will permit a multiple expansion of credit by those financial institutions for which it acts as a reserve constraint.

In the absence of inflation, the government of a developing country can expect to get finance from the central bank. This will be equal to the increment of the stock of primary money (currency) held by the public plus a share in the increment of the bank deposits of private banks.

The magnitude of the potential share of the public sector in the increment in the stock of deposit money has received little attention. Data from the IMF's *International Financial Statistics* show that the proportion of government securities to the total assets of banks in developing countries varies considerably, ranging between zero and 0.5 in the sixty-eight countries for which the figures are available. The 0.5 can probably be considered as the limit to which banks will be willing to sacrifice yield as a *quid pro quo* of their retention of their implicit 'charters' to create money. But this constraint is only binding on the marginal share, after the maximum is reached. In 1972, the Uganda Government acquired 0.98 of the total money increment but this was in a political climate which was hardly encouraging to private borrowers. Similar figures obtained in Nigeria during the civil war, when the government's share of the money increment averaged 0.89 between 1966 and 1969. But Idi Amin and oil-motivated civil wars aside, a marginal share of 0.5 is clearly a feasible figure. Such utilisation of bank finance will either involve the government in the cost of issuing securities, the marginal yield of which is equal to that of the least profitable private assets held by the banks, or, if the share is obtained under duress, displacement of private demand for bank finance and an increase in bank credit.

Taking 0.5 as the government share in bank money and using the median value for the currency/money ratio in *International Financial Statistics* of 0.46, the government's share in the total money increment will be $0.46 + 0.5(1 - 0.46) \Delta M$ which equals $0.73 \Delta M$.

The magnitude of the non-inflationary increment in the money stock will be a function of the growth of real income, generally supplemented by a long-term upward trend in the function itself, as monetisation increases. Median figures derived from a study of inflationary finance (Newlyn, 1977) give 4.34 for the income/money ratio $(k)$ and 0.51 for the rate of real growth $(\dot{y}_r)$. Assuming no growth of $k$, the increment in money stock is 5.1 per cent which is 1.17 per cent of income. If the median value of 0.02 for the growth of money stock $(\dot{k})$ is incorporated, then the money increment is increased by the factor $1 + (\dot{k} + \dot{k}/\dot{y}_r)$ to 1.67 per cent of income.

It is well known (particularly to governments trying to maximise public-sector financial resources) that the amount of finance derived from monetary expansion can be increased by inflation. Moreover, history shows that restrictions in central bank charters need be no constraint on the use of the 'inflation tax' – so-called because it has been the currency element (seignorage) which has featured in the literature. This literature has consisted of hypothetical estimations of the maximum finance obtainable, in most cases using equations of the form which was successfully used in an analysis of hyper-inflations.

The maximum revenue obtainable, as with conventional taxes, will be at the point at which the elasticity of the tax base (real balances) to the rate of tax (the rate of inflation) is minus one. The crucial relationship is therefore the elasticity of the money–income ratio (or velocity) to the rate of inflation. Hypothetical use of Kagan-type demand functions has resulted in very low estimates of the maximum revenue achievable. Their general use is, however, inconsistent with observation and evidence (Brown, 1955) of the insensitivity of velocity to relatively high rates of inflation, as well as to low rates.

The results reported here are from a study (undertaken with the hypothesis that there is a threshold to sensitivity in mind (see Newlyn, 1977). This used a regression analysis of time series to estimate the effect of the rate of inflation: on the velocity of currency plus demand deposits ($V1$); on the velocity of currency plus total deposits ($V2$); and on the rate of increase of velocity, using linear, semi-log and double-log forms. The sample consisted of forty developing countries for which consistent price and income data were available for at least ten, and mostly fifteen, years.

The sensitivity of velocity to inflation was higher, in all specifications, for $V1$ than $V2$. This reflected shifts from currency plus demand deposits to interest-bearing deposits, but did not involve a reduction in total money. Hence, $V2$ was taken as the appropriate measure for further investigation.

Table 6.1 shows the distribution of significant results for the linear form (generally the best) of the regression of $V2$ on the rate of

TABLE 6.1    SENSITIVITY OF V2 AND THE RATE OF INFLATION

| Rate of Inflation % | | Number of Countries | |
|---|---|---|---|
| Overall average | Average highest 3 years | Significant | Not |
| Over 30 | 50+ | 9 | 1 |
| | 30–50 | 1 | Nil |
| 20–30 | 40+ | 1 | Nil |
| 15–20 | 20–30 | 1 | 1 |
| 10–15 | 15–20 | 1 | 1 |
| 5–10 | 5–10 | Nil | Nil |
| | 10–15 | 4 | Nil |
| Under 5 | 5–10 | 4 | Nil |
| | Under 5 | 5 | 11 |
| Total | 37* | 21 | 16 |

* Three of the forty countries were significant only in respect of VI.
  *Source:* Necolz (1977).

inflation. The five significant cases (at under 5 per cent) refute the absolute form of the hypothesis of a threshold below which sensitivity is zero. But the eleven cases in which the coefficient is not significantly different from zero suggest that the chance of it being positive is one in three. Furthermore, there is no systematic relationship between the values of the coefficients and the rate of inflation.

Figure 6.1 shows, in respect of the significant results of the equation for the rate of growth of velocity, the percentage of GNP ($Y$) obtained at rates of inflation up to 60 per cent. The values of the coefficient are shown against each curve. Only in Greece does the potential increment in inflationary finance reach its maximum below 60 per cent inflation. Greece is also the extreme case where a low rate of inflation is combined with a high coefficient of sensitivity. This is consistent with the conclusion that the sensitivity of velocity tended to be high where there had been previous experience of hyperinflation.

From the significant results from the linear regression of $V2$ on the rate of inflation, median and maximum values of the coefficients are used, in combination with alternative values of the associated parameters to determine the magnitude of potential inflationary finance derived from the study. The results are shown in Table 6.2.

This presentation excludes as improbable the combinations giving the limiting values of the range – which are 1.6 and 17.8 per cent of income. Each of the numbered pairs of outcomes 1 to 4 in Table 6.2 could be regarded as presenting a set of options appropriate to the parameters of four countries with differing basic potential. But there is uncertainty as to which value of the V-coefficient is more likely to emerge from venturing away from the non-inflationary certainty of zero inflation, assuming that that is taken as the starting point. The table is confined to inflation rates up to 30 per cent, which would seem to be the highest rate any government would seriously contemplate generating deliberately.

But do governments really take deliberate action to generate inflation in order to obtain the proceeds from the inflation tax? Or do they make less strenuous efforts to contain such inflation as occurs as a result of structural change or world inflation? They may be aware that there is evidence that inflation has a positive effect on private investment, at least within the 30 per cent range, and that the rate of growth is a most powerful factor in stimulating private saving (Singh, 1972). On the other hand, what is intended as a sharp injection of inflationary finance to stimulate growth, may initiate a two-way

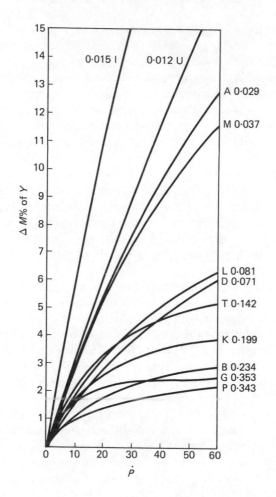

| Country | Key | Average $\dot{P}$ | Average highest 3 years $\dot{P}$. |
|---|---|---|---|
| Argentina | A | 20.6 | 27.2 |
| Bolivia | B | 5.2 | 8.8 |
| Dominican Republic | D | 2.4 | 11.9 |
| Greece | G | 2.5 | 3.2 |
| Ireland | I | 3.8 | 5.9 |
| Korea | K | 15.4 | 26.0 |
| Libya | L | 4.6 | 10.3 |
| Morocco | M | 4.1 | 5.5 |
| Paraguay | P | 4.7 | 10.8 |
| Taiwan | T | 4.1 | 8.3 |
| Uruguay | U | 5.15 | 96.6 |

*Source:* Newlyn (1977), p. 58, figure II, 2; p. 54, table II, 2.

FIGURE. 6.1 Incremental finance and rate of growth of velocity of money

TABLE 6.2 INCREMENTAL MONETARY FINANCE
(*Initial Velocity Vo = 4.34*)

| | $\dot{Y}r$ | $k$ | $b$ | $p = 0$ | $p = 5\%$ | $p = 10\%$ | $p = 30\%$ |
|---|---|---|---|---|---|---|---|
| 1i | 0.051 | 0.02 | 0.353 | 1.65 | 2.38 | 2.79 | 3.45 |
| ii | | | 0.081 | | 3.07 | 4.27 | 7.93 |
| 2i | | 0.05 | 0.353 | 2.39 | 3.46 | 4.06 | 5.02 |
| ii | | | 0.081 | | 4.47 | 6.27 | 11.09 |
| 3i | 0.085 | 0.02 | 0.353 | 2.46 | 2.86 | 3.09 | 3.45 |
| ii | | | 0.081 | | 3.68 | 4.72 | 7.60 |
| 4i | | 0.05 | 0.353 | 3.21 | 3.73 | 4.03 | 4.50 |
| ii | | | 0.081 | | 4.82 | 6.16 | 9.93 |

*Note:* All $\Delta M/Y\%$ values are inversely proportional to $V$, and can therefore be scaled to obtain data of values for any value of $Vo$.
*Source:* Newlyn (1977), p. 59, Table II,4.

relationship between inflation and the deficit to be financed, as a result of a lag of revenue on expenditure. This possibly self-defeating process, first formulated by Olivera (1967) was recently confirmed by the application of a model to four countries with differing rates of inflation (Aghevli and Khan, 1978). Moreover, governments deliberating on these matters should, if concerned at all about distribution, take into account the regressive nature of a tax on the holding of money balances. But they should be especially aware of the nature of the external constraint operating in open economies. Any domestic expansion requires an increase in the capacity to import in order to maintain external balance and, taking domestic multiplier effects into account, it may require an equal amount of exports to offset an expansion in investment or in public sector expenditure (Newlyn, 1977). Given this very severe external-balance constraint, domestic credit expansion greatly in excess of real growth requirements is certain to lead to controls on imports and on external payments. These will add to the domestic inflation effect of the excessive credit expansion and will risk initiating a 'shallow finance' regime (Shaw, 1973).

## IV TAXATION

Taxation represents a compulsory transfer from the private sector to the government. The justification for this, in respect of the provision of public goods, is that these must of necessity be provided for by the government. Any increase in taxation beyond the level necessary to cover the generally accepted categories of public goods such as defence and civil order should, according to formal welfare analysis, yield a marginal social benefit greater than that of the private expenditure which is displaced. Governments of developing countries can be deemed to believe this condition to be satisfied both in respect of merit goods such as health and education and of any other expenditure which is capacity-creating even though it is classified as consumption in the national accounts. Pressure to cover the growth of such 'development expenditure' with recurrent revenue, and to generate savings to finance investment in the face of constraints on domestic borrowing, will induce them to increase taxation. Success in doing so has come to be termed 'tax effort'.

Clearly the crude ratio of tax revenue to GNP (tax-ratio) is a very poor indicator of tax effort, if only because it does not reflect the wide variation in the economic characteristics determining a country's capacity to raise tax revenue. This has led to a number of attempts to incorporate some measure of taxable capacity. The most used method has been regression analysis of a large cross-section of countries, in an attempt to identify proxy variables for the economic characteristics which have the most significant effect on the tax ratio. The equation which performs best, statistically, for this purpose is then used to determine each country's tax-raising capacity. The deviation of the country's actual tax ratio is then expressed in an index, in which equality between the actual and estimated ratios is expressed as unity.

Three successive studies of this kind have emanated from the IMF. The first of these (A) reported results obtained in the original study of a sample of forty-seven countries (Chelliah, 1971) and related to an average of the years 1966–8. These results were (B) up-dated to 1969–71 (Chelliah, Bass and Kelly, 1975). More recently, study (C) has appeared (Tate, Gratz and Eichengreen, 1979). This study updates the previous results to 1972–6 and applies the same set of five equations as in the original study to a larger sample – of fifty-three countries. The authors rightly point out that 'tax effort' is an inappropriate term because countries seeking to equate the marginal social benefits of public and private goods services may, *ceteris paribus*, exhibit different tax ratios: they therefore substitute the term International Tax Comparisons (ITC).

Five estimating equations which have previously been used are all specified in terms of the ratio of total tax revenue to GDP. They exclude social security contributions and they cover all levels of government, except where local revenues count for less than 10 per cent of the total. The results (three sets for each of the five equations) are given in the Appendix. The principal points which emerge from a comparison are as follows.

In all equations except one, the $\bar{R}_2$ values are higher in the successive studies A and B and the increase is greater still for the larger sample in C. The exception is the only equation which does not have an export or trade variable. In all the other equations, the increase in $\bar{R}_2$ is associated with substantial increases in the coefficient values for the export or trade variables, however specified; the same features are more strongly reflected in the equations of the larger sample (C).

On the basis of this statistical performance, the authors selected equation (2) for the construction of the International Tax Comparison Index. This equation includes non-export income per capita; share of mining in GDP; and the export-ratio, excluding minerals. The $\bar{R}_2$ was 0.581 in the C version, which is remarkably high given the numerous socio-political factors involved.

Figure 6.2 and 6.3 reproduce charts from the study. Those show, respectively, the 1969–71 ratio and the ITC index, against the percentage increase in these over the period 1969–71 to 1972–6. Each of the charts thus combines information on relative levels of taxation with what has previously been called tax effort.

The next issue is the possibility of an adverse effect on aggregate saving, as suggested in the Please hypothesis (Please, 1967). This increased taxation might cause government consumption to rise by more than the amount by which private consumption was reduced.

A number of studies made to test this have been reviewed by Brothwell (1977). He shows that the evidence refutes the hypothesis and, in his own regression analysis of thirty-six developing countries, he confirms the general finding that a substantial decrease in total consumption is associated with an increase in the tax rate. He also ran an equation regressing the government-investment ratio on the tax-ratio and obtained a significant positive result.

Brothwell then extended the scope of the analysis by applying it to government development expenditure, which he defined as government investment plus expenditure on goods and services, minus expenditure on defence and civil order. The regression of his development expenditure over GNP on the tax-ratio produced a significant coefficient of 0.472. The further inclusion of private investment increased the coefficient to 0.482, which implies a positive effect of the tax-rate on private investment.

Governments of developing countries, having been reassured about

Tax Ratio 1966-68

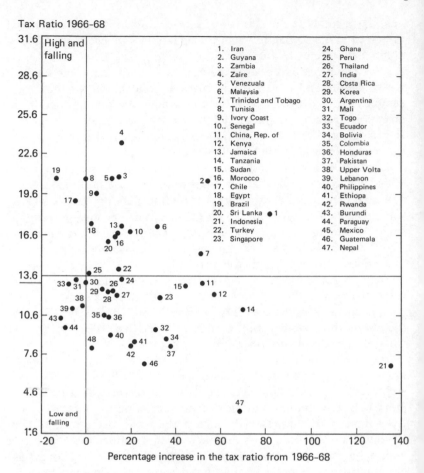

FIGURE. 6.2 Tax ratios

*Source:* Tait, Gratz and Eichengreen (1979), p. 132.

the possibility of adverse effects of their tax effort on savings and investment, will want to be reassured about a possible adverse effect on income distribution. Unfortunately, the standard method of measuring the effect of the impact of the tax system on pre-tax income distribution of households, gives the wrong answer to the question it asks. And it cannot ask the question posed above.

It can be demonstrated (Newlyn, 1981) that by assuming that the tax system impacts on a 'no-tax' situation in the year of the study, and thus applying any shifts of the impact-adjustment burden to the

ITC Index 1966–68

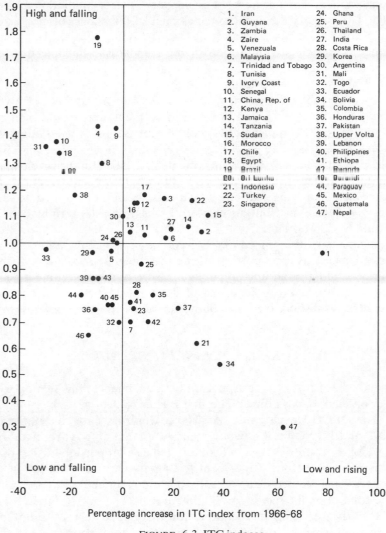

FIGURE. 6.3 ITC indeces

*Source:* Tait, Gratz and Eichengreen (1979), p. 135.

whole of the current revenue of the particular taxes, the shifts are grossly overestimated. This is due to the failure to distinguish between (i) the magnitude of the discretionary changes in revenue, which are the sole cause of adjustment shift; and (ii) the buoyancy of tax revenue, which is a function of nominal growth of income and consumption. Furthermore, it is apparent that a methodology designed to identify the economic incidence of the impact of new taxes on incomes and prices cannot answer the quite different question, which is relevant to household living standards. That question is: who bears the actual burden of paying the taxes, given the current level of incomes and prices?

However, the effects of tax effort clearly require comparison over time, and the use of a combination of both concepts would then be appropriate. The impact-shifts could be correctly estimated annually from the appropriate discretionary increases in revenue; and the effect of the sum of these increments, adjusted for price change, could be applied to the base year, pre-tax income distribution. A combination of this with the payments incidence, applied to the pre-tax income distribution in both the base and the terminal year, would be appropriate.

Incidentally, the sum of the discretionary increments, adjusted for price change, as a proportion of the increment in revenue over the period could give an unambiguous measure of the government's tax effort. It would do so in terms of deliberate decisions to increase taxation, as distinct from the buoyancy reflected in the tax-ratio.

## V  FOREIGN FINANCIAL RESOURCES

Since other papers cover aspects of external finance, this section will be confined to two points. The first relates to debt service.

The OECD Development Assistance Statistics show that between 1970 and 1979 Official Development Assistance (ODA) received by developing countries from all sources fell as a proportion of the total flow of finance from 43 per cent to 34 per cent. Such a dilution of concessional finance clearly has implications for the service cost of the total of public-sector foreign finance.

But the servicing implications for the public sector cannot be separated from the implications of private sector borrowing; and the ratio of total debt service to ODA debt service has grown from 7.78 in 1970 to 33.8 in 1979. The remission of profits has to be added to this to get the gross reverse-flow of financial resources. Its magnitude is about one-third of total debt service.

Although the private sector generates its own interest and profits in domestic currency, these combine with public-debt service in the demands upon foreign exchange. It is the transfer problem, implicit in the pervasive difficulty that developing countries have in transforming domestic resources into marketable exports, which constitutes the basic problem. Rescheduling of public sector debt-servicing can play only a minor role in this context, because it constitutes less than one-third of total reverse-flow.

The second point is this. There is evidence of the persistence of a belief that it has been demonstrated that an increase in foreign-resource inflows causes a reduction in the savings of the host country, particularly via the behaviour of the public sector. This belief is based upon misinterpretations of the results of regression analysis, designed to test this relationship. In all studies which the writer has been able to locate, the results of regressing savings ($S$) on total foreign inflows ($F$), however specified, have shown a significant negative association. The modal value of the coefficient is $-0.5$ and it never exceeds unity. This result has frequently been reported as 'substitution of $F$ for $S$' and in some cases the reduction in savings has been rationalised in terms of plausible behaviour, such as relaxed tax effort and an increase in the proportion of public-sector resources consumed. The correct interpretation of a negative coefficient not exceeding one is that it measures the propensity to consume out of $F$: and the difference between the coefficient value and one measures the propensity to save out of $F$. It thus adds to domestic savings and contradicts any behavioural reduction. The negative coefficient reflects the accounting identity $Sn = Y - C$ and not, as is usually the case, a behavioural reduction in the dependent variable. The perverse sign results from incorrect specification of the behavioural equation. This should be $St = a + bY + cF$; and the corresponding identity is $St = Y + F - C$, where $St$ is the sum of savings out of $Y$ and $F$.

Areskoug's study of the effect of foreign finance which relates explicitly to public-sector borrowing regresses investment and consumption on official borrowing, GNP and total resource inflows minus official borrowing. The result is a coefficient of 0.57 for investment, and a coefficient of 0.34 for consumption. It is noteworthy that the coefficients do not add to unity. This could well reflect the effect of reverse-flow on investment and/or consumption. In my own study, the total resource-inflow was disaggregated and the reverse-flow of debt service included as an additional variable. Its negative effect on both consumption and investment was highly significant, in three different specifications.

REFERENCES

Aghevli, B.B. and Khan, M.S. (1978) 'Government Deficits and Inflationary Process in Developing Countries', IMF Staff Papers (Washington DC; IMF) Sept.
Brothwell, J.F. (1972) 'Government Finance', in W.T. Newlyn, *The Financing of Economic Development* (Oxford: Oxford University Press).
Chelliah, R.J. (1971) 'Trends in Taxation in Developing Countries', *IMF Staff Papers* (Washington DC; IMF) July.
Chelliah, R.J., Bass, J. and Kelly, M.R. (1975) 'Tax Ratios and Tax Effort in Developing Countries, 1969–71, *IMF Staff Papers* (Washington DC; IMF) Mar.
Newlyn, W.T. (1977) *The Financing of Economic Development* (Oxford: Oxford University Press), chapters 2, 4, and 5.
Newlyn, W.T. (1981) *Tax Burden Analysis; Critique and Reformulation*. Discussion Paper No 9 Development Economics Research Centre (Warwick: University of Warwick).
Olivera, J.H.G. (1967) 'Money Prices and Fiscal Logs: A Note on the Dynamics of Inflation', *Banca Nazionale del Lavoro, Quarterly Review*, Sept.
Please, S. (1967) 'Saving Through Taxation – Reality or Mirage?' in IMF and World Bank (eds) *Finance and Development* (Washington, DC; IMF and World Bank).
Prest, A.R. (1969) 'Compulsory Lending Schemes', *IMF Staff Papers*, Mar.
Shaw, E.S. (1973) *Financial Deepening in Economic Development* (New York: Oxford University Press).
Singh, S.K. (1972) *The Determinants of Aggregate Savings*, Economic Staff Working Paper, 127 (Washington DC: International Bank for Reconstruction and Development).
Tait, A.A., Gratz, L.M. and Eichengreen, B.J. (1979) 'International Comparisons of Taxation for Selected Developing Countries, 1972–76' *IMF Staff Papers* (Washington DC: IMF) vol. 26, Mar.
Wai, U. Tun and Patrick, H.T. (1973) 'Stock and Bond Issues and Capital Markets in Less Developed Countries', *IMF Staff Papers* (Washington DC; IMF) July.

# Appendix

## FIVE TAXABLE CAPACITY EQUATIONS

1. The Lotz–Morss equation (per capita GNP and share of foreign trade in GNP)

A. 1969–71(47) $T/Y$ = 11.65 + 0.002$Y_n$ + 0.06$X + M/Y$
(7.77)   (0.50)   (2.36)
$R^2$ = 0.110

B. 1972–76(47) $T/Y$ = 9.9683 + 0.0003$Y_p$ + 0.1108$X + M/Y$
(6.02)   (0.18)   (3.91)
$R^2$ = 0.267    $F(2.44) = 9.378$

C. 1972–76(63) $T/Y$ = 6.5775 + 0.003$Y_p$   0.1457$X + M/Y$
(3.75)   (1.20)   (5.28)
$R^2$ = 0.343    $F(2.60) = 17.200$

2. The CBK 1969–71 equation (non-export income per capita, share of mining and non-mineral exports in GNP)

A. 1969–71(47) $T/Y$ = 11.47 + 0.001$(Y_p - X_p)$ + 0.44$N_y$ + 0.05$X_y'$
(7.84)   (0.38)   (5.45)   (1.17)
$R^2$ = 0.376

B. 1972–76(47) $T/Y$ = 9.9949 − 0.0008$(Y_p - X_p)$ + 0.4068$N_y$ + 0.1938$X_y'$
(6.15)   (0.34)   (5.41)   (3.12)
$R^2$ = 0.413    $F(3.43) = 11.80$

C. 1972–76(63) $T/Y$ = 7.1134 + 0.0024$(Y_p - X_p)$ + 0.5700$N_y$ + 0.2218$X_y'$
(4.82)   (0.94)   (9.31)   (4.17)
$R^2$ = 0.581    $F(3.59) = 29.69$

3. Non-export income per capita and share of exports in GNP

A. 1969–71(47) $T/Y$ = 10.36 + 0.005$(Y_p - X_p)$ + 0.15$X_y$
(6.31)   (1.32)   (3.35)
$R^2$ = 0.178

B. 1972–76(47) $T/Y$ = 8.4022 + 0.0005$(Y_p - X_p)$ + 0.3037$X_y$
(5.54)   (0.22)   (6.49)
$R_p$ = 0.470    $F(2.44) = 21.37$

C. 1972–76(63) $T/Y$ = 7.3663 + 0.003$(Y_p - X_p)$ + 0.3025$X_y$
(4.41)   (0.94)   (6.19)
$R^2$ = 0.375    $F(2.60) = 19.58$

*continued on page 114*

APPENDIX *continued*

## FIVE TAXABLE CAPACITY EQUATIONS

4. Shares in GNP of mining, agriculture and exports

A. 1969–71(47) $T/Y$ = 14.46 + $0.32N_y$ + $0.07A_y$ + $0.04X_y$
                          (8.12)        (3.85)        (2.04)        (1.10)
          $R^2$ =  0.445

B. 1972–76(47) $T/Y$ = 8.0840 + $0.2119N_y$ + $0.01581A_y$ + $0.2452X_y$
                          (4.08)        (2.82)        (0.36)        (4.91)
          $R^2$ =  0.542                                    $F(3.43) = 19.16$

C. 1972–76(63) $T/Y$ = 9.1859 + $0.3550N_y$ − $0.0240A_y$ + $0.1903X_y$
                          (4.88)        (5.51)        (−0.61)        (4.30)
          $R^2$ =  0.593                                    $F(3.59) = 31.12$

5. Shares of mining and agriculture in GDP

A. 1969–71(47) $T/Y$ = 15.66 + $0.35N_y$ − $0.08A_y$
                          (11.07)       (4.44)        (2.37)
          $R^2$ =  0.442

B. 1972–76(47) $T/Y$ = 14.3579 + $0.3555N_y$ − $0.3018A_y$
                          (7.67)        (4.15)        (−0.57)
          $R^2$ =  0.302                      $F(2.44) = 10.94$

C. 1972–76(63) $T/Y$ = 14.2423 + $0.4521N_y$ − $0.0.571A_y$
                          (8.54)        (6.59)        (−1.30)
          $R^2$ =  0.475                      $F(2.60) = 29.01$

---

$T/Y$ = Tax ratio (excluding social security contributions)
$Y_p$ = per capita GNP in US dollars
$X + M/Y$ = ratio of exports and imports to GNP
$Y_p - X_p$ = per capita non-export income in US dollars
$N_y$ share of mining in GDP (including petroleum)
$A_y$ = share of agriculture in GDP
$X_y$ = export ratio
$X'_y$ = export ratio excluding mineral exports
$\bar{R}^2$ = adjusted $R^2$ estimate
$F$ = $F$-statistic
The figures in parentheses below the coefficients are $t$-ratios.

*Source:* Tait, Gratz and Eichengreen (1979), p. 128.

# 7 Inflation and the Financing of Alternative Development Strategies

**Alfredo J. Canavese** and
**Luisa Montuschi**

UNIVERSITY OF BUENOS AIRES,
ARGENTINA

## I INTRODUCTION

Among countries which have followed industrialisation policies based on import substitution, Argentina is probably the one which adhered to this strategy over the longest period of time. It is possible to identify an early process of import substitution during the first stages of Argentina's economic development. Up to the Second World War industrialisation was mainly connected to the ups and downs of the exporting sector. The war forced Argentina to develop a much more diversified industry while the economic policies carried out after the war were aimed at protecting this sector. With changing emphasis, this strategy lasted until 1976–7, but it failed as a growth policy. Inflation was a by-product and, as a consequence, the capital market lost its importance as a source of financing, both the private and public sectors finding subsidised bank credit a convenient substitute. Financial repression was an outstanding characteristic of the use of subsidised bank credit.

In 1976–7, there was a major economic reform which implied opening-up the economy and liberalising financial markets. Changes in the tax system consistent with this policy were also enacted. Since this financial reform was intended to end the financial repression that characterised the earlier import substitution policy, Argentina provides a good example for analysing the inter-relationships between interest rates, inflation and the financing of different development strategies.

## II IMPORT-SUBSTITUTING INDUSTRIALISATION

In its early growth, the Argentine economy developed a strong complementary relationship with that of Britain – a consequence of the resource endowments of the two countries. The UK was both Argentina's main supplier of capital and also the main customer for her exports. The performance of the agrarian sector determined the pattern and the trend of Argentine growth (Vázquez-Presedo, 1971). The rural sector entered a period of virtual stagnation after 1918, implying a reversal of the impressive growth of Argentine exports in 1900–10.[1] This may be partly explained by the gradual deterioration of Argentina's terms of trade.

After 1918, the structure of the world economy changed and the USA replaced the UK as the world's main financial and economic centre. Unfortunately, the American economy was similar to that of Argentina, so that the latter could no longer follow its previous patterns of international trade in the new framework. The UK continued to be Argentina's main customer, but the USA became her main supplier of raw materials and capital (Vázquez-Presedo, 1978).

The beginning of Import-Substituting Industrialisation (ISI) in Argentina is usually identified with the great depression of the 1930s, or with the Second World War. However, by 1938, Argentina already had an important industrial sector; the share of manufacturing in GDP amounted to 27.8 per cent, when the contribution of agriculture to GDP was 24.2 per cent (Banco Central de la República Argentina, 1966). This early development was partly due to a tariff on imports. Enacted in 1870, its main objectives were to raise funds for the Federal Government and to solve balance of payments problems. Nevertheless, its structure allowed the development of some import-substituting industries and new tariffs in 1891 and 1905 deepened this process. The new-born industries were not only linked to traditional agrarian production but also produced a variety of manufactured goods for internal consumption.[2]

Around 1950, the Economic Commission for Latin America (ECLA) favoured long-run development of Latin American countries based on

ISI policies which ECLA described as a growth strategy. Empirical studies show a high positive correlation between increases in per capita income and in the evolution of the relative share of industry in GDP (Chenery, 1960). Although this does not necessarily imply a special causal relationship, ISI advocates assume that the causal direction is from industrialisation to income growth. Due to an 'export pessimism', they believe that the economy's import capacity cannot grow quickly enough to finance the increased imports necessary to sustain a satisfactory growth rate for industrial output (ECLA, 1950). Since this makes the external sector the main constraint on economic growth, a successful ISI should reduce the imports/output ratio, because a fall in a country's international reserves, or an increase in its external debt, can be considered only as short run alternatives. In a way, the first stages of Argentine industrialisation could be considered a successful ISI.

A wide variety of policy instruments are usually applied to carry out an ISI strategy. Protectionism is a common feature of any ISI policy, and may assume many forms: exchange controls, multiple exchange rates, exchange permits, quotas, prohibitions, tariffs, advance deposits, etc.[3] Fiscal incentives and credit facilities are also important instruments devised to promote industrialisation.

Although post-war industrialisation in Argentina was not strictly based on ECLA's ideas, an ISI that was rather a consumption and employment policy than a growth strategy was followed.

Exports and imports declined sharply during the Second World War. Argentina's traditional markets in Europe had been almost totally closed and imports from the USA limited through a system of quotas established by the latter for a set of 'essential' goods. Many new industries developed as a consequence and finance for them was provided partly by the newly created Banco de Crédito Industrial Argentino.[4] By 1945, exports to the USA had increased remarkably. International reserves, not tied to compensation agreements, began to grow and it was believed that increasing traditional exports would now be sufficient to match the industrial sector's growing import needs. Raw materials, fuel, intermediate goods, capital goods and new technology were badly needed to ensure a satisfactory rate of industrial growth. Nevertheless, the concomitant opening-up of the economy to international competition made the future development of new industries uncertain. A particular external constraint resulted from export restrictions by Argentina's traditional suppliers, which limited output growth and induced rises in the prices of imported inputs. These higher prices were accommodated by an easy credit policy, which also ratified wage increases. An inflationary process began.

In 1946, Perón took over the government, supported by the vast majority both of the working class and of the new industrial entrepreneurs. One outcome was a radical change in economic policy: an inward-looking strategy replaced the outward-looking pre-war model. The new economic aim was to avoid dependence on imports and exports,[5] but it was perhaps really devised to adapt the economy to a well-defined political project as well as to the conditions by prevailing in the international setting. The political project sought to favour the new urban classes which were dependent upon industrialisation. Workers were pleased by a programme that made important reforms in social security and promoted income redistribution. Entrepreneurs enjoyed a régime that protected them from external competition and provided a growing level of internal consumption to absorb their production.

The post-war international setting conditioned Argentina's economic development, because of its neutrality maintained almost up to the end of the war.[6] Most international reserves, accumulated late in the war, were used to buy railways and other public utilities owned by British capital. The external debt was repatriated. The Central Bank was nationalised and the deposit régime modified. External trade was centralised by the government. Argentina's growth performance was outstanding during the period 1946–8,[7] but this ended in 1949, with a major balance of payments crisis, caused by these economic measures. Exports declined sharply during that period.[8] In part, the decline could be explained by increased internal consumption. This followed the growth of urban income and was encouraged by subsidised consumer prices under a compulsory purchasing programme for crops, adopted by the Instituto Argentino de Promoción del Intercambio (IAPI) – the government agency which monopolised external trade. Complementing this internal demand-side effect was a fall in supply due to discriminatory credit and price policies which discouraged agricultural production. Fertilizers and agricultural equipment could not be imported because of discriminatory exchange controls.[9] Imports were also regulated to protect local industry. Apart from quotas (for a limited range of goods) the instrument of regulation was exchange controls.

After August 1947, when the pound sterling was declared inconvertible, import permits were required for all goods, under a priority system of the Central Bank. Even so imports, severely restricted during the war, increased remarkably after it. But the effect of

TABLE 7.1     THE STRUCTURE OF IMPORTS

|  | *Percentages* | | |
| --- | --- | --- | --- |
|  | *1947* | *1948* | *1949* |
| Consumer goods | 12 | 10 | 6 |
| Raw materials and intermediate goods | 40 | 48 | 52 |
| Machinery and equipment | 23 | 20 | 23 |
| Transport equipment | 20 | 11 | 11 |
| Fuel and lubricants | 5 | 11 | 8 |

*Source:* Banco Central de la República Argentina, Annual Reports, various dates.

controls is clear when the structure of imports is analysed. The share of consumption goods declined; that of raw materials and intermediate goods increased (see Table 7.1). The 1949 balance-of-payments crisis called attention to the perverse consequences of agricultural policy.

Similar ISI policies were followed until 1976. The nominal level of protection increased steadily and, despite occasional foreign-exchange liberalisation, a more diversified set of protective instruments was developed.[10] New capital equipment for industry was inadequate because of the constraints on imports; and too little foreign exchange was released by the substitution of local for imported consumer and intermediate goods. As a result, technological advance was slow. Stagnant productivity and a smaller domestic market together meant high costs by international standards.

The way that both the public and private sectors financed their economic activities changed dramatically after the war. Equity financing almost disappeared, to be replaced by subsidised bank credit. Financial policies and inflation played a fundamental role in this change, whose outcome was 'financial repression' (McKinnon, 1973; Arnaudo, 1981).

## III     INFLATION AND STRUCTURAL CHANGE

Inflation was at the roots of the financial repression phenomenon. Argentina has experienced a long history of inflation whose origins can be traced back to the post-war years (Table 7.2).

During the pre-war years, price increases were associated with high levels of economic activity, low rates of unemployment and expansionary monetary policies. The same was true in 1946–8, when the government, which came to power in 1946, relied heavily on Central

TABLE 7.2  ANNUAL RATES OF INFLATION AND OUTPUT
GROWTH

| | Annual Averages (per cent) | | |
|---|---|---|---|
| Years | Consumer prices | Wholesale prices | GDP |
| 1936–44 | 2.6 | 8.0 | |
| 1945–8 | 16.0 | 11.0 | 4.6 |
| 1949 | 31.1 | 23.1 | −4.6 |
| 1950–1 | 31.1 | 34.6 | 5.9 |
| 1952 | 38.5 | 31.2 | −5.0 |
| 1953–8 | 14.8 | 17.5 | 5.1 |
| 1959 | 113.2 | 133.3 | −6.5 |
| 1960–1 | 20.4 | 12.0 | 7.5 |
| 1962 | 26.0 | 30.3 | −1.6 |
| 1963 | 26.0 | 28.8 | −2.4 |
| 1964–72 | 26.9 | 26.9 | 5.5 |
| 1973–4 | 42.2 | 35.0 | 5.4 |
| 1975 | 182.9 | 192.5 | −0.9 |
| 1976 | 442.0 | 499.0 | −1.7 |
| 1977 | 175.9 | 149.4 | 4.9 |
| 1978 | 175.6 | 146.0 | −3.4 |
| 1979 | 159.5 | 149.3 | 8.4 |
| 1980 | 100.8 | 75.4 | −0.2 |

*Source:* Instituto Nacional de Estadística y Censos and Banco Central de la República Argentina.

Bank credit to finance a large fiscal deficit and a rapid expansion of commercial bank loans. A number of across-the-board wage increases decreed during these years, together with higher prices for imported inputs, added further inflationary pressure. Increases in the general price level in 1946–8 could easily be explained by the general monetarist model, with its assumption that excess demand in the goods market can exist only if the money supply is greater than the demand for cash balances. This implies an excess supply of financial assets, which spills over into the markets for goods and services. Excessive wage claims and higher prices for imported inputs require only an accommodating money supply to add to inflation.

We have noted that 1949 was a key year: the link between expansionary monetary policy and inflation weakened from then on. In 1949, 1959, 1962, 1975, 1976 and 1978 recession was positively correlated with an acceleration in the rate of inflation. Argentina's industrialisation is closely connected with this changing pattern of

TABLE 7.3   IMPORTS/OUTPUT RATIO

| | *(per cent)* | | |
| --- | --- | --- | --- |
| *Years* | *Ratios* | *Years* | *Ratios* |
| 1945 | 4.7 | 1963 | 8.8 |
| 1946 | 8.0 | 1964 | 7.6 |
| 1947 | 14.3 | 1965 | 6.4 |
| 1948 | 13.8 | 1966 | 6.0 |
| 1949 | 9.9 | 1967 | 7.2 |
| 1950 | 8.5 | 1968 | 7.5 |
| 1951 | 10.4 | 1969 | 8.3 |
| 1952 | 8.5 | 1970 | 9.1 |
| 1953 | 4.7 | 1971 | 9.6 |
| 1954 | 5.4 | 1972 | 8.8 |
| 1955 | 6.7 | 1973 | 7.9 |
| 1956 | 11.7 | 1974 | 8.7 |
| 1957 | 11.9 | 1975 | 9.2 |
| 1958 | 10.0 | 1976 | 6.9 |
| 1959 | 11.1 | 1977 | 8.4 |
| 1960 | 11.3 | 1978 | 7.9 |
| 1961 | 11.0 | 1979 | 10.8 |
| 1962 | 11.9 | 1980 | 14.2 |

*Source:* 1945–9 Olivera, J.H.C. (1968)
1950–69 Banco Central de la República Argentina (1975)
1970–80 Ministerio de Economía, Hacienda y Finanzas (1981)

inflationary performance. During the first stages of Argentina's industrialisation, resources from agriculture were smoothly transferred
to industrial activity. Agricultural sectors, whose markets are usually
fairly competitive, are flex-price ones. Hence, a relative price change,
induced to favour the reallocation of resources, was compatible with a
general price level stability. Nominal prices of industrial goods rose,
while those of agricultural goods declined. The ISI policies failed to
reduce the import/output ratio (Table 7.3). The anti-export bias characteristic of these policies (Krueger, 1981) pervaded the whole period
(Berlinski and Schydlowsky, 1977), together with falling prices for agricultural goods that led to stagnating production and lower exports.
Recurrent balance-of-payments crises were unavoidable. Devaluation, aimed at changing relative prices to encourage agricultural
production, was a remedy usually applied. Unfortunately, the highly
protected industrial sector which was tailored, under ISI policies, to
cater exclusively for the domestic market, developed a remarkable

oligopolistic behaviour.[11] Falls in demand resulted in quantity reductions rather than price falls.[12] Any change in relative prices
necessarily implied an increase in the general price level. Transmission mechanisms always magnified the initial inflationary shock,
generated by the need to accommodate relative prices. Nominal
wage increases were closely linked to increases in the prices of the
agricultural goods that are a major component or the urban worker's
consumption basket. Higher labour costs and higher prices for imported inputs jointly led to higher industrial prices. Hence, the
original change in relative prices was partly offset and the desired
resource reallocation could not be achieved. A further balance-of-
payments crisis arose and the whole process restarted at a higher
price level (Olivera, 1968).

Although such a 'structural' process is typical of Argentine inflation, and that of some other Latin American countries, it must not be
seen as the only source of the inflationary pressure that plagued
Argentina. In some years, a fiscal deficit and expansionary monetary
policies could also be blamed for reinforcing inflation. ISI policies did
cause inflationary spurts, but we must remember that some authors
have noted that ISI policies lead to more permanent excess demand.
This occurs when the import/output ratio is reduced because of a fall
in consumption-goods imports not accompanied by a corresponding
reduction in the marginal propensity to consume (Felix, 1965).

Inflation was the outcome of this oscillating process of resource
reallocation which was, in turn, required by a new-born economic
structure. While intended to cope with changes in the internal and
external frameworks, this was not successful enough to loosen the
external constraints on economic growth.

## IV   THE ARGENTINE FINANCIAL SYSTEM

Financial repression was also associated with the financial policies
that Argentina followed after the end of the war and until 1977.
These were implemented by the Central Bank, which was created as
a semi-private institution in May 1935. From then on, its Charter and
Banking Law were the framework for the development of the Argentine financial system. The 1935 Charter entrusted three main tasks to
the bank. They were: (a) to accumulate and manage the gold and
foreign exchange reserves, so as to damp the effects of capital
movements and export fluctuations on money, credit and commercial
activity and hence to stabilise the value of money; (b) to control the

amount of credit and means of payments and so to adapt them to the level of economic activity; and (c) to promote the liquidity and to smooth the performance of the commercial banking system. To achieve these goals, the tools were: to manage rediscounting; to fix the rediscount rate; to perform some open-market operations; to provide short-term advances to the commercial banks and Treasury; to regulate new entries into banking; and to control the structure of banks' assets and liabilities. A special law established minimum fractionary reserves to be kept by commercial banks on each kind of deposit and limited the interest paid on them by linking it to the rediscount rate. The Central Bank was to keep a gold and foreign exchange reserve amounting to 25 per cent of its notes and sight liabilities. This arrangement was abandoned in 1949, but into convertibility to gold which was enacted by law, never became effective.

In 1946, the Central Bank was nationalised and its tasks were widened. It was to encompass control over economic activity so as to maintain high employment and promote the balanced growth of the economy 'in order to raise the standard of living of the population'. The deposit régime was modified: a guarantee to insure depositors against banking risks was established and all deposits were transferred to the Central Bank, for which the commercial banks acted. Rediscounting became the only credit instrument and was extensively used to allocate funds according to the Central Bank's promotional goals.[13] All expenses incurred in handling deposit accounts, including interest, were paid by the Central Bank while a commission on loans was received by commercial banks, which therefore found *any* credit operation profitable. Selective credit controls were used to ration loans. With the nominal interest rate fixed by the Central Bank, and with the high rate of inflation, loans were made at negative real interest rates. Subsidised banking credit became the main source of finance for business firms' investment and working capital.

Inflation had destroyed the capital market, which had been the traditional source of investment finance for both private businesses and the public sector. A specialised agency, Banco de Crédito Industrial Argentino, granted credit to industry at an interest rate lower than the return on preference shares. The Bank was also a lenient lender.[14] Financing of housing, previously made through a traditional bond, traded in the Stock Exchange, the Cédula Hipotecaria, became the object of another specialised agency: the Banco Hipotecario Nacional, whose credit again implied a subsidy for borrowers.

These policies led to evident excesses. In 1955–6 the Central Bank tried to encourage financing from non-banking sources. In 1955, credit support was refused to businesses which had not covered a 'reasonable' proportion of their financial needs with profits, and in 1956 banking credit to finance new capital was limited to 50 per cent of the estimated costs of investment (Banco Central de la República Argentina, 1956 and 1957). In 1957 the Central Bank's charter was reformed again. The main 1946 objectives regarding full employment and growth were maintained. In addition, targets for the regulation of the money supply and for credit policy were also stressed. The aim was to keep a stable price level and to manage the gold and foreign exchange reserves so as to avoid fluctuations in economic activity, due to external imbalance. The banking system returned to a fractionary reserve régime. The Central Bank kept the legal right to establish nominal interest rates and was also entrusted with fixing reserve requirements on deposits. Real rates on deposits and loans continued to be mainly negative in 1957–6. (Table 7.4). So the situation concerning the financing of business firms did not change (Fiel, 1971). Inflation also eroded depreciation reserves.

There was clearly financial repression, whose natural outcome was a steady decline in the intensiveness with which money was used. In the 1940s, this had reached the same level as it has today in the 'mature industrial economies', as measured by the $M_2/pY$ ratio (McKinnon, 1981). Financial repression fragmented the capital market, where an important group of *financieros* – paying interest rates well above those of banks – appeared. Their existence was officially recognised in 1960, and a law of 1964 put them under the regulation of the Central Bank. This regulation introduced control of the asset and liability structures as well as of maximum active and passive interest rates. The new interest rates were lower than those previously ruling and further regulations were later enacted, extending control over the extra-banking financial sector.[15]

During this period, financial repression was such that one of the Annual Reports of the Central Bank complained that credit was insufficient even for the working capital needs of business firms. They were consequently obliged to turn to internal savings, with an obvious deterioration in investment capacity.

## V   LIBERALISATION OF THE ECONOMY

The overall performance of the ISI strategy was disappointing. The accumulated annual average rate of growth of GDP in 1946–76 was a mere 3.7 per cent. The economy evolved through a pattern of stop–go cycles, due to heavy dependence on exports for growth. This pattern, closely associated with devaluations, caused fluctuating income redistribution among productive sectors, and also among groups of income earners. The high and non-selective level of protection for domestic economic activity and the general availability of subsidised credit, led to misallocation of productive resources. Despite a satisfactory rate of domestic saving, only a reduced investment rate could be achieved because of distorted relative prices.[16] The financial repression that was one of the outcomes of the ISI policy can be easily identified through the negative real interest rates that prevailed during 1950–76 (Table 7.4). These implied redistribution of income from lenders to borrowers, as estimated in Table 7.4. The tax imposed on depositors by the negative return on savings equalled 1.7 per cent of GDP in the 1950s, 0.6 per cent in the 1960s and reached a peak of 2.0 per cent in 1971–6. Its burden can be appreciated by comparing it with an income tax revenue/GDP ratio of 1.7 per cent in 1971–6 (Gaba, 1977).

In 1976 a major economic reform began, aimed at liberalising the economy. It included both fiscal and financial reform and a gradual opening-up of the economy. According to one theoretical viewpoint, such changes in economic policy must be considered as a whole. R. McKinnon (1973) has presented a liberalisation proposal for semi-industrial LDCs which, by following an ISI strategy, are suffering from financial repression with moderate rates of inflation, chronic foreign exchange shortages and poor growth performance. Such liberalisation could be carried out in four stages: financial reform; a new tax system; liberalisation of external trade; and, eventually, removal of exchange controls on foreign capital movements.

Financial reform aims to allow interest rates to reflect real capital scarcity; this should increase both absolute savings and the proportion of these channeled into the banking system, thus allowing more efficient investment allocation. Tax reform should help to eliminate the fiscal deficit[17] and remove any bias against exports and/or imports. The target of trade liberalisation is to remove the anti-export bias that protectionism implies. Such liberalisation can take place without recession only when reallocation of resources from import-substituting industries to potential export industries is rapid and smooth. Free capital movements should come last in the liberalisation process, to avoid possible perverse effects on high-powered money and on the exchange rate, which could offset existing achievements.

TABLE 7.4    FINANCIAL REPRESSION INDICATORS

| Year | (1) | (2) | (3) | (4) | (5) | (6) |
|------|-----|-----|-----|-----|-----|-----|
| 1940 | 0.457 | 0.234 | | | | |
| 1941 | 0.432 | 0.212 | | | | |
| 1942 | 0.387 | 0.181 | | | | |
| 1943 | 0.396 | 0.175 | | | | |
| 1944 | 0.397 | 0.167 | | | | |
| 1945 | 0.449 | 0.180 | | | | |
| 1946 | 0.433 | 0.166 | | | | |
| 1947 | 0.463 | 0.165 | | | | |
| 1948 | 0.474 | 0.159 | | | | |
| 1949 | 0.503 | 0.153 | | | | |
| 1950 | 0.472 | 0.136 | −16.1 | −11.6 | 2.1 | 21.6 |
| 1951 | 0.370 | 0.094 | −31.8 | −28.1 | 2.8 | 35.0 |
| 1952 | 0.332 | 0.082 | −13.5 | −9.3 | 1.3 | 20.1 |
| 1953 | 0.352 | 0.087 | 3.7 | 8.6 | −0.2 | −4.8 |
| 1954 | 0.387 | 0.098 | −11.2 | −7.4 | 1.3 | 17.7 |
| 1955 | 0.387 | 0.098 | −4.2 | −0.1 | 0.6 | 6.7 |
| 1956 | 0.352 | 0.089 | −11.7 | −6.0 | 1.2 | 13.0 |
| 1957 | 0.317 | 0.081 | −17.8 | −12.6 | 1.6 | 18.1 |
| 1958 | 0.270 | 0.067 | −30.3 | −26.5 | 2.1 | 31.5 |
| 1959 | 0.183 | 0.039 | −47.8 | −45.0 | 2.2 | 34.0 |
| 1960 | 0.197 | 0.043 | −11.3 | −6.8 | 0.6 | 8.3 |
| 1961 | 0.207 | 0.049 | −8.8 | −4.8 | 0.6 | 7.9 |
| 1962 | 0.185 | 0.047 | −17.3 | −13.0 | 0.9 | 14.4 |
| 1963 | 0.179 | 0.052 | −11.4 | −5.6 | 0.8 | 11.9 |
| 1964 | 0.184 | 0.060 | −7.0 | −1.0 | 0.6 | 5.0 |

Incentives to invest in order to promote growth are created, under an ISI strategy, because the domestic market is closed to external competition. Sometimes they are reinforced by subsidised credit. Under liberalisation, however, investment incentives rest on the possibility of obtaining enough funds from the banking system to finance indivisible projects, the real returns from which make it possible to pay the higher interest rates ruling after financial reform. The size of the financial system, measured by $M_2/pY$, will grow as higher interest rates increase the attractiveness of accumulating money – the so-called 'complementarity' between money and physical capital (McKinnon, 1973).

The external sector is usually the main constraint on the economic growth of semi-industrialised LDCs. Liberalisation of trade aims to remove this constraint by increasing the flow of exports – the expected outcome of eliminating bias against them. Many profitable

TABLE 7.4 *continued*

| Year | (1) | (2) | (3) | (4) | (5) | (6) |
|------|------|------|------|------|------|------|
| 1965 | 0.182 | 0.062 | −20.4 | −15.4 | 1.5 | 15.8 |
| 1966 | 0.193 | 0.066 | −15.2 | −10.0 | 1.2 | 14.2 |
| 1967 | 0.200 | 0.070 | −13.5 | −8.3 | 1.1 | 14.4 |
| 1968 | 0.234 | 0.085 | 0.3 | 6.6 | 0.2 | −1.7 |
| 1969 | 0.258 | 0.102 | 2.9 | 8.8 | −0.1 | −4.4 |
| 1970 | 0.250 | 0.103 | −9.8 | −5.4 | 1.3 | 12.3 |
| 1971 | 0.216 | 0.091 | −18.8 | −15.4 | 2.0 | 23.1 |
| 1972 | 0.165 | 0.071 | −27.1 | −25.3 | 2.4 | 30.7 |
| 1973 | 0.179 | 0.076 | −17.1 | −14.8 | 1.6 | 20.0 |
| 1974 | 0.249 | 0.109 | −16.7 | −12.4 | 2.1 | 18.4 |
| 1975 | 0.118 | 0.047 | −71.3 | −67.6 | 5.7 | 47.9 |
| 1976 | 0.083 | 0.022 | −65.1 | −62.0 | 1.7 | |

Column (*1*) $M_2/pY$
Column (*2*) $D/pY$
*Source:* Banco Central de la República Argentina.

Column (*3*) Average passive real rate of interest.
Column (*4*) Average active real rate of interest.
Column (*5*) Tax on deposits/GDP (per cent).
Column (*6*) Subsidy on loans/Domestic private investment (per cent).

The tax on deposits has been computed as the loss suffered by depositors assuming a 2.0 per cent equilibrium real rate of interest.

The subsidy on loans has been computed as the transference payment made to borrowers assuming a 5.0 per cent equilibrium real rate of interest.

*Source:* Gaba, E. (1977).

indivisible investment projects, financed by the increased domestic credit, will be connected with exports. Domestic financing is preferable to external credit, since the latter might reduce the real exchange rate and so result in a new anti-export bias.

Such a liberalisation programme assumes that financial reform may help to control inflation and avoid a recession. Under the general monetarist model, inflation is caused by an excess supply of money. A higher real return on money will increase the demand for $M_2/p$. With the nominal money supply growing at a decreasing rate, this increase will allow a decline in the inflation rate without implying a fall in the real amount of loanable funds available for business – an important input to the productive process in the short periods of time over which stabilisation occurs (Maynard and Van Ryjckeghem, 1968). Though non-monetary inflationary pressures are not considered in this liberalisation programme, one may assume that they will dwindle with the improved competitiveness of the industrial sector, which is an outcome of the opening-up of the economy.[18] That, in turn, will reduce the downward inflexibility of nominal prices.

Although partial liberalisation of the Argentine financial market was already underway, a complete financial reform was undertaken in June 1977 in line with McKinnon's proposals.[19] Interest rates on loans and deposits were now freely determined in the financial market and the banking sector returned to a fractionary reserve system. The money-intensiveness of the economy had reached its lowest-ever level in 1976. It began steady growth after 1977.

Regressions for the demand for money in Argentina were run for the period 1950–73 to test the 'complementarity' hypothesis. The dependent variables $D/pY$ (the ratio of time- and saving-deposits to GDP),[20] and $M_2/pY$ (the ratio of demand-deposits and currency plus time- and saving-deposits to GDP) were correlated with the real interest rate ($i$), the share of household and corporate savings in GDP ($S/pY$) and the rate of inflation, measured as the rate of change of the overall wholesale price index ($\dot{p}$). It was assumed that short-run demand adjusts to long-run demand according to an adaptive pattern

$$x_t - x_{t-1} = c(x_t - x_{t-1}), \quad c > 0$$

Here, $x$ denotes the variable being studied, $t$ is a time index, $x$ is the desired level of $x$ and $c$ is a constant coefficient of adjustment.

The dependent variable in a demand-for-money test of the complementarity hypothesis should strictly be the investment/output ratio, but the savings/output ratio was used. This was on the assumption that savings acted as a constraint on capital accumulation, since the interest rate was set below its equilibrium level (Fry, 1978). The actual real rate of interest was taken to be the expected rate of interest, because some empirical evidence had shown that the coefficient representing the speed of adjustment of actual to expected rates in an adaptive-expectations scheme was very close to one (Baliño, 1977).

The results (Table 7.5) support to some extent the hypothesis tested, where the variable to be explained is $D/pY$. Since Argentina suffered steady inflation during the period covered by the test, one can assume that the ratio of currency plus demand deposits to GDP had been driven to a level that could not be further compressed without reverting to barter.

Although $M_2/pY$ had been observed to increase, it did not reach the previous (1949) maximum. Besides, a large proportion of $D/pY$

TABLE 7.5 COMPLEMENTARITY HYPOTHESIS TEST

| Equation | $a$ | $b$ | $c$ | $d$ | $R^2$ | $s$ |
|---|---|---|---|---|---|---|
| $M_2/pY = a + bi + c\,S/pY + d(M_2/pY)_{-1}$ | 0.018 (0.591) | 0.003 (7.853) | 0.0⬜ (1.4⬛) | 0.916 (18.569) | 0.967 | 0.016 |
| $D/pY = a + bi + c\,S/pY + d(D/pY)_{-1}$ | 0.017 (1.958) | 0.001 (8.655) | 0.0⬜ (1.5⬛) | 0.811 (15.938) | 0.941 | 0.006 |
| $ln(M_2/pY) = a + bi + c\,ln(S/pY)$ $+ d\,(M_2/pY)_{-1}$ | -0.096 (0.580) | 0.009 (7.199) | 0.0⬜ (0.37⬛) | 0.917 (15.128) | 0.957 | 0.066 |
| $ln(D/pY) = a + bi + c\,ln(S/pY)$ $+ d\,ln(D/pY)_{-1}$ | 0.456 (2.978) | 0.014 (10.399) | 0.1⬜ (1.6⬛) | 0.871 (17.847) | 0.954 | 0.067 |
| $ln(D/pY) = a + bp + c\,ln(S/pY)$ $+ d\,ln(D/pY)_{-1}$ | -0.632 (3.538) | -0.005 (8.725) | 0.14⬜ (1.7⬛) | 0.851 (15.226) | 0.939 | 0.077 |

*Source:* Calculated by author.

was very short-term deposits (thirty days and under). This was perhaps because the inflation rate was highly variable, which made it almost impossible to guess the actual real return on deposits.[21] The performance of the interest rate suggests that the variability of the expected inflation rate was smaller than that of the actual rate. Depositors enjoyed being able to revise their decisions frequently. This short-term structure of bank liabilities allowed banks to make only high-turnover loans. One might therefore assume that credit was used mainly to finance the working capital needed for businesses. This could hardly be considered a shortcoming where an active capital market was providing a steady flow of investment funds, but the Argentine capital market never recovered its earlier importance.

Despite a growing $M_2/pY$, the anticipated steady reduction in the rate of inflation, was not achieved.[22] It remained both high and very variable. A possible explanation may be the persistence of non-monetary inflationary pressures. Distorted relative prices may be traced back to the officially imposed maximum nominal prices which ruled from June 1973 to April 1974 (Montuschi and Canavese, 1975). In 1976, economic policy was aimed at restoring equilibrium relative prices, even though additional distortions were added in 1977 with the so-called *tregua de precios* (price freeze).[23] According to the process described earlier, the unavoidable result of any accommodation of relative prices is an increase in the general price level. The varying speed of adjustment of different nominal prices and changes in economic policy might also explain the high oscillation in the inflation rate.

Liberalisation of trade was carried out by eliminating export taxes and gradually reducing import duties. By November 1976, the foreign exchange market was unified. Before April 1976, two official foreign exchange markets had co-existed, whose gradual unification meant an implicit devaluation. In 1976–9 movements in the real exchange rate and lower import duties mainly affected the tariff redundancy (Wogart and Marquez, 1980). New import tariffs were devised for use in 1979–84. The aim was a reduction both in the average rate of nominal tariff protection and in its sectoral dispersion, so as to change the productive structure of the economy.

Persistent inflation obliged the government to adopt a new anti-inflationary policy late in 1978. It consisted of pre-announced nominal values for a set of key variables, including minimum wages, public utility prices and a decreasing exchange rate devaluation. Aimed at influencing the expectations of economic agents, the programme assumed that, in an open economy with a fixed exchange rate, the domestic inflation rate must eventually tend to the international rate plus the rate of exchange devaluation. This assumption takes for granted that home-goods prices follow the trend of traded-goods prices, which make up the bulk of domestic production. For some goods, the government decided to speed up tariff reductions and so to accelerate the convergence of the domestic and international rates of inflation, by strengthening competition from abroad.

The impact on the inflation rate was first felt only in late 1979. This lag may be explained by: difficulties in setting up adequate import channels and grasping new import opportunities on the supply side; and by the time it usually takes for customers to react to new, imported products on the demand side. After September 1979, consumer prices increased systematically faster than the wholesale price index because of the incidence of home goods on consumer prices (Table 7.6). This shows that the key assumption of converging prices for traded and home goods was not fulfilled; it precluded the desired convergence between internal and international rates of inflation.

High domestic nominal interest rates, the failure of inflation rates to converge and the active pre-announced decreasing crawling-peg in Argentina after 1979 resulted in badly aligned domestic and foreign rates of interest. The high nominal interest rates in Argentina were actually high real rates for foreign investors (Table 7.6). An inflow of short-term foreign capital was unavoidable. The money supply became manifestly passive, ratifying the continuing inflation that was led by prices of domestic goods. The real exchange rate fell continuously. Even though the 1980 current account of the balance of payments was in deficit, capital inflows reduced the pressure to devalue. A new anti-export bias built up progressively and some previously protected sectors faced deepening adjustment problems, not offset by increased domestic demand. At the end of 1980, the impending recession made real the threat of regression to a protectionist régime.

## VI CONCLUSIONS

Some useful conclusions about the ISI strategy and about attempts at liberalisation can be drawn from Argentine experience.

The domestic market in an LDC is small, so that industries developed under ISI strategies in order to cater for those markets usually

TABLE 7.6

| Month | (1) | (2) | (3) | (4) | (5) | (6) | (7) |
|---|---|---|---|---|---|---|---|
| *1979* | | | | | | | |
| Jan | 12.8 | 10.0 | 5.2 | 6.8 | 7.6 | −5.3 | −2.2 |
| Feb | 7.4 | 8.0 | 4.8 | 6.4 | 7.1 | −1.0 | −0.8 |
| Mar | 7.7 | 8.1 | 4.7 | 6.4 | 7.0 | −1.3 | −0.9 |
| Apr | 7.0 | 6.5 | 4.6 | 6.4 | 7.1 | −0.5 | 0.6 |
| May | 6.9 | 9.0 | 4.6 | 6.5 | 7.1 | −0.4 | −1.7 |
| Jun | 9.7 | 10.5 | 4.4 | 6.7 | 7.3 | −2.8 | −2.9 |
| Jul | 7.2 | 7.5 | 4.1 | 7.0 | 7.6 | −0.1 | 0.1 |
| Aug | 11.5 | 14.7 | 3.9 | 7.3 | 7.9 | −3.7 | −5.9 |
| Sep | 6.8 | 5.3 | 3.7 | 7.4 | 8.0 | 0.5 | 2.6 |
| Oct | 4.3 | 1.1 | 3.4 | 7.2 | 7.9 | 2.7 | 6.8 |
| Nov | 5.1 | 3.4 | 3.3 | 6.2 | 7.0 | 1.1 | 3.4 |
| Dec | 4.5 | 2.5 | 3.1 | 5.9 | 6.8 | 1.3 | 4.1 |
| *1980* | | | | | | | |
| Jan | 7.2 | 4.3 | 2.9 | 5.8 | 6.6 | −1.3 | 2.3 |
| Feb | 5.3 | 4.1 | 2.7 | 5.2 | 6.0 | −0.1 | 1.8 |
| Mar | 5.8 | 3.9 | 2.5 | 4.8 | 5.6 | −0.9 | 1.6 |
| Apr | 6.2 | 3.9 | 2.3 | 4.5 | 5.2 | −1.6 | 1.3 |
| May | 5.8 | 5.4 | 2.1 | 4.5 | 5.4 | −1.2 | 0.0 |
| Jun | 5.7 | 7.3 | 2.0 | 5.4 | 6.4 | −0.3 | −0.9 |
| Jul | 4.6 | 2.9 | 1.7 | 6.0 | 7.0 | 1.4 | 3.9 |
| Aug | 3.4 | 2.9 | 1.5 | 5.0 | 5.9 | 1.5 | 2.9 |
| Sep | 4.5 | 2.9 | 1.3 | 4.3 | 5.5 | −0.2 | 2.5 |
| Oct | 7.6 | 5.4 | 1.1 | 4.3 | 5.2 | −3.0 | −0.2 |
| Nov | 4.7 | 2.6 | 1.0 | 4.6 | 5.4 | −0.1 | 2.7 |
| Dec | 3.8 | 0.8 | 1.0 | 5.4 | 6.3 | 1.5 | 5.4 |

Column (*1*) Consumer Price Index (Monthly rate of change-per cent).
Column (*2*) Wholesale Price Index (Monthly rate of change-per cent).

*Source:* Instituto Nacional de Estadística y Censos.

Column (*3*) Monthly rate of dollar devaluation (per cent).

*Source:* FIEL, *Indicadores de Coyuntura,* various issues.

Column (*4*) Monthly passive nominal rate of interest (per cent).
Column (*5*) Monthly active nominal rate of interest (per cent).
Column (*6*) Monthly passive real rate of interest (per cent).
Column (*7*) Monthly active real rate of interest (per cent).

*Source:* Banco Central de la República Argentina.

have oligopolistic features. These features lie at the roots of the non-monetary inflationary pressures that bring about financial repression. Lack of domestic funds obliges countries to resort to external financing in order to sustain a satisfactory rate of growth. Experience shows that, in the long run, foreign financing (including foreign direct investment) can worsen the characteristic external constraints of ISI strategies.

The attempt at liberalisation carried out in Argentina supports McKinnon's warnings on the necessity of matching the opening-up of the economy with financial reform. The increasing availability of domestic funds should allow the economy to avoid the generalised use of foreign capital. However, financial reform is not enough to get rid of inflation in countries leaving the ISI stage. The liberalisation of trade, while loosening the external constraint, will increase the economy competitiveness. So it looks like an adequate instrument to control non-monetary inflationary pressures. To avoid the possible perverse effects of foreign capital movements, the proper way to accomplish the opening-up of the economy is to manoeuvre tariffs and to keep the real exchange rate at a level where exports balance imports.

NOTES

1. In 1912 the value (FOB prices in sterling) of Argentine exports was approximately three times that in 1900. (Cf. Vázquez-Presedo, 1971.)
2. Flour mills, packing plants, sugar refineries, wineries and breweries are usually mentioned, but textile plants, metallurgical manufacturing, rubber and papers mills, rubber plants and electrical-appliance factories also existed. (Cf. Vázquez-Presedo, 1978.)
3. Official import prices are used to compute import duties.
4. This bank was founded in 1944 and from 1946 to 1951 it contributed to the establishment and financing of more than 20 000 industrial enterprises.
5. According to official thought, this dependence 'points out clearly the necessity of developing a domestic market until it prevails over the external one'. (Cf. Banco Central de la República Argentina, 1947.)
6. For example, Brazil obtained massive external aid from the USA which was denied to Argentina, which also failed to qualify as a source for most Marshall's Aid purchases of agricultural products. (Cf. Vázquez-Presedo, 1977 and Schwartz, 1967.)
7. Growth in GDP in 1946–8 was 15.1 per cent, as compared with the 14 per cent in the previous four years. (Cf. Banco Central de la República Argentina, 1966.)
8. Exports dropped by 20.9 per cent between 1946 and 1948 and by 41. 1 per cent between 1946 and 1949. The share of exports in GDP fell from

17.6 per cent in 1946 to 12.1 per cent in 1948 to 9.4 per cent in 1949. (Cf. Banco Central de la República Argentina, 1966.)

9. During the period 1946–55, the total area planted had declined steadily for most export crops.

10. S. Macario reckoned that Argentina's import duties were the highest in Latin America during the period 1958–60. (Cf. Macario, 1964.)

11. Montuschi estimated that 63.4 per cent of industrial production was traded in oligopolistic markets in 1953, a proportion which increased to 69.9 per cent in 1963. (Cf. Montuschi, 1976.)

12. This phenomenon is usually referred to as 'downwards rigidity in nominal prices'.

13. The official point of view was that the Central Bank should support any businessman needing financial aid to produce goods and services to cover the population's needs. (Cf. Banco Central de la República Argentina, 1948.)

14. The yearly interest rate charged on loans by the Banco de Crédito Industrial Argentino was 5.5 per cent and the return on preference shares amounted to 6.0 per cent per year. According to the Annual Report of the Central Bank, in 1957 nearly 14 per cent of the portfolio of that Bank was frozen. (Cf. Schwartz, 1967.)

15. In 1969 the regulations concerning the whole financial system were summarised in a single law. (Cf. Banco Central de la República Argentina, 1965, 1966 and 1970.)

16. 'Current peso accounts indicate that Fixed Gross Domestic Investment averaged approximately 20 per cent of Argentine GNP during the period from 1946 through 1958. In terms of 1935–7 prices, however, such investment amounted to only 12 per cent of the national product'. (Cf. Schwartz, 1967.) Díaz Alejandro came to the same conclusion on the basis of alternative estimates covering a longer period. (Cf. Díaz Alejandro, 1970.)

17. In LDCs indirect taxation is the main source of government revenue. A high proportion of indirect tax revenues comes from foreign-trade taxation. As a consequence of ISI strategies, the indirect tax system becomes less income-elastic. Since government expenditures are elastic to income growth, it is necessary to build more income elasticity into a reformed tax system. (Cf. McKinnon, 1973.)

18. This does not preclude the possibility that other non-monetary inflationary pressures, such as those described in the so-called 'Scandinavian model', might eventually appear. (Cf. Canavese, 1979.)

19. The organisation of the Argentine banking system in 1973–7 was similar to that ruling during the period 1946–57.

20. In Argentina, only time- and savings-deposits yield interest.

21. The monthly average passive nominal interest rate on thirty days deposits for the period June 1977–December 1980 was 6.61 per cent and its standard deviation 1.50. For the same period, the monthly average rate of change of wholesale prices was 6.65 per cent and its standard deviation 3.21.

22. Even though a fiscal reform was not enacted until October 1980, by 1976 the fiscal deficit had been sharply reduced as a proportion of GDP and, after 1977, it reached the same level as in the first years of the decade.

This reduction was achieved by increasing the pressure of taxation and reducing government expenditure. (Cf. Ministerio de Economía, 1981.)
23. The government's objective was to dampen inflationary expectations.

## REFERENCES

Arnaudo, A.A. (1981) *El crecimiento financiero argentino en los últimos cuarenta años* (Buenos Aires).

Baliño, T.J.T. (1977) 'Algunos resultados sobre la demanda de dinero en la Argentina', *Ensayos Económicos*, March.

Banco Central de la República Argentina Memoria Anual (Annual Reports) for 1946, 1947, 1955, 1956, 1957, 1964, 1965, 1966 and 1969. (Buenos Aires: Banco Central de la Republica Argentina).

Banco Central de la República Argentina (1965) *Origen del Producto y* Cuentas Nacionales del Gasto Nacional (Buenos Aires).

Banco Central de la República Argentina (1975) *Producto e Ingreso de la Argentina*, Vol. 2, (Buenos Aires).

Berlinski, J. and Schydlowsky, D.M. (1977) *Incentives for Industrialization in Argentina*, unpublished, International Bank for Reconstruction and Development, Washington, D.C.

Canavese, A.J. (1979) 'La hipótesis estructural en la teoría de la inflación', *Ensayos Económicos*, September.

Chenery, H.B. (1960) 'Patterns of Industrial Growth', *American Economic Review*, vol. 50, September.

Díaz Alejandro, C.F. (1970) *Essays on the Economic History of the Argentine Republic* (New Haven and London: Yale University Press).

Economic Commission for Latin America (1950) *The Economic Development of Latin America and its Principal Problems* (New York: United Nations).

Felix, D. (1965) *Industrialización sustitutiva de importaciones y exportación industrial en la Argentina*, unpublished, Instituto T. Di Tella, Buenos Aires.

Fiel (1971) *La financiación de las empresas industriales en la Argentina*, unpublished, Buenos Aires.

Fry, M.S. (1978) 'Money and Capital or Financial Deepening in Economic Development', *Journal of Money Credit and Banking*, vol. 10, November.

Gaba, E. (1977) 'Indexación y sistema financiero', *Revista Argentina de Finanzas*, June.

Krueger, A.O. (1981) 'Interactions between Inflation and Trade Regime Objectives in Stabilization Programs', in Cline W.R. and Weintraub, S. (eds) *Economic Stabilization in Developing Countries* (Washington DC: Brookings Institution).

Macario, S. (1964) 'Protectionism and Industrialization in Latin America', *Economic Bulletin for Latin America*, ECLA, March.

Maynard, G. and Ryjckeghem, W. van (1968) 'Stabilization Policy in an Inflationary Economy: the Case of Argentina', in G. Papanek (ed.) *Development Policy. Theory and Practice* (Totawa, NJ: Barnes and Noble).

McKinnon, R.I. (1973) *Money and Capital in Economic Development* (Washington DC: Brookings Institution).

McKinnon, R.I. (1981) 'Financial Repression and the Liberalization Problem Within Less-Developed Countries', in Grassman S. and Lundberg, E. (eds) *The World Economic Order: Past and Prospects* (New York: St. Martin's Press).

Ministerio de Economía, Hacienda Y Finanzas (1981) *Informe Economicó, Reseña Estadística 1970–1980* (Buenos Aires: Ministry of Economics).

Montuschi, L. and Canavese, A.J. (1975) 'Efectos redistributivos del pacto social', *Anales*, Asociación Argentina de Economía Política, vol. 2.

Montuschi, L. (1976) 'Concentratión y trabajo asalariado en la industria manufacturera argentina, 1953–1963', in *Lecturas de* Microenomía por Economistas Argentino (Buenos Aires).

Olivera, J.H.G. (1968) *Causas no monetarias de inflación en la Argentina*, (unpublished). Instituto de Investigaciones Económicas, Universidad de Buenos Aires.

Schwartz, H.H. (1967) *The Argentine Experience with Industrial Credit and Protection Incentives, 1943–1958*, unpublished doctoral dissertation, Yale University.

Vázquez-Presedo V. (1971) *El caso argentino. Migración de factores, comercio exterior y desarrollo 1875–1914* (Buenos Aires).

Vázquez-Presedo, V. (1977) 'Aspectos de las vulnerabilidad económica argentina durante la Segunda Guerra Mundial', *Anales*, Asociacion Argentina de Economía Política, vol. 2.

Vázquez-Presedo V. (1978) *Crisis y retraso. Argentina y la economía internacional entre las dos guerras* (Buenos Aires).

Wogart, J.P. and Marques, J.S. (1980) 'Price Stabilisation Through Trade Liberalization in Latin America', Segunda Conferencia Internacional sobre América Latina y la Economía Mundial, unpublished OAS and Instituto T. De Tella, Buenos Aires.

# Part Three
# Foreign and
# International Financing

# 8 The Flow of Public and Private Financial Resources to Developing Countries: Recent Trends

**Helmut Führer**

OECD*

## I INTRODUCTION

This paper provides a broad quantitative picture of recent trends in the flow of financial resources to developing countries. The period covered is the last decade. Most of the data presented are derived from the statistical reporting systems of the OECD and the statistical concepts and country categories used are also those of the OECD. The paper discusses trends in: overall resource flows (Section II); major types of resource flows (Section III); resource flows to different groups of developing countries (Section IV); financial terms of resource flows (Section V); geographic origin of resource flows (Section VI); government policies for resource flows (Section VII).

---

* The Author is an official of the OECD. The views expressed in this paper are those of the author and should not be attributed to the organisation. The figures presented in two tables are drawn from data published by the OECD in its annual review 'The Development and Cooperative Effects and Sources of Two Members of Two Development Resistance Committee' and in the 'Geographical Distribution of Financial Flows to Developing Countries', issued in December 1981 and February 1982.

## II  TRENDS IN OVERALL RESOURCE FLOWS

The 1970s have seen a major increase in the use of external financing by developing countries (see Table 8.1). Combined external receipts[1] from all sources by all developing countries (including OPEC countries) increased from \$19bn in 1970 to \$54bn in 1975 and \$87bn in 1980: that is with an average annual rate of increase of over 16 per cent. Much of this, however, is a reflection of inflation, which must, of course, be allowed for in interpreting the statistical information and in trying to identify significant trends. For the analysis in this paper the average OECD GNP deflator has been used throughout as a rough measure of world inflation.[2] During the period it rose at an annual average rate of 11 per cent. On this basis, the average annual rate of increase in the use of external resources by developing countries, over the decade, was of the order of 5–6 per cent.[3] This is roughly in line with the average annual growth rate of the GNP of developing countries over the decade, of somewhat under 6 per cent. Total external resource receipts – as a percentage of the GNP of developing countries – were, therefore, maintained at somewhat over 4 per cent.

The most spectacular increase during the decade took place in 1975, following the 1973–4 oil price hike. Major increases occurred in that year, in virtually all types of concessional and non-concessional resource flows. What is particularly remarkable is the major upturn in official aid and multilateral financing. An important factor was the prompt aid response by the OPEC aid donors following the large increases in their oil receipts, but OECD donors and multilateral agencies also reacted with astonishing vigour by accelerating disbursements and by taking a liberal attitude to non-project and cost-overrun financing. On the non-concessional side, major increases came from commercial bank lending and export credits. (The sharp increase in private investment in 1975 is partly spurious since it followed major Middle East disinvestment in 1974.)

A good part of the total real increase in resource flows over the decade is thus concentrated in the jump to a new level that occurred between 1974 and 1975, and was followed by a much more gradual rise and subsequent levelling off.

The increase in the use of external resources by developing countries during the 1970s was considerably faster in real terms than that recorded during the 1960s. During that decade external resource flows to developing countries are estimated to have increased at an

TABLE 8.1 OVERALL TRENDS IN EXTERNAL RESOURCE FLOWS TO DEVELOPING COUNTRIES 1970–80

| | 1970 | 1971 | 1972 | 1973 | 1974 | 1975 | 1976 | 1977 | 1978 | 1979 | 1980 |
|---|---|---|---|---|---|---|---|---|---|---|---|
| | | | | | | $bn at current prices | | | | | |
| Total external resource flows | 18.97 | 21.09 | 23.17 | 31.37 | 35.04 | 53.67 | 57.5 | 63.55 | 79.83 | 83.86 | 89.11 |
| ODA | 8.04 | 9.29 | 9.88 | 11.62 | 15.33 | 19.33 | 19.0 | 20.16 | 23.75 | 28.91 | 33.62 |
| Non-concessional | 10.93 | 11.80 | 13.29 | 19.75 | 19.71 | 34.34 | 38.5 | 43.39 | 56.08 | 54.95 | 55.49 |
| | | | | | | $bn at 1980 prices[a] | | | | | |
| Total external resource flows | 52.55 | 54.50 | 54.01 | 57.77 | 62.57 | 84.79 | 87.9 | 89.01 | 96.06 | 91.55 | 89.11 |
| ODA | 22.27 | 24.01 | 23.03 | 21.40 | 27.37 | 30.54 | 29.0 | 28.24 | 28.58 | 31.56 | 33.62 |
| Non-concessional | 30.28 | 30.49 | 30.98 | 36.37 | 35.20 | 54.25 | 58.8 | 60.77 | 67.48 | 59.99 | 55.49 |
| For reference: OECD GNP Deflator | 36.1 | 38.7 | 42.9 | 42.9 | 56.0 | 63.3 | 65.5 | 71.4 | 83.1 | 91.6 | 100.0 |

[a] Deflated by GNP deflator of OECD countries combined.

average annual rate of roughly 4 per cent in real terms, considerably less than the developing countries' GNP growth during this period which exceeded 6 per cent.

## III   TRENDS BY MAJOR TYPES OF RESOURCE FLOW

Major shifts in the composition of resource flows, in terms of different types of capital, have taken place during the 1970s, as can be seen from Tables 8.2 and 8.3.

There were significant increases over the decade in real terms in all major types of resource flows, Official Development Assistance (ODA) and non-concessional. ODA increased substantially, in real and absolute terms, at an average annual rate in real terms of 4 per cent over the decade. However, the largest increases were in the form of non-concessional resource flows which account for almost 70 per cent of the total absolute increase over the period.

The fastest relative expansion was in the form of multilateral flows (concessional and non-concessional flows from the World Bank, regional development banks and United Nations development programmes) and in commercial bank lending. Both multilateral lending and commercial bank lending grew at the extraordinary average annual rate of 10 per cent in real terms over the decade.

The low direct investment figure for 1980 is exceptional, since the basic trend over the decade was upwards. Export credits (net) grew at an average annual rate of 7 per cent in real terms, which is still rather less fast than the expansion in exports.

As a result of the differences in rates of expansion, the overall pattern of financing has changed (see Table 8.3). The share of official development assistance and of direct investment has declined slightly; that of commercial bank lending and multilateral financing has considerably increased. Dramatic changes in financing patterns occurred in the earlier half of the decade; since then, however, the relative importance of the various types of financing has remained remarkably stable.

## IV   TRENDS IN RESOURCE FLOWS TO DIFFERENT GROUPS OF DEVELOPING COUNTRIES

Data on resource flows to the totality of developing countries combined are of limited analytical significance. The notion 'developing

TABLE 8.2  TOTAL NET RESOURCE RECEIPTS OF DEVELOPING COUNTRIES FROM ALL SOURCES

| Net disbursements ($bn) | 1970 | 1971 | 1972 | 1973 | 1974 | 1975 | 1976 | 1977 | 1978 | 1979 | 1980 |
|---|---|---|---|---|---|---|---|---|---|---|---|
| Official Development Assistance | 8.05 | 9.29 | 9.88 | 11.62 | 15.33 | 19.33 | 19.12 | 20.16 | 23.75 | 28.91 | 33.62 |
| I. Bilateral |  |  |  |  |  |  |  |  |  |  |  |
| (a) DAC countries | 5.66 | 6.33 | 6.63 | 7.09 | 8.23 | 9.81 | 9.50 | 10.08 | 13.12 | 15.91 | 17.64 |
| (b) OPEC countries | 0.36 | 0.37 | 0.48 | 1.22 | 3.02 | 4.92 | 4.54 | 3.94 | 3.25 | 4.93 | 6.11 |
| (c) CMEA countries | 0.96 | 1.26 | 1.38 | 1.35 | 1.26 | 0.73 | 1.05 | 1.09 | 1.28 | 1.75 | 1.80 |
| (d) Other countries |  |  |  |  |  | 0.03 | 0.05 | 0.08 | 0.10 | 0.12 | 0.20 |
| II. Multilateral agencies | 1.07 | 1.33 | 1.39 | 1.96 | 2.82 | 3.84 | 3.57 | 4.97 | 6.00 | 6.20 | (7.87) |
| of which: OPEC financed |  |  |  |  | 0.12 | 0.16 | 0.42 | 1.23 | 0.96 | 0.26 | 0.26 |
| Non-concessional flows | 10.94 | 11.80 | 13.29 | 19.75 | 19.71 | 34.34 | 38.57 | 43.39 | 56.08 | 54.95 | 55.49 |
| I. Bilateral |  |  |  |  |  |  |  |  |  |  |  |
| (a) Direct investment | 3.69 | 3.31 | 4.23 | 4.72 | 1.89 | 11.51 | 8.54 | 9.59 | 11.83 | 13.62 | 9.69 |
| (b) Bank sector[a] | 3.00 | 3.30 | 4.80 | 9.70 | 10.00 | 12.00 | 15.00 | 15.50 | 22.87 | 19.67 | (18.00) |
| (c) Bond lending | 0.30 | 0.30 | 0.52 | 0.58 | 0.28 | 0.42 | 1.22 | 3.20 | 2.67 | 1.14 | (2.00) |
| (d) Private export credits | 2.09 | 2.71 | 1.44 | 1.15 | 2.40 | 4.42 | 2.21 | 9.11 | 10.22 | 9.49 | 12.20 |
| (e) Official export credits | 0.59 | 0.71 | 0.75 | 1.18 | 0.86 | 1.22 | 1.39 | 1.48 | 2.15 | 1.72 | 2.46 |
| (f) DAC other official | 0.15 | 0.28 | 0.43 | 0.90 | 0.65 | 0.56 | 0.57 | 0.48 | 1.27 | 0.95 | 2.24 |
| (g) OPEC countries[b] | 0.20 | 0.19 |  | 0.14 | 0.92 | 1.50 | 1.5 | 0.89 | (1.01) | (1.00) | (1.00) |
| (h) Other countries[c] | 0.10 |  |  |  | 0.79 | 0.04 | 0.1 | 0.09 | 0.87 | (3.20) | (3.10) |
| (i) CMEA countries | 0.11 | 0.10 | 0.11 | 0.10 | 0.09 | 0.09 | 0.1 | 0.11 | 0.10 |  |  |

continued on page 144.

TABLE 8.2 *Continued*  TOTAL NET RESOURCE RECEIPTS OF DEVELOPING COUNTRIES FROM ALL SOURCES

| Net disbursements ($bn) | 1970 | 1971 | 1972 | 1973 | 1974 | 1975 | 1976 | 1977 | 1978 | 1979 | 1980 |
|---|---|---|---|---|---|---|---|---|---|---|---|
| II. Multilateral | 0.69 | 0.90 | 1.01 | 1.28 | 1.83 | 2.58 | 2.68 | 2.94 | 3.09 | 4.16 | (4.80) |
| of which: OPEC financed | | | | | 0.02 | 0.06 | 0.13 | 0.27 | 0.16 | 0.22 | 0.14 |
| Total receipts | 18.97 | 21.09 | 23.17 | 31.37 | 35.04 | 53.67 | 57.59 | 63.55 | 79.83 | 83.86 | (89.11) |
| Memorandum Items: | | | | | | | | | | | |
| Private sector grants | 0.86 | 0.91 | 1.04 | 1.37 | 1.22 | 1.34 | 1.35 | 1.49 | 1.65 | 1.95 | 2.31 |
| IMF Purchases, net[d] | 0.34 | 0.05 | 0.30 | 0.36 | 1.74 | 3.24 | 2.98 | -0.43 | -0.93 | | 2.61 |
| IMF Trust Fund (incl. under ODA II above) | | | | | | | | 0.18 | 0.86 | 0.68 | 1.64 |

[a] Excluding (i) bond lending and (ii) export credits extended by banks which are included under private export credits. Includes loans by branches of OECD banks located in offshore centres, and for 1980 participation of non-OECD banks in international syndicates.

[b] Official flows only; no information is available on private flows.

[c] Includes Ireland, Luxembourg, Spain, Yugoslavia, India, Israel.

[d] Drawings minus repayments including reserve tranches (amounting to $103m in 1979 and $309M in 1980) but excluding loans by the IMF Trust Fund included under multilateral ODA above.

*Note:* Figures concerning non-DAC Member countries are based as far as possible on information released by donor countries and international organisations, and completed by OECD Secretariat estimates based on other published and unpublished sources. It has therefore not been possible fully to verify that they comply in all respects with the norms and criteria used by DAC Members in their statistical reports made directly to the OECD Secretariat.

TABLE 8.3 COMPOSITION OF EXTERNAL FINANCIAL RECEIPTS
OF DEVELOPING COUNTRIES BY TYPES OF FLOW:
1970, 1975, 1979, 1980
*(Percentage shares in total receipts)*

|  | 1970 | 1975 | 1979 | 1980 |
|---|---|---|---|---|
| ODA | 42.4 | 36.0 | 34.5 | 37.7 |
| (a) DAC bilateral | 29.8 | 18.3 | 19.0 | 19.8 |
| (b) OPEC bilateral | 1.9 | 9.2 | 5.9 | 6.9 |
| (c) CMEA countries, bilateral | 5.1 | 1.4 | 2.1 | 2.0 |
| (d) Other countries, bilateral |  | 0.1 | 0.1 | 0.2 |
| (e) Multilateral agencies | 5.6 | 7.1 | 7.4 | 8.8 |
| of which: OPEC financed |  | 0.3 | 0.3 | 0.3 |
| Non-concessional flows | 57.6 | 64.0 | 65.5 | 62.3 |
| (a) Multilateral | 3.6 | 4.7 | 5.0 | 5.4 |
| of which: OPEC financed |  | 0.1 | 0.3 | 0.2 |
| (b) Direct investment | 19.5 | 21.4 | 16.2 | 10.9 |
| (c) Bank sector | 15.8 | 22.4 | 23.5 | 20.2 |
| (d) Bond lending | 1.6 | 0.8 | 1.4 | 2.2 |
| (e) Private export credits | 11.0 | 8.2 | 11.3 | 13.7 |
| (f) Official export credits | 3.1 | 2.3 | 2.0 | 2.8 |
| (g) DAC – Other official | 0.8 | 1.0 | 1.1 | 2.5 |
| (h) OPEC bilateral | 1.1 | 2.8 | (1.2) | (1.1) |
| (i) CMEA countries | 0.6 | 0.2 |  |  |
| (j) Other | 0.5 | 0.1 | 3.8 | 3.5 |
| Total receipts | 100.0 | 100.0 | 100.0 | 100.0 |

countries' encompasses a vast variety of countries and they differ greatly in relative levels of per capita income and development, resource endowment, growth and investment potential, debt servicing capacity and degree of integration into the international trade and financing system.

For the purposes of this analysis, developing countries have been grouped into four categories:

(i) The Newly Industrialising Countries (NICs). This is a group of countries at a relatively advanced level of economic development, with a substantial and dynamic industrial sector and with close links to the international trade finance and investment system (Argentina, Brazil, Greece, Hong Kong, Korea (Rep.), Mexico, Portugal, Singapore, Spain, Taiwan and Yugoslavia).

(ii) The Middle-Income Countries (MICs). These are defined as developing countries (other than NICs and OPEC countries) with a per capita income in 1979 exceeding $500. This group includes many countries in Latin America, a number of countries in South-East Asia (such as the Philippines, Thailand, Malaysia), Mediterranean countries, (such as Israel, Morocco and Tunisia) and some sub-Saharan African countries (e.g. Ivory Coast, Liberia, and Nigeria). Also included in this category are most of the remaining overseas dependencies.

(iii) The Low-Income Countries (LICs). This includes countries with per capita income in 1979 under $500. They are essentially the least-developed countries; mainly Bangladesh and sub-Saharan Africa, Egypt, the Indian sub-Continent and Indonesia and Vietnam. China is excluded throughout.

(iv) The OPEC countries – other than Indonesia (a LIC) and Nigeria (a lower MIC). The OPEC countries (even excluding Indonesia and Nigeria) are a highly heterogenous group, comprising major net capital exporting countries (such as Saudi Arabia, Kuwait and the other Gulf States) as well as capital importing countries, such as Algeria, Ecuador, Gabon, Iran and Venezuela.

The analysis of resource flows by types of country is hampered by serious statistical problems, since significant resource flows cannot be geographically allocated. This is true, especially, for bank lending and private investment. The share of geographically unallocated transactions equals some 10 per cent of total flows, but this was much higher at the beginning of the 1970s – of the order of 30–40 per cent. It affects different types of resource flow, and consequently affects types of developing country, differently. It is, therefore, quite difficult to compare growth rates in resource flows and changes in resource-use patterns for different groups of developing countries.

Table 8.4 shows the direction of resource flows to the four groups of country categorised. Almost 70 per cent of total resources flow to middle-income countries and NICs. These account for 35 per cent of total Third World population and 64 per cent of its total GNP. The share of OPEC countries has tended downwards, and now stands at some 9 per cent. The LICs as a group receive only some 22 per cent of total resource flows; far below their population share of 61 per cent.

Just over half of ODA is directed to the LICs, substantially less than their population share. With more than twice this share of LDC population, MICs are also major recipients of ODA. But the NICs and OPEC countries have stopped being significant recipients. The

TABLE 8.4   TOTAL RESOURCE FLOWS TO DIFFERENT CATEGO-RIES OF DEVELOPING COUNTRIES IN 1979[a]

|  | NICs | MICs | OPEC | LICs | Total |
|---|---|---|---|---|---|
| Total resource flows |  |  |  |  |  |
| in billion $ | 24.3 | 26.5 | 6.4 | 16.4 | 73.6 |
| percentage share | 33.0 | 36.0 | 8.7 | 22.3 | 100 |
| ODA |  |  |  |  |  |
| in billion $ | 0.6 | 11.2 | 0.4 | 13.3 | 25.5 |
| percentage share | 2.4 | 43.9 | 1.6 | 52.2 | 100 |
| Non-concessional |  |  |  |  |  |
| in billion $ | 23.8 | 15.3 | 6.0 | 3.1 | 48.2 |
| ꙮꙮꙮ ꙮꙮꙮ | 19.1 | 31.7 | 12.4 | 6.4 | 100 |
| Bank lending | 62.1 | 26.7 | 11.0 | 0.2 | 100 |
| Bonds | 47.4 | 23.7 | 23.7 | 5.3 | 100 |
| Export credits | 34.8 | 25.5 | 26.3 | 13.4 | 100 |
| Direct investment | 61.8 | 32.4 | 8.1 | −2.3 | 100 |
| Multilateral | 39.6 | 40.6 | 1.2 | 18.6 | 100 |

[a] Allocated amounts only.

comparatively large proportion of ODA (including OPEC ODA) going to MICs is the result of the large aid receipts of a limited number of MICs, including Syria, Israel, Jordan, Morocco and overseas territories with constitutional links. Remaining concessional aid to the NICs – 2 per cent of the total, down from 13 per cent at the start of the 1970s – consists primarily of technical assistance (and some capital assistance) for such countries as Korea and Portugal. Half of the total non-concessional flows to all developing countries go to the eleven NICs; only 6 per cent to the LICs and the remainder to the MICs and OPEC countries. The concentration on the NICs is even more pronounced for commercial bank lending and direct investment (60 per cent). Few developing countries have been able to gain access to bond markets. In 1979–80 these were primarily Spain, Brazil, Morocco, Algeria, Venezuela and Malaysia.

Table 8.5 summarises changes in the geographic distribution of ODA and non-concessional flows over the decade. What emerges first is that the NICs have received a growing share of total resource flows to developing countries. Since much of the increase in total resource flows was in non-concessional form, the LICs have lost ground in the total resource-distribution. Although the declared intention of aid donor countries is to increase the share of ODA to

TABLE 8.5   SHARE OF DIFFERENT GROUPS OF DEVELOPING COUNTRIES[a] IN EXTERNAL RESOURCE FLOWS

| | 1970 | | | 1975 | | | 1979 | | |
|---|---|---|---|---|---|---|---|---|---|
| | ODA | Non-conc. | Total | ODA | Non-conc. | Total | ODA | Non-conc. | Total |
| NIC | 9.2 | 38.2 | 24.0 | 3.1 | 38.5 | 22.9 | 2.2 | 49.3 | 33.1 |
| MIC | 34.7 | 40.5 | 37.7 | 31.6 | 30.6 | 31.0 | 44.2 | 31.7 | 36.0 |
| LIC | 52.5 | 6.8 | 29.2 | 62.8 | 18.2 | 37.9 | 52.1 | 6.5 | 22.2 |
| OPEC | 3.6 | 14.5 | 9.1 | 2.5 | 12.6 | 8.2 | 1.5 | 12.4 | 8.7 |
| All developing countries[a] | 100.0 | 100.0 | 100.0 | 100.0 | 100.0 | 100.0 | 100.0 | 100.0 | 100.0 |

[a] Allocated amounts only.

the poorer countries, the total share of the LICs has remained roughly constant, though with major shifts within the group. There has been a large increase, particularly to the group of least-developed countries, Egypt, Burma, Kenya and Sri Lanka, but there have been declines, or at best stability, in aid (in current dollar) to India, Indonesia and Vietnam (a major recipient of United States aid in the early 1970s).

Table 8.6 shows the external financing pattern of the identified country groups; i.e. the relative importance of each different type of resource transfer for each of these groups. For LICs the main source of external financing is clearly concessional aid. Over 80 per cent of their external financing consists of ODA. Use of non-concessional resources is, nevertheless, necessary, and has been rising. Officially guaranteed private export credits, often on subsidised terms, have always been drawn on to finance industrial projects, but private investment, which contributes to natural-resource development, plays a limited role in resource transfers to these countries.[4] Multilateral non-concessional lending has been used, to blend with multilateral concessional aid. Only a few low-income countries have had access to commercial bank lending: e.g., India, Pakistan, Egypt, Kenya and Indonesia.

The MICs as a group now rely on non-concessional resources for roughly 60 per cent of their total external financing. Commercial bank borrowing alone accounts for almost 30 per cent of external financing. MICs which have been able to use sizeable amounts of bank lending include the Philippines, Malaysia, Thailand, Chile, Columbia, Morocco, Bolivia, Peru, Ivory Coast, Nigeria and Turkey.

For the NICs, the principal single source of external financing now is commercial bank lending, which in 1979 accounted for almost half of the total borrowing. Other major sources are direct investment and export credits.

OPEC countries have traditionally been major users of export credits and bank credits, which together represent 80 per cent of their external finance. Public authorities and private firms, even of the capital-exporting countries, have availed themselves of access to relatively cheap export credits. In addition, direct investment in OPEC countries is still substantial, despite heavy repatriation of oil investment funds following takeovers. The major recipients of non-concessional flows are Algeria, Libya, Saudi Arabia and the United Arab Emirates. Up to 1978, Iran was one of the largest capital importers. More recently, its repayments on earlier borrowing have exceeded its uptake of new finance.

TABLE 8.6 ODA DISBURSEMENTS TO LLDCs AND NON-LLDC LICs, IN 1980

| Countries | ODA to LLDCs[a] (including imputed multilateral flows) | | ODA to non-LLDC LICs[a] (including imputed multilateral flows) | |
|---|---|---|---|---|
| | % of total ODA | % of GNP | % of total ODA | % of GNP |
| Australia | 13.5 | 0.07 | 27.4 | 0.13 |
| Austria | 5.6 | 0.01 | 50.6 | 0.11 |
| Belgium | 22.5 | 0.11 | 44.5 | 0.22 |
| Canada | 27.2 | 0.12 | 34.1 | 0.14 |
| Denmark | 37.9 | 0.27 | 38.4 | 0.28 |
| Finland | 35.3 | 0.08 | 33.5 | 0.07 |
| France | 14.6 | 0.09 | 17.0 | 0.10 |
| Germany | 27.3 | 0.12 | 27.6 | 0.12 |
| Italy | 35.2 | 0.56 | 38.0 | 0.07 |

| | | | | |
|---|---|---|---|---|
| Japan | 24.6 | 0.08 | 4_ | 0.15 |
| Netherlands | 27.3 | 0.27 | 3_3 | 0.36 |
| New Zealand | 12.1 | 0.04 | 1_1 | 0.06 |
| Norway | 33.9 | 0.28 | 3_ | 0.30 |
| Sweden | 30.1 | 0.23 | 3_ | 0.30 |
| Switzerland | 34.4 | 0.08 | 2_ | 0.05 |
| United Kingdom | 27.8 | 0.09 | 3_7 | 0.11 |
| United States | 17.5 | 0.05 | 3_7 | 0.08 |
| Overall Average | 22.6 | 0.08 | 3_7 | 0.12 |

[a] Allocated amounts only.

*Note:* The imputed multilateral values used in this table are based on the geographical distribution of multilateral organisations' concessional flows in 1979.

TABLE 8.7  COMPARATIVE ACCESS OF DIFFERENT CATEGORIES
OF DEVELOPING COUNTRIES TO EXTERNAL
FINANCIAL RESOURCES – 1979

|  | NICs | MICs | OPEC | LICs | Total |
|---|---|---|---|---|---|
| Share in total resource flows (%) | 33 | 36 | 9 | 22 | 100 |
| Share in total LDC GNP (%) | 42 | 22 | 18 | 18 | 100 |
| Share in total LDC population (%) | 16 | 19 | 5 | 61 | 100 |
| Resource receipts as % of GNP | 3.4 | 6.8 | 1.9 | 5.2 | 4.1 |
| Resource receipts per capita ($) | 70 | 63 | 63 | 12 | 33 |
| Average per capita income ($), 1979 | 2 140 | 960 | 3 010 | 230 | 790 |
| GNP annual real growth rate 1970–9 (%) | 6.1 | 5.6 | 7.4 | 3–5 | 5.7 |

Table 8.7 summarises the comparative access of different categories of developing countries to external financial resources. The outstanding impression is the predominant role of the NICs.They combine sheer economic weight with major investment needs and opportunities and with international creditworthiness. With only 16 per cent of total Third World population (excluding China) these eleven countries account for 40 per cent of Third World GNP. For them, resource receipts as a percentage of GNP were 3.4 per cent in 1979. For the MICs, external resources use, in relation to GNP, was much higher at almost 7 per cent. This reflects, on the supply side, a combination of continuing access to ODA and new access to non-concessional flows; and, on the demand side, investment opportunities and urgent current balance of payments requirements.

Because of the statistical problems mentioned above, it is not really possible to assess the relative rates of growth in external resource use for these countries over the decade. They were however, clearly faster than the average for all developing countries of 5–6 per cent. For the NICs and MICs, the relative use of external resources has rapidly increased and the average ratios of external resource use to GNP are now more than twice as large as they were at the beginning of the decade. This probably also means that external resource use grew at a somewhat faster rate than investment, reflecting a growing use of external resources for financing current imports.

For the LICs, access to external financing is still essentially a matter of the available supply of ODA. ODA growth has been significant, at some 4 per cent, but much slower than growth of non-concessional flows. External resource receipts of the LICs are relatively high in relation to GNP, at more than 5 per cent. However, on a per capita basis, these receipts are less than 20 per cent of those of the other developing countries. External resource flows have thus exacerbated, rather than compensated for, the differences in the investment capacity of the stronger and poorer developing countries which, arises from differences in their domestic savings capacity.

There are much more pronounced differences in relative access to external resources among LICs than among the other groups of developing countries. For instance, for the LLDCs, for Egypt and for Sri Lanka external resource receipts are of the order of 10 per cent of GNP; for India, they are only 1 per cent.


## V  FINANCIAL COMPOSITION OF RESOURCE FLOWS

There has been a considerable shift in emphasis during the last decade towards more expensive forms of external financing. The share of non-concessional flows has increased, from just over half to more than 70 per cent of total resource receipts. The shift towards less-concessional forms of external financing was particularly pronounced for the MICs, where it increased from 40 per cent in the 1970s to almost 60 per cent now. In addition to the relatively heavier use of more expensive types of external financing, there was a general upward movement in interest rates. Considering world inflation rates, however, the impact of the rise in real interest rates has remained limited until recently.

Table 8.8 compares nominal interest rates for different types of financing and their evolution over time. The actual interest costs of total external resources used depend, of course, on the relative use of the various financing flows. Table 8.9 shows this for developing country groups.

It has to be emphasised that the LICs and MICs have obtained substantial amounts of grants so that actual average external resource

TABLE 8.8  NOMINAL INTEREST RATES BY TYPE OF CREDITS[a]

| Categories of outstanding debt | 1972 | 1976 | 1978 | 1979 | 1980 | 1981 |
|---|---|---|---|---|---|---|
| A. Fixed-interest debt | | | | | | |
| 1. ODA | 2.5 | 2.4 | 2.3 | 2.2 | 1.9 | 1.8 |
| 2. Official export credits | 6.0 | 6.3 | 6.2 | 6.3 | 6.8 | 7.3 |
| 3. Private export credits | 6.6 | 7.6 | 8.1 | 8.3 | 8.6 | 8.9 |
| 4. International financial institutions[b] | 5.2 | 5.5 | 6.2 | 6.2 | 6.6 | 7.3 |
| of which: concessional | 3.6 | 3.3 | 3.0 | 2.8 | 2.7 | 2.7 |
| non-concessional | 7.5 | 8.4 | 8.9 | 9.1 | 9.3 | 9.7 |
| 5. Bonds | 4.9 | 5.0 | 7.0 | 7.3 | 8.3 | 9.0 |
| 6. Other private debt | 8.5 | 8.5 | 8.6 | 9.2 | 9.8 | 10.5 |
| 7. Non-DAC total bilateral | 2.6 | 3.0 | 3.3 | 4.0 | 4.5 | 5.0 |
| Total weighted fixed interest debt | 4.2 | 4.8 | 5.2 | 5.5 | 5.7 | 6.2 |
| B. Floating interest debt[c] | 7.9 | 8.5 | 9.0 | 12.3 | 15.3 | 18.0 |
| C. Total debt[d] | 4.6 | 6.6 | 7.5 | 8.0 | 9.2 | 10.5 |

[a] Interest payments as a percentage of average outstanding debt adjusted for exchange rate discrepancies and arrears of interest payments.

[b] World Bank plus regional development banks.

[c] Weighted average annual cost to debtors, including spreads and fees, assuming, 6-months . . . . .(?)

TABLE 8.9  NOMINAL INTEREST COST BY GROUPS OF DEVELOPING COUNTRIES[a]
(*percentages*)

| | 1972 | 1976 | 1978 | 1979 | 1980 (*est.*) | 1981 (*est.*) |
|---|---|---|---|---|---|---|
| LICs | 2.8 | 2.9 | 3.3 | 3.5 | 3.7 | 4.0 |
| MICs | 4.1 | 4.6 | 6.3 | 6.8 | 7.8 | 8.6 |
| NICs | 7.0 | 8.9 | 9.4 | 9.7 | 11.5 | 13.3 |
| Total non-oil developing countries | 4.8 | 5.8 | 6.7 | 7.2 | 8.4 | 9.5 |

[a] Interest payments as a percentage of average outstanding debt.

costs are lower. For the LICs and MICs, the costs of external-resource receipts have remained significantly below world inflation rates. Moreover, some of these countries have on balance benefited from the recent trend towards borrowing at floating interest rates, since their floating interest holdings exceed their floating interest debt. However, the NICs, and especially Brazil and Mexico which rely heavily on borrowing at floating rates, were dramatically hit by the increase in interest rates in 1981.

## VI  TRENDS IN THE GEOGRAPHIC ORIGIN OF RESOURCE FLOWS

The geographic origin of external flows to developing countries is shown in Table 8.10. The main sources are, not surprisingly, the major industrial and financial centres. The United States, the United Kingdom, Japan, West Germany and France together account for 65 per cent of total resource flows to developing countries. This is slightly more than their share in the combined GNP of the capital-exporting countries listed in the table – of 61 per cent. The share of the Big Five in non-concessional flows is over 70 per cent; in ODA, only 54 per cent.

The relative importance of a number of countries as sources of ODA far exceeds their relative importance in world GNP. This is true, especially, for the Nordic countries, the Netherlands, France, Belgium and Australia and, even more, for the Arab capital-surplus countries. This comes our more clearly from a comparison of ODA as a percentage of GNP with their share of world GDP for the countries in Table 8.11.

Non-concessional capital exports to developing countries reached a remarkable size relative to their GNP for such countries as Switzerland, the United Kingdom, Belgium, Italy and France. The first two are, of course, major international banking centres; the data for them, as for other countries, refer to transactions of resident banks, irrespective of their ownership (which may be foreign) or of the origin of the deposits on which their lending operations are based, which need not be domestic.

Flows of non-concessional resources from OPEC oil-surplus countries are probably significantly understated, due to the absence of complete statistical recording. Further, as regards the identification of the geographical origin of international bank lending, it is not

TABLE 8.10   RESOURCE FLOWS BY COUNTRIES OF ORIGIN 1978–9 AVERAGE $bn

| | Total flows | ODA | Non conc. | Export credits | Direct investment | Other | Share in world GNP % |
|---|---|---|---|---|---|---|---|
| *DAC* | 73.0 | 21.2 | 51.8 | 12.4 | 12.3 | 27.1 | 77.5 |
| United States | 17.4 | 5.2 | 12.2 | 0.4 | 6.8 | 5.0 | 28.6 |
| United Kingdom | 11.1 | 1.8 | 9.3 | 1.7 | 1.3 | 6.3 | 4.6 |
| Japan | 9.1 | 2.4 | 6.7 | 1.1 | 1.0 | 4.6 | 12.6 |
| France | 8.3 | 3.0 | 5.3 | 1.9 | 0.5 | 2.8 | 6.6 |
| West Germany | 7.4 | 2.8 | 4.6 | 1.2 | 0.9 | 2.5 | 9.0 |
| Switzerland | 4.6 | 0.2 | 4.4 | 0.7 | 0.3 | 3.4 | 1.2 |
| Italy | 3.7 | 0.3 | 3.3 | 3.0 | 0.3 | 0.1 | 3.7 |
| Netherlands | 2.3 | 1.2 | 1.1 | 0.2 | 0.3 | 0.6 | 1.8 |
| Canada | 2.3 | 1.0 | 1.3 | 0.3 | 0.3 | 0.7 | 2.7 |
| Belgium | 2.6 | 0.6 | 2.0 | 0.6 | 0.2 | 1.1 | 1.3 |
| Nordic countries | 2.7 | 1.7 | 1.1 | 0.6 | 0.2 | 0.2 | 3.7 |
| Other | 1.4 | 0.9 | 0.6 | 0.7 | 0.1 | -0.2 | 1.7 |
| *OPEC*[a] | 6.2[a] | 5.3 | 0.9 | (0.9) | | | 4.7 |
| Saudi Arabia | | 1.9 | | | | | 0.9 |
| Kuwait | | 1.0 | | | | | 0.3 |
| Other | | 2.4 | | | | | 3.6 |
| *CMEA* | 1.6 | 1.5 | 0.1 | (0.1) | | | 17.8 |
| USSR | | 1.2 | | | | | 12.9 |
| Other | | 0.3 | | | | | 4.9 |
| *Total* | 80.8 | 28.0 | 52.8 | 13.4 | 12.3 | 27.1 | 100.0 |

[a] Non-concessional consequently total flows understated; see text.

TABLE 8.11    ODA AND NON-CONCESSIONAL RESOURCE FLOWS AS
A PERCENTAGE OF GNP OF CAPITAL-EXPORTING COUNTRIES,
1979–80 AVERAGE

| *ODA* | | *Non-concessional* | |
|---|---|---|---|
| Qatar | 5.14 | Switzerland | 5.38 |
| UAE | 4.88 | UK | 2.07 |
| Kuwait | 3.97 | Belgium | 1.36 |
| Saudi Arabia | 3.39 | Italy | 0.94 |
| Netherlands | 0.96 | France | 0.85 |
| Norway | 0.87 | West Germany | 0.69 |
| Sweden | 0.84 | Norway | 0.68 |
| Denmark | 0.73 | Canada | 0.67 |
| France | 0.61 | Sweden | 0.65 |
| Belgium | 0.52 | Denmark | 0.47 |
| Australia | 0.50 | Japan | 0.41 |
| Canada | 0.44 | Netherlands | 0.41 |
| West Germany | 0.43 | USA | 0.39 |
| UK | 0.42 | Finland | 0.20 |
| New Zealand | 0.31 | Australia | 0.18 |
| Japan | 0.29 | Austria | 0.13 |
| USA | 0.24 | New Zealand | 0.12 |
| Switzerland | 0.22 | | |
| Austria | 0.21 | | |
| Finland | 0.21 | | |
| USSR | 0.14 | | |
| Italy | 0.13 | | |

possible to show to the credit of OPEC oil-surplus countries that part
of their large short-term deposits, held with banks in OECD countries, which the latter transform into long-term loans to developing
countries. Even if more detailed statistical information were available, there would be no way to estimate which particular deposit had
been embodied in to which particular loan. Moreover, while the
OPEC countries are the economic source of the savings deposited
with OECD banks, the transformation risk is carried by these banks.
There has also been some direct OPEC bank lending to developing
countries, but statistical information is inadequate to identify this.

## VII   GOVERNMENT POLICIES FOR RESOURCE FLOWS

The size, nature and direction of international resource flows is
determined by a mixture of market decisions and by government

policies in both capital exporting and importing countries. Governments themselves have become substantial sources of international financing, and they influence capital flows through a variety of policies, facilities and regulations.

The provision of official development assistance constitutes, of course, the most direct involvement by governments in international resource-transfers. In addition to bilateral ODA, an array of government-financed and government-supported multilateral financing institutions now act as channels of ODA and for long-term capital taken up on the markets against government guarantees. Government aid and multilateral lending constitute about 40 per cent of the total net resource receipts of developing countries, and for many of them it is the essential source of external capital.

Governments are heavily involved in export credits, which constitute an important source of the external financing of all groups of developing countries (roughly 15 per cent of total net receipts). Most export credits are guaranteed by governments against political and commercial risks and government institutions are important sources of finance for export credits – including significant direct or indirect interest subsidies. The difference between actual interest rates on export credits given by OECD was substantially higher in 1981. In addition, a growing volume of export credits and indeed bank loans are extended under various mixed-credit and co-financing arrangements, with government and multilateral financing.

Most OECD governments offer guarantees against political risk for certain types of direct investment in developing countries. Roughly 10 per cent – some $10bn – of the outstanding stock of foreign direct investment in developing countries is covered by guarantees.

By and large, developing countries have non-discriminatory access to international private capital markets. Much international bank lending in any case escapes direct government control. There has been a tendency towards closer prudential surveillance by the monetary authorities, but the regulatory environment has remained generally liberal. Much more important factors are financial market conditions, as determined by general economic and monetary policies. Sustained increases in interest rates are bound, over time, to spread to all forms of borrowing and would reduce the ability of developing countries to supplement internal savings by external financing.

The immediate consequences for developing countries of the oil-price rises and higher costs of imported food and capital goods, on the one hand, and slackening export earnings as a result of stagnation in the OECD, on the other, are major increases in their current-account deficits and balance-of-payments adjustment problems. While rising energy costs have exacted a heavy economic toll on oil-importers, there is now a large pool of world savings arising from OPEC surpluses. They are potentially available, if the right policies are followed by all concerned, to step up growth-promoting productive investments in developing countries.

What is required to achieve reasonably satisfactory growth in the developing countries during the difficult period of adjustment ahead, is a combination of effective mechanisms for external financing and determined pursuit of policies:

(i) by developing countries to contain inflation through cautious monetary and fiscal policies and to step up productive investment as part of coherent structural-adjustment and longer-term development programmes;

(ii) by OECD countries to maintain open markets and to accept and facilitate structural adjustments that help the affairs of developing countries to expand their exports, in addition to policies that will create the conditions necessary for resumed non-inflationary growth.

The international financial institutions, especially the World Bank and the IMF, have an important role to play in encouraging effective adjustment policies and in providing financial assistance. These institutions should, therefore, have the fullest possible support both for their policies and in financial terms. Various possibilities of further strengthening the lending capacity of the multilateral institutions for development lending are being explored. But the political climate for major new institutional initiatives, and indeed for the replenishment of the existing programmes at anything like the major increases in the past few years, is not propitious.

The outlook for official development assistance is a problem of particular concern. A number of donor countries have firm plans for increasing their aid programmes. However, prospects for a significant increase in overall ODA from OECD countries are affected by the restraints on aid which an increasing number of donor countries have felt obliged to introduce, as part of their efforts to reduce government expenditures. On present indications, maintaining the annual average rate of growth in real terms at the 4 per cent, recorded over the last decade, must be ragarded as an optimistic forecast.

NOTES

1. All figures are for long-term flows, i.e. funds with repayment periods of more than one year and are *net* of repayments. Flows from developing countries, other than OPEC countries, to other developing countries are not included.
2. Real resource flows calculated by using the GNP deflator measure the cost in real terms to the *source* economy of providing the resources conveyed (which may or may not be equivalent to the benefit to the recipient). The implicit assumption is that the prices of the goods and services financed by aid and other resource flows move in line with the GNP deflator. Other special-purpose deflators have been constructed, e.g. for Official Development Assistance. Over a period of years, there is little difference on an annual average basis between the movements of the various deflators, although they have occasionally diverged markedly in individual years. As constructed, deflator values apply to data expressed in current dollars, and include the effect on dollar prices of changes in the value of the dollar *vis-à-vis* other currencies. Were some other numeraire used, e.g. the SDR, the deflator figures would differ by a transformation equal to the change in the value of the dollar against the SDR.
3. The actual 1970–80 increase was 5.4 per cent. However, the 1980 data are distorted by unusually low private investment figures. Up to 1979 the increase was 6.4 per cent.
4. The negative figure for 1979 in Table 8.4 is due to large disinvestments in Indonesia.

# 9 The Role of International Financial Markets in the Financing of Development

**T. M. Rybczynski**

LAZARDS, LONDON, UK

## I INTRODUCTION

For some time now the problems of economic development and the way it can be financed have been very much to the fore, not only for policy-makers and students of economic growth and development but also for members of the world financial community. The increasing importance of these problems in recent years has been evidenced by the attention given to them both in policy formulation and implementation, as well as in the enormous flow of articles in learned journals, books and semi-official and official reports examining the issued involved.

The aim of this paper is in essence a modest one; to examine briefly how the international financial markets have contributed to the process of economic development; their role in mobilising financial resources for this purpose; how this differs from finance from other sources; and the implications of using these sources for the future.

To provide a reasonably comprehensive view, Section II provides a highly compressed description of the international financial markets, their role and functions in financing the internal and external deficits of the developed and developing countries. Section III comments briefly on deficit financing, its relationship to economic development and to the international financial markets, and Section IV considers some implications of recent developments. Some concluding remarks are contained in Section V.

162

## II  INTERNATIONAL FINANCIAL MARKETS AND DEFICIT FINANCING

International financial markets comprise the international credit markets and international bond markets.

1. *Credit Markets*: the international credit markets form an integral part of total world credit markets. They accept deposits (retail and wholesale) be they interest bearing or non-interest bearing, and including CDs. They re-lend to borrowers. International credit markets differ from domestic credit markets in that, first, they are undertaken by banks which raise the funds they use in currencies other than the currency of the country in which they are located. Second, they are not in principle subject to the prudential and other regulations applicable to operations in the domestic markets of the countries in which they are situated. To that extent operations in the international currency markets, generally described as the Euro-currency markets, are, in principle, not subject to national rules and regulations regarding capital, liquidity and risk ratios. They also offer opportunities for higher profit margins than do domestic operations, with which they are, however, closely linked.

Funds employed in domestic credit markets can and do move into international credit markets when opportunities in the latter are more attractive, and vice versa. This is why we can say that the two segments form an integral part of a large, unified world credit market. The link is reflected in a close relationship between interest rates in the various national credit markets and in the relevant sectors (i.e. dollar, DM, Yen, etc.) of the international credit market.

2. *Capital Markets*: primary international capital markets handle the issue of, and trade in, marketable securities denominated in currencies other than the currencies in which the investment bankers sponsoring and underwriting them operate. These markets are also a part of the worldwide capital markets (primary and secondary). Like international credit markets they are characterised by being unregulated: that is, they are outside the jurisdiction of national regulatory bodies as regards the provision and scope of underlying information, etc. They are also closely linked to domestic capital markets, but the scale of their operations is rather limited in that they are concerned only with debt obligations with maturities of, say, up to twelve years, and with convertibles but not with ordinary shares. The terms, that

is, the effective interest rates, of the debt and allied obligations dealt with by international capital markets are related closely to those in the relevant domestic markets.

The role of the total world credit and capital market, and of its international segments, has undergone a profound change in the last thirty or so years, and especially since the first oil-price shock, when the absolute and relative size of the net deficits to be financed increased significantly. The combined deficits of the free-world economies averaged, between 1950 and 1973, about three-quarters of 1 per cent for the combined gross national product. This proportion increased to about 1.5 per cent in the seven years ending in 1980. Table 9.1 gives the details.

Even before the doubling of the total deficits in the free world, the relative significance of total world credit and capital markets had already been growing. Such estimates as can be made suggest that the relative importance of total world credit and in financing deficits more than doubled between the 1950s and 1960s, when that share increased to about 25 per cent of the deficit financing. The share again more than doubled between the 1960s and the period 1970–3, which was, of course, before the first oil shock. This raised the relative contribution to about 50 per cent of total deficit financing. However, and this is rather interesting and important, there has been no significant change in the share of the financing of deficits accounted for by the total world credit and capital markets since the first oil shock. This remained at about 55 per cent of total deficit financing in 1974–80 (see Table 9.2).

This change in the relative importance of total world credit and capital markets (that is to say, both domestic and international credit and capital markets) in financing the deficits of the free-world economies in the last thirty years has been accompanied by a very rapid increase in the relative significance of the international credit and capital markets. These markets were of negligible importance in the 1950s, but their contribution rose to about 50 per cent of total financing in the 1960s, increased in 1970–3 to 60 per cent and amounted to three-quarters of the total in 1974–80, following the first oil shock. Table 9.3 gives a further breakdown.

In short, three outstanding features have characterised the behaviour of the free world's deficits and the role of financial markets (and especially of their international segment) in the last thirty years or so. These are, first, a doubling of the relative size of deficits since 1970;

TABLE 9.1   AGGREGATE DEFICITS ON CURRENT ACCOUNT
1959–80[a]

|  | *1950–9* | *1960–9* | *1970–3* | *1973–80* |
|---|---|---|---|---|
| Annual average $bn | (10.1) | 12.7 | 21.1 | 103.2 |
| % of GNP of free-world economies | (1.1) | 0.75 | 0.68 | 1.55 |

[a] Excluding official transfers.

*Source:* IMF, OECD, UN, IBRD and Bank of England Quarterly Review.
*Note:*   The figures above are estimates, subject to a considerable degree of error and must be regarded only as indicative of broad orders of magnitude. They cover all countries, other than the planned economies, including both developed and developing countries. Full details of countries included are given in the Appendix.

TABLE 9.2   FINANCING OF DEFICITS AND CHANGES IN OFFICIAL
RESERVES[a]

|  | *1960–9* | *1970–3* | *1974–80* |
|---|---|---|---|
|  | | *% of total* | |
| 1. Official transfers and concessionary loans | 21 | 17 | 11 |
| 2. Direct investment | 21 | 18 | 2 |
| 3. Financial markets | 25 | 56 | 54 |
| 4. Other capital | 10 | 3 | 4 |
| 5. Official financing[b] | 23 | 6 | 29 |

[a] The sum of deficits on current account, excluding official transfers.

[b] Includes changes in official holdings of gold and foreign currencies, borrowings from the IMF, other reserve borrowings, allocations of SDRs, gold monetisation and any counterpart to valuation adjustments, but excludes compensatory borrowings by the authorities from the international financial markets and US liabilities which have formed part of oil-exporting countries' reserves since 1972.

*Source:* IMF, OECD, BIS and IBRD.
*Note:*   The figures above are estimates, subject to a considerable degree of error and must be regarded as indicative of broad orders of magnitude only.

second, a rapid growth in the share of deficit financing accounted for by total credit and, capital markets before the first oil shock; and, third, a marked and continual rise (since the 1950s) in the relative importance of the international credit and capital markets, which as yet shows no sign of slowing down.

TABLE 9.3   SHARES OF FOUR SECTORS OF WORLD CREDIT AND
CAPITAL MARKETS IN FINANCING WORLD DEFICITS

|  | *1960–9* | *1970–3* | *1974–80* |
|---|---|---|---|
|  |  | *% of total* |  |
| 1. *International Markets* |  |  |  |
| (a) Credit markets | 40 | 43 | 58 |
| (b) capital markets | 10 | 17 | 17 |
| 2. *Domestic Markets* |  |  |  |
| (a) Credit markets | 50 | 40 | 25 |
| (b) Capital markets |  |  |  |
| Total | 100 | 100 | 100 |

*Source:*   IMF, IBRD, OECD, BIS and UN.
*Note:*    The figures above are estimates, subject to a considerable degree of error and
         must be regarded as indicative of the broad orders of magnitude only.

## III   THE INCREASING IMPORTANCE OF INTERNATIONAL FINANCIAL MARKETS IN DEFICIT FINANCE

The two questions which arise from this development are these: why
did the role of total credit and capital markets increase so rapidly
until 1973 but then stop doing so? and why has the relative importance of international credit and capital markets continued to grow
until the present?

Broadly, two basic factors appear to be responsible for these
fundamental changes in the financing of the world's deficits. The first
is a rapid expansion in financial intermediation, both domestically
and internationally, increasingly involving more multilateral financial
flows and consequently also deficit financing. The second, which has
emerged only since the first oil crisis, is a marked difference in the
liquidity and risk preferences of the new creditors, as compared with
creditors before 1973. This is the development which has imparted
additional momentum to financial intermediation and, above all, to
international financial intermediation.

The rapid expansion of financial intermediation domestically is by
now a well-known phenomenon, which has been analysed and studied extensively in recent years. In addition to the classical function of
collecting savings and channeling them to various users (for both

consumption and investment) financial intermediation performs two other basic functions. These are: the transformation of the maturity debt; and the diversification, pooling and consequently transformation of risk. In principle, the transformation of debt maturity is undertaken by credit markets, but not by capital markets. Deposit banks borrow short and lend, on the average, longer; in the process of doing so they change the length of debt in a way that reconciles the liquidity preferences of the ultimate fund providers and the ultimate fund users. In doing this, banks incur a risk relating to liquidity. The extent of this liquidity risk depends on the difference in the maturities of their lending as compared with their borrowing.

Capital market operations do not, in principle, involve any maturity transformation of the debt instruments they deal with. Debt instruments issued in primary markets normally have a fixed maturity date, which can be changed only at additional cost to a borrower. The risk capital instruments with which they are concerned, and those falling between pure debt obligations and pure risk instruments, as a rule do not involve maturity transformation.

Alongside the function of transforming debt maturity deposit banks also have a separate risk-bearing function, in that the debtor to whom they lend may not repay the debt. The risks so arising are both commercial and financial. Though risks are reduced by pooling, they are nevertheless important and real.

Intermediaries involved in capital market operations (i.e. those issuing securities in primary markets and those dealing in them in secondary markets) do not in principle incur any commercial or financial risk. Participants in the capital markets include, in addition to individuals, a number of savings-collecting, non-bank financial institutions such as insurance companies, pension funds, unit trusts, etc. These endeavour to make collectives and to diversify their commercial and financial risks by appropriately structuring their portfolios, but they do incur financial and commercial risks.

It should perhaps be pointed out here that only in the USA is the deposit-banking business, comprising operations in credit markets, separated formally from investment banking business involving operations in the primary capital markets. Such informal separation also existed in the UK until recently, but has been giving way, though gradually, to the involvement of deposit banks in underwriting. In all other industrial countries in Europe and Japan, deposit banks also undertake underwriting business (i.e are involved in primary capital market operations). In all industrial countries, deposit banks are either participants in the secondary markets by way of managing funds (in a fiduciary capacity) on behalf of individuals and of savings-collecting bodies, such as pension funds.

The increase in domestic financial intermediation started to gain momentum in the late 1950s and early 1960s. It involved the collection of savings from various units within the personal, company and public sectors, and their re-channeling to other uses in the same and other sectors. Accompanying this development has been a similar development internationally. Stimulating it have been the acceptance of convertibility obligations, mandatory under the IMF rules; increasingly free access to domestic credit and capital markets in the developed countries; and a growing awareness on the part of deposit banks and those involved in the operations of primary and secondary capital markets, of the profitability advantages of operating in the international financial markets with their absence of regulations.

We have already seen that the increase in the relative importance of international financial markets (credit and capital) which was already under way before the first oil shock in 1973, has continued uninterrupted. However, in strong contrast to the 1970–3 experience prior to the first oil shock, its expansion in the last seven years has been to a large extent at the expense (in relative terms) of expansion in domestic credit and capital markets.

The main reasons underlying this development since 1973 are these. There has been a fundamental change in the pattern of world savings and investment, associated with the emergence of OPEC surpluses, and with marked differences in the liquidity and risk preferences of the new generators of net savings as compared with those before the first oil shock. There have also been the opportunities for financial intermediaries operating in the international financial markets to reconcile the liquidity preferences of savers and borrowers and to offer some cover against political risk, as well as some tax and allied advantages which seem to be of greater appeal to the new net savers.

The new pattern of world international deficits and savings which has come into existence since 1973 is well known. It has involved, first, a doubling of the relative size of international deficits (i.e. in relation to the total GNP of the free world); second, it involved a replacement of the industrial countries as net exporters of capital (i.e. net providers of savings) both to developing countries and to planned economies. Their place has been taken by the OPEC or, more specifically, by the six

TABLE 9.4    DISPOSITION OF CASH SURPLUS OF OIL-EXPORTING
COUNTRIES 1974–80

|  | $bn | % of total |
|---|---|---|
| Current account surplus | 357 | |
| Plus oil sector transactions and net borrowing | 31 | |
| Cash surplus | 388 | 100 |
|  |  |  |
| Disposition | | |
| Bank deposits and direct placements | 27 | 6.9 |
| Euro-currency deposits | 127 | 32.7 |
| Short-term government securities[a] | 10 | 2.5 |
| Long-term government securities | 20 | 5.1 |
| Other capital flows[b] | 144 | 37.2 |
| IMF and World Bank[c] | 8 | 2.1 |
| Flow of funds to developing countries[d] | 52 | 13.4 |
|  | 388 | 100 |

[a] Mainly US and UK Treasury bills.

[b] Comprising net acquisition of long-term government securities, (including those issued in international capital markets by government and international organisations), corporate stocks and bonds, real estate, direct investment and bilateral loans.

[c] Including direct purchases of World Bank bonds.

[d] Bilateral grants and loans.

*Source:* IMF, IBRD, BIS and OECD.

*Note:* The countries defined as oil exporters here include, in addition to six chronic surplus members, Algeria, Indonesia, Iraq, Iran, Nigeria and Venezuela.

persistent-surplus OPEC members (Saudi Arabia, Kuwait, United Arab Emirates, Qatar, Oman and Libya).

The liquidity and risk preferences of the oil-exporting countries which have become providers of net savings have favoured holdings of assets with high liquidity and small (commercial) risk. As is shown in Table 9.4, out of their total cash surplus of $388bn in 1974–80, nearly 40 per cent was placed in the form of bank deposits, and nearly 10 per cent in short-term and long-term government securities, with the IMF and with the World Bank. Only slightly less than 40 per cent went into other assets, including long-term bonds issued in international capital markets.

Thus, in retrospect, we can specify the growing role of total world credit and capital markets, and above all of international credit and

capital markets, in financing external imbalances. This can be attributed to a rise in world deficits (and surpluses), in relative and absolute
terms, to a shift in their pattern, and, above all, to the markedly different
liquidity and risk preference of the new savers.

In contrast to the other institutional changes that have occurred, the
credit and capital markets could have, and have, transferred savings
from economic units unable to use them to those wishing to employ
them. They could do this by undertaking the function of debt-maturity
transformation as well as that of risk-pooling and diversification in a
way that accorded with the preferences of the ultimate providers and
users of funds.

Let me now turn to the developing countries, taken here to cover
those now defined by the IMF as non-oil developing countries. They
comprise all countries, except for twenty-one industrial countries,
twelve oil exporters, and the planned economies (for classification, see
Appendix A). We first summarise the main features of the financing of
their external deficits.

For these non-oil developing countries since 1973, in common with
the broad trends in the world economy outlined previously, finance
from private sources (excluding, however, direct investment) has come
to play an increasingly important part in deficit financing. Here again, its
role had been increasing previously, though at a rather slow pace.

Reliable information is available only for the period since 1973. A
comparison of the position in 1974–80 with that in 1973 can, however,
be taken as indicative of the developments in the preceding five or so
years. It is illuminating and instructive.

We take four main sources of deficit financing for all non-oil
developing countries – non-debt creating flows including official
transfers; long-term capital from official sources; long-term private
capital; and other capital flows (Table 9.5). The shares of two
elements rose from 24 per cent in 1973 to an average of 46 per cent in
1974 to 1980. These were: long-term finance from private sources, of
which financial markets and especially international financial markets
are the largest component; and other capital flows, among which
private short-term market finance is dominant and accounts for about
three-quarters to four-fifths of the total. In contrast, the share of non-
debt creating flows fell, in the same period, from 75 to 44 per cent.

Taking long-term private capital and 'other capital flows' together,
their relative importance as a source of deficit financing increased
most for 'other non-oil importers' (i.e. mostly middle-income countries, exporting primary products). For them, it rose from 3.2 per

TABLE 9.5 FINANCING OF CURRENT ACCOUNT DEFICIT AND CHANGES IN RESERVES OF NON-OIL DEVELOPING COUNTRIES[a]

| | 1973 | | 1974–80 | |
| --- | --- | --- | --- | --- |
| | | Annual | average | |
| Current account deficit $bn | −11.5 | | 45.6 | |
| Increase in reserves | 9.7 | | 7.8 | |
| | 21.2 | | 53.4 | |
| Financed by: | | % of | | % of |
| | $bn | total | $bn | total |
| Non-debt creating flows[b] | 10.4 | 49.0 | 15.4 | 28.8 |
| Long term capital from official sources | 5.7 | 26.9 | 13.4 | 25.1 |
| Long-term capital from private sources[c] | 5.7 | 26.9 | 19.4 | 36.3 |
| Other capital flows[d] net | −0.6 | −2.8 | 5.2 | 9.8 |
| | 21.2 | 100 | 52.4 | 100 |

[a] Excluding official transfers.

[b] Official transfers, direct investment and SDR allocations, gold monetisation and valuation adjustment.

[c] Borrowings from financial institutions and other lenders with original maturity of more than one year.

[d] Use of reserve-related facilities (i.e. official finance, excluding direct use of reserves), short-term borrowings and errors and omissions.

Source: International Monetary Fund.

cent in 1973 to over 50 per cent in 1974–80. It also rose from nearly 43 per cent to about 63 per cent for major exporters of manufactures, or by about half; and by as much for the net oil exporters – from 22 to 35 per cent. However, for low-income countries it fell, in the same period, from nearly 27 to some 25 per cent.

Similar development is noticeable in relation to long-term private capital only. Its relative importance increased for the same three sub-groups of developing countries, net oil importers, net oil exporters and major exporters of manufactures – from 11 to 35 per cent and 42 to 43 per cent respectively. It fell for low-income countries from 5.5 to 3.75 per cent (see Table 9.6 for details).

These differences between the four groups of the developing countries as regards the pattern of deficit financing, including funds for development, are not surprising. They are indicative of the different nature of their problems, which are commented upon briefly

TABLE 9.6  RELATIVE IMPORTANCE OF DIFFERENT SOURCES OF FINANCING OF CURRENT ACCOUNT DEFICIT[a] AND ADDITIONS TO RESERVES FOR NON-OIL DEVELOPING COUNTRIES

| | 1973 | | | | 1974-80 (Averages) | | | |
|---|---|---|---|---|---|---|---|---|
| | Non-debt creating flow | Official long-term capital | Private long term capital | Other | Non-debt creating flows | Official long-term capital | Private long-term capital | Total |
| | % of total | | | | % of total | | | |
| Net oil-exporters | 57.5 | 20.1 | 29.0 | −6.6 | 40.4 | 28.8 | 49.8 | −19.1 |
| Major exporters of manufactures | 39.4 | 17.8 | 42.4 | 0.3 | 23.7 | 13.4 | 43.0 | 19.9 |
| Low income countries | 42.9 | 30.4 | 5.4 | 21.4 | 38.7 | 46.3 | 3.7 | 11.4 |
| Other net oil-importers | 57.2 | 39.6 | 10.8 | −7.6 | 25.5 | 24.0 | 35.6 | 14.9 |

[a] Excluding Official transfers.

Source:  International Monetary Fund.

Note:  For classification of various groups see Appendix.

TABLE 9.7   NON-OIL DEVELOPING COUNTRIES: SHARE OF CRE-
DIT AND CAPITAL MARKETS IN LONG-TERM FINANCING
(*Average 1974–80*)

| | International financial markets | | Domestic financial markets | | |
|---|---|---|---|---|---|
| | Euro-currency % | Euro-bonds % | Credit markets % | Bond markets % | Total % |
| Net oil exporters[a] | 84 | 4 | 8 | 3 | 100 |
| Major exporters of manufactures | 55 | 1 | 19 | ? | 100 |
| Low income | 94 | neg. | 6 | | 100 |
| Other net oil importers | 86 | 5 | 9 | neg. | 100 |

[a] Including other private sources.

*Source:* Author's calculations

later. To complete the picture of the deficit financing (and additions to reserves) on non-oil developing countries, very rough estimates of the shares of international and domestic credit and capital markets in providing long-term private capital and for the four groups are shown in Table 9.7.

This shows that international financial markets accounted for over 90 per cent of the private capital going to three groups of non-oil developing countries, net oil exporter, low-income developing countries and other net-oil importing developing countries. Only for major exporters of manufactures was its share as low as 55 per cent. Furthermore, the bulk of funds obtained from international financial markets came from credit markets – the share of international capital markets being very small indeed.

These very rough estimates understate the contribution made by the international financial markets. First, they do not include the finance provided by international development intitutions such as the IBRD and its regional counterparts, such as the Asian Development Bank, etc. Their borrowings in the international financial market, mainly for re-lending to developing countries, have increased significantly, and such rough estimates as can be made suggest that the funds re-lent by them have made an important contribution to financing the deficits of developing countries.

Second, a growing proportion of other sources of deficit-financing for the developing (and indeed developed) countries can be said to have a counterpart in their borrowings from the international (and domestic) financial markets. This is true of non-debt creating financial transactions and, above all, of direct investment by the private sector of the developed countries, which has increasingly raised funds in international financial markets. Large multinational companies have been important here, as have 'official sources' in industrial countries. These have. not infrequently supplemented their resources by making borrowings in international financial markets and passing them on to developing countries, by way of aid and concessionary loans.

## IV   ECONOMIC DEVELOPMENT AND ITS FINANCING

What are the implications of a greater reliance by developing countries on funds for the financing of their development from financial markets, and above all international financial markets, especially since 1973?

It may be helpful to look at this question by stating, first, that despite significant and important advances made in the last twenty-five years there is as yet no unified theory of economic development and of the place of external finance in it. What is generally agreed is that the process of economic development involves the mobilisation of the financial resources needed for the acquisition both of directly productive assets and of indirectly productive resources. The latter are needed for the improvement of the managerial and technical skills that are indispensable if productivity and output are to increase.

For the developing countries, domestically generated financial resources (reflecting, of course domestic savings) are inadequate for investment in physical and human resources, so that they must be supplemented by additional financial resources from overseas (i.e. excess foreign savings). These are then transmitted, by way of aid and long-term lending from official and private sources, to cover a structural deficit in external account. Such a deficit must be distinguished from a cyclical deficit which is financeable, when it occurs, by recourse to funds from private and official sources, but repayable within a short period.

What is a 'structural deficit in external accounts' and how should it be financed? These are two important questions which were debated following the Second World War and are debated again now. At the risk of drastic simplification, one can say that a 'structural' deficit, for the developing countries, is a deficit bigger than the cyclical deficit which is necessary to raise domestic investment and total absorption, so as to accelerate the rate of growth of productivity and total output. To be a viable part of development policy, a 'structural' deficit has to be sustained over a number of years and to be financed by 'autonomous' capital movement – to use Meade's terminology – as distinct from an accommodating capital flow which covers cyclical disequilibria.

Until the late 1960s, autonomous capital movements were interpreted as long-term capital movements from public and private sources plus, of course, official transfers. The phrase 'long term' referred to the maturity of debt which tended to be interpreted as having an original life of, say, more than twenty years.

Broadly speaking, until the late 1960s the developing countries could obtain such funds from the World Bank and similar institutions and from the issue of debt in the US capital market. This dominated the world scene at that time, the US having previously been a large exporter of capital to the rest of the world.

The World Bank's policy, notwithstanding a short-lived debate after it was set up, was to link such loans to specific investment projects, a policy also adopted by similar institutions. Loans were floated on capital markets by some developing countries, but they were few in number, small in size, and restricted to countries in the middle-income group with good records. They were, however, untied.

Supplementing long-term development finance of the 'autonomous' type from these sources, there was also until the late 1960s a relatively modest amount of medium-term bank finance, with original life of up to about seven years. This also can be said to have been 'autonomous', but it did tend largely to represent government-guaranteed export credits.

Thus, until the late 1960s, the shift by developing countries towards a greater reliance on financial markets for deficit financing appears to have conformed to the then conventional approach. This was that such funds should, in essence, represent 'autonomous' capital movements and should take the form predominantly of long-term debt, partly project-oriented and partly for general balance of payments support. It should, however, be regarded by financial markets as self-liquidating over a number of years.

As outlined previously, the position has changed fundamentally since the first oil shock, inasmuch as deficit financing by the developing countries now includes a much greater proportion of funds raised in the financial markets, and especially international financial markets. This comprises to a large extent debt of medium-term maturity for general balance of payments support, rather than project-oriented funds in the form of long-term debt.

Can these funds be regarded by developing countries as 'sustainable autonomous capital flows' to cover structural deficit in external accounts, in the same way that overseas funds previously used for development purposes were, and if not, how does the change in their character bear on the development policy?

The answer to these questions is complicated by the fact that the original nature of such funds is not long term but medium term and that they now cover to a large extent general balance-of-payments support. It therefore depends essentially on the view taken, first, of the availability of such funds in the future; and, second, on the extent to which those in the financial markets will be prepared to continue to re-channel such funds to the developing countries.

These two issues are closely interlinked. If participants in the financial markets do not consider the developing countries sufficiently creditworthy, and if they consequently restrict and reduce their lending to them, the size of the structural deficits that could be financed by using financial markets will still have to be diminished. This may be achieved by forced changes in domestic policy, which will decrease the structural deficits, mainly by reducing imports. In turn, such forced changes in domestic polices would reduce world savings and investment, reflecting the view of the financial intermediaries that they cannot undertake the functions of transforming debt maturity, or of risk pooling and diversification, any further.

Thus the availability of funds from financial markets is now to a large extent determined by the assessment which those in them make of the creditworthiness of the developing countries. This is likely to continue to be true in the future, because of the likelihood that the six chronic-surplus oil exporters will remain in this position for some time.

In essence, whether or not financial markets will make funds available to the developing countries for structural deficit financing, and on what terms, will depend on three factors. The first is the growth in the number of participants in such markets; the second is the pace of expansion of their total operations; and the third is their individual assessment of the creditworthiness of the potential borrowers, as reflected in the degree of exposure (in relation to total assets) that they are prepared to accept.

One of the characteristic features of the international financial market in recent years has been a steady rise in the number of institutions operating in international credit markets and to a smaller extent those involved in international capital market operations. To the extent that this trend will continue, as it is likely to do, finance from such sources can be expected to be available as part of the structural-deficit financing of the developed countries.

Likewise, an increase in the capital base of the banks resulting from retention of profits and from capital-raising operations, can be expected to continue to increase the total size of their assets, including lending to the developing countries. At the same time, additions to the total assets of non-bank financial institutions and of individuals can be expected to provide scope for increasing the debt of developing countries.

It is the assessment of the creditworthiness of potential borrowers by financial markets, however, that is of overriding significance. In assessing 'country risk', fund providers apply a number of different tests. Among these, the debt-service ratio is the most important (i.e. the proportion of current account receipts absorbed by the service of debt). The debt-service ratio, as well as other ratios applied by different private-fund providers, need not be the same, and indeed may differ from time to time. It is nevertheless true that, beyond a certain point, lenders are likely to change their behaviour. First, they will increase the 'spread'. Later they will lose interest altogether in providing funds until this ratio (and other ratios) improve as a result of deliberate policy changes. If these ratios are beyond acceptable levels, the transfer of voluntary savings from abroad will not take place. Thus, the view of debt-service capacity is likely to be crucial in determining the extent to which funds will be available for the developing countries to cover their structural debt.

In other words, a 'country risk' evaluation has now become central to the provision of funds to help the development strategies of developing countries by financial markets, and especially international financial markets. This is especially true of the financing of structural deficits in their external accounts.

'Country risk' assessment by financial markets takes as its starting point a significantly shorter time-horizon than that taken by official and similar lenders. It also places greater emphasis on the nature and speed of structural adjustments, above all as regards external accounts.

To continue to attract funds from financial markets to cover structural deficits, a country's development strategy, if it is to be viable, must therefore shift the emphasis away from financing. It must move towards more rapid structural adjustment and aim explicitly at reducing the rate of growth of both imports and exports in relation to GDP. Evolution of a new approach along these lines by the developing countries must inevitably require a reassessment of demand management, of supply-oriented policies and of the relationship between them, as well as of the role of fiscal, monetary and exchange-rate policies and the appropriate 'mix' between these too.

## V  SOME IMPLICATIONS FOR DEVELOPMENT STRATEGY

The exact nature of the changes in development strategies needed to achieve more rapid structural adjustment will vary. They will depend on individual developing countries and their salient characterisitics. Certain basic features that must be incorporated into the new approaches will be common to all of them. Yet there are sufficient differences to pose a challenge to the members of the economic profession, which needs to provide a detailed programme to take account of them.

The changes in the nature of the economic policies pursued by the developing countries, arising from a greater dependence on deficit financing by recourse to financial markets, must be seen in a wider perspective – that of changes in the financial pattern in the free world as a whole in the last twenty or so years.

In that period, the financing of industry and commerce in the industrial countries has also moved away from long-term finance towards medium-term finance from the banks. That is, it has moved away from the traditional 'Anglo-Saxon' approach towards the 'Continental-cum-Japanese' approach. 'Structural' deficit financing by some of these countries has likewise assumed the same form.

The changes which have occurred in the pattern of deficit financing in the developing countries may be in essence no different from those which have occurred in the world at large, and may carry similar consequences for economic policy. Yet the developing countries' position is less favourable. This is because their foreign assets/liabilities position is worse than that of the industrial countries and has been deteriorating more rapidly. It is also because the success of their development policies depends to a large extent on the pace of the growth and the trade policies of the industrial economies. To that extent, the problems of readjusting their policies are more formidable and urgent.

If the world economic climate is reasonably propitious and if development strategy of the developing countries is adjusted accordingly, they should be able to contain their debt service and other ratios within a range regarded as acceptable by financial markets. They should then be able to look upon these sources of finance as willing and able to provide a 'sustainable flow of structural-deficit financing'.

The question of how development policies should be changed to accelerate the pace of structural change, of what use should be made of various policy instruments, and of the assessment of their impact presents a new, urgent and formidable challenge to the members of the economic profession. If the challenge is taken up and if the answers produced are satisfactory, the benefits to the developing countries and to the world at large will be immense.

# Appendix

*COUNTRY CLASSIFICATION USED IN THIS CHAPTER*

1 INDUSTRIAL COUNTRIES

| | | |
|---|---|---|
| Australia | West Germany | New Zealand |
| Austria | Iceland | Norway |
| Belgium | Ireland | Spain |
| Canada | Italy | Sweden |
| Denmark | Japan | Switzerland |
| Finland | Luxembourg | United Kingdom |
| France | Netherlands | United States |

2 DEVELOPING COUNTRIES: OIL-EXPORTING COUNTRIES

| | | |
|---|---|---|
| Algeria | Kuwait | Qatar |
| Indonesia | Libya | Saudi Arabia |
| Iran | Nigeria | United Arab Emirates |
| Iraq | Oman | Venezuela |

3 NON-OIL DEVELOPING COUNTRIES

*I   Net Oil Exporters*

| | | |
|---|---|---|
| Bahrain | Egypt | Peru |
| Bolivia | Gabon | Syria |
| Congo | Malaysia | Trinidad and Tobago |
| Ecuador | Mexico | Tunisia |

*II   Major Exporters of Manufactures*

| | | |
|---|---|---|
| Argentina | Israel | Singapore |
| Brazil | South Korea | South Africa |
| Greece | Portugal | Yugoslavia |
| Hong Kong | | |

## III   Low-Income Countries

| | | |
|---|---|---|
| Afghanistan | Guinea-Bissau | Niger |
| Bangladesh | Haiti | Pakistan |
| Benin | India | Rwanda |
| Burma | Kampuchea | Senegal |
| Burundi | Kenya | Sierra Leone |
| Cape Verde | Laos Republic | Somalia |
| Central African | Lesotho | Sri Lanka |
|   Republic | Madagascar | Sudan |
| Chad | Malawi | Tanzania |
| China (People's | Maldives | Togo |
|   Republic) | Mali | Uganda |
| Cameroon | Mauretania | Upper Volta |
| Ethiopia | Nepal | Vietnam |
| The Gambia | | Zaire |
| Guinea | | |

## IV   Other Net Oil Importers

Remaining 27 non-industrial and non-oil exporting members of the IMF.

# 10 How to Manage a Repressed Economy*

## Ronald I. McKinnon

STANFORD UNIVERSITY, USA

### I INTRODUCTION

Chile from 1974 to the present is one of the few recent examples of a sustained economic liberalisation; fiscal, exchange-rate and monetary policies were manipulated more or less correctly (with the possible exception of wage indexing) to secure free trade, an unrestricted domestic capital market, rapid real growth and a stable currency.

Argentina, on the other hand, ostensibly began in 1976 to follow – with some initial success – foreign trade and financial policies similar to those being carried out in Chile. By 1980, however, Argentina's programme of economic liberalisation was in severe difficulty. A loss of financial control resulted in ongoing price inflation, serious over-valuation of the peso and massive bankruptcies. This was followed in 1981 by forced devaluations, a sharp escalation of price inflation and a negative rate of growth. Regression to more import restrictions and to more direct controls on domestic commerce and finance seemed likely – in the mode of most countries in Latin America.

Rather than analyse the whole liberalisation process, the complex transition from an economically 'repressed' to a 'liberalised' state,

---

* I would like to thank Donald Mathieson of the International Monetary Fund and Philip Brock of Stanford University for their great help in setting up the equation system underlying the formal model of financial control presented in this paper. In his Stanford Ph.D. dissertation, Brock has worked out a more general model of monetary control for a repressed economy than that presented here.

the aim of this paper is more modest. First, certain critical economic conditions, if full liberalisation is to be feasible, are identified. Second, supposing that these conditions for foreign trade and domestic financial processes are *not* met, how can one deal efficiently with the resulting, ongoing economic repression, while avoiding premature moves towards full liberalisation, in the mode of some (although not all) recent policies in Argentina?

The most fundamental difference betwen Chile and Argentina seems to be the control, or lack of control, over fiscal policy. Relatively early in its liberalisation process, Chile curbed government expenditures and increased tax collections to the point where the Treasury accounts began to show large cash surpluses – between 1–4 per cent of GNP between 1976 and 1900. Equally importantly, large credit subsidies – funnelled mainly through the discount window of the central bank and the state owned commercial bank – to both industry and agriculture were virtually eliminated by 1979. Thus the swing from deficit to surplus in the 'true' government accounts, where the monetary system is appropriately consolidated with the Treasury, is remarkable by any standard and was a necessary condition for fully liberalising the Chilean economy.

In Argentina, on the other hand, the military take-over in March 1976 resulted in modest subsequent fiscal improvement. The combined public sector deficits – including those of state governments and of nationalised enterprises – fell about 10 to 5 per cent of GNP up to 1979. But the formal accounting deficit in the public sector accounts remained large relative to the real size of the domestic financial system. More importantly, the Argentinians were much less successful in phasing out credit subsidies, chanelled through the monetary system to favoured claimants in the nationalised and private sectors, that are not formally included in the public sector accounts. Indeed, with the great strain on Argentinian industry in late 1979 and throughout 1980, from the overvaluation of the peso, a series of actual and threatened bankruptcies forced the central bank greatly to extend these implicit and explicit credit subsidies. The result is a large increase in effective government expenditure in Argentina, much of which must be financed domestically. This lack of fiscal control should have inhibited the Argentinian authorities from preceeding with a full-scale financial liberalisation similar to that undertaken in Chile, and from prematurely slowing the rate of devaluation of the peso.

In the formal theoretical model to be developed below, it is assumed that the government authorities make a *realistic* estimate of the ongoing, consolidated fiscal deficit for which the central bank is called on to provide domestic finance, by issuing base money. Then, monetary technicians at the central bank choose the best combination of exchange controls, interest ceilings, and reserve requirements to enable them to minimise the use of the inflation tax (as an instrument of public finance), while limiting the inevitable crowding out of private capital formation. The equations are set up as if the economy remains in a steady state where financial repression is associated with the fiscal deficit, and no attempt is made to analyse the transition to a more liberalised state as would be possible if fiscal policy were to improve in the Chilean mode. Even so, a steady-state analysis of financial repression seems applicable to most LDCs at present. Uncovered domestic fiscal deficits are more common than surpluses.

Once one has specified an appropriate financial strategy for imposing the inflation tax and/or extracting seigniorage from the domestic financial system, a complementary and rather passive foreign exchange policy – based on indexing and restrictions on capital flows – follows naturally. In addition, it is assumed that the flow of foreign commodity trade is also significantly repressed by quotas, licenses and redundantly high tariffs. As with most countries in Latin America and Asia, this repression of foreign trade is biased against exporting and leads to general resource misallocation and reduced per capita real income. However, in the face of an ongoing domestic inflation tax, these trade restrictions have the incidental advantage of making exchange-rate indexing somewhat easier. Correspondingly, this repression of foreign trade, or merely incomplete and uncertain trade liberalisation, militates against the use of an actively pegged exchange rate as an acceptable instrument through which the government can try to reduce domestic price inflation (McKinnon, 1981b) – as with the unfortunate Argentinian overvaluation of the peso in 1979–80.

Before spelling out our formal model of optimal financial control, however, let us sketch in more detail the main characterisitics of a repressed economy.

## II   THE REPRESSED ECONOMY

Economists are generally aware of the highly protectionist foreign trade policies followed by most LDCs in the post-war period. Recently, a ten-country NBER study under the editorship of Jagdish Bhagwati (1978) and Anne Krueger (1978) established that protectionism commonly takes the form of direct quantitative restrictions (QRs) on imports and on some exports. Besides imposing a wide variety of direct quotas and prohibitions on the importation of specific goods, these 'QR regimes' often impose exchange controls on purchases of foreign currency that make it more difficult to import goods and services otherwise not specifically restricted. Although protective tariffs are sometimes important in unrestricted categories, QRs may well dominate most of the import bill.

In order to placate politically powerful urban groups, natural export goods in the form of domestically produced foodstuffs may face quantitative restrictions on sales abroad. Similarly, the export of industrial raw materials – such as natural textile fibres usable in urban industry – is occasionally restricted. Generally, the domestic terms of trade are turned against agriculture and other exporters in order to protect urban industry and urban consumers.

When foreign trade is rather broadly repressed by quantitative restrictions (or high tariffs) on both the import and export sides, the prices of most goods produced and consumed are determined mainly by domestic demand and supply considerations – and in the first instance are rather insulated from exchange-rate changes. Similarly, the domestic financial system is usually insulated by exchange controls on the capital account of the balance of payments. In contrast to the very different situation facing a small open economy (to be treated below), therefore, we may reasonably begin analysing fiscal and financial policy in a prototype repressed economy *as if* it were closed to foreign trade.

Economists are less familiar with the syndrome of 'financial repression' (McKinnon, 1973; Shaw, 1973), although this is equally common and equally important in LDCs by comparison with restraints on foreign trade. Those firms, individuals or industries – private or nationalised – that receive protection on what they produce from potential imports, and favourable allocations of import licenses for what they use, are often the recipients of officially designated bank credits at negative real rates of interest – once domestic price inflation or anticipated exchange depreciation are taken into account. Official interventions in the allocation of credit may be as pervasive, detailed and bewildering as the proliferation of QRs on foreign trade. Often private borrowing and lending at equilibrium rates of interest is completely pre-empted: there may be no open, organised capital market where borrowers and lenders can freely contract at a market clearing rate of interest.

Institutionally, how does such financial repression arise? In developing countries, open markets for primary securities are usually insignificant. This situation does not itself constitute a distortion but merely reflects the low level of per capita income and the resulting small scale of individual acts of saving and investment. Information is insufficient for small farmers or merchants to issue either their own notes or publicly traded shares, that can easily attract resources from small savers.

Thus the monetary system in LDCs has a relatively important role as an intermediary between savers and investors. Private financial savings in developing countries are largely held in the form of currency and deposits – claims on central banks, commercial banks, savings and loan associations, financieras (development banks), postal savings depositories and so on, that are indeed potentially attractive to small savers. Influence on the flow of loanable funds arising out of the issue of currency and such deposits – money in the broad sense of $M_2$ – assumes critical importance in the development process. What is purely a concern for supervisory and monetary control over their banking systems by governments in most industrial countries becomes a highly activist credit-allocating role in LDCs.

There is a fiscal root to this apparent philosophical difference regarding the conduct of monetary policy. Most LDC governments feel constrained in the amount of the revenue they can raise from conventional sources – taxes on income, sales, and property – to support desired levels of expenditure on both current and capital account. The absence of open markets in primary securities means that the Treasury cannot directly market non-monetary debt outside the banking system – unless it relies on capital inflows from abroad.

However, forced sales of government debt to the banking system – through an elaborate system of *reserve requirement* – gives the government direct access to banks' loanable funds. In LDCs, reserve requirements of 50 per cent or more on deposits in commercial and savings banks are not uncommon. Less directly, comprehensive *usury restrictions* on both lending and deposit rates of interest allow regulatory authorities to give credit subsidies to preferrred claimants – without these appearing in the official Treasury accounts. If, with a stable price level, insufficient resources are mobilised to cover these explicit and implicit deficits in the public finances, inflation develops. It then interacts with the reserve requirements and usury restrictions to provide even more revenue to the government – as we shall see below.

The whole process of extracting revenue from the banking system is much too complicated to be captured in a single diagram. However, the diversion of bank loanable funds to the government (the central bank) from the imposition of reserve requirements is portrayed in Figure 10.1. With this very substantial resource flow at its disposal, the central bank channels cheap credits to various specialised banking agencies (A, B, C, D in Figure 10.1). They in turn lend at low, disequilibrium rates of interest for export promotion, credit for small farmers, industrial projects the government wishes to subsidise, and so forth. Because the government may have very detailed credit allocations in mind, these agencies decentralise the potentially huge administrative burden. Or, central bank credits can flow directly to the ministry of finance (see Figure 10.1) to cover explicit current-account deficits in the government's budget.

One consequence of taxing the monetary system in this way is to reduce the monetary tax base *and* the flow of loanable funds in the economy; the size of $M_2$ in GNP is truncated. Typical economies in Latin America, where such policies are commonplace, may have a ratio of $M_2$ to GNP of about 0.20, and in Asia about 0.24; whereas the same ratio for industrial economies is closer to 0.6 – although they also have significant markets in primary securities. Taiwan, one of the few LDCs with a long history of maintaining a liberalised financial structure, has a remarkable $M_2$ to GNP ratio of over 0.7 – whereas Japan's is even higher (McKinnon, 1981).

A second consequence is that the trickle of bank lending that does occur is badly distorted by the fragmented structure of interest rates. Investors favoured by the official agencies may borrow at negative real rates of interest that often reflect the quality of their investment projects; other potential borrowers with high yield projects are severely rationed.

That said, however, the repression of both foreign trade and domestic finance often persists in the same economies for long periods of time. It is politically feasible neither to eliminate protection in foreign trade nor to raise taxes and cut government expenditures so as to liberalise domestic financial process. As we shall see, a certain mutual consistency between repression in both sectors makes it more difficult to liberalise one without the other. Given these common political constraints, let us first sketch an 'optimal' programme of financial and exchange-rate management for a typical

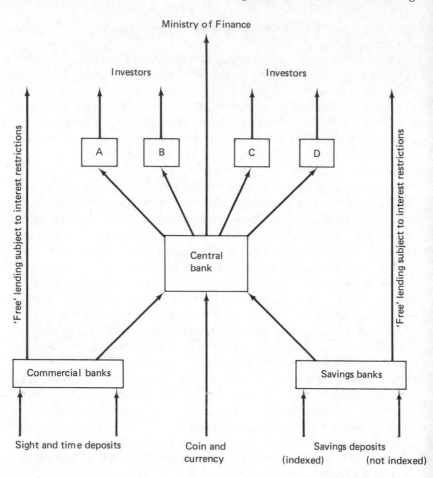

PRIMARY SAVERS

FIGURE 10.1 Bank intermediation in a typical semi-industrial LDC

*Note:* A, B, C, D, E and so on are specialised credit agencies (banks) that get cheap finance from the central bank. A could be the export promotion fund; B the agricultural bank; C the central mortgage bank; and D the industrial development bank.

repressed economy as if it were in a steady state that would last indefinitely. Besides being intrinsically interesting, such a programme provides a natural starting point, or a consistent set of initial conditions, from which to examine the liberalisation problem if and when the underlying political constraints in fiscal and foreign trade policy are altered.

## III  UNCONTROLLED FISCAL DEFICITS AND OPTIMAL INFLATIONARY FINANCE

Consider the financing problem facing the government of a repressed economy. Let us hypothetically consolidate (i) the official uncovered Treasury deficits; and (ii) the unofficial subsidy element in the flow of low-cost credits to preferred borrowers through government controls over the banking system. Let $Z$ be the resulting total *flow* of revenue (seigniorage) to be extracted from the domestic banking system:

$$Z = G - T \qquad\qquad \text{Nominal fiscal deficit.} \qquad (1)$$

Here, $G$ is our inclusive measure of government expenditures, and $T$ the flow of ordinary taxes collected. $Z$ is stated in purely nominal terms, say pesos, and will of course vary with the price level. To avoid specifying a complete macromodel of domestic income determination, and the way public finance are embedded in it, simply assume that the government's need for real finance from the domestic monetary system is given exogenously:

$$Z/P = \alpha Y_t + v_t \qquad\qquad \text{Real seigniorage.} \qquad (2)$$

Here, $P$ is a general price deflator, $Y_t$ is a scale factor in terms of exogenously given real income (GNP), and $v_t$ is random stochastic disturbance, reflecting lack of official control over the fiscal system. In principle, $\alpha$ could be treated as a policy parameter. A reduction in $\alpha$ could signal, say increased ordinary tax collections or increased official determination to reduce credit subsidies to preferred borrowers. However, to reflect *steady-state* financial repression, we assume that $\alpha$ is a positive constant and that $v_t$ has significant variance. In effect, an ongoing and somewhat variable fiscal deficit is pre-determined, and simply dumped into the laps of the monetary technicians at the central bank. They must design an overall financial policy to make the best of the situation.

What objective function should be imposed on the technicians? To simplify the analysis greatly, suppose that the goverment instructs the technicians to minimise the rate of expected price inflation in the steady state – subject to the constraint that the ongoing fiscal deficit is indeed financed. Apart from the credit subsidies to officially designated borrowers which are part of the government deficit in equation (2), the technicians are not otherwise constrained to maintain general interest-rate controls (usury laws) unless these prove useful in reducing the rate of price inflation. Moreover, the technicians remain

* free to manipulate reserve requirements on all classes of deposits without any direct concern for the 'crowding out' of private borrowers.[1] In this context of a repressed economy, therefore, how best should the instruments of financial policy be manipulated in order to minimise the inflation rate?

The government effectively taxes the financial system through its control over the supply of non-interest bearing base money. (To avoid unnecessary complications, required bank purchases of government bonds at below-market rates of interest are ignored here.) First, because currency is part of non-interest bearing base money, suppose the technicians decide that demand deposits – which compete directly with currency as a means of payment – will also be non-interest bearing. Official reserve requirements against demand deposits are set at a very high level – close to 100 per cent – and this is roughly tailored to absorb abnormal bank profits after the costs of servicing checking accounts have been deducted. Although somewhat repressive, this 'suboptimisation' strategy has the advantage of maintaining the margin of substitution between currency and demand deposits in the portfolios of money holders – despite possible variability in the rate of price inflation or in rates of interest on other financial assets.

Second, suppose the technicians allow banks of all classes to issue one other type of liability: thirty-day term deposits that are unrestricted in the rate of interest that may be paid to depositors. Moreover, the net proceeds from attracting such deposits may be lent out in the 'free' part of capital market, with no restrictions on interest charged to various borrowers. However, a non-interest bearing reserve requirement of $k$ per cent is imposed on all such thirty-day deposits, whether these be in commercial banks, saving banks or various classes of 'non-bank' intermediaries, such as money market mutual funds. The idea is to make this $k$ per cent tax, on all capital-market transactions, as general as possible. Thus $k$ becomes the key monetary control variable, responding to different levels of the fiscal deficit. (We ignore the additional financial complexity associated with low-interest savings deposits – which are hardly different from demand deposits under high inflation; also, deposits of maturity longer than thirty days are omitted, because financing is very short term in an inflationary environment.) Simplicity is a virtue both analytically and institutionally – and this two-asset strategy rougly corresponds to Chilean financial policy in the mid-1970s when inflation was still severe.

On the central bank's balance sheet, all 'narrow' money usable for making payments to third parties is aggregated into the variable $C$, and all reserves against term deposits are denoted by $R$. The accumulated sum of past government deficits is the central bank's only asset in this, as yet closed-economy, approach.

|  | Central Bank |
| --- | --- |
| Government debt $\Sigma Z_t$ | $C$ Currency and reserves against demand deposits |
|  | $R$ Reserves against term deposits |
|  | $M$ Monetary base |

In a current flow sense, the real revenue accruing to the government from the issue of base money must be:

$$Z/P = \dot{M}/P = (\dot{M}/M)(M/P) = \mu(M/P) \tag{3}$$

where $\dot{M}$ is the absolute rate of change in the money supply, and $\mu$ is its proportional rate of change. Equation (3) yields the conventional result that real revenue from the banking system is the percentage change in nominal money times the real monetary base, whose scale in the steady state roughly depends on the level of real income ($Y$). If initially, in our analysis, we assume an exogenously given steady growth in real income, then:

$$\pi = \mu - \gamma \qquad \text{Steady state inflation,} \tag{4}$$

where $\pi$ is the ongoing rate of price inflation ($\dot{P}/P$), and $\gamma$ is income growth.

What is unconventional is to partition the demand for base money into two components: currency (plus demand deposits) and $k$ per cent of term deposits. Such disaggregation is necessary because the demand for currency is negatively related to the rate of interest, $i_d$, on the term deposits;[2] whereas the derived demand for reserves held against term deposits is positively related to $i_d$. The two basic demand functions are:

$$C/P = f(\underset{-}{\pi}, \underset{-}{i_d})Y \qquad \text{Demand for currency} \tag{5}$$

and

$$D/P = q(\underset{-}{\pi}, \underset{+}{i_d})Y \qquad \text{Demand for term deposits,} \tag{6}$$

yielding

$$M/P = kD/P + C/P \qquad \text{Demand for base money.} \qquad (7)$$

Note that the demand for term deposits is *not* homogeneous of degree zero in $\pi$ and $i_d$. One cannot specify this demand purely in terms of the 'real' deposit rate, $r_d = i_d - \pi$, because equal percentage-point increase in $\pi$ and $i_d$ will still attract depositors away from holding currency – for which there is no interest rate to adjust.

An additional distinguishing feature of our analysis is the importance of the demand for unsubsidised loans in the 'free' part of the capital market. Based on resources attracted through the issue of term deposits, commercial banks are free to lend and charge whatever interest rate (denoted by $i_1$) that they can get:

$$L/P = h(\pi, i_1) \qquad \text{Real loan demand.}^3 \qquad (8)$$
$$\phantom{L/P = h(}+ \ - $$

However, imposing the non-interest bearing reserve requirement, $k$, on term deposits *drives a wedge* between open-market rates of interest on deposits and on loans. If we assume that the domestic commercial banking system is competitive, and we also ignore the returns to factors of production employed in banking, then the intermediaries in term deposits are constrained to making zero profits:

$$i_1(1 - k) - i_d = 0 \qquad \text{Zero profit constraint.} \qquad (9)$$

The incidence of the inflation tax on reserves is distributed between depositors – whose yields are driven down – and borrowers – whose costs are driven up. The way in which ongoing price inflation interacts with the reserve requirement to make the wedge bigger can be illustrated by rewriting equation (9) in terms of the real rates of interest $r_d$ and $r_1$ (McKinnon, 1981a). Substitute $r_d + \pi$ for $i_d$, and $r_1 + \pi$ for $i_1$, to get

$$r_1 = \frac{k\pi}{1 - k} + \frac{r_d}{1 - k} \qquad \text{Real loan rate.} \qquad (9')$$

*The real* loan rate is a weighted average of the rate of change in *nominal* prices and the *real* deposit rate. The tax effect of price inflation on real deposit and loan rates varies directly with $k$. Putting the same point somewhat more forcefully, we rearrange the terms in $(9')$ to show the wedge between either nominal or real rates of interest:

$$r_1 - r_d = \frac{k}{1 - k}(\pi + r_d) = i_1 + i_d \quad \text{Wedge effect.} \qquad (9'')$$

For a given real return to depositors, the wedge between borrowing and lending rates is positively associated with the rate of price inflation: as $\pi$ increases and $i_d$ rises equally, the government implicitly appropriates (through its reserve requirements) a larger share of the proceeds from lending by widening the wedge. How much $r_1$ increases absolutely and $r_d$ falls absolutely depends on the elasticity of demand for loans *vis-à-vis* the elasticity of supply of deposits – presuming that both markets clear.

Conversely, if the governments were to put a ceiling on $i_d = \bar{\imath}_d$, $r_d$ would decline by as much as $\pi$ increased: the wedge remains invariant to the rate of inflation, if the zero profit condition is maintained.[4] Indeed, the real loan rate actually falls, if a commensurate ceiling on nominal lending rates of interests is imposed in order to restrict bank profitability. Of course, the demand for loans will then exceed the available supply of loanable funds and some form of credit rationing will become necessary.

If inflation increases in the presence of these general interest ceilings on deposits and loans, government 'revenue' from the term deposit part of the system could be severely reduced: $r_d$ and $D/P$ decrease more because no part of the tax is shifted forward to borrowers. This loss in financial efficiency from general usury restrictions implies that price inflation could be much higher, for any given size of the fiscal deficit, than it needs to be. Moreover, the crowding out of private borrowing becomes a more acute policy problem. If the government must subsidise specific classes of borrowers, far better to isolate them with direct-interest subsidies that are counted formally as part of the budget deficit. Then, general ceilings on deposit and loan rates of interest can be relaxed, thus opening the capital market to a significant degree.

Henceforth, we analyse the choice of an optimal $k$ *as if* the government were proceeding efficiently by removing interest ceilings from term deposits and loans. Even for a 'repressed' economy, the maintenance of interest ceilings on all monetary assets is unwise, and it is best discarded in favour of this degree of partial financial liberalisation.

For alternative inflationary steady states, our constrained macroeconomic optimisation procedure may now be reduced to its bare essentials:

Minimise $\pi$ with respect to $k$, (10)

subject to the market-clearing conditions:

$$L/P = (1- k)D/P \qquad\qquad \text{Private loanable funds} \qquad (11)$$

$$= h(\pi, i_1) = (1-k)q(\pi, i_d)$$

and

$$Z/P = (kq + f)\,(\pi + \gamma) \qquad\qquad \text{Official deficit finance} \qquad (12)$$

and

$$i_1(1 -k) - i_d = 0 \qquad\qquad \text{Bank competition.} \qquad (13)$$

From the three equations, this optimisation procedure determines that the endogenous variables are $i_1$, $i_d$ and $\pi$. Starting from equation (12), the real government deficit $Z/P$ is exogeneously given and must be financed by issuing base money against both term deposits and (100 per cent reserve) currency. As $k$ increases, the relative tax burden is shifted towards the term-deposit part of the market; how much, depends on the elasticity of response of depositors *and borrowers*. The more inelastic are the $q$ and $h$ functions in response to a fall in $i_d$ and a rise in $i_1$ (for a given $\pi$), the greater is the optimal $k$. Conversely, the more inelastic is the demand for currency imbedded in the function $f$, the lower will be optimal $k$, as more of the inflation tax burden is shifted towards currency holders. According to commonly accepted canons of public finance, one taxes where the inelasticity of demand is most pronounced – in order to minimise the erosion of the tax base. Of course, the more inelastic the demand for either financial asset, the lower the necessary $\pi$. Similarly, from equation (12), the higher the 'natural' real rate of growth and the flow of seigniorage in the economy, the lower will be the minimum inflation rate.

A full algebraic development of the macroeconomic optimisation contained in equations (10) to (13) – where interior solutions are distinguished from corner solutions – is too lengthy and tedious to present here. Instead, Figure 10.2 illustrates the more important ways in which the optimum reserve requirement, the inflation rate and different levels of the exogenously given fiscal deficit, are likely to interact. Each $Z$ represents a given current level of real income and prices, but a different level of fiscal deficit. Our only decision variable $(k)$ ranges between zero and one. If $k$ is set at zero, the government gets no revenue from the term-deposit part of the system. Similarly if $k =1$, so that the nominal yield on term deposits falls to zero, everybody will abandon term deposits in favour of more liquid demand deposits and currency. Again, government revenue from the term-deposit part of the system moves to zero. For each possible fiscal deficit, therefore, the graph relating $\pi$ to $k$ must be U-shaped, with an 'interior' solution for minimising $\pi$ where $k$ is positive but less than one.

For $Z = 10$, the optimum solution is at point C, where the reserve requirement is set at fairly high level to minimise the relatively high inflation rate. If the monetary technicians set reserve requirements either too low (as at point $A$) or too high (as at point $B$), the inflation rate experienced rises above the minimum ($C$). Intuitively, this is easily understood for point $A$, because $k$ is too low and term deposits are insufficiently taxed. Thus a higher inflation tax is forced on currency holders. However, that higher price inflation should result when $A$ is increased beyond $C$ to $D$ may seem counter-intuitive to many readers. Yet, setting reserve requirements 'too high' shrinks the term-deposit part of the system unduly and also diminishes real government revenue based on it. Contrary to what simple text-book models of the money multiplier might suggest, increasing reserve requirements may be inflationary rather than deflationary![5] But the apparent paradox is resolved if one considers choosing the optimal $k$ as an exercise in the theory of optimum taxation for which the elasticities of response of depositors and borrowers are correctly weighed.

An equally serious error would be to leave large segments of the financial system with no reserve requirements at all. Important classes of deposit-taking financial institutions could then be mistakenly classified as 'non-banks', not subject to the central bank's control. Then real deposits would shift towards these unregulated intermediaries, people would avoid the inflation tax, and an unduly high rate of inflation would result – as depicted by $A'$ in Figure 10.2.

As the size of the government's consolidated budget deficit is reduced, the U-shaped curves in Figure 10.2 shift downward and to the left: the optimum ($\pi$, $k$) solutions shift from $C$ to $D$ to $E$. Of course, the minimum rate of inflation falls, but also the optimum reserve requirement ($k$) becomes progressively smaller in order to maintain the correct tax balance between the market for currency and the market for term deposits. If we have substantial economic growth, the minimum-necessary rate of price inflation can fall to zero before the public sector deficit is eliminated: point $E$ along the curve $Z = 3$. Growth itself generates seigniorage, $(C/P + kD/P)\gamma$, which is just sufficient to finance $Z = 3$ in a non-inflationary fashion (Friedman, 1971), for given levels of prices and income. Indeed, further

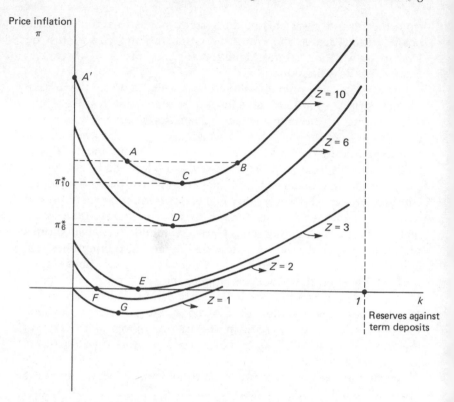

FIGURE 10.2  Inflation, the fiscal deficit and optimum required reserves

*Note:* Income growth, and the current levels of income and prices are given. $Z$ denotes various levels of the fiscal deficit.

*Source:* This is a simplified version of a similar diagram in Philip Brock's Ph.D. dissertation, Stanford University (unpublished).

cuts in $Z$ would generate price deflation in the economy (as shown by the point $G$) if the monetary technicians stuck to the pure strategy of minimising inflation by maintaining $k$ at a significantly positive level.

In the interest of securing price stability without falling prices, however, one might want to truncate the optimising procedure outlined in equations (10) to (13). Impose the additional condition that price deflation be avoided. Then, as $Z$ is further reduced below 3, the authorities respond by simply reducing $k$ rather than letting $\pi$ become negative. In Figure 10.2, reserve requirements are reduced from $E$ to $F$ to 0, with the significant additional advantage (not part of our formal optimising procedure) of further liberalising the capital market. At the origin, where $k$ is zero, $Z$ has been arbitrarily set at one in Figure 10.2: seigniorage from the currency part of the system is just sufficient to provide non-inflationary finance for a deficit of this rather modest size.

Further reductions in $Z$ below one would again cause deflationary pressure, unless the monetary technicians reduce reserve requirements against demand deposits (not incorporated in our formal optimisation procedure) *or* extended modest domestic credit from the central bank to the commercial banks. Either method would be sufficient to ensure that base money expanded fast enough to prevent outright deflation, as the public finances improved in the context of general economic liberalisation.

A *sine qua non* of a repressed economy, however, is high and unstable fiscal deficits, as portrayed in Figure 10.2 by the neighbourhood around point $C$. Together with an appropriate foreign exchange policy, to be discussed in Section IV, the repressed economy can limp along at points of minimal inflation such as $C$ – unless the consolidated public sector finances, inclusive of hidden credit subsidies, go wildly out of control.[6]

## IV  THE CASE FOR EXCHANGE CONTROLS

In a repressed economy, how best might foreign exchange policy complement the domestic financial strategy outlined above? On the one hand, the monetary technicians will wish to ensure that the ongoing inflation tax does not fall unduly heavily on the foreign sector: exporters should be protected. On the other hand, given the quota restrictions and high tariffs on international commodity arbitrage, the management of the foreign exchanges should not create additional monetary instability in the economy. We suggest that these goals can best be accommodated by: (i) imposing strict exchange controls on outflows *and* inflows of capital; and (ii) indexing the exchange rate to the domestic price level by a passive downward crawl. Consider, first, the case for two-day exchange controls on international flows of *private* capital. Part of the ongoing fiscal deficit could be financed abroad by the government negotiating directly with foreign creditors. We assumed above, however, that a substantial proportion of the ongoing fiscal deficit had to be financed by taxing the domestic financial system. Obviously, real yields on currency and term deposits, denominated in domestic money, say, pesos, are thereby depressed. Depositors would purchase substitute financial assets denominated in a 'hard' foreign money (usually dollars), unless prevented from doing so. Hence exchange controls on capital outflows from repressed economies are quite common – and tight controls are appropriate as long as the domestic financial system is being taxed.

What is less obvious, however, is that potential private *borrowers* from the domestic banking system can evade the tax by obtaining foreign credits. In the domestic market for term deposits and loans, we showed that reserve requirements interacted with the rate of inflation to drive a wedge, equation (9″), between bank lending and deposit rates. By forcing higher interest rates on to borrowers, the government extracts more revenue for a given rate of inflation, *and* real yields to depositors hold up somewhat better. If, instead, businesses could freely borrow abroad, the domestic real loan rate would be reduced, along with revenue to the government and yields to depositors. In effect, the term-deposit part of the domestic monetary tax base ($kD/P$) would be unduly eroded unless such private foreign borrowing was restricted.

Because the governments of repressed economies often consider themselves to be short of foreign exchange, they are more likely to encourage rather than discourage inflows of private capital – even though such inflows are artificially stimulated by the domestic inflation tax. Indeed, if the government is fixing the exchange rate (see below), such private capital inflows directly augment official exchange reserves. In this case, the loss of real revenue from the domestic financial system is manifest in the higher rate of base-money creation (inflation) coming through the foreign component of the domestic monetary base. Thus, if private capital inflows are not restricted outright, they should be taxed by reserve requirements or similar measures, so that the net tax burden on firms that borrow abroad is roughly equated to the 'wedge effect' imposed on those that must borrow domestically.

To get its hand on foreign exchange, the government should borrow directly under official auspices – rather than depend on using private borrowers as financial intermediaries. Although private borrowing may give the appearance of augmenting official exchange reserves, it effectively lessens proceeds from the domestic inflation tax.

Modern examples abound of countries taxing their domestic financial systems, while not realising the importance of two-way exchange controls for maintaining the tax base. To cite but two examples:

(1) In late 1977, *Israel* precipitously abolished exchange controls on residents holding foreign currency deposits or borrowings abroad – but the real size of its fiscal deficit remained unchanged. The domestic rate of inflation, which had been running at about 30 per cent per annum over 1974–6, then accelerated to over 100 per cent per annum in 1978–80. The smaller size of the domestic financial system required that the rate of price inflation be much higher to extract the same real revenue.

(2) While still running a substantial (consolidated) fiscal deficit, *Argentina* in 1977 and 1978 loosened its controls on capital inflows and outflows. Moreover, in 1979–80, Argentina reduced reserve requirements on all classes of bank deposits. These premature measures eroded the real size of the taxable part of the domestic financial system. The resulting inflationary explosion was temporarily forestalled in 1979–80 by fixing the exchange rate, which inevitably became overvalued. But, in 1981, the fixed exchange rate system broke down, and domestic inflation accelerated dramatically.

As a postscript to these rather sad episodes, observers should remember that allowing an (untaxed) foreign-currency component of the domestic financial system to develop *within* the country is just as bad as allowing free international inflows and outflows of capital. Not only Israel and Argentina, but also countries such as Peru, Mexico and Uruguay, have permitted substantial 'dollarisation' of their economies to occur. This then greatly narrows the local currency part of the domestic financial system, and sets the stage for unnecessarily violent inflationary explosion if and when fiscal control is lost. If the government develops an uncovered fiscal deficit that can no longer be financed abroad or by issuing dollar securities at home, then the necessary issue of base money in local currency will lead to much greater price inflation.

Allowing (untaxed) dollar bank accounts to develop within the country can often be justified on the grounds of short-run expediency – for example, in encouraging migrant workers or capitalists to remit their foreign exchange earnings. But, once in place, a large foreign currency component in the domestic financial system has the characteristics of an economic 'time bomb'.[7]

Clearly, monetary technicians should view exchange controls as an integral part of the financial management of a repressed economy.

Only *after* very substantial fiscal, monetary and foreign trade measures have been taken to relieve that repression, should such restrictions on international inflows and outflows of capital be removed. It remains doubtful, however, whether free transactions in foreign-currency deposits and loans within the domestic economy could ever be justified. Even the ultra-liberal Chilean government restricts domestic banks from offering residents dollar term deposits at market rates of interest.

## V  INDEXING THE EXCHANGE RATE: THE 'PASSIVE' DOWNWARD CRAWL

An immediate consequence of imposing exchange controls in a repressed economy is that the central bank must 'make' the market for foreign exchange. Private foreign exchange dealers, banks or multinational firms cannot do so, because the exchange controls prevent them from moving capital into or out of the country. Potential private dealers cannot freely assume positive or negative positions in foreign exchange (against the domestic currency) and thus are not collectively capable of establishing a market-clearing exchange rate. 'Non-speculative' merchants are not by themselves capable of making a stable foreign exchange market (McKinnon, 1979, ch. 7). Without direct government participation, therefore, the exchange market would be highly illiquid and hopelessly unstable.

Given the necessity of intervention, should the government establish an official parity or be a market maker within a no-par regime? How often, and by what procedure, should the exchange rate be adjusted – if ever? We suggest that the foreign exchange rate in a repressed economy should be unified and *passively* adjusted to whatever degree of inflation tax – possibly zero – is being levied on the domestic financial system. Unlike the situation in an open economy, a passive downward crawl need not add to the dynamic instability of an inflation-prone economy, in which foreign trade is substantially restriced by quotas and high tariffs and in which capital flows are blocked by exchange controls. Consider how a number of countries – Chile, Brazil, Peru, Portugal and others – have sometimes indexed against domestically generated price inflation by continuously adjusting the 'nominal' exchange rate in order to stabilise the 'real' one.

Suppose $E$ is the nominal exchange rate in pesos per dollar, and $P^*$ is the foreign price level in dollars, and $P$ is the domestic price level in pesos. Even if $P$ and $P^*$ are based on internationally tradable goods, commodity arbitrage is too weak to link foreign and domestic price levels at the prevailing exchange rate. The prevalence of quota restrictions (QRs) and redundantly high tariffs implies that the 'law of one price' need not hold naturally:

$$P \neq EP^* \qquad \text{Imperfectly commodity arbitrage.} \qquad (14)$$

In effect, QRs convert most potentially tradable goods – whose domestic prices would normally be determined by international arbitrage – into 'pseudo non-tradables' whose domestic prices are determined mainly by national supply and demand considerations (McKinnon, 1979). Hence, domestic price inflation, as measured by the left hand side of equation (11), may proceed independent of the right-hand side, unless the authorities consciously manipulate $E$ to offset it. Why might they wish to do so?

Most such economies still depend heavily on unprotected export activities that must sell their products at world prices. In addition, some import substitution industries may still face unrestricted competition from abroad. To stabilise the cost–price relationships for these few genuinely tradable activities national authorities would like to maintain the 'real' exchange rate at a predictable level.

$$e - EP^*/P \qquad \text{Real exchange rate.} \qquad (15)$$

For a given foreign price level, any upward movement in $P$ could be quickly offset by an upward adjustment in $E$. The competitive position of exporters is then protected: the rigid real exchange rate ensures that a variable inflation tax does not fall unduly heavily on them. Exporters are taxed (along with everybody else) in so far as they hold domestic currency or borrow from the domestic financial system, but they are *not* taxed when foreign exchange is translated back into the domestic currency. There is not an unpredictable cycle of overvaluation (high domestic inflation and a fixed exchange rate) coupled with discrete massive devaluation and a period of currency undervaluation.[8] In effect, an official commitment to indexing gives exporters valuable forward assurance that their domestic prices will not change capriciously relative to their costs of production. Because of this insulation from monetary or foreign exchange instability, investment in export activities can be undertaken more efficiently.

In the presence of ongoing and independently determined inflation in domestic prices, such indexing implies a passive and variable downward crawl in the exchange rate – a continual increase in $E$. Yet the authorities cannot announce the official exchange rate on a completely mechanical basis. First, there may be more than one price index for measuring '*P*'. A broadly based index of tradable-goods prices would be preferable. However, a consumer price index may be the only comprehensive one available, and still worth using if price inflation is at all significant. Then there is the question of what adjustment should be made for 'international' inflation in *P**. Often the price levels of trading partners do not move in unison: nevertheless, some appropriately simple weighting system is not difficult to establish.

Secondly, the authorities should not adjust the exchange rate discretely every month. Rather, if the domestic price index jumped 6 per cent in a month, as announced on a particular day, the resulting 6 per cent adjustment in the exchange rate would best be smoothed over thirty days, with adjustment of, say, 0.2 percentage points per day. In the classic mode of the crawling peg, this would minimise the propensity of traders to undermine the exchange controls and to speculate on discrete exchange-rate changes. Each small movement in the rate is not worth the transactions costs of taking a speculative position.

If discrete changes in the monthly price indices are highly variable – say 6 per cent one month and 2 per cent the next, and the authorities can rationalise why any one month might be 'unusual' – then some *ad hoc* inter-month smoothing of the variable crawl is warranted. However, the basic objective should be well advertised: to adjust the nominal exchange rate at deliberate speed by the extent to which domestic price inflation exceeds that of the trading partners to which the currency is pegged.


## VI  CURRENCY SUBSTITUTION AND FINANCIAL INSTABILITY: REPRESSED VERSUS OPEN ECONOMIES

Would not such a variable downward crawl further exacerbate domestic financial instability? Besides being an important political symbol, a fixed exchange rate is often deemed necessary to stabilise price-level expectations and to give confidence in the government's financial future. While more or less correct for a fully open economy, this traditional view is invalid for a repressed economy that is insulated from financial and commodity arbitrage with the outside world and must resort to the inflation tax. Far better to regularise the inevitable exchange adjustment in a series of small steps that are reported only in the back pages of the newspapers – rather than to endure the periodic massive devaluation, following an earlier squeeze on exporters, that is a threat to both political and economic stability.

First, consider why exchange controls on capital accounts facilitate the management of an indexed exchange rate. Suppose our hypothetical price index is published on 1 August and shows 6 per cent inflation for the month of July – a substantially higher rate of inflation than the monthly average of 3 per cent experienced in the first half of the year. Everybody now knows that the government is committed to speeding up the rate of mini-devaluation – the downward crawl in the 'near future'.

Despite the continuing domestic price inflation, suppose the authorities were operating this indexing procedure for a completely open economy *without exchange controls*. In the first half of the year, firms and individuals would have adjusted their portfolio holdings of currency and term deposits, and the rate of interest on term deposits and loans would be determined endogenously, on the basis of a relatively low anticipated rate of inflation and exchange depreciation. On 1 July, however, the expected (smooth) rate of exchange depreciation suddenly increases. Because individuals are unrestricted in their foreign currency holdings, the demand for domestic money will fall sharply in favour of foreign exchange assets. For an open economy, the demand functions for currency and term deposits – equations (5) and (6) – would have to be respecified to include the expected rate of exchange depreciation, $\dot{E}/E$, as an important determining variable. The upshot would be that destabilising currency substitution (in either direction) would occur continually as the government varied the rate of downward crawl without imposing exchange controls. (These short-run effects would be additional to the 'long-run' shrinkage of the domestic monetary base, due to individuals avoiding the domestic inflation tax by holding foreign exchange assets.

International currency substitution, in response to predictable exchange-rate changes in an open economy, may occur both directly and indirectly. *Direct substitution* out of domestic currency (and demand deposits) into foreign currencies is one channel, but it is one mainly confined to international traders with working cash balances,

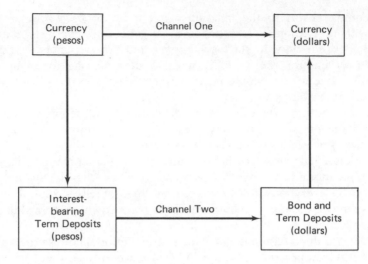

FIGURE 10.3 International currency substitution in an open economy

both at home and abroad. Currency, narrowly defined, does not bear any (protective) market-equilibrating rate of interest which can dampen such switching.

Less obviously, *indirect substitution* occurs within the domestic financial system as people move from currency to term deposits. With free international financial arbitrage, domestic nominal rates of interest on term deposits and loans will increase in response to the anticipation of more rapid exchange depreciation. This induces the broad mass of domestic transactors to move out of currency – which has a high reserve requirement – into term deposits, with a lower reserve requirement. Through this second, and probably more important channel, the demand for domestic base money again falls and capital flows out. Both channels are portrayed in Figure 10.3.

Clearly, given *predictable* alterations in the speed of downward crawl in the exchange rate, unrestricted international currency substitution would seriously destabilise the short-run demand for domestic base money. And our proposed indexing procedure would be predictable. Such a system may well be dynamically unstable, unless the government maintains the strict exchange controls on both capital inflows and outflows that are appropriate for managing a repressed economy.

Similarly, international arbitrage in the *commodities market*, through an indexed exchange rate, has different implications for an open economy compared to a repressed one. Consider again a small increase in the domestic price index that induces offsetting (indexed) devaluations. In an open economy, these are more likely to cumulate over time because there are no quota restrictions or licenses to inhibit international commodity arbitrage. The resulting mini-devaluations quickly feed back into domestic prices and accentuate the initial inflationary impulse – whether this is random or not. This requires further mini-devaluations, according to our indexing procedure. The rate of domestic price inflation is now no longer an independent datum to which the exchange rate passively adjusts. Rather, the exchange-rate movements themselves directly accentuate domestic price fluctuations as well as destabilising the demand for money (as described above). For an open economy, the intuitive opposition of government officials to such an indexing procedure is well founded.

For a repressed economy, however, international commodity arbitrage is (by definition) blocked. Feedback effects, from passively adjusting the exchange rate to the domestic price level, are largely absent – except for the influence of those few 'open' categories of exportables and import substitutes that the government wishes to protect by maintaining their real exchange rate. Otherwise, domestic prices of the more typical quota restricted goods are well insulated from the *immediate* consequences of exchange-rate changes. Instead, the economic rents accruing to quota holders – giving the implicit or explicit market value of a license to import – fluctuate with the exchange rate.

This simple point is illustrated in Figure 10.4 where a typical quota restricted import good, $X$, is considered in a partial equilibrium situation. $E$ is the domestic currency price of foreign exchange; $P^*$ is the foreign price of good $X$; $t$ is the ad valorem licence premium; and $D$ net excess demand for $X$. Only 500 units of $X$ may be imported over the time period for which its net domestic demand, $D$, is drawn. At point $A$, $D_1$ is such that the domestic price is exactly equal to the foreign price at the beginning exchange rate $E_1$: the value of an import licence is exactly zero.

Now suppose an inflationary surge in demand to $D_2$, that raises the domestic price of $X$ and all similar goods. At point $B$, if the old exchange rate $E_1$ holds, then a premium of $t$ per cent develops on a licence to import $X$. However, if our indexing procedure comes into play, the exchange rate is adjusted upward from $E_1$ to $E_2$. Notice that the only effect of this exchange rate increase is to eliminate the licence premium: there is no further upward movement in the dom-

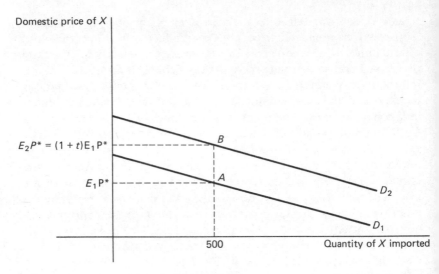

FIGURE 10.4

estic price of the commodity. Hence, the exchange-rate adjustment does not contribute to the inflationary momentum in the prices of such pseudo non-tradables.

Unlike their colleagues in open economies, the monetary authorities in a repressed economy seem well in placed to manage an indexed exchange rate. Moreover, to keep the inflation tax as 'pure' as possible, other officially controlled prices in the economy could be subject to the same quantitative indexing procedure. If the government is maintaining price ceilings on a few basic foodstuffs, official prices for public utilities, or minimum wages, all should be subject to continual small changes of a similar nature. However, this presumes that *most* domestic prices are not set directly by the government, so that continuing market-determined price inflation can provide an *independent* datum for the indexing authority.

## VII   A CONCLUDING DISCLAIMER ON ECONOMIC REPRESSION

In LDCs, the repression of foreign trade and of the domestic financial system is commonplace. International agencies and foreign academic advisors often react to this situation by advocating the liberalisation of trade, financial and fiscal processes. If this difficult transition to a liberalised economy could be successfully effected, the empirical evidence does indeed suggest that the economic welfare of the average citizen would improve dramatically.

But what is 'rational' and devoutly to be wished in a successfully liberalising economy, may be counter-productive in a repressed one. For a given fiscal deficit, financial guidelines have therefore been proposed for minimising the necessary rate of price inflation without penalising exporters unduly and without crowding-out the private capital market more than is necessary. The main elements in this second-best strategy for managing a repressed economy are:

(i) Nominal interest restrictions should be replaced by direct interest subsidies from the fiscal authority to specifically preferred borrowers. The resulting 'true' fiscal deficit could then be calculated more accurately, once interest rates are freed.

(ii) In the 'open' part of the capital market, a comprehensive non-interest bearing reserve requirement against term deposits should vary directly with the size of the fiscal deficit.

(iii) Both inflows and outflows of private capital to the rest of the world should be subject to exchange controls or reserve requirements.

(iv) The exchange rate should be indexed, through a passive downward crawl, if the minimum necessary rate of domestic inflation exceeds that of the country's principal trading partners.

If the basic fiscal constraint – the continuing deficit – is not eliminated, it could be economically disastrous to 'liberalise' by reducing reserve requirement, by removing exchange controls, or by slowing the rate of depreciation to below what the indexing procedure would warrant. Securing adequate control over the domestic price level by slowing depreciation or fixing the exchange rate, requires a fiscal surplus and a concurrent movement to free trade – if serious overvaluation is to be avoided.

By thus avoiding premature liberalisation, our repressed economy can still limp along in a second-best way without becoming dynamically unstable. The principal continuing costs are a 'wedge' in the domestic capital market between deposit and lending rates of interest; a rigid real exchange rate that reflects the economy's inability automatically to adjust the trade balance to capital flows; and the ongoing microeconomic distortions in the import competing and export sectors, with which we are so familiar.

NOTES

1. Somewhat surprisingly, it turns out that no necessary conflict exists between minimising inflation and limiting crowding out. To be sure, the fiscal deficit ensures that there will be some crowding out and some inflation. As long as the monetary technicians allow the banking system to issue term deposits that are free of interest ceilings (but not reserve requirements), however, minimising the inflation rate need not lead to undue crowding out – as will become clearer later on.
2. Remember, in a repressed economy there is no open-market rate of interest on 'bonds' that is the opportunity cost of holding 'money', in the conventional sense of Keynesian liquidity preference analysis.
3. The deposit rate of interest has been left out of the function describing the demand for loans, and the loan rate of interest has been left out of the demand for deposits, because the qualitative direction of either effect is unclear.
4. I would like to thank Leslie Lipschitz for pointing this out.
5. The inappropriate but standard textbook model of the money multiplier may be an important reason why Chilean authorities in 1976 and 1977 kept reserve requirements too high despite the marked improvement in their fiscal situation.
6. Our analysis of optimal inflationary finance omitted the important random or stochastic elements in the consolidated public sector deficit. For a given $k$, the wedge between deposit and loan rates of interest will be sensitive to inflationary pressure, and will thus accommodate unexpected changes in such pressure to a limited extent. The absence of general interest ceilings on the term-deposit part of the market gives the system additional flexibility.
7. A felicitous phase owed to Jacob Frenkel.
8. This argument is a bit oversimplified. In so far as there exist substantial ongoing restrictions on imports coming into the domestic economy, even an equilibrium exchange rate associated with balanced trade will be biased against exporters. This bias can only be eliminated under full trade liberalisation. An indexed exchange rate merely avoids additional (cyclical) unplanned bias against exporting.

REFERENCES

Bhagwali, Jagdish (1978) *Anatomy and Consequences of Exchange Control Regimes* (New York: National Bureau of Economic Research).
Brock, Philip L. (1982) *Optimal Monetary Control during an Economic Liberalisation: Theory and Evidence from the Chilean Financial Reforms*, unpublished Ph.D. thesis, Stanford University.
Friedman, Milton (1971) 'Government Revenue from Inflation', *Journal of Political Economy* 79, July/August, pp. 846–56.
Krueger, Anne (1978) *Liberalisation Attempts and Consequences* (New York: National Bureau of Economic Research).

Mathieson, Donald (1979) 'Financial Reform and Capital Flows in a Developing Economy', *IMF Staff Papers*, September, pp. 450–89.

McKinnon, Ronald I. (1973) *Money and Capital in Economic Development* (Washington DC: Brookings Institution).

McKinnon, Ronald I. (1979) *Money in International Exchange: The Convertible Currency System* (New York: Oxford University Press).

McKinnon, Ronald I. (1979) 'Foreign Trade Regimes and Economic Development: A Review Article', *Journal of International Economics*, August, pp.429–52.

McKinnon, Ronald I. (1981a) 'Financial Repression and the Liberalisation Problem Within Less Developed Countries' in S. Grassman and Lundberg E. (eds) *The Past and Prospects for the World Economic Order*, (London: Macmillan). pp. 365–86.

McKinnon, Ronald I. (1981b) 'Monetary Control and the Crawling Peg', in John Williamson (ed.) *Exchange Rate Rules: The Crawling Peg Past Performance and the Future Prospects* (London: Macmillan).

Shaw, Edward S. (1973) *Financial Deepening in Economic Development* (Oxford: Oxford University Press).

# 11 Oil Surplus Funds: The Impact of the Mode of Placement

## Hazem El-Beblawi

UNIVERSITY OF ALEXANDRIA, EGYPT AND
INDUSTRIAL BANK OF KUWAIT

## I INTRODUCTION

The increases in oil prices in 1973–4 and 1979 led to a large body of literature, attempting to trace and understand their effects on the world economy. Frequently the analysis focused on the cost effects of higher-priced energy, with little attention given to the macroeconomic effects of the redistribution of world income and of the emergence of oil-surplus funds.

I present a different macroeconomic analysis, by emphasising the resulting income redistribution. The analysis will centre on the changed behaviour of world investment and savings aggregates rather than on the changes in oil prices themselves.

It has been suggested that economic analysis would gain increased insight, once the emphasis was laid on the asset concept as an analytical tool (Boulding, 1950). Nowhere has this been as imperative as in this case. To the extent that they do not spend on goods or services, OPEC countries actually transform their real asset (oil) into overseas financial assets. From OPEC's view point, no income is earned; there is only an exchange of assets.

Broadly speaking, assets are real or financial. Every financial asset creates liabilities of equal value, and the real assets are the ultimate wealth. Financial assets are merely claims on these real assets; in

210

particular, on the stock of capital goods. The impact of the asset concept on flow-aggregates is more significant than is usually assumed. In particular, the interactions of financial assets with savings and investment have far-reaching ramifications; the more so with the oil-surplus funds which affected both the stock of financial assets and the world's propensity to save.

The following is a macroeconomic analysis of the world economy, inspired by Keynes. The differences are, however, quite substantial. First, the savings function used here differs from the Keynesian function, with savings a function of both the distribution *and* the level of income, since the effect of redistributing world income is paramount with the oil-price increases. Second, the adjustment mechanism makes wider use of the interaction of stock and flow concepts, that is, financial assets and investment and savings flows. Third, while the whole world is a closed economy, international relations complicate the picture. In particular, balance-of-payments surplus/deficit relationships bring to the fore equilibrating forces, in a different manner from that in a closed, national economy.

The two major increases in oil prices followed a period of remarkable stability. Following a price of US$1.20 at the beginning of the century, the oil price was only about US$1.60 a barrel in 1969. The Teheran agreement in September 1970 paved the way for changes. The first round of major increases began with the October 1973 war. After quadrupling in 1973–4, oil prices remained relatively stable up to 1978, but a second round of increases was triggered by the Iranian Revolution and they increased in steps through 1979, roughly doubling by December.

The analysis here mainly concerns the first round (i.e. 1974–8), a period long enough for economic forces to work out the necessary adjustment. My basic premise is that, save for income redistribution, the world economy has undergone no *real* fundamental change, since 1973–4. *Nominal* changes in oil prices were matched by no similar real changes in the underlying resource allocation. The opposition – real/nominal – will therefore loom large here.

The world's available resource-base and technology remained largely unchanged after 1973–4, as did final demand and tastes. The world's real economy remained almost the same. Available resources, know-how used and human wants served remained more or less unchanged.

The 1973–4 oil-price increases nevertheless brought about a dramatic increase in oil revenues, and changed the oil terms of trade, and hence the world income-distribution. From no more than \$15.2bn in 1972, oil revenues reached more than \$110bn in 1974 (International Petroleum Encyclopædia, 1975). This is no place to justify the increase in oil prices, which had been artificially suppressed for over seventy years. Nor is it necessary to recall the need for a sustained price increase to make the use of exhaustible resources more rational (Solow, 1979).

The Gulf oil-producing countries enjoyed high per capita incomes prior to the oil price increase and already had a remarkably high propensity to save,[1] which the price increase could only increase. Sparsely populated and with few other resources, their domestic absorptive capacity is very limited. The increase in their domestic savings appeared, accordingly, in balance-of-payments disequilibria which gave rise to the oil-surplus funds. There are, therefore, additions to world savings in the form of foreign financial assets.

The additions are, moreover, relatively quite substantial. World oil trade increased in value from \$28bn in 1970 to \$535bn in 1980, or from 7 per cent of world trade to 21 per cent. This increase is considerably larger than the current share of West Germany or the USA in world trade: the change in the oil bill is equivalent to paying for all the exports of another USA or West Germany (IBRD, 1981). Any such change is bound to affect the functioning of the world economy. In 1974, oil-surplus funds added more than \$65bn to world savings. We may again note that in the world's largest economy – the USA – exports and private gross fixed capital formation were respectively \$110bn and \$205bn in the same year (IMF, 1974). In summary, OPEC's external savings (Petrofunds) represented over 50 per cent of US exports and 30 per cent of its private investment in 1974. True, these savings then declined to reach their low point in 1978. These developments can be considerably attributed to the mode of placement of the oil-surplus funds.

## II   OPEC'S SAVINGS: POSSIBLE SCENARIOS

Since the oil-surplus funds have added substantially to world savings, the new situation which has thus emerged needs to be fully grasped. I analyse it by starting from the Keynesian identity of *ex-post* savings and investment. This does not necessarily imply full agreement with Keynesian economics, now assaulted from almost every side. Theorists may differ on what determines savings and investment or how the economy responds to *ex-ante* changes in either of them; all agree that *ex-post*, realised savings must equal realised investment. Thus the *ex-post* equality is an accounting identity and one which has acquired a *droit de cité* in all systems of national accounts.

There is no doubt that OPEC countries increased their savings after 1973–4. Yet each act of saving is matched, *ex-post*, by parallel investment. Three possible scenarios can then be constructed in the face of the increase in OPEC savings. There could be:

(i) a parallel increase in the rate of world *real* investment;
(ii) nominal *dis*-saving elsewhere to offset the increased OPEC savings, i.e. no change in world net savings and investment; or,
(iii) an increase in financial assets, giving rise to increased *nominal* investment.

I call Scenario (i) 'the investment case', Scenario (ii) 'the distribution of wealth case' and Scenario (iii) 'the placement case'. These labels need little explanation, though we need to distinguish the French term 'placement' from 'investment'. By 'placement' I mean the purchase of financial assets: by 'investment' the use of finance to add to capital goods (Robinson, 1956, p. 8). Investment adds to productive capacity; placement only to financial assets.

It is not necessary that only one of these scenarios should result from OPEC's new savings. A combination of elements from different scenarios is always possible and, indeed, likely. It is useful, however, to analyse each case separately in order to emphasise its particular outcome.

We may note first that these scenarios differ not only in the behaviour of investment and savings but also in the relationship of financial to real assets. Whereas this relation remains largely unaffected in Scenarios (i) and (ii), it is substantially distorted in (iii), giving rise to a new structure of financial/real assets. The different character of (iii) would thus justify more detailed discussion. We now consider the scenarios in turn.

1  SCENARIO (I): THE INVESTMENT CASE

This is very interesting because it represents the ideal outcome for OPEC countries and the world at large. It implies temporary sacrifices during a transitional period, for resource reallocation.

Here, there will be a *real* response to the increase in the world propensity to save; the allocation of resources between consumption and investment shifting in favour of investment. The immediate effect of the oil-price increase would be a reduction in consumption equal to the increase in OPEC savings. There is no reason, however, why the decrease in consumption should be distributed equally between countries. It is likely that it would be distributed somewhat in relation to oil imports.

This is the true meaning of the assertion that oil-price increases imply a transfer of real resources. What is at issue is not the transfer of real resources from oil-importing countries to OPEC, as is usually maintained (Noreng, 1958, p. 133); rather it is their reallocation from consumption to investment. What is important is not who forgoes resources and to whom they go; rather, to what uses resources are allocated. It is natural, nonetheless, that the oil exporters would have substantial claims on any additional investment (in ownership and/or debt).

The reduction of real consumption in this case need not be permanent. With a higher rate of capital formation, the world would grow richer. Accordingly, previous consumption levels would, in time, be resumed and even surpassed. The world economy would move to a higher growth path (Pollack, 1975, p. 12), the transition to which would inevitably imply distortions in prices, employment, etc., before full adjustment.

The important thing about Scenario (i) is not to visualise the final outcome, but rather to identify the mechanism at work. Here, the relation between financial and real assets is of prime importance. Financial and real assets (real investment) grow together: but there is also a cause–effect relationship between them.

The logic assumes that an expansionary process is triggered by the injection of new financial assets. In fact, the increase in the OPEC surplus would increase loanable funds, that is, financial assets. When placed, these would affect the credit market, so that it 'would generally tend to be easier. Real investment would tend to increase because the desired long-term capital stock tends to increase with lower interest rates' (Hansen, 1976, p. 119). Thus the increase in world savings, following the emergence of OPEC surpluses, would mean that 'interest rates would fall just sufficiently to increase that amount of real investment' (Hansen, 1976).

It is not difficult to observe a neoclassical framework here. The interest rate plays a strategic role, reflecting the real forces in the economy and maintaining an independent behaviour *vis-à-vis* the monetary authorities. Alternatively, it is assumed that 'the monetary system operates in such a wise as to interpret and not distort the influence of real forces'. Interest rates would depend on 'the demand for and supply of investable funds. Behind the former stand the forces of productivity, behind the latter that of thrift' (Robertson, 1951, p. 193).

To sum up: in Scenario (i), increased OPEC savings (financial assets) will be matched by an increase in real investment. Financial assets would probably increase proportionately to the increase in real investment. 'With real investments running at a higher level, a continued inflow of oil exporters' funds might thus take place without further increase in the price of financial assets' (Hansen, 1976 p. 112). Changes in the rate of interest will bring about the desired increase in real investment, which assumes that both savings and investment are interest-sensitive. It is by no means necessary, in Scenario (i), that there should be a general price increase. There might be a once for all change in prices to bring about the necessary reallocation of resources, but there would be no inherent need for continuous price increases.

## 2  SCENARIO (II): THE DISTRIBUTION OF WEALTH CASE

Here, there will be no net change in global situation; only a redistribution of wealth. Scenario (ii) reflects, substantially, the general, popular feeling in the wake of the oil-price increases. A minority share in Krupp purchased by Iran; a Kuwaiti purchase of real estate in South Carolina; Libya's investment in Italy's Fiat, etc., gave support to such feelings.

This scenario does assume that increased OPEC wealth is accompanied by some impoverishment of oil-importing countries. The former will save more and the latter less. The allocation of resources between investment and consumption will remain largely unaffected; only the holders of claims on wealth will change. OPEC surplus countries will have more financial assets, the rest of the world less.

This is an extreme simplification. Some changes in industrial allocation are conceivable, indeed likely, with the change in asset holders. There is no reason to suppose that the new asset-holders will necessarily perpetuate the 'old' demand. The main feature of this case is that the *overall allocation* of resources between investment and consumption will remain unchanged, regardless of the change within each of them. The world as a whole would be neither richer nor poorer, only the distribution of wealth would have changed.

If real consumption, savings and investment remain unchanged, as this suggests, so would the volume of financial assets. There is no inherent reason why the rate of flow of financial assets should increase, nor why general prices should change. There is a change only in holders of financial assets.

Although this outcome is simple to conceive, it is difficult to think of a mechanism to bring it about. What is needed is a mechanism whereby oil-importing countries would have to finance their oil deficit by handing to OPEC financial claims on their domestic wealth.

In fact, most oil-importing countries would resist this situation. OPEC countries would also be extremely reluctant to accept it; they have shown great discretion in these matters. Scenario (ii) was therefore very unlikely to take place. It is difficult to think of a smooth mechanism to bring it about: and all the interested parties were opposed to it. The most publicised scenario is thus the least likely.

In the two previous cases, financial assets were introduced in a non-fundamental way. The world economy adjusted through changes in real aggregates; the increase in real investment in (i) and the redistribution of wealth in (ii). Nevertheless, financial assets were instrumental in bringing about real adjustment. In these two scenarios there is a direct relationship between real investment and the flow of financial assets. Financial assets increase with the increased real investment in Scenario (i): they remained constant – though in different hands – in Scenario (ii). In both (i) and (ii) the relationship between financial and real assets remained roughly the same.

3 SCENARIO (III): THE PLACEMENT CASE

The characteristic feature here is that the relationship between real investment and the flow of financial assets is broken. Financial assets would increase independently of real investment and set the world economy in motion; they are, therefore, introduced more *fundamentally*. Adjustment to OPEC savings is financial, rather than real.

Scenario (iii) assumes both a largely unchanged overall allocation of resources between investment and consumption after the oil-price increase *and* that no *apparent* dis-saving elsewhere follows the increase in OPEC's savings. The scenario opens a new course of action through the behaviour of financial assets and its impact on *nominal* rather than *real* aggregates.

Given a general reluctance to transfer wealth to OPEC and/or to reduce consumption levels, deficit countries would issue *new* financial assets which OPEC countries would hold. The supply of new financial assets would thus be matched by a new OPEC demand for them. On the face of it, everything seems to be in order. OPEC countries increase their savings and hold a preferred form of wealth, free of political animosity; oil-importing countries minimise the transfer of real resources. But this cannot be the whole story. OPEC savings seem to be increasing with no corresponding increase in real investment or any offsetting dis-savings. This is impossible, since the *ex-post* accounting equality of investment and savings must always hold. If real aggregates fail to react to the change in OPEC savings, we are left with nominal changes which bring costs and prices to the forefront.

An increase in the financial assets held by OPEC means a corresponding increase in deficit countries' *financial liabilities*. If OPEC countries choose to hold their savings in the form of new financial assets, it is because they intend to receive a reasonable return on them (for a similar argument, see Pasinetti, 1974, p. 106). Since we assume that the real capital stock has not changed with the issue of new financial assets, that capital stock will be owned more widely.

The new wealth-owners are obviously entitled to a nominal return on their assets equivalent to that on the 'old', that is, new financial assets produce the same nominal yields as 'old'.

How do these new nominal returns compare with the old? One could argue that this increase in loanable funds would depress nominal returns, but one must then refer back to the initial situation (see Hansen, 1976). Starting from a 'quasi-equilibrium', the increase in oil import bills caused a higher demand or loanable funds. The issue of new financial assets started, then, from a situation of financial squeeze, not excess liquidity. It is therefore hardly conceivable that the nominal yields of the new financial assets should settle below prevailing ones; eventually they would be higher. Also, a well-known lesson of monetary history is that any economic disturbance leads to a crisis of confidence and a rise, not a fall, in interest rates (Robinson, 1971, p. 84). The banking system would probably generate the required liquidity. The military/political situation when the 1973-4 oil-price increase took place, with the accompanying oil embargo is, probably, an economic and confidence crisis *par excellence*. We may therefore assume that the increase in financial assets with the emergence of OPEC's savings does not reduce nominal returns on them but rather that these would increase. We are faced with a downwards stickiness of nominal returns, a phenomenon not very different from Keynes's assumption of downward rigidity of money wages. It follows that there will be a corresponding increase in absolute nominal earnings from property titles (loosely defined as the share of profit). This cannot fail to affect the structure of output distribution and of factor earnings.

Empirical investigation shows a remarkable historical constancy in three basic macroeconomic ratios; the rate of profit; the capital/ output ratio; and the share of profit (wages) in output. The merit of the Cambridge/neo-Keynesian school is to have drawn attention to this constancy and to have developed growth models accounting for it (Kaldor, 1957). Since these ratios are mutually interdependent, the system is overdetermined: the constancy of two ratios implies that of the third. Moreover, given the historical constancy, we can reasonably assume that all three ratios remain constant.

We cannot reconcile our two assumptions – the rigidity of nominal returns on financial assets and the constancy of these basic ratios – without introducing other changes, that is, in prices and costs. Under the first assumption, an increase in financial assets (liabilities) with rigid nominal returns, should increase the share of profit. Under the second assumption, this should not affect the constancy of the basic ratios. The only way out is for prices to change so as to increase the *nominal* values of other aggregates sufficiently to give both the absolute nominal increase in financial returns and the constancy of the ratios. A general price increase can both maintain the ratios constant and simultaneously service larger returns on financial assets. This is *inflation*. Changes in the stock of financial assets cannot avoid having an impact on the nominal values of output and investment.

Even those who challenge the statistical validity of the aforementioned constancy concede the following. The unstylised facts about capital output ratios justify little more than an agnostic conclusion about the distribution of income. But there is quite strong and general evidence that labour benefits at the expense of capital, rather than that distributive shares are stable (Hacche, 1979, p. 299). With this assumption, the previous conclusion will be more imperative and the general price increase more pronounced. Prices have to rise even further, to give the absolute nominal increase in returns on financial assets (share of profit), while allowing for a growing relative, and absolute, share of wages in income.

Prices are thus introduced as the final element in a chain of reactions to the increase in OPEC savings. Though real investment does not increase, nominal investment, under inflation, does grow. The sacred identity between saving and investment is rescued, albeit in nominal terms.

Here we find inflation built into Scenario (iii) in order to bring about the equality of savings and investment. Failing to increase real investment or to effect parallel dissavings, the only possibility is to increase *nominal* investment. Inflation is the villain of the drama, but without it there would be no drama at all.

The precise mechanism for propagating inflation can differ. It can be channelled through monetary, fiscal instruments or both. The financial assets (liabilities) increase can be bank deposits, treasury bills, bonds or similar instruments. In either case the money supply or budget deficit will grow substantially, causing inflationary pressures.

I emphasise that in this scenario the role of inflation is different from that under the much-publicised allegation that oil-price increases are responsible for world inflation. It is not the oil-price increase *per se*, but a particular mode of investment of oil surpluses, that is responsible for inflation. In 1974, only 2.4 per cent of the US increase in prices could be explained by oil-price increases, and similar conclusions have been reached for other OECD countries (Merklein and Hardy, 1977). Ours is a macroeconomic interpretation of inflation based on the need to increase nominal rather than real investment, so as to match the increase in OPEC savings. This differs from a microeconomic cost-push approach, which attributes the increase in inflation to increased energy cost. The difference also extends to the cure. If inflation were the villain it could be controlled, according to the microeconomic approach, simply by reducing oil prices and, according to the macroeconomic approach, by increasing world real investment.

Before proceeding, a word of warning is necessary. It would be a grave mistake to lose a sense of proportion. Inflation is a world problem to which various factors contribute; domestic factors are the most prominent. Since I deal with oil funds and their investment, it is natural to focus on their impact on inflation.

## 4 INSUFFICIENT INVESTMENT AND INFLATION

What I am trying to convey in Scenario (iii) seems at odds with established Keynesian doctrine, which holds that an increase in *ex-ante* savings over investment is deflationary, not inflationary. Scenario (iii) suggests, on the contrary, that if not matched by an increase in real investment, OPEC's increased savings are inflationary. We should have expected the opposite.

This is a very serious point indeed. The clue to the apparent contradiction may, however, lie in the origin of OPEC's savings.

They are realised through a change in income distribution and forced exogenously upon the system.

Since there has been no major, short-period change in the distribution of income in industrial countries, standard Keynesianism though recognising the importance of income distribution, would postulate savings as a more or less stable function of the *level* of income.

In a nutshell, Keynesian economics sees investment as an independent variable, invariant to changes in savings. But savings depend on income. Hence, if investment were to fall short of *ex-ante* savings, income would have to decline to bring savings down. This decline (deflation) is necessary to bring *ex-post* equality of savings and investment.

But if increased savings result from a redistribution of income and not a rise in income, deflation is not inevitable. By analogy, if investment fell short of savings, a reverse distribution of income should take place to undo the excess savings. A general price increase, particularly for non-oil commodities, could well reverse a redistribution of income brought about by increased oil prices. An increase in financial assets and the revaluation of nominal returns on them could be the trigger-mechanism. With inflation, a new mechanism to reverse the change in income distribution is set up.

Whatever the source of OPEC's increased savings, savings remain a function of income. The traditional Keynesian diagnosis is not altogether irrelevant and an excess of savings over investment is still deflationary. The fact that increased OPEC savings are due to income redistribution does not preclude the simultaneous dependence of savings on income. The 'income distribution' variable supplements, but does not supplant, the 'level of income' variable and this accounts for the ambivalent impact of increased OPEC savings. They are mainly inflationary, but also partially deflationary. To undo OPEC's excess savings would require both a reversal of the distribution of income, and a decline in its level. Thus, in Scenario (iii) OPEC savings are stagflationary, with more pronounced inflationary pressures (El Beblawi, 1981).

## III   WORLD EXPERIENCE 1974–8

I shall not give a comprehensive survey of world economic experience since 1973–4, much less a thorough statistical analysis. A bird's-eye view can, however, help to fix our ideas on world economic adjustment to the oil-price increases. Observation suggests that, of my three scenarios, the 'placement case' probably gives the best description of the adjustment process in 1974–8. Data on investment rates, inflation, financial asset-flows and OPEC surpluses provide ample support for this.

After 1975, world real investment showed no marked rise, following the rise in OPEC savings. On the contrary, it was disappointingly low. It became almost a ritual for international economic organisations to regret the low rate of fixed investment, particularly in the OECD countries which received the bulk of OPEC savings. I quote from IMF annual reports;

> [The] further deceleration or decline in the volume of private investment during the latter part of 1971 and early 1975 was the most direct and obvious manifestation of monetary restraint. (IMF *Annual Report*, 1975)

> Real gross fixed investment (including residential construction) declined sharply in each of the past two years. (IMF, *Annual Report*, 1976)

> A major factor in this outturn was the disappointing behaviour of private gross fixed investment which had been showing its customary cyclical lag behind the rise in general economic activity . . . the unusual behaviour of private investment must in general be attributed to investors' cautiousness in face of inflation and other economic or political uncertainties. (IMF, *Annual Report*, 1977)

> In most of the industrial countries, levels of private fixed investment during 1977 and the first half of 1978 were very low in a medium-term perspective. (IMF, *Annual Report*, 1978)

IMF reports are, by no means, a lone voice. The same message is found in reports of the OECD, IBRD, BIS and GATT as well as of central banks. Real investment showed no perceptible increase after the oil-price increase; rather it slackened.

A 'transfer of wealth case' also seems remote from experience.

Although concern was expressed at one time that the newly rich oil-producing countries would buy up massive blocs of American business, this in fact has not happened. Reflecting their desire for safe, relatively liquid investments and for anonymity, they have placed most of their excess financial reserves in bank deposits, short-term Eurodollar loans, etc., although it seems reasonable to expect them to move increasingly in the future toward government bonds and other longer-term portfolio investments. (US Department of State, 1976)

Other evidence suggests that this remained true for almost all OPEC surplus countries in 1974–8.

Against sluggish GDP growth and slack real investment, flow of financial assets increased enormously. Since the total spectrum of financial assets is very broad indeed, it is difficult to survey the development of all forms of financial assets – a task commensurate to constructing a flow-of-funds statement for the world economy. With small variations, however, the amounts of different financial assets move in the same direction. It suffices, therefore, to study simple indicators for the increase in world financial assets. The growth of the Euro-currency market and of individual countries' indebtedness indicates, to some extent, what happened. These two indicators are, incidentally, directly related to OPEC surplus funds. Both show that the value of financial assets has been soaring, following the increase in OPEC savings.

Statistics on the size of the Euro-currency market differ greatly, depending on the definitions used (gross, net), area covered, etc. It is estimated that the gross value of Euro-currency passed the $1trn mark in June–September 1979 (International Herald Tribune, 1981). Its net size grew from $12bn in late 1964 to $475bn in December 1979 (IMF, 1980). Since 1973, the average annual rate of growth in the Euro-currency market has been about 22 per cent. It is probably ironic to recall that when the IMF met at Nairobi in late 1973, it was widely believed that Euro-currencies would soon disappear (Healey, 1979–80). In fact, the Euro-market was preparing a giant step forward.

The increase of public foreign debt, particularly of the Third World, was no less dramatic. From less than $70bn in 1970, the outstanding medium- and long-term debt of the LDCs reached $438.7bn in 1980 (World Bank, 1981).

The behaviour of interest rates is also worth noting. Concurrently with the increased flow of financial assets, interest rates went up substantially. The United States, the major beneficiary of OPEC funds, set the pace. In the spring of 1974, US rates rose to what was then a record high level. They were: 8 per cent for the discount rate; 13.5 per cent for Federal Funds; about 12.5 per cent for deposits; and around 13 per cent for the bankers' prime lending rate (BIS, 1975). Rates of 18–21 per cent have since become commonplace in the USA and other countries followed suit.

As for price stability, it is true that world prices – especially for food – were already moving up before the 1973–4 oil shock. However, only since then have we witnessed a sustained price increase. From less than 7 per cent in 1973, already high by previous standards, the rate of inflation in industrial countries averaged 13.5 per cent in 1974 (IMF, 1974). Despite a fall in 1975, it remained rapid through the late 1970s (IMF, 1976).

Two-digit inflation, once the prerogative of Latin American economies, became an everyday phenomenon, Latin Americans being promoted to three-digit inflation. There are, of course, great disparities among nations, but everywhere an upward trend was introduced. The Swiss were best with a low growth ratio, the Germans were second with about 5.3 per cent. The UK and Italy trailed behind the rest of the industrial countries, while the USA, long accustomed to price stability, had to accommodate itself to a 13–15 per cent annual rate of inflation.

OPEC's savings were affected adversely by inflation. From about $65bn in 1974, the OPEC current account balance declined steadily. In 1978, it was estimated at $18bn before official transfers, and only $5bn after them. The decline in OPEC surpluses does not result only from increased real imports; it is also the result of a downward trend in the real oil price (Willett, 1979). It is estimated that OPEC prices declined in real terms by 25 per cent against the dollar between 1974–8; by 40 per cent against the Deutsche Mark; and by 30 per cent against the Yen (Brown and Kahn, 1980). It thus seems plausible to conclude that the world reacted to the increased OPEC savings in a 'placement case' mode.

## IV  THE IMPACT OF THE MODE OF PLACEMENT

The emergence here of the 'placement case' is not fortuitous. It is related to the way OPEC savings are used and in particular whether they were placed (in DCs) or invested (in LDCs). This basic decision has far-reaching effects on the world economy and on how OPEC's savings can themselves be sustained. What is important is where the savings are used *initially*.

Out of an estimated $180bn of OPEC surplus funds at the end of 1978, only $30bn – less than 20 per cent – seems to have been allocated directly or indirectly by OPEC, through the World Bank and other multilateral lending institutions, to LDCs (see, *Financial*

*Times*, 1978 and IMF, 1977).[2] The rest went to OECD countries and their financial institutions.[3]

It is fairly easy to find the reasons for this. Partly it was a matter of necessity. The increased oil prices surprised everyone, including OPEC countries. Few, if any, LDCs were prepared to absorb a large amount of the new wealth. The breadth and depth of financial markets in the OECD countries, and especially the USA, made it much easier to place funds with them. Moreover, conventional wisdom advocated that OPEC countries would gain enormous economic benefits by investing in the OECD. Opportunities for investment are greater, techonology is available, creditworthiness is much higher and more secure, and financial markets are highly organised. The LDC's situation is almost the opposite (El-Beblawi, 1982). Large-scale recycling 'to less developed countries soon would be faced with demands for lower interest rates, moratoria and so forth that would challenge the very principle on which all these schemes are based, i.e., loans at commercial rates' (Hansen, 1976, p. 47). There is, of course, no denying the badly needed *political* leverage that OPEC countries can obtain from investment in LDCs. However, this should be weighed against the *economic* advantage that OPEC countries obtain from investment in OECD countries. The trade-offs determine the mix of oil funds invested in the two areas. This is, broadly, the conventional wisdom and it is largely shared, usually implicitly, by officials responsible for using OPEC funds. In the event, the major share of OPEC funds was placed in the DCs – 'the placement case'.

Choosing whether to recycle oil funds into DCs or LDCs amounts, in fact, to opposing Keynes' 'effective demand' against 'Say's Law'. It has been argued that while Keynesian economics approximates the situation in DCs, classical economics better describes the LDCs Rao, 1959). For Keynes, investment is the exogenous variable that is determined independently: savings will adjust to it. For the classics, on the contrary, once savings are available, investment seems to follow suit, whence their insistence on the savings decision. To Keynes, 'A fresh act of saving' means a net reduction in effective demand. Future demand, implicit in the behaviour of savers, is not effective demand to which investment can respond. It gives producers no 'signals' that could tell them where to re-employ resources freed from producing consumer goods (Leijonhufvud, 1969, p. 37). This is, more or less, the case of DCs, but the situation in LDCs is diametrically opposite. Many investment projects are held back for lack of finance. Demand, effective or otherwise, is not really their problem, because the supply of available resources limits their investment. If savings are available, investment will not be a real problem. This does not, of course, mean the Third World development depends only on the availability of finance. Development is a complex process involving institutional, cultural and political changes as well as finance. It remains true, however, that the possibilities for increasing real investment in LDCs are huge, but need finance in order to be started up.

It follows that placing OPEC funds in the OECD countries cannot increase real investment without changing effective demand in favour of more investment goods. Failing to do this, the OECD countries cannot increase real investment simply because financial resources happen to be available. An increase in financial assets would trigger inflation, much as in our 'placement case'. This is a matter of structure, not policy.

Investing OPEC funds in LDCs would, however, have brought the missing link. Given the existence in LDCs of huge investment needs lacking finance, OPEC savings would have been used to increase real investment. This would, inevitably, have led to enhanced demand for OECD capital goods and, given enough time, capital goods industries in OECD countries would have expanded – our 'investment case'. It is not far-fetched to conclude that the world has realised 'the placement case' rather than 'the investment case' largely because we have recycled oil funds to DCs not LDCs. The latter not only receive aid for political reasons; they could also be indispensable agents for bringing about the necessary shift in effective demand and hence matching OPEC's savings with increased real investment. OPEC's need to recycle its savings to developing countries does not stem from political considerations alone; it is of major economic significance for maintaining the real value of OPEC's wealth. The partnership of OPEC and the LDCs is more fundamental than appears at first sight.

It is ironic, however, that wherever OPEC chooses initially to place its funds, OPEC will end up with the LDCs as its partners. The need for a deal between them becomes more imperative.

## V  THE INCREASING DEFICIT OF THE LDCs

It seems that there was, before the oil shock, a relatively constant structure of trade relations. OECD countries as a group had a favourable current account; non-oil LDCs incurred the counterpart

TABLE 11.1    SHIFTS IN THE GLOBAL CURRENT ACCOUNT
BALANCE

|  | 1967–72 | *average* | |
|---|---|---|---|
|  |  | *At 1977* |  |
|  | *Actual* | *prices* | *1977* |
| Major oil-exporting countries | 0.7 | 3 | 42 |
| Industrial countries | 10.2 | 30 |  |
| Non-oil developing countries | −9.8 | −33 | −39 |
| Total | 1.1 |  | 3 |

*Source: IMF World Survey*, May 1977.

deficit. OPEC countries were in balance – with a small deficit in 1970 and a surplus of about $5bn in 1973. This surplus averaged $10bn in the years 1967–73. Non-oil LDCs incurred a deficit almost as large.

This situation was suddenly disrupted after 1973–4. The OECD countries, being the major oil importers, shifted from a surplus of about $9.5bn in 1973 to a deficit of $28bn in 1974. The deficit of the non-oil LDCs doubled to $20bn in 1974. (Chenery, 1975, p. 247). OPEC countries were, of course, the beneficiaries, their 1974 current surplus jumping to over $60bn.

All these figures are, of course, subject to the usual shortcomings of error, omission and different statistical definitions, with resulting discrepancies between figures for individual countries and for the whole world. The important thing is that these figures trace the broad direction of change.

The immediate changes in world trade, in 1974–5, were only a *first step* in the long process of evolution to a new structure. Less than five years later, OECD countries had adjusted in such a way that they reached virtual balance in 1978 (*Economist*, 1979).

Non-oil LDCs were the losers. OECD countries still took more than three-quarters of world oil imports, while maintaining an almost balanced current account in 1978. The LDCs, with an unchanged share in oil imports, ran a 1978 deficit of $34bn (Table 11.1).

The new structure of the world's current accounts thus seems to have settled down to rough balance for the OECD countries; a more manageable OPEC surplus; and a corresponding LDC deficit (Bhattacharya, 1977, p. 11). Hence it is natural that financial flows will move to the LDCs. This is what has happened. During 1974–5, OECD commercial banks financed about 45 per cent of the LDCs' current deficit: the annual amount of their new financing for LDCs has not since fallen below this level (World Financial Markets, 1979). Of OPEC's net deposits of $30bn in the international banking system in 1979, some $24bn was rechannelled to LDCs (BIS, 1980).

Clearly, OPEC surpluses are largely used to offset LDC deficits. OPEC funds placed *initially* in OECD financial institutions were partly channelled to the LDCs.

How far does this affect our argument? To answer this, we need to remember two concepts about economic systems. The first is the concept of process. Economic activity proceeds as a sequence of actions and reactions; every action calls forth a specific set of economic forces from which emerges the final outcome. Initial conditions are important. The second concept is that of a circuit; different sectors are linked through the interaction in the economy – the old *tableau economique*.

## 1 THE ECONOMIC PROCESS

The path of the world economy is affected by the different economic forces involved. It cannot be indifferent to the initial actions.

We have shown that injecting oil funds initially into the LDCs would enhance world demand for capital goods, reallocating resources between consumption and investment. The world would move along a new path, with higher real investment giving rise to increased LDC imports of capital goods from OECD countries. The OECD would therefore benefit from oil funds indirectly.

This is a different path from that resulting from initially placing oil funds in the OECD, which would aggravate inflationary pressures, with increased financial assets (liabilities) raising financial charges and hence fuelling inflation. The world would move along a different path, with worldwide inflation *en route*. LDCs would now be affected by oil funds indirectly, through imported inflation and deteriorating of terms of trade, with the oil funds rechannelled to finance their balance-of-payments' deficits, not their increased investment.

The final outcome is not indifferent to the initial conditions. The way in which oil funds are placed *initially* is decisive.

## 2 SURPLUS–DEFICIT RELATIONS

It is always easy to overlook simple facts. The surplus–deficit situation is, after all, a zero-sum game. The surplus exists so long as the deficit is permitted to persist. This may seem trivial; it happens to be very important.

Broadly speaking, DCs are better able than LDCs to correct imbalances in their external accounts. Hla Myint, in a now classic article (Myint, 1958), distinguished two kinds of external vulnerability: (i) stems from the 'productivity theory of trade' where 'a country has adapted and reshaped its productive structure to meet the requirements of the export market through genuine process of specialisation'; (ii) is related to his 'vent for surplus'. A country 'happens to possess a sizeable surplus productive capacity which it cannot use for domestic production'. This implies 'an inelastic domestic demand for the exportable commodity and/or a considerable degree of international immobility and *specificness* of resources'. In general, DCs exhibit the first kind of vulnerability; LDCs suffer the second.

Increased productivity in (i) and high rigidity in (ii) largely explain the ability of OECD countries to adjust their external accounts, in due time, to the oil-price shock and the failure of the LDCs to cope with it.

In such adjustment, OECD countries have far larger flexibility than LDCs. The OECD countries' ability to redress their external account with OPEC must be limited, but they maintain a tremendous economic superiority over other LDCs. Changes in terms of trade seem to be directly related to the degree of economic development. Though their share of oil imports remained modest, LDCs were seriously hit because of the deterioration in their terms of trade. This was more true with the lower-income, oil-importing LDCs. These countries had shown a quite impressive performance, increasing the *volume* of their manufactured exports by 90 per cent during the 1970s. In terms of export purchasing power, more than two-thirds of this volume-increase was offset by a decline in relative prices. Middle-income oil-importers among LDCs raised the volume of their manufactured exports by almost 300 per cent and lost less than one-third of this through relative price decline. For all oil-importing LDCs, the unit purchasing-power of their non-fuel primary exports fell by 28 per cent; of their manufactured exports by 24 per cent. The low-income oil-importers were hit harder by low prices (World Bank, 1981). The IMF Managing Director was thus able to assert that for LDCs

> on a terms of trade basis, the cumulative loss incurred in the seven-year period 1973–79, was of the order of $80 billion. Although much stress has rightly been laid on the effect of oil price increases on the import bills of developing countries, it should be

borne in mind that oil still accounts for only about one-fifth of the current account deficit of the LDCs. Thus, the current account deficits of the LDCs have also been raised considerably by the general inflation in countries which export manufactures.[4]

It therefore seems that, given the actual world economic structure and the dominant economic status of the OECD, it is the LDCs that are bound to incur, in the final analysis, the counter-deficit of the OPEC surplus. Acknowledgement of this is bound to be of utmost importance to OPEC investment policy. 'It is the poorest industrial countries and the LDCs which have had to carry the largest share of the importing countries' deficit' (US Senate, 1977).

The LDCs are, in fact, the ultimate debtors for OPEC's financial claims, whose real value cannot be separated from the creditworthiness of the LDCs. OPEC countries thus have a definite economic interest in the prosperity of the LDCs. Financial institutions are so closely interwoven that any default or failure of substantial magnitude by the LDCs will undoubtedly affect OPEC financial assets. The same financial institutions that receive the bulk of OPEC surplus funds extend loans to the LDCs. Any disruption of the international financial market will set in motion a chain reaction, similar to the 'domino-effect' in political theory. Indeed, OPEC countries have a direct stake in the economic health of the LDCs.

OPEC countries would indeed be called upon to assist the LDCs in case of any serious failure by LDCs to honour their obligations. Since the world cannot afford a serious upheaval in international economic affairs, a possible reason behind the so-called 'Witteveen facility' was the increase in the borrowing by some LDCs (e.g. Zaire) from the international capital market. Its extent was such that it could have affected some major international and American banks. The OPEC countries are of course *en tête* with countries contributing to this facility. It is therefore probably an illusion to think that OPEC's risks are reduced by the intermediary role played by OECD financial institutions.

## VI CONCLUSION

OPEC surplus countries, particularly in the Arabian Gulf, emerged in 1973–4 as a world financial power. The oil-price increases introduced far-reaching financial and monetary rearrangements worldwide.

Money and finance are undoubtedly powerful instruments for affecting real resources, which alone are ultimate wealth. However, without a parallel rearrangement in real resources, they risk remaining sterile.

Establishing a new international order based 'less on power and status, more on justice and contract, less discretionary, more governed by fair and open rules' (Brandt Commission, 1980), is no doubt a meritorious undertaking. My intention here is less ambitious and more down to earth. Rather than reforming the world in a philanthropic vein, I discussed OPEC's external investment from a perspective of self-interest. This could be less noble, but stands on firmer ground.

Developed countries seem to offer OPEC surplus countries better opportunities to invest. Yet reality is far more complex than appears at first sight. What appears to be common sense may turn out to be utter nonsense.

As oil-based economies, the Gulf States' future depends on their ability to conserve their wealth. The only rational policy to enhance their interests is to follow a *conservation policy* in a large sense. This does not necessarily imply holding oil in the ground; it means, in particular, being able to conserve the real values of all assets, be they oil or financial claims.

With financial assets, this cannot be realised unless they maintain their value in terms of real assets. From the economic point of view, what matters is not the accumulation of financial assets *per se*, but the implicit deferred transfer of real assets involved. For OPEC surplus countries, what matters is their ability to transform, in the future, their financial wealth into goods and services without loss. Inflation is thus the *bête noire* for any holder of financial assets, particularly a major holder of nominal securities as with OPEC countries.

The DCs can only perpetuate the financial character of OPEC financial wealth. The easy façade of investing oil funds in rich, creditworthy and secured OECD countries conceals their eventual erosion. Motivated by self-interest, their placement in the OECD countries is self-defeating. The LDCs, with all their shortcomings, can offer OPEC surplus countries a chance of transforming the *financial* phenomenon of oil into a *real* phenomenon. What seems to be a disinterested act of moral commitment towards brotherly poor countries may be the only way to preserve the value of OPEC's financial wealth.

This is not all. Regardless of what they do with their surplus funds, OPEC surplus countries will anyway be left with developing countries as their ultimate debtors. The fate of the one depends then on the prosperity of the other.

Keynes once introduced the 'widow's cruse' and the 'Danaid jar' legends into economic literature, to depict situations in which entrepreneurs would stand to gain what they spent and to lose what they withheld (Keynes, 1930, reprinted 1971, p. 125). OPEC surplus countries seem to be in a similar situation. They gain what they 'give' to the poor and lose what they 'invest' commercially. Only an imaginative and unconventional policy for investing oil funds – to bring about a real as opposed to a financial restructuring of the world economy – can promote the interests of both OPEC and the LDCs.

'The new international economic order' is not only the fight of non-oil LDCs; it is the condition for the consolidation of OPEC gains in oil prices. A new *oil order* is not separated from it: OPEC surplus countries can play a leading role in bringing about this new order. If they do not, other will.

The LDCs are not, of course, the promised land for investment. Their development record – quite impressive in the 1960s, but less so in the 1970s – leaves much to be desired. The odds against secure and successful investments in the LDCs are substantial. Not only the inadequacy of infrastructures and lack of qualified manpower, but particularly inefficient management and political instability, impede any sustained development effort in the LDCs. A single country – even an oil-rich country – cannot assume all the hazards of investment in the LDCs. *Collective OPEC action is needed.*

The challenge is formidable, yet the rewards promise to be worthwhile!

NOTES

1. In Kuwait, for example, the propensity to save in 1950–70 was between 40 and 45 per cent of GNP (see Ragei El Mallakh (1968) *Economic Development or Regional Cooperation: Kuwait* (Chicago: Chicago University Press), p. 81.
2. See also Senator J. Javett's speech on the floor of the Senate, *Danger on the International Economic Front*, 8 February 1978.
3. See *World Financial Markets* (1979) July. Saudi Arabia, for instance, has chosen to invest around 85 per cent of its funds in the USA and in deposits in Euro-banking markets; see Fred Bergsten (1980) *U.S.-Saudi Economic Interests* (New York: American Association for Commerce and Industry).
4. See the address by J. de Larosière, the IMF Managing Director before the Economic and Social Council of the United Nations, Geneva, 4 July 1980. *IMF Survey*, 7 July 1980.

REFERENCES

*Bank for International Settlements* (1975) Annual Report, no. 45.
Bank for International Settlements (1980a) cited in *International Herald Tribune*, 25 February.
Bank for International Settlements (1980b) Annual Report, no. 50.
Bhattacharya, A.K. (1977) *The Myth of the Petropower* (Lexington. Mass: Lexington Books).
Boulding, Kenneth E. (1950) *A Reconstruction of Economics* (New York: Wiley).
Brandt Commission (1980) *North–South, A Programme for Survival* (Brandt Report), (London: Pan Books).
Brown, William and Herman Kahn (1980) 'Why is OPEC Vulnerable', *Fortune*, 14 July.
Chenery, Hollis B. (1975) 'Restructuring the World Economy', *Foreign Affairs*.
*The Economist* (1979), 17 March.
El Beblawi, Hazem (1981) *International Finance Markets: The End of Stability?* Bulletin of the Industrial Bank of Kuwait, no. 2.
El Beblawi, Hazem (1982) 'The Predicament of the Arab Gulf States: Individual Gains and Collective Losses', in *Rich and Poor States in the Middle East* (ed.) M. Kerr and S. Yassin, (Boulder, Col: Western View Press).
Financial Times (1978) *Banking Survey*, 22 May.
Healey, Denis (1979–80) 'Oil Money and Recession', *Foreign Affairs*.
Hacche, Graham (1979) *The Theory of Economic Growth* (London: Macmillan).
Hansen, Bent (1976) 'The Accumulation of Financial Capital by the Middle East Oil Exporters: Problems and Policies', in A.L. Udovitch (ed.) *The Middle East: Oil, Conflict and Hope* (Lexington, Mass: Lexington Books).
IBRD (1981) *Annual Report*, p. 17.
*IMF (1974) Annual Report*, p. 1.
*IMF (1976) Annual Report*, p. 4
IMF (1977) World Financial Survey, (Washington DC: IMF).
International Monetary Fund (1980) *International Capital Markets,* Occasional Paper, no. 1 (Washington DC: IMF).
International Petroleum Encyclopedia (1975) (Oklahoma Petroleum Co.).
Kaldor, N. (1957) 'A Model of Economic Growth', *Economic Journal*, vol. 61.
Keynes, J.M. (1971) *A Treatise on Money*, vol. 1; 1st edn. 1930 (London: Macmillan).
Leijonhufvud, Alex (1969) *Keynes and the Classics* (London: Institute of Economic Affairs).
Merklein, Helmut A. and Hardy, W. Carey (1977) *Energy Economics* (Texas: Gulf Publishing Co.).
Myint, Hla (1958) 'The Classical Theory of International Trade and Underdeveloped Countries', *Economic Journal*, vol. 68.

Noreng, Oystein (1958) *Oil Politics in the 1980s* (New York: McGraw Hill).
Pasinetti, Luigi L. (1974) 'Growth and Income Distribution', in *Essays in Economic Theory* (Cambridge: Cambridge University Press).
Pollack, Gerald (1975) *Are the Oil Payments-Deficits Manageable?* Princeton Essays in International Finance, no. 111). (Princeton NJ:
Rao, V.K. (1959) 'Investment, Income and the Multiplier in Underdeveloped Countries', in Agrawala and Singh (eds) *Economics of Underdevelopment* (Oxford: Oxford University Press).
Robertson, Dennis H. (1951) 'Some Notes on the Theory of Interest', in *Money, Trade and Economic Growth*, Essays in honour of John Williams (New York: Macmillan).
Robinson, Joan (1956) *The Accumulation of Capital* (London: Macmillan).
Robinson, Joan (1971) *Economic Heresies, Some Old-Fashioned Questions in Economic Theory* (London: Basic Books).
Solow, Robert M. (1979) 'The Economics of Resources or the Resources of Economics', *American Economic Review*, vol. 69, May.
US Department of State (1976) *The United States and the Third World*, Discussion Paper (Washington DC: US Government Printing Office).
US Senate (1977) *International Debt, the Banks and U.S. Foreign Policy*, Committee on Foreign Relations, Sub-Committee on Foreign Economic Policy, a staff report (Washington DC: US Senate), p. 33.
Willet, Thomas D. (1979) 'Structure of OPEC and the Outlook for International Oil Prices', *The World Economy*, vol. 2, no. 1.
World Bank (1981) *Annual Report*, p. 12, 15.

# 12 External Financing and the Level of Development: A Conceptual Approach

**Robert Z. Aliber**

UNIVERSITY OF CHICAGO, USA

## I INTRODUCTION

One of the most striking differences between the developing and the industrial countries involves the structures of their financial systems. As per capita incomes increase, financial structures expand rapidly. Thus, in the developing countries, the ratio of money to national income ranges from 10 per cent at low levels of per capita income to 30 per cent at higher levels. Similarly, the ratios of financial assets to national income and of indirect finance to direct finance are also significantly higher in the industrial countries than in the developing ones. The counterpart to a modest financial structure in countries with low levels of per capita income is extensive reliance on self-finance. Increases in these ratios, as per capita incomes increase, are associated with changes in the institutional financial structure; banks and non-bank financial intermediaries are relatively more important in the economies of the industrial countries. Moreover, the facilities for trading in various risks, including various business risks, are much more comprehensive in the industrial countries than in the developing ones.

A somewhat parallel set of statements can be made about the size of the current-account deficits of individual developing countries, and the way these deficits are financed. At low levels of per capita income, most of the financing of current-account deficits takes the form either of official economic assistance or of direct foreign investment; in both cases, these flows avoid the market processes. At higher levels of per capita incomes, however, a larger proportion of the current-account deficits are financed by market-related flows, including short-term bank funds, trade credits and long-term debt; these debt issues are sold by governments, government agencies and private firms. Finally, equity shares in the enterprises in the developing countries may be acquired by foreign investors.

Despite the strong association between the expansion of the financial sector and increases in per capita income, the dominant analytic strain in development economics slights the relationship between financial structure and economic growth. These models project an equilibrium path for the growth of income on the basis of a savings–income ratio and an investment–income ratio. Among the assumptions implicit in these models are that there is one homogeneous investment good, one borrower-investor, one saver, and that this saver acquires debt sold by the investor, without being deterred by transaction costs or by a concern with various types of risk. Such models illustrate the macroconditions necessary for steady-state growth; these models ignore that the sufficient conditions for growth are not met, as well as the distortions within the financial sectors. Moreover, these models posit current-account deficits of the size associated with steady-state growth, but ignore the capacity of the country to finance the requisite deficits.

Both in industrial and in developing countries, the financial sector acts as a proxy for conditions in the 'real' economy. The financial sector of the economy might be considered developed if Paretian-type equivalence relationships were satisfied both among savers and among borrowers, as well as between individual borrowers and individual savers. Thus, the rate of return on any one investment would not differ significantly (especially when judged on a risk-adjusted basis) from rates of returns on all other investments. Similarly, returns to any one saver would not differ significantly from returns to all other savers, again on a risk-adjusted basis. Moreover, returns to savers as a group would not differ significantly from returns to investors as a group. Finally, rates of return on domestic investment would not differ significantly from those on comparable foreign investments.

Financial markets are integrated to the extent that these Paretian conditions are satisfied; there are then few 'corners of inefficiency' where returns are significantly higher, or significantly lower, than those generally available in the economy. Financial markets in the developing countries are characterised by extensive segmentation; savers face limited options and frequently realise negative real returns, while funds are allocated to borrowers on a basis other than the size of the potential rates of return they might earn on new investments. There is more self-finance and less reliance on the market; financial flows are 'internalised' within economic units. Finally, rates of return in many developing countries, especially those with relatively high rates of growth of per capita income, appear significantly higher than rates of return in the industrial countries, and there are significant differences in the returns available in different industrial countries – say, USA, Sweden and Japan.

Financial development consists of enlarging the scope of market opportunities available to savers and to investors by reducing and eliminating their segmentation, both in a domestic and an international context. Integrating the segments of the financial markets contributes to the increases both in levels of income and in the growth of income. It does so both by leading to distributions of savings and investment that are more nearly Paretian-efficient, and by leading to an increase in the savings ratio.

The association between increases in per capita income and the expansion of the financial sector raises a number of critical policy issues. The emphasis in policy partly depends on whether a demand-side or a supply-side explanation for the relative expansion of the financial sector is more nearly relevant. The demand-side explanation is that higher ratios of money, financial assets and indirect finance to income are a result of the increase in investor-demand for these assets which occur as per capita incomes increase; the institutional structure responds to these changes in investor-demand for money and other financial assets. The supply-side explanation for the expansion of the financial sector is that the increases in the supplies of these assets generated by the financial institutions is a response to a reduction in the costs and the risk of financial intermediation as per capita incomes increase. Similarly, the increase in the size of the current-account deficits of individual developing countries, as their per capita incomes increase, might be a result either of an increase in the demand for external funds, or, alternatively, of a reduction in estimates of the costs and risks associated with flows of external finance of different types.

This paper develops the parallelism between the expansion of domestic financial structures as per capita incomes increase and the changes that occur in the size and the financing of the current-account deficits of individual developing countries. Section II discusses the economic consequences of distortions in domestic financial markets and on the boundaries between domestic and external markets. It considers possible causes of these distortions, both those due to market imperfections and those due to government policies. Section III develops a typology for changes in the size of the current-account deficits of individual developing countries as their per capita incomes increase, and for changes in the pattern of financing of these deficits.

## II  THE CONSEQUENCES AND SOURCES OF FINANCIAL SEGMENTATION

The reason why the ratios of money to income and of financial assets to income are lower in developing than in developed countries – for a given level of saving – is that savers and firms 'internalise' rather than 'externalise'. Savers acquire real assets on their own, rather than acquire financial assets issued by banks and other financial institutions. Hence anticipated rates of return on financial assets are lower than anticipated returns on real assets purchased directly. This preference for self-finance must indicate that savers attribute costs and risk to the acquisition of assets such that these dominate the advantages of liquidity and diversification. Somewhat similar costs and risks may deter flows of funds across national borders, and lead to an unusually large share of direct foreign investment – the international counterpart of self-finance – in the flows that occur.

If the savings ratio is taken as given, the segmentation of financial market results primarily in a misallocation of savings and of investment. Some investors are able to borrow less than they would be able to do in a Paretian world, but others are able to borrow more. Segmentation affects the composition of investment; certain investors are 'subsidised' by the segmentation of financial markets, while others are 'taxed'. To the extent that there is a shortage of term loans, or working capital, or equity capital, or agricultural credit within a developing country, there must be a corresponding surplus of credit for housing, or industry or for some other sector. Similarly at the international level, segmentation affects the distribution of investment among countries, but not the aggregate worldwide level of investment. The consequences of such segmentation on the aggregate level of income both within countries and among countries, is the product of the difference between the marginal rates of return earned by those investors who are 'taxed' and those who are 'subsidised'.

The larger the tax-subsidy impacts resulting from the segmentation of financial markets, the more untenable the assumption that the savings rate can be taken as given. If segmentation were extensive, the average rate of return on investment would increase, the rate of return to savers would increase, savers would acquire more financial assets and, indeed, the savings rate would increase. Moreover, if segmentation were less extensive, the flow of external funds to the developing countries should increase.

Segmentation distorts numerous margins: between private borrowers and public borrowers; among private borrowers because of differences in their effective tax rates; between self-finance and indirect finance; between indirect finance and direct finance; between debt finance and equity finance; between inflationary finance and non-inflationary finance; and between domestic finance and external finance.

The significance of these distortions at various margins could readily be analysed with the McDougall argument about the gains from international investment. The costs of segmentation depend on differences between the marginal products of low-productivity undertakings and the marginal products in higher-productivity undertakings.

The segmentation of financial markets might be a result of market imperfections or of government policies. The function of finance is to collect savings from a multitude of households, and allocate these savings to a much smaller number of investors. The channels for these flows include self-finance, indirect finance and direct finance. Indirect finance involves banks and non-bank financial intermediaries. Direct finance involves open-market paper, term loans, bonds and equities. Changes in the relative importance of these components of financial flows, as levels of per capita income increase, might reflect several factors. The first is that investor-demand for different types of asset may change as incomes increase; the implicit assumption here is that the relative supply prices of different channels of finance are constant. The second is that relative rates of return or risk on different types of asset change because of changes in the cost of intermediation or because of changes in risk assessment.

One source of segmentation involves transactions costs. These market-oriented costs might include the difference between the price at which an asset can be purchased and the price at which the same asset can be sold. These transactions' costs should be considered separately from the costs of intermediation. The transactions' costs are incurred both when savers acquire assets issued by banks and other financial intermediaries, and when these assets are sold. Even if there are no apparent transactions' costs the issuer of securities incurs these costs, and adjusts the returns paid to investors accordingly. Transaction costs thus reduce the return on direct finance relative to that on indirect finance. At national borders, transactions' costs involve the costs of buying and selling securities issued by borrowers in the developing country, whether denominated in their own currency or in the dollar, mark, or any other international currency.

A second market-type factor leading to segmentation is the cost of intermediation. This cost reflects the difference between the interest rate that the intermediaries receive when they lend, over the interest rate that they pay savers. The higher this cost, the greater the encouragement to self-finance and to direct finance. This cost might be high either because the absence of effective competition means that intermediaries within the developing countries realise some benefit of monopoly profits, because the intermediaries are inefficient or because they are subject to a declining cost-function.

Intermediaries (indirect finance) provide numerous advantages relative to direct finance: they provide investors with greater liquidity, lower transactions costs and risk diversification. Nevertheless, investors may prefer self-finance if the risks and costs of indirect finance are high. Savers are concerned with the future returns available on indirect finance because many of the borrowing firms will be new and untested. Moreover, savers may have no good way of 'policing' the management and owners of the intermediary institutions, in order to be sure they do not favour themselves at the expense of investors.

In addition to these market sources of segmentation, there may be some policy sources, as a result of government intervention in various markets. Thus, government-imposed reserve requirements are a tax on the deposits of the institutions which sell the issues in question, and lead to an increase in the costs of intermediation. Government ceilings on interest rates distort margins. Government tax policy may lead to significant difference in the pre-tax returns on different investments. Government intervention in the foreign exchange market may distort rates of return on both domestic and foreign investments; the maintenance of an overvalued currency increases the return to labour and reduces the return to capital, and thus constrains the incentive for private capital-flows internationally. Moreover, uncertainty about future exchange rates creates an incentive for capital to flow out to profit from anticipated devaluations.

## III   THE LEVEL AND COMPOSITION OF FLOWS OF EXTERNAL FINANCE

The unanticipated development in the flow of funds to the developing countries has been the surge in the availability of finance, mostly since the sharp increase in the price of crude petroleum in 1973–4. The increase in the current-account deficits of many of the developing countries has exceeded the increase in their oil import bills, despite the loss of real income associated with the adverse movement in the terms of trade. While the developing countries were adversely affected by the increase in the price of oil, they benefited from changes in world financial structures attributable to OPEC surpluses. What must be explained is why the OPEC shock appears to have been associated with such a sharp increase in the flow of external funds to developing countries. The oil-price shock may have quickened a change in the pattern of flows of funds to the developing countries that was otherwise inevitable. What must be explained is whether the sharp increase in that flow of funds was more a response to the increase in the supply of funds, or to the increase in the demand for them.

The international counterpart of the explanation of this expansion of the domestic financial structure as per capita incomes rise is a typology of flows of different kinds of external fund to various developing countries, as the levels of per capita income change. This typology indicates the changes in the magnitude of the current-account deficits of individual countries at different stages of development, as well as the changes in the relative importance of the various flows of external funds – official assistance, direct foreign investment, bank credits and portfolio capital – that finance the current-account deficits.

The domestic counterpart to changes in the current-account deficit involves the relationship between the level of per capita income and the savings ratio, while the domestic counterpart to the second issue is how much of national saving is allocated in self-finance, how much in indirect and how much in direct finance.

Over the long run, the volume of financing for the current-account deficits must match the size of these deficits. In short periods, however, a country increases its holdings of international reserves if the volume of financing exceeds the current-account deficit; in contrast, if the volume of financing is smaller than current-account deficit, the country's holding of international reserves declines. Changes in holdings of reserves occur because the current-account balance is determined by the international competitiveness of domestic goods, while the flows of particular types of external funds are determined by anticipated yields on each of these types of investment relative to the risks.

Each developing country has access to a worldwide pool of capital, which is extremely large relative to its own needs for external funds. The flow of funds to each developing country during any one period is determined by the relation between the yields on the various types of investment available in this country and the yields on similar investments available both in other developing countries and in industrial countries. Most international flows of funds, except for official assistance, are responsive to yield differentials. And the age of flows of official assistance is inversely related to the ability to attract external funds on the basis of yield; for as countries demonstrate that they have greater ability to attract funds on the basis of yields, the volume of official assistance is reduced. In effect, countries are 'graduated' into the market.

Flows of funds to the developing countries encounter unique risks not associated with domestic finance flows. These include foreign exchange risk, which involves uncertainty about changes in exchange rates, and political risk, which involves uncertainty that changes in exchange controls will delay or prevent payments of interest and principal; the borrower may have adequate funds denominated in his own currency available for these payments, but may still lack access to foreign exchange. Moreover, sovereign risk involves uncertainty about the stability of the government, and whether successor regimes will honour the external financial commitments of their predecessors. The one risk in common both to domestic and foreign loans is project risk: will the borrowers be able to earn enough on the investments to repay the external loans on schedule? The key question about flows of international finance is whether these risks are appropriately priced. If not, the policy question is whether measures might be undertaken to reduce investors' assessments of these risks.

The flow of funds to each developing country reflects the financial yields available in that country and the risks associated with these investments. The structure of financial yields in each of the developing countries appears to be related both to the level of per capita income and to its rate of growth. Rates of growth of per capita income are low in countries with low levels of income, below $300 per capita. As levels of per capita income rise from the $500 to $3000 range, their growth rates also appear higher. These countries are in the early stages of industrialisation, and there is a rapid shift of labour from agriculture into industry, producing standardised products for both the home and world market. At per capita income levels above $3000 to $4000, growth rates appear to decline, perhaps because there are fewer opportunities for achieving productivity gains by shifting labour from agriculture to industry.

The implication of golden-rule models is that the level of the structure (i.e the whole complex) of financial yields in each country parallels its rate of growth of per capita income. At low levels of per capita income, the growth rate of income is low; so is the level of the structure of financial yields. Yields are determined by the return on investment (the ability to pay), not by the availability to pay. The current-account deficit is small because the country has little ability to finance such deficits. As rates of growth of per capita income increase, the level of the structure of financial yields rises and the current-account deficit increases, because the country can attract relatively large amounts of external funds.

One stylised fact about flows of funds to the developing countries is that most of the flows to the poorest and smallest of them involve official financial assistance, usually on concessional terms. Flows of yield-sensitive funds are trivial or non-existent, because levels of yield are too low relative to risks. Direct foreign investment may occur if there are resources to develop; the value of the natural-resource deposit (or of the concession to exploit the resource) is then determined after payment of the return required to compensate foreign investors for the risks of the investment. In effect, investors determine the amount that they will bid for the concessions on these investments on the basis of their own estimates of the value of the resources and of their own supply-price for capital on a risk-adjusted basis.

Direct foreign investment is the international equivalent of self-finance. Flows of direct foreign investment, perhaps like self-finance domestically, are a second-best option. Usually, the investing firms would prefer to borrow within the countries in which they have the projects, and so to avoid the foreign exchange risk and the political risk of the investment. However, the funds available to subsidiaries in the host country are too limited and too costly. These foreign firms take on these risks because the interest rates they would have to pay on loans in the developing country are too high, relative to the interest rates these firms pay when they borrow at home. They engage in direct finance from parent to subsidiary in the host country, because they believe that the market has 'overpriced' the risk – both the exchange risk and the political risk. The overpricing is reflected in the excess of interest rates on loans available in the developing countries relative to the interest rates on similar loans available in the industrial countries. Portfolio investors in the industrial countries still find this interest-rate differential insufficiently high to compensate for the risks involved in selling liabilities denominated in the currency of one of the industrial countries and using the funds to acquire investments in the developing countries. Before interest-rate differentials increase to the level at which these portfolio flows occur, firms internalise these flows. In effect, managers in these firms believe that portfolio investors require such a high return for bearing the exchange and political risks that they prefer to carry these risks on their own, self-finance occurs internationally because the costs of indirect finance are deemed too high. One consequence is that the return on the intrafirm loan may in fact 'subsidise' the return to the firm's project activities.

As levels of per capita income rise, and as industrialisation becomes greater, direct foreign investment in manufacturing – both for the domestic market and then perhaps for the world market – may increase. Again the foreign firms might prefer to borrow within the developing country, but interest rates seem too high relative to the rates at which they can borrow abroad.

Over time, as the rate of growth of per capita incomes in a developing country increases, relatively more of the external finance flows through the market, and relatively less involves self-finance. Changes in the level and mix of flows of funds to individual developing countries reflect changes both in anticipated yield differentials and in the estimates of foreign exchange risk and the political risk. These risks are unavoidable on all flows of external finance, except that project risks are not relevant for loans to governments, only to businesses. The story of international finance involves changes in distribution of these several risks among borrowers, lenders and financial intermediaries. Changes in anticipated yields reflect increases in the overall level of the yield structure, as the rate of growth of per capita income increases. Moderate increases in the growth rate can be associated with significant increases in the differentials between yields in a developing country and in various industrial countries; at the same time, as both borrowers and lenders develop experience with the risks involved in these flows of external finance, the assessment of risks may decline.

The assessment of risk is a function of the extent of the investment experience that the developing countries have had with international investors. These lenders engage extensively in credit rationing, rather than greatly increase the interest rate they charge borrowers with whom their experience is limited: they charge 'moderate' mark-ups, but ration the flow of funds extensively. Lenders' assessments of the risks associated with loans and credits to particular developing countries change, and usually decline, as they develop more experience with individual borrowers in particular countries. The ostensible reason for credit rationing is that lenders have a very limited basis for determining appropriate mark-ups for individual borrowers.

The growth of indirect finance, initially in the form of bank loans to governments and state-controlled enterprises, reflects two factors. One is that the returns in the developing countries may rise as the rate of growth of per capita incomes increases, and as the estimates of risk attached to loans to borrowers in these countries decline. Usually the government and government agencies are among the first to borrow from foreign banks, almost always on the basis of loans denominated in dollars or in the currency of some other industrial country. Borrowing abroad may require the approval of the exchange-control authorities, and governments usually place themselves at the head of the queues for such approvals. Moreover, a government can always ensure that it obtains the domestic currency with which to buy the foreign exchange, so that the political risk on such loans is smaller than on loans to non-governmental borrowers. The inference is that borrowers believe that the foreign exchange risk is overpriced; so they sell loans denominated in the dollar or the currency of another industrial country and acquire the foreign exchange risk. Most of these risks are relatively short term, although some may be on term loans with floating interest rates. At the same time that borrowers acquire the foreign exchange risk, lenders acquire both 'sovereign risk' and 'project risk'. Borrowers would acquire more of the foreign exchange risk if they could borrow more at the same interest rate but, because of credit rationing, they do not. In effect, they believe that the exchange risk is overpriced. They are less reluctant than lenders to bear the foreign exchange risk, and for two reasons. One is that they may believe they have offsets to this risk, and the other is that they may believe that the risk is socialised.

Subsequently, the lenders may buy loans from non-governmental borrowers, and at higher interest rates than those on the loans to governments. Lenders are attracted to these non-governmental loans because the additional interest income on them dominates both the incremental project risk and the political risk. Loans to non-governmental borrowers incur the risk that the borrowers may not be able to detain the foreign exchange needed to meet debt-service payments on schedule.

At some stage, banks with headquarters in the developing countries sell debt to the banks in the industrial countries, as an alternative both to the use of their own interbank market and to reliance on their central bank. These flows of indirect finance involve two sets of financial intermediaries: banks in the industrial countries and banks in the developing countries. Financial intermediaries in the industrial countries specialise in raising funds or selling deposits, while financial intermediaries in the developing countries specialise in the assessment of project risk in their own market areas. Loans by the banks in the developing countries are therefore to small and somewhat less well-known borrowers that do not have access to lenders in the industrial countries.

As individual borrowers in the developing countries develop credit experience records, direct finance to them is likely to increase: both borrowers and lenders will seek to 'capture' the mark-up formerly realised by banks. The increase in the share of direct finance certainly reflects this fact. One reason why indirect finance is initially more important than direct finance in flows of external assistance is that the banks may have more experience in assessing the sovereign risk and the project risk than individual lenders do: another is that banks can more readily diversify. In effect, the banks receive the mark-up over LIBOR (London Inter-bank Offer Rate) for providing these risk assessments, as well as for providing lenders with liquidity and diversification. Governments in some developing countries may sell bonds of ten or fifteen years' maturity, and denominated in the foreign currency. Non-governmental borrowers in developing countries might sell securities denominated in one of the currencies of the industrial countries; these securities would have longer maturities than those associated with loans from banks. Moreover, some lenders with headquarters in the industrial countries may begin to acquire directly securities issued by project borrowers in the developing countries as a way to profit from carrying the foreign exchange risk.

Changes in the composition of flows of funds to the developing countries thus reflect several factors. The decline in the relative importance of official assistance reflects the increase in the value of marked-induced flows. The decline in the absolute level of these flows is then a result of a weaning or 'graduation' process: just as these countries were once shifted from concessional to non-concessional funds, so they are subsequently 'graduated' from non-concessional assistance. The changes in the composition of market-sensitive flows reflects changes both in yield-differentials and in the assessment of various risks. Initially, these risks are taken by the foreign firms involved in direct ownership; subsequently borrowers acquire the foreign exchange risk. Lenders then begin to acquire the political risk. Finally, non-bank lenders begin to acquire both risks.

There is a parallelism between the patterns of domestic financial development and of international financial development. The initial reliance on self-finance reflects the fact that the costs of 'using the market' are judged to be too high; in the domestic case, high transactions' costs and high costs of assessing project risks induce the move to self-finance. At the international level, the high costs of the foreign exchange risk and the political risk lead to reliance on self-finance. The increased importance of indirect finance, and especially in loans to governments, then reflects the fact that banks are better able to assess project risks than individual investors are, and that lenders want to avoid project risks. Subsequently, loans to non-government borrowers are undertaken in order to obtain the advantage of the incremental returns on project risks.

We may ask why the sharp increase in the price of crude petroleum was associated with a significant increase in the flow of funds to the developing countries, especially in the form of bank loans suggested by this typology. The answer is that the price rise caused yield-structures in the oil-importing countries that are also developing countries to increase, relative to yield-structures in the industrial countries. This inference derives from changes in the rates of growth of per capita incomes. In the industrial countries, these declined from an unusual average of 3.9 per cent in the 1960s to 2.4 per cent in the 1970s. For the oil-importing developing countries as a group, the decline was from 3.1 per cent to 2.9 per cent (U.N. *World Development Report*, 1980, p.111).

The international banks' role as financial intermediaries increased significantly in the 1970s because the OPEC countries had strong preferences for acquiring various types of bank liabilities. Their preference was explainable in terms of a desire for diversified portfolios and their inexperience in the evaluation of credit risks. Moreover, indirect finance encountered political problems that were far less evident as compared with those associated with direct finance. As their deposits increased, the international banks increased their loans to those borrowers best able to pay the risk-adjusted interest rates. These banks had a modest preference for acquiring relatively more loans from the developing countries; rather they established risk-adjusted interest rates for various borrowers, and at these rates borrowers in the developing countries sold relatively more loans than those in the industrial countries.

This surge in loans to the developing countries has involved the assumption of sovereign risk and, to a much lesser extent, political and project risk by lenders in industrial countries. The next step in the evolving pattern of financial flows to the developing countries implies increased reliance on direct finance; lenders in the industrial countries supply funds to developing-country borrowers and to banks with headquarters in the developing countries.

From the point of view of each individual developing country, there is an infinite supply of capital. The policy problem is to attract more of it, both by raising the returns available to foreign investors and by reducing the risks encountered by borrowers and lenders. Raising the level of the yield structure is closely linked with increasing the rate of growth of per capita income. The problem may seem circular: it may seem intractable to raise the growth rate of income without an increase availability of foreign capital. Reducing investors' estimates of the risks attached to various types of capital flow may also seem intractable. Inevitably, the rate at which investors revise these risk assessments downward is likely to seem too slow from the viewpoint of the development authorities. There may, however, be a few techniques which might be used to reduce these risk assessments. Major contributions towards reducing them would come from preventing currencies from becoming overvalued, thus limiting investors' estimates of foreign exchange risk. Similarly, investor estimates of political risk would tend to decline if the authorities limited or reduced reliance on exchange controls.

## IV CONCLUSION

Flows of external funds for economic development encounter unique risks, especially the foreign exchange risk, the political risk and the sovereign risk. Investors' estimates of these risks segment financial markets in the developing countries from the worldwide market: the only risk common to both is the project risk – the risk of default or business failure. One of the central questions is whether the 'market in international financial flows' is efficient or whether, instead, it is inefficient, so that risk premiums associated with carrying these risks are excessively high.

As rates of growth of per capita income in individual developing countries increase, their current-account deficits increase. They do so because the ability to finance them increases. That increase in ability to finance deficits reflects two factors: (i) a rise in yields in the developing countries, associated with the increase in the rate of growth, and (ii) a reduction in investors' estimates of the several risks attached to these flows. Again, as the rate of growth of per capita incomes increases, the composition of the financing of the current-account deficits changes in a way that parallels the expansion of domestic financial structures as per capita incomes increases. Thus, there is an increase in the importance of indirect finance and a reduction in the amount of self-finance in the form of direct foreign investment. This is largely because of a decline in the risks and costs of using financial intermediaries. Subsequently, the share of direct finance increases relatively to that of indirect finance, as lenders seek to acquire the mark-up for diversification, liquidity, and risk-evaluation formerly taken by the financial intermediaries. The increased importance of direct finance begins to arise as investors reduce their estimates of the risks attached to securities issued by borrowers in the developing countries.

# 13 Foreign Indebtedness and Economic Growth: Is there a Limit to Foreign Financing?*

**Armin Gutowski**

HAMBURG INSTITUTE FOR INTERNATIONAL ECONOMICS, WEST GERMANY

The capacity of a country to incur debts depends, as it does for a private enterprise, on whether or not it has at its disposal profitable investment opportunities which could at least meet the interest rate demanded on the international capital market. It is obvious that the country will only then receive a loan if potential creditors are convinced that such investment opportunities exist.

## I INITIAL ANALYSIS

Let us commence by considering a simple case: a poor developing country, whose economy is in equilibrium, has as yet had no access to foreign capital. Let us assume that it has been engaged in foreign trade to a limited degree, exporting perhaps some agricultural goods and importing some textiles, and that its balance of trade is in equilibrium. For the sake of simplicity, we regard the population as being constant. Savings are considered as negligible, even with a

*I am grateful to R. Erbe, K. Fertig, H.H. Härtel, M. Holthus and S. Schattner, all at the HWWA-Institut für Wirtschaftsforschung-Hamburg, for their assistance in the preparation of this paper.

growing national income. The total labour force is assumed to be necessary to produce, directly or through international trade, those goods which are required for basic survival.

Is this country in a position to be granted a loan? Suppose there is a choice between two investment projects: the first project, a road, would primarily entail the involvement of the indigenous labour force; the second project, a textile factory, would primarily require foreign capital goods.

The amount of the loan considered would be the same for both projects. A cost-benefit-analysis may prove that both projects are profitable enough to yield the interest rate prevailing on the international capital market. If, however, the road project would induce a greater increase in the net domestic product than would the textile factory project, the country would choose to build the road and use the loan to buy foreign consumer goods, previously produced in the country itself. This would make sufficient manpower available for road construction. The new capital stock, in this case the road, would thus be a result of the utilisation of domestic physical resources ($K_d$). Should the cost-benefit-analysis come out in favour of the textile factory, the loan would be used for importing capital goods (textile machinery) produced by foreign physical resources ($K_f$). In both cases the investment is financed by foreign savings. If the road construction proves to be more profitable than the textile factory, this implies that the productivity of $K_d$ is greater than that of $K_f$, and vice versa.

After completion of the investment operation, the now-existing capital stock (financed by foreign savings) gives rise to an increase in the domestic product the value of which is greater than the amount of interest owed.[1]

(i) This increment can either consist of goods which are suitable for exporting. If investment was in a textile factory, textile goods would be exported. The foreign exchange revenue from these exports could then be used to pay interest. If investment was in road construction, transport costs in the country would be reduced. With the division of labour being improved and resources in transport being saved, more agricultural goods can be produced and exported, again the export revenue being used to pay interest.

(ii) Or the increment can consist of goods suitable for import-substitution. Textile goods, for example, which formerly had to be imported, would now be produced in the new textile factory; the foreign exchange proceeds from agricultural exports would no longer be needed to pay for imports of textile goods and could now be made available for the payment of interest. The road construction project could also lead to import-substitution, if, for example, the resources now set free by a more efficient division of labour were employed in the conventional production of textiles, thus making some textile imports superfluous.

Whichever the case, be it increased exports or import-substitution, the balance of trade must, on completion of the investment operation, come out with a surplus sufficient to cover the annual amount of interest payable, bringing the current account into balance. If other imports have to be increased because certain raw materials and intermediate products cannot be produced domestically (for example, cotton for the textile factory), these additional imports must always be balanced by additional exports or additional import-substitution, in order to maintain a trade surplus equal to the amount of interest owed.

(iii) Finally, the increment of the domestic product can take on a third form, which leaves the balance of trade unaffected. Here, no additional consumer goods would be produced for either export or import-substitution purposes; instead additional capital assets could be produced by utilising those domestic physical resources made available in the course of the investment (road or textile factory). In this case, the interest owed can be paid only if a creditor is found abroad who is willing to grant a loan on the additional capital stock. Of course, he will do this only if he is convinced that this additional capital stock will cause the domestic product to increase by an amount which is at least equal to the interest payable on the additional loan.

If this third way of utilising the domestic physical resources gained by investment is chosen, on account of its superior macroeconomic profitability as compared to increasing exports or substituting for imports, this does not mean, of course, that the problem of future interest payments is solved. Rather, in the next period, interest charges will be greater still due to the additional inflow of foreign capital. If, then, there is a lack of new projects profitable enough to meet the international capital market's interest rate, a trade surplus will eventually have to be created in order to pay the interest on the loans used to build the capital stock. The question is, at what stage does this occur?

## II   OPTIMAL LEVEL AND OPTIMAL COMPOSITION OF CAPITAL STOCK

As reality shows us, over a given period of time quite a number of investment projects can be carried out, utilising partly foreign and partly domestic physical resources, all of which will be profitable enough to reach the international capital market's interest level. The limit of a country's capacity to absorb foreign savings is reached when the rate of return on the last dollar invested in the creation of capital assets, using domestic physical resources $(K_d)$, is equal not only to the rate of return on the last dollar invested in foreign capital goods $(K_f)$ but also to the international interest rate $(r)$.

Let us assume this to be the case in year $n$. The capital stock has then acquired its optimal level and optimal composition:

$$K_{f,\,n} : K_{d,\,n} = opt.; \quad \frac{dY}{dK_d} = \frac{dY}{dK_f} = \frac{dY}{dK} = r.$$

The condition that the capital stock is optimal only when its marginal productivity is equal to the prevailing interest rate on the international capital market, is, of course, valid for all countries and not only for developing ones. The essential difference is that a developing country, due to its low saving capacity, is generally unable to achieve this optimal capital stock on its own and therefore needs to attract foreign savings to do so. This phenomenon is referred to in the relevant literature as the savings gap. In general, however, the fact that the existence of a savings gap can be established only by comparing domestic profitability with the foreign interest rate is left unconsidered. A country may well be poor and have a low propensity to save; if at the same time it has not projects which would at least yield a rate of return equal to the international interest rate, then there is no savings gap. A savings gap in one country always corresponds to a savings surplus in other countries, in which the marginal rate of return on capital would be lower than the international interest rate, if all the savings were used domestically.

Another condition – also valid, of course, for all countries – that the composition of capital stock can be regarded as optimal only if the marginal productivities of both the capital stocks, namely those created by domestic and by foreign physical resources, are the same. This poses a particularly serious problem for developing countries. On the one hand, they would not be in a position to produce the foreign capital goods themselves if they had to. On the other hand, both an unfavourable endowment of natural resources and a lack of flexibility in the structure of their economy make it possible for them to increase exports or to substitute imports in order to be able to import the necessary capital goods. The need for foreign capital independent of the savings gap is referred to in the literature as the foreign exchange gap. This gap is assessed by estimating import requirements and deducting potential exports from this estimate. To avoid a merely technical interpretation of the foreign exchange gap, one has to consider the economic aspect. Foreign indebtedness can then be justified if it can be convincingly claimed that at present (i) it would be more profitable for the country to run up debts than to finance import requirements by exporting more or by substituting for imports; and (ii) that domestic product minus interest payable to foreign creditors would still be greater than domestic product without foreign indebtedness.

## III POSSIBLE STAGES IN THE PROCESS OF INCURRING DEBTS

What are the possible stages which indebtedness could go through in a developing country, and what risks are involved therein? Let us stick to our assumption that there are no national savings ($S_d = 0$) and no consumption on credit terms. Thus total national income is consumed ($Y' = C$) and total investment is financed through foreign savings ($I = S_f$).

Let us accept the equation

$$Y = C + I + X - M \tag{1}$$

and also assume that no incomes are payable to foreign factors except interest payments on foreign debt ($Z$), that is, net domestic product equals the sum of net national product and interest payments ($Y = Y' + Z$). It follows that:

$$I = M - X + Z. \tag{2}$$

We know that $I = \Delta K_{f_k} + \Delta K_d$. Alternatively, $\Delta K_f = M^k$, which represents the import of capital goods. This means that $M - M^k = M^s$, namely, the import of all other (non-capital) goods. It then follows that:

$$\Delta K_f + \Delta K_d = M^k + M^s - X + Z \text{ and that} \tag{3}$$

$$\Delta K_d = (M^s - X) + Z. \tag{4}$$

From this, it can be seen that, before an economy reaches the optimum, the development of the course of indebtedness varies. This depends on whether it is more profitable to raise the net domestic product (i) via the production of export goods and the substitution of imports or (ii) by creating additional capital stock from domestic physical resources. We shall illustrate this with the help of two extreme cases:

Let us assume the first extreme to be case 3, as described above. The increase in total domestic production as a result of the initial investment takes the form of additional capital stock produced by domestic physical resources, instead of increased exports or decreased imports as the case may be. The growth of the capital stock created by domestic resources is then in any given year $t$ – prior to reaching the optimum –

$$\Delta K_{d,\,t} = (M_t^s - X_t) + r(K_d + K_f)_{t-1}. \tag{5}$$

It is easiest to imagine such a development taking place in a country with a very low level of development. Particularly in the early stage of indebtedness we can then expect an improvement in the infrastructure, achieved by utilising domestic resources, to have high productivity. The country will therefore import relatively few foreign capital goods ($\Delta K_f$), using the borrowed foreign capital to finance the import of consumer goods ($M_t^s - X_t$ = positive). It will augment its capital stock ($K_d$) by utilising domestic resources released from the former production of consumer goods. Provided that it is advantageous to increase the capital stock ($K_d$), then there is no harm in a country not yet being able to produce profitably export goods or products for import-substitution. It can then proceed to borrow an additional amount of foreign capital, equal to the amount of interest due.

The more developed the infrastructure has become, the more probable is a shift in the optimal composition of the growing capital stock, in favour of that part which is created by using foreign resources ($K_f$). Since the capital stock created by the use of domestic physical resources is assumed to grow in line with the continually increasing amount of interest, the import of consumer goods in order to make additional domestic physical resources available for the increase of capital stock ($K_d$) will become less and less advisable. ($M_t^s - X_t$) will therefore decrease to zero. Foreign capital goods will be imported instead. To maintain the optimal composition of the capital stock, $K_f$ must increase at a faster rate than $K_d$ until – with diminishing marginal productivity of both partial capital stocks – $K_d$ and $K_f$ finally reach the same levels of marginal productivity which, at the same time, is equal to the interest rate in the international capital market.

A further increase in capital stock is now no longer profitable, but the annual obligation to pay interest still remains. The country is in 'structural' difficulties. Devaluation of the country's currency would now be the most appropriate solution. It is true that this would make importing more difficult, facilitate exporting and make domestic resources cheaper by comparison with foreign capital goods. However, real national income would also be decreasing. The country could find itself in a severe indebtedness crisis if the substitutability of $K_d$ for $K_f$ is low and if its capacity for the production both of exportable goods and of goods substitutable for previously imported products is limited. This could occur, even allowing for a considerable deterioration in the terms of trade.

This need not be the case, though. Devaluation, with all its implications, can be avoided within the process of development if enough effort is made (and enough money is spent) to improve domestic resources. The effort must be directed in such a way that the productivity of the capital stock created by domestic physical resources ($K_d$) and therefore also its volume (with $K_f$ now growing more slowly) increases. The capital stock, foreign indebtedness, interest to be paid abroad and domestic incomes could then grow over a longer period and to a greater extent before additional exports or additional substitution of domestic output for imports become necessary for the payment of interest.

The other extreme case occurs if it proves to be more profitable to produce the increment necessary to pay interest, at all times and exclusively, in the form of import-substitution, or in the form of export products or as a mixture of both. This would particularly apply to countries where primary products are available which can be produced at comparatively low cost and for which world demand might even be expected to increase; those countries with fertile land suitable for the production of agricultural products which up to now have had to be imported, are in a similar position.

Such a country need not run into debt as much as in the previous case in order to achieve the same increase in income. Its capacity for indebtedness and its ability to create capital stock depends on the extent to which sufficient extra exports and import-substitutes can be produced to pay interest on the debt incurred. The composition of the capital stock is also relevant here, since its marginal productivity is again at its peak when an optimal combination of the two types of capital stock, $K_d$ and $K_f$, has been achieved. Once this is reached, however, no problems arise in maintaining this optimal composition while further investments are made until the country arrives at the limit for absorbing foreign savings, that is, when the marginal productivity of the total (optimal) capital stock has fallen sufficiently to correspond to the interest level on the international capital market. Any further increase in foreign borrowing, made in order to add to the existing capital stock, would then no longer be economic.

As opposed to the case previously described, indebtedness at the limit does not here pose any transfer problems, since interest due can continually be paid either from continuously earned export receipts or because of the sustained reduction of imports. The country's balance of trade will always have been improved sufficiently to allow for a continuously balanced current account, even though interest payments were continuously increasing. Even in a stagnating economy, interest payments are thus covered by the surplus in the trade balance. Again, further economic growth is possible only if the quality of domestic resources can be improved so that further capital investment becomes profitable. Of course, various combinations of these two extreme cases are possible.

In both of these cases there is not only an increase in net domestic product but also in national income (which by definition is lower than net domestic product by the interest paid to foreign countries). We can expect increasing income to lead to an increase in savings. Let us therefore remove the assumption that national savings remain at the zero level. This would mean that instead of equation (2) we have

$$I = M - X + Z + S_d \tag{6}$$

and instead of equation (4) we have

$$\Delta K_d = (M^s - X) + Z + S_d. \tag{7}$$

This means that, in all cases presented, the foreign indebtedness needed for the formation of $K_d$ can be reduced by the amount of national savings. National income then increases more rapidly, even if net domestic product increases no faster than in the cases where there are no national savings. If the optimum has been reached and saving continues, then the interest rate on national savings tends to fall below the international capital market level. Residents will react to this development by trying to invest their money in foreign currency which leads to a devaluation of the domestic currency. Capital goods and other imported goods become more expensive. It becomes profitable to increase exports, to substitute more domestic products for imported goods and to increase the utilisation of domestic physical resources to increase the capital stock. The price to be paid for this, however, is less growth (or even a reduction) in the national income, due to terms-of-trade effects. Nevertheless, a high propensity to save need not lead to payments problems.

The following however again applies: if the deterioration in the terms of trade is to be avoided, the quality of domestic resources must be continually improved. In the end, the capacity of a country to absorb more domestic and foreign savings in order to enlarge its capital stock and also its capacity for indebtedness may be limited. They can be repeatedly enhanced (beyond that level determined by the technological progress incorporated in imported capital goods) only if technological and organisational progress is achieved in the use of domestic physical resources for current production and for investment. Still, the quality of domestic resources can be improved either in order to raise exports, or to increase substitution of imports or to provide indigenous capital stock ($K_d$). These three possibilities compete, but they do not exclude each other. Unfortunately, this does not facilitate an assessment of a country's capacity to incur debts. Nor does it provide specific recipes for making decisions about what to do in order to improve the chances of growth-cum-debt, in order to avoid an indebtedness crisis. Traditional indebtedness models and criteria offer little, if any, help in this respect.

## IV RESEARCH ON THE SUBJECT

The significance of foreign capital for development has been a frequent subject of research. With respect to underdeveloped countries it received particular attention after the Second World War, when many of these countries gained independence. Primary interest at this time was directed towards foreign aid and not towards indebtedness on the international capital market; interest and amortisation payments were not taken into consideration.[2] The aim was not to find answers to such sophisticated questions as what was the optimal level and the optimal development of foreign indebtedness. The intention was rather to find out, by using models of a relatively simple type, how much foreign capital a country would need in order to achieve a given, target rate of growth.

These models were, however, also used in attempting to establish whether or not developing countries were in a position to incur debts. The basis for such models was a Harrod–Domar type of growth function, where the growth rate of domestic product is determined by the size of the investment ratio, the productivity of capital being taken as constant. As soon as the investment ratio is increased, the growth rate increases proportionately. The amount of foreign capital needed is then the difference between the amount of investment necessary to achieve the desired growth rate and domestic savings. The absorptive capacity for capital which will lead to the desired growth rate is regarded as given. The assumption of a constant marginal productivity of capital implies that the country is *either* in a position to accept an unlimited amount of foreign capital (if $dY/dK > r$) or *no* capital whatsoever (if $dY/dK < r$).

Dragoslav Avramovic,[3] in a study which can be regarded as classic, also assumed in his models a firm link between capital stock and domestic product. Making the assumption of a Keynesian-type savings function, he presented the typical stages in the process of indebtedness. He elucidated how an economy could, within one generation, attain a more successful growth path by means of borrowing, and subsequently pay back all of its foreign loans out of the increased domestic savings due to an increase in income. Such analyses made it apparent that the indicators of indebtedness usually used, above all the debt–service ratio, are not of great value. Even with the most favourable assumptions – which allow for the complete elimination of indebtedness within thirty-six years – the debt–service ratio would at times exceed values which are regarded today, as they were then, as critical.

This is hardly surprising, since these indicators and their critical values were established not by a dynamic analysis of the process of indebtedness but simply by observing economic aggregates in those countries which were forced to reschedule their debt.[4] Such rescheduling may have been the result of a rapid decrease in capital productivity or of an insufficient increase in domestic savings. In other words, it came about because the assumptions on which the country's plans relating to indebtedness were based, proved to be incorrect.

The indicators of indebtedness have been obtained by 'measurement without theory'. A mere look at the facts reveals that there are indeed countries (and always have been) that have long exceeded the critical values of such indicators, and yet still enjoy healthy growth and considerable creditworthiness. If creditors had, in fact, based their decisions on these indicators then they would have stopped granting loans, even though such countries could and should have further indebted themselves, since they had sufficient profitable projects at their disposal. The more seriously such indicator systems are taken, the more likely is the danger of 'self-fulfilling-prophecy'.

Avramovic, for his part, demonstrates a series of factors which could endanger the 'growth-cum-debt' process. The critical interest rate which he deduces from his model is, however, not very convincing, since the assumed savings function does not (as in Keynes' function) solely refer to national savings but also incorporates payment of interest on foreign capital.

The second 'classic' model comes from Chenery and Strout (1966). The main difference from the Avramovic model is that new growth-limiting factors are introduced, which result from the limited structural flexibility of developing countries. The authors assume that the volume of investment cannot simply be automatically increased from any one year to the next if complementary domestic factors are lacking (for example, human capital). Such a lack imposes a limit on the capacity to absorb capital. Growth is further limited by the fact that exports are not sufficient to pay for imports, even if sufficient domestic savings are available for financing investment (the foreign exchange gap). This model, too, gives little help in assessing the extent to which foreign indebtedness is justified and in giving guidance to policy-makers on how to increase a country's borrowing power.

Admittedly, Chenery and Strout have tried to take limited export or import-substitution capacity into consideration within the framework of their model. However, in their assumptions of a constant growth rate for exports, of a fixed relationship between domestic product and imports, and of a constant capital–output ratio, they ignore important factors. They do not bear in mind that a developing country, albeit not in the short run, has a choice between producing export goods, commodities that substitute for imports and non-tradeable goods, and that it must take its decisions according to relative profitability. The now commonly used concept of the foreign exchange gap is therefore confusing: either there are profitable projects, in which case creditors who would be willing to supply the foreign exchange necessary should be found. Or there are no such profitable projects, in which case no additional foreign loans should be granted.

Due to the assumption of limiting production relationships for the economy as a whole, none of these models is able to give information on the absorptive capacity of developing countries and, consequently, on limits to indebtedness. It is only in recent studies that this assumption has been abandoned in the interest of using functions with positive, yet diminishing, marginal productivity of capital and which give due consideration to technological progress.

With the aid of a CES production function Desai (1979), for example, takes a look at the Soviet Union and, comparing the interest rate to be paid to the internal rate of return (measured as the marginal productivity of the foreign-resource inflow), demonstrates that foreign loans should be accepted only on 'soft terms'. An exception could be made if an increase in the productivity were made possible by importing goods with a high level of technology. Desai differentiates here between the productivity of domestic and of foreign capital goods. This differentiation is not, however, found embodied in his model.

A number of authors have established in empirical investigations[5] that the inflow of foreign capital can be negatively correlated to national savings. This aspect, interpreted in the literature as a process of substitution, has been added to Desai's model by Levy (1980). Taking Egypt as an example, Levy demonstrates that part of foreign capital enters into consumption. In order to establish the limit to foreign financing, Levy relates the additional domestic product to the additional *foreign* capital and not to the increase in the capital stock. In Egypt's case there is a marginal return on foreign capital of 7 per cent, only 60 per cent of foreign capital actually being used for investment. The marginal productivity of the total capital stock, on the other hand, is 25 per cent. Capacity for indebtedness would therefore be considerably greater if all foreign credits were to be used for investment purposes. This is an interesting observation, which has to be taken into account by economic policy-makers.

## V   THE NATURE OF THE PRODUCTION FUNCTION

These recent models of Desai and Levy represent a definite improvement, in that the Cobb–Douglas and other CES production functions allow for the marginal productivity of capital and therefore permit a key factor in the capacity for indebtedness to be estimated. However, sensitivity tests reveal that the level and the development of an 'optimal foreign indebtedness' react in a very sensitive way to variations in the value of parameters in the production function. Specification of the production functions must therefore always be sufficiently precise. From our theoretical analysis of the capacity for indebtedness, we find that there are several minimum requirements for a production function. They relate both to the right-hand side of the equation (factors of production) and to the left-hand side (composition of output).

First, it would appear to be important not only to incorporate the aggregate level of capital stock into the production function, but also to differentiate between capital stock resulting from the use of domestic physical resources ($K_d$) and capital stock created by the utilisation of external physical resources ($K_f$). We are not concerned here with the financial aspect, or with property relationships, but solely with ascertaining the more technological characteristics of the different resources. Taking the factor of production 'labour' explicitly into account, the production function would then read as follows:

$$Y = f(K_d, K_f, L). \tag{8}$$

Second, the fact that, due to technological and organisational change, the production function changes over time must be taken into account. Reasons for an increase in capital productivity are:

- improvements in the quality of the capital goods imported from abroad
- an increase in the technological level of capital goods produced domestically or
- improvements in the qualification and motivation of the labour force, in management and in the allocation of resources, enabling bottlenecks to be eliminated.

The extent to which such possible components of progress in production will materialise depends considerably, of course, on the overall economic policy.

The difficulty in quantifying such sources of output growth generally leads to the incorporation of technological progress into the production function as an exogenous factor, regarded as a residual component. The results would be more informative if one could express at least some of the components of progress in an explicit manner, for example, the improvement in the average quality of domestic labour by an increase in the share of skilled workers in the total labour force. Supposing this can be done and taking the different indicators of progress $(F_1)$ into account, the production function then reads:

$$Y = f(K_f, K_d, L, F_1, F_2, \ldots F_n). \tag{8a}$$

Third, one must bear in mind that the left-hand side of the production function (total output) is not homogenous. Rather, it consists of the value added by different industries and enterprises. There are, of course, narrow limits to the possibility of disaggregation. Suppose one wants to make a successful attempt at answering the question: which development strategy can best take advantage of foreign financing? One would, at least, have to split up the production function into two partial functions; one would relate to the foreign-trade industries, including those industries which are able to produce exportable goods or goods for import substitution $(Y^A)$; the other would relate to the domestic sector, including all other industries $(Y^B)$.[6] The general economic production function would then consist of two partial production functions:

$$Y^A = f^A(K_f^A, K_d^A, L^A, F_1^A, F_2^A, \ldots F_n^A), \text{ and} \tag{8aa}$$

$$Y^B = f^B(K_f^B, K_d^B, L^B, F_1^B, F_2^B, \ldots F_n^B). \tag{8ab}$$

These partial production functions reveal the same characteristics as the aggregate production function. The factors of production used in the individual industries add up to the total factor-endowment.

Fourth, one must remember that the production function supplies information only on the relationships between factor quantities and the volume of output. For the discussion of the capacity for indebtedness, however, the quantitative relationship is not the relevant one. Even if models of indebtedness were to be developed in real terms, i.e. assuming a constant price level, one would still have to bear in mind that relative prices are subject to change. Of particular interest to any discussion on foreign indebtedness are differences in the movement of domestic prices and of international prices for goods produced and for capital goods employed. The capital productivity resulting from the production function must be corrected to take account of changes in the terms of trade; only then can capital productivity be compared to the real interest rate on foreign capital.

If statisticians and econometricians could work out a production function for a developing country which would meet these four requirements, one would be able to establish to what extent the capital stock derived from (a) domestic and (b) foreign physical resources would have to grow in order to maintain the optimal combination. One could then also state how investments ought to be distributed between the sectors producing tradeable and non-tradeable goods in order to guarantee an optimal composition of the capital stock, with marginal productivity the same wherever capital is used. Only if a country uses foreign credits for investment, and if it maintains this double optimum, will it be able to draw maximum benefit from foreign indebtedness. But if a country wishes to continue this growth-cum-debt process for as long as the relative improvement in the quality and efficiency of domestic resources makes it profitable, that will affect the structure of investment. The composition of the capital stock ($K_f$ and $K_d$), as well as the sectors and industries where the investment takes place, will have to change more or less continuously over time. And this change may not be brought about by market forces alone. It may have to be supported by an appropriate change of economic strategies.

During the early stages of a country's development and indebtedness, the production function will probably often indicate that foreign loans should be used primarily to extend and improve the basic infrastructure, e.g. in the rural sector. After a time it may turn out to be more profitable to direct new investment towards the production of goods that are import substitutes, or even goods for export, depending on the country's endowment with exploitable natural resources and other factors. For a country which has little or no natural resources and insufficient good agricultural land, it might be better to continue to invest in more sophisticated infrastructure and in the improvement of knowledge and skills of the working population for a longer period of time. This would enable the country to produce goods of a higher technological standard until it becomes profitable to establish capacity for the production of export goods.

There is no simple time pattern of strategies for developing a country's economy. The more the quality of domestic resources can be improved in relation to the improvement of foreign resources the better. This can be done in two ways: either by way of technological or by organisational progress, or by enhancing the skills and motivation of the labour force. Whichever the course chosen, the better are the prospects for accelerating the growth of national income by utilising foreign savings, i.e. by incurring foreign debt.

If a country succeeds in continuously narrowing the gap between the quality and efficiency of its own resources and that of resources in highly-industrialised countries, the share of its growing capital stock which has been built up by using domestic resources will probably increase and/or its exports of investment goods will rise. It will then no longer have to be considered a developing country.

We cannot expect to learn enough about a country's capacity to incur debt solely by looking at its production function, derived from available statistics. But we can hope to gain more information which will be a better assessment of the use of foreign financing. We can do so by detailed studies of the growth and indebtedness processes which individual developing countries (with different factor endowments) have experienced at different stages of their development. One important point, however, has always to be borne in mind. This is that the capacity for indebtedness is greatly determined by the economic policies pursued. The success of specific measures in development planning is uncertain. In assessing the limits to foreign financing one has, therefore, also to consider the ability of a country to correct wrong decisions and to cope with external disturbances.

When will the limit to foreign indebtedness be reached? This is a question far too complex to be answered simply by looking at commonly used indicators or by applying growth-cum-debt models of the types in general use.

# Appendix

### PRINCIPAL VARIABLES AND PARAMETERS

| | |
|---|---|
| $K_d$ | Capital stock resulting from the utilisation of domestic physical resources |
| $K_f$ | Capital stock resulting from the utilisation of foreign physical resources |
| $Y$ | Net Domestic Product |
| $Y^A$ | Value added of the foreign trade industries |
| $Y^B$ | Value added of all other industries |
| $S_d$ | Net national savings |
| $S_f$ | Net borrowing abroad |
| $C$ | Consumption |
| $I$ | Net investment ($\hat{=} \Delta K$) |
| $Z$ | Interest payments |
| $X$ | Exports |
| $M$ | Imports |
| $M^k$ | Import of capital goods ($\hat{=} \Delta K_f$) |
| $M^s$ | All other imports |
| $r$ | International interest rate |
| | Rate of return on real capital |
| $L$ | Total labour force |
| $F$ | Technological progress |
| $F_1, F_2, \ldots F_n$ | Indicators of technological progress |

NOTES

1. Amortisation is not discussed during this paper; we assume revolving borrowing for reinvestment purposes to be always possible. This does not imply that borrowing to cover repayments and reinvestments does not entail problems of its own.
2. See United Nations (ed.) (1949) Measures for the Economic Development of Underdeveloped Countries (New York: United Nations); Millikan and Rostow (1958); P.G. Hoffmann (1960); Tinbergen (1962);

P.N. Rosenstein–Rodan (1961) 'International Aid for Underdeveloped Countries', *The Review of Economics and Statistics*, vol. 43, no. 2, p. 107ff; Chenery, H. and Strout, A (1965) *Foreign Assistance and Economic Development*, AID Discussion Paper, no. 7, June.

3. See Avramovic *et al.* (1964). The contributions presented here refer back to G.M. Alter, 'The Servicing of Foreign Capital Inflows by Underdeveloped Countries', in International Economic Association (1961) *Economic Development for Latin America*, (London: Macmillan).

4. See R.Z. Aliber (1980) *A Conceptual Approach to the Analysis of External Debt of Developing Countries*, World Bank Staff Working Paper, no. 421, (Washington: World Bank) October. Petersen, H.J. (1977) '*Zur Früherkennung kritischer Verschuldungslagen von Entwicklungsländern*' (On the Early Recognition of Critical Debt Situations in Developing Countries), in *Vierteljahreshefte zur Wirtschaftsforschung*, vol. 3, p. 180ff. For criticism of such early warning systems cf. Erbe, R. and Schattner, S. (1980) 'Indicator Systems for the Assessment of the External Debt Situation of Developing Countries', in *Intereconomics*, no. 6, p. 285ff.

5. See, for example, Griffin, K.B. and Enos, J.L. (1970) 'Foreign Assistance: Objectives and Consequences', in *Economic Development and Cultural Change* vol. 18, p. 313ff; Rahman, A. (1968) 'Foreign Capital and Domestic Savings: A Test of Haavelmo's Hypothesis with Crosscountry Data', *Review of Economics and Statistics*, vol. 50, p. 137ff; Weisskopf, T. (1972) 'The Impact of Foreign Capital Inflow on Domestic Savings in Underdeveloped Countries', *Journal of International Economics*, vol. 2, no. 1, p. 25ff; Chenery, H.B. and Eckstein, P. (1967) *Development Alternatives for Latin America*, Centre for International Affairs, memorandum no. 29 (Cambridge, Mass: Harvard University); Papanek, G.F. (1972) 'The Effect of Aid and Other Resource Transfers on Savings and Growth in Less Developed Countries', in *Economic Journal*, vol. 82, no. 327, p. 934ff.

6. Nelson (1970) elaborated upon Chenery and Strout by splitting production into consumer goods, capital goods and export goods. However, Nelson does not differentiate in the production function between $K_d$ and $K_f$.

REFERENCES

Avramovic, D. *et al.* (1964) *Economic Growth and External Debt* (Baltimore: Johns Hopkins University Press).

Chenery, H. and Strout, A. (1966) 'Foreign Assistance and Economic Development', *American Economic Review*, vol. 56, no. 2, p. 179ff.

Desai, P. (1979) 'The Productivity of Foreign Resource Inflow to the Soviet Economy', *American Economic Review*, vol. 69, no. 2, p. 70ff.

Hoffman, P.G. (1960) *One Hundred Countries: One and One Quarter Billion People* (Washington DC: Albert and Mary Lasker Foundation).

Levy, V. (1980) *The Productivity Gap and the Productivity of Egypt's inflow of Foreign Resources* (Jerusalem).

Millikan, M.F. and Rostow, W.W. (1958) *A Proposal: Key of an Effective Foreign Policy* (New York: Harper and Row).

Nelson, R. R. (1970) 'The Effective Exchange Rate: Employment and Growth in a Foreign Exchange Constrained Economy', *Journal of Political Economy*, vol. 70, no. 3, p. 546ff.

Tinbergen, N. (1962) *Shaping the World Economy* (New York: McGraw Hill).

# 14 Exchange-Rate Policy, International Capital Movements and the Financing of Development

**Alexandre Kafka**

INTERNATIONAL MONETARY FUND,
WASHINGTON DC, USA

## I SUMMARY AND CONCLUSIONS

The topic assigned to me is potentially vast. Of the many ways of cutting it down, I have thought it most interesting to choose an impressionistic one: namely, to address a few points which seemed particularly interesting from a policy point of view. There is some empirical evidence (particularly relating to 'developing countries'), but much of the discussion is merely taxonomic. There are, consequently, no firm conclusions. It does not appear, however, that either the exchange-rate system or the exchange rate is a particularly apt instrument for stimulating capital flows and financing development.

The first group of points refers to the relationship between exchange-rate policy and international capital flows (Section II). An examination of a series of devaluation of nominal exchange rates suggests that they have a short-term positive effect on capital inflows, presumably via the real balance effect, and a delayed (also positive) short-term effect on the current account. The empirical work of others suggests a longer-term effect of an analogous kind (specifically, overvaluation of the effective real exchange rate resulting in long-term capital outflows) through a different mechanism. But then a puzzling question is discussed: the capital flows to LDCs in 1970s were admittedly not as dramatic when deflated for real growth and inflation as they appear in nominal terms. Were they the cause of what may appear as widespread overvaluation of LDC exchange rates, or was the causal chain reversed?

There follow a few taxonomic points on the exchange rate system (Section III). Next, there is a brief discussion about the possible relationship between capital flows and domestic saving (Section IV). It appears that there was no 'crowding out' of domestic saving by capital imports. Finally (Section IV) there are some taxonomic comments on the relationship between exchange rates and types of capital flows.

Two matters should be explained. The discussion is concerned with the finance of development and not the promotion of development as such. Also, there is no discussion of the manner in which the available instruments for setting the exchange rate operate or how they may directly affect international capital movements or the financing of development.

## II EXCHANGE RATES AND INTERNATIONAL CAPITAL MOVEMENTS

In a recent article, Marc A. Miles (1979, pp. 600–20) suggests that the trade balance is not improved by devaluations, but that the balance of payments (the change in reserves net of SDR allocations) is temporarily improved. From this he concludes that the capital account is temporarily improved by devaluation (Miles, 1979, pp. 606–8). In the Annex to my papers, Mrs Marianne Schulze examines the nominal devaluations, relative to the US dollar, of a group of developing countries.[1] Her examination, like that of Miles, refers to effects on (i) the overall balance of payments, and (ii) unlike Miles, to effects on the current account rather than on the trade balance.

(i) On the basis of regression equations, the exchange-rate variable is insignificant at a 5 per cent level throughout the sample so far as concerns the current account. It is significant for the balance of payments only in four cases, and has the expected sign only in two.

(ii) On another test (the residuals test) the overall balance of payments in Mrs Schulze's sample behaves, on average and at first sight, differently than in Miles's sample. The average residual for the overall balance of payments, if government expenditure is *excluded* from the regression equations, does not become positive in the year after devaluation, but it does become slightly less negative in that year. The residuals test for the overall balance of payments, where government expenditure is *included* in the regression equations, does turn very moderately positive in the year after devaluation. The residuals test for both sets of regressions becomes increasingly negative in the year of devaluation itself, as compared to the preceding year. One should not make too much of this, however. One would assume that devaluation was undertaken because of a deteriorating balance of payments, but the devaluation may well come too late in the year of devaluation to swing the residuals from negative to positive.

Contrary to Miles's findings for the trade account there is, in Mrs Schulze's sample, a marked improvement in the year following devaluation in the average residuals for the current account on the other hand. These average residuals become more negative than previously in the year of devaluation itself. It is also true that in Mrs Schulze's sample, in the year of devaluation, the average residual for the overall balance of payments, even when negative (rather than barely positive), is far less negative than the average residual for the current account. This suggests an initial 'J' curve effect combined with a rapid improvement in the capital account.

(iii) After obtaining unsatisfactory results in an attempt to apply Miles's equations directly to the capital account, Mrs Schulze developed an alternative model. The estimated capital-flow equations are reduced forms, derived from a simple three-asset portfolio equilibrium model (Kouri and Porter, 1974, pp. 443–67a). Domestic residents alone hold domestic money; they also hold domestic and foreign interest bearing assets; and domestic interest-bearing assets are also held abroad. The capital flow equation applied has as arguments the monetary base, the foreign interest rate and income growth at home and abroad, plus the exchange rate. Because of statistical problems the usual wealth term was excluded. The results are interesting. The exchange rate coefficients have the expected signs in five out of ten cases and are statistically significant at the 1 per cent level. The residuals test bears out this result.

The average residual turns positive in the year of devaluation, this is followed by a strong swing to a negative figure in the subsequent year.[2]

(iv)   In sum, devaluation appears not to have much influence on capital flows; in so far as there is an influence, it is of short duration and favourable. This is what one would expect in the presence of a real-balance effect.

Can one, nevertheless, find longer-term effects? John Makin (1974) shows that overvaluation of the US dollar precipitated sizeable long-term capital outflows from the United States during the 1960s, by a mechanism different from that of the real-balance effect. The mechanism is the substitution of capital flows for trade, i.e. investment and production abroad replace exports, or domestic production of import-type goods. One might conclude from this experience that underdevaluation would have the opposite effect. Obviously, however, there is no reason to expect that the undervaluation (i) could be sustained for any length of time, or (ii) would not be offset by short-term outflows. In case (ii), the change in the structure of the supply of capital may, nevertheless, be considered an improvement.

The apparently positive but short-term association of devaluation with capital inflows (or of overvaluation with long-term capital exports) mentioned so far should be examined in the light of the recent experience of non-oil developing countries as a group. After the first and second oil shocks, the current account deficits of the non-oil LDCs rose sharply. They were financed mostly by increased capital inflows of a medium- and long-term nature rather than by reserve losses. (IMF, 1981).[3] Moreover, these capital inflows were provided by both official and private sources and were obtained by both official and private borrowers, including private borrowers that did *not* benefit from government guarantees.[4] Thus, the increased capital inflow cannot be ascribed simply to government intervention.

There is one interesting thing about the capital inflows that took place in the 1970s, into the non-oil LDCs as a group and were large (even when deflated for world price rises and for the real GDP growth of the recipient countries). They occurred during a period when the currencies of some of the most important recipients could be argued to have been, in some significant sense, overvalued and had not simply appreciated (as compared to the past or to what the rate would have been in the absence of the capital inflows). Overvaluation (like any state of disequilibrium) is characterised by its unsustainability, given the underlying conditions. What, then, were the signs of overvaluation?

The non-oil LDCs as a group lost reserves only in one year, 1975. But a major decline in reserve accumulation took place after each oil shock and reserves fell in relation to imports, even though they did not do so in absolute terms. In an inflationary and growing world, one might be tempted to call such a relative decline in reserves unsustainable and a sign of overvaluation, especially since the earlier accumulation had been by no means particularly impressive compared with the historical levels of reserves as a share of imports.[5]

Moreover, throughout the period, the perception of the international financial community was that the non-oil LDCs were not adjusting their current account deficits rapidly enough. This also would seem to imply a perception that the currencies of these countries were in some sense overvalued.

Before proceeding further, it may be well to note a corollary here. Unless one accepts that overvaluation prevailed in non-oil LDCs during the period of the oil shocks, one cannot very well accuse these countries of failure to attempt to adjust their balances of payments. If, in tolerating enlarged current account deficits, they were simply reacting to an increased supply to them of international capital, they were not mismanaging their economies. One could say that they were piling up problems for themselves for the future, when and if the supply to them of international capital would shrink. But that raises a different question, namely, what is the appropriate period over which economic management is to be judged? The fact that, in the 1970s and up to now, there were very few important debt crises among non-oil LDCs would tend to support the view that the LDCs were not particularly shortsighted.

If one accepts the association of exchange-rate movements – whether appreciation as defined above, or overvaluation in some relevant sense – with increased capital imports, one is naturally tempted to ask in which direction the causation may have run.

Was there in some sense a spontaneous rise in capital inflows into non-oil LDCs? During the period under review, the expansion of the size of the international capital market was greatly accelerated – largely, of course, as a result of the oil shocks. Moreover, the period following the first oil shock and until recently is generally considered to have been characterised by negative real interest rates.[6] Two considerations would seem to cast at least some doubt on the significance of this observation. First, in the sources quoted, real interest rates are calculated as the difference between nominal interest rates and contemporaneous price movements; it is doubtful whether this concept is a meaningful proxy for the 'real' rate which is presumed to influence behaviour. Second, there was certainly no close association between capital flows to LDCs and the real rate shown in the sources quoted (or any other real rate that I am aware of).[7]

It is, therefore, by no means clear that one can simply argue that negative interest rates stimulated capital flows and thereby brought about the exchange-rate movement. However, the increase in the size of the capital market may well have led to a greater propensity of the market to accept risks. It may thereby have brought about larger capital flows and appreciation relative to the past, or to equilibrium amounts in the absence of increased capital flows. Capital flows as a cause of appreciation was the relation shown to exist by Viner (1924).

If, however, one accepts overvaluation rather than merely appreciation, one is faced with the question; by what mechanisms could overvaluation have been associated with a capital inflow rather than with an outflow (or, at least, with a reduction in the rate of inflow as compared to the past, or to equilibrium)? In the conditions prevailing in many non-oil LDCs after the first oil shock, the otherwise discouraging effects of overvaluation on capital inflows (whether through a real-balance effect or through the type of mechanism described by Makin with respect to long-term capital inflows) might very well have been more than offset by a different mechanism. The rising current-account deficits of the oil shocks were widely attended by increases in import tariffs or in restrictions of various kinds. Under these conditions, the exchange rate could provide a stimulus to imports of goods that were not affected by restrictions, especially capital goods. The exchange rate would be overvalued in the sense that it was sustained by the existence of restrictions and, sometimes, of subsidies. Furthermore, the stimulus to the import of goods would also stimulate capital imports to finance the import of goods. Normally, overvaluation would engender an expectation of devaluation, which could be expected to discourage capital imports. But in so far as the adjustment mechanism was perceived to be based on restrictions, this expectation would not prevail or at least not be as effective as otherwise. What could happen then would be that, in the absence of a strong expectation of a corrective devaluation, there would be a strong expectation of rising prices for the goods that were to be produced with the help of the imports of capital and, hence, an expectation of particularly high profitability.

Moreover, one must consider whether the expectation of a corrective devaluation would not engender expectations of relative price changes that would stimulate capital imports. If the import content of capital goods exceeds that of consumer goods, then a corrective devaluation will lower the expected profitability of future production of the latter with future capital goods, but it would *raise* the expected profitability – as long as the present capital goods did not have to be replaced.

It seems quite likely that something of the kind described above prevailed after the first oil shock. The disadvantage of restrictions which are a condition for circumstances in which overvaluation will stimulate capital imports would, however, presumably be this. They would discourage the use of overvaluation as a deliberate long-term policy of stimulating capital inflow, even in so far as it could be expected to add to the supply of capital.

The effects of a uniform over- or under-valuation of a unitary exchange rate are obviously indistinguishable (except for practical complications) from the effects of taxes or subsidies applied uniformly to transactions between domestic and foreign residents. No comments will be made here on the effects on capital flows of the indefinitely large number of possible combinations of non-uniform taxes and subsidies.

## III   THE EXCHANGE RATE SYSTEM

At first sight it would seem that there should be a lot to say about the effects on capital flows and the financing of development of the change to the present system from the Bretton Woods system. For example, it has been shown that 'floating' produces greater exchange-rate instability than par values (see Helleiner, 1981, Tables 3 and 4).

But what is one to make of this fact? Greater instability need not mean greater unpredictability or uncertainty.[8] In so far as it does, there is likely to be somewhat less international trade and capital flows in relation to world product than there would be, *ceteris paribus*, under less uncertainty. There is no question that the growth of the volume of world trade has declined since 1973 (see IMF, 1981, Table 6, p. 115) when the Bretton Woods system finally collapsed. It would, however, be odd to ascribe the decline in the growth rate of the volume of world trade to that collapse. In any case, the (real) value of international capital flows has risen greatly since then.[9]

Before the collapse of the Bretton Woods system, it was popular to claim that 'floating' – even if it discouraged capital flows by creating increased uncertainty – would nonetheless, on balance, stimulate them by preventing restrictions (on trade and capital flows). It would, however, be odd to claim that the rise in capital flows after 1973 was due to floating, or even that 'floating' was a necessary condition of the rise. The growth of the Euro-currency market, was, in fact by no means slow before floating and after 1973 the market's growth was greatly influenced by the oil shocks.[10]

## IV  INTERNATIONAL CAPITAL MOVEMENTS AND DOMESTIC SAVING

We come now to two distinct but related questions. First, the direct effect of exchange rate policy on domestic saving, second, the effect of international capital flows on domestic savings.

One would expect overvaluation and undervaluation of the real exchange rate to lower and raise domestic saving, respectively as a result of the real-balance effect. But this is not the only mechanism by which exchange-rate policy may produce a direct effect on domestic saving. Saving is a matter of the relative price of present and future goods, given time preference and, presumably, exchange-rate policy will not affect time preference. But the prices of present goods would be lower in relation to future goods in the case of overvaluation, and the reverse would apply in the case of undervaluation. Hence, this second mechanism, based on changes in the relative prices of present and future goods, would tend to reaffirm the real-balance effect. However, an overvaluation which was expected to be corrected could have a more complicated effect on domestic saving. If the correction of overvaluation was expected to raise the prices of capital goods in the future more than those of consumables, there would be a tendency for domestic saving to be stimulated in order to purchase investment goods now, when they are particularly cheap in relation to the future goods which they will produce. Since the prices of capital goods in many developing countries may be more sensitive to the exchange rate than are the prices of consumables (because the import content of capital goods is likely to be higher than that of consumer goods), such an effect is not at all unlikely. (The opposite would apply to undervaluation which was expected to be corrected)[11]

A separate matter is the effect (if any) of capital inflows as such on domestic savings: that is, are the latter likely to be 'crowded out' by the availability of foreign savings?[12] Data for one country,[13] which I was able to assemble with reasonable confidence that they are meaningful, do not suggest that there has been any 'crowding out' of domestic saving by foreign capital inflows. I use the term in an analogous sense to that intended when one speaks of the crowding out of private investment by public sector deficits: i.e. less saving in relation to GNP than when there was less capital inflow. In so far as inflows reflect government borrowing and in so far as the latter's saving does not obey the same incentives as does that of private agents, there is no reason why there should be crowding out in the sense of less domestic saving than *there would have been, all other things being equal*, in the absence of the capital inflows. But this is not the important thing; that is rather whether the capital inflow brings about a net addition to the sum of domestic saving plus net capital inflows and there is no reason why it should not – and no proof that it did not.

## V   MICROECONOMIC ASPECTS

We have still to make some reference to microeconomic effects, that is, the effects of exchange-rate policy on different types of international capital movements and different types of domestic-saving flows. The statistical material available is simply not of a quality to permit anything definite to be said on this, but a few observations may nevertheless be permissible.

The likelihood that the misvaluation of the real exchange rate will be undone could be expected to increase with its extent and with time; but the latter only up to a point. In the longer run everything else also becomes uncertain. The effect of a correction of a misvaluation, even if firmly expected, is therefore likely to be quite minor. Hence, one might expect very short-term flows and very long-term flows to be relatively immune to the effects which might otherwise result from misvaluation of the exchange rate.

Since direct investment (and the loans associated with it, from the mother company to its subsidiaries) is generally undertaken with the expectation of a long period of investment, one would expect these types of capital flows to be less affected than (other) loans.

One might also ask whether the present exchange-rate system is likely to have had any effects on the relative importance of different types of capital flow. One could assume that by increasing instability, and probably uncertainty, in the short run it would bear more heavily on short-term flows than on long-terms flows, particularly on direct investment.

TABLE 14.1 BALANCE OF PAYMENTS OF NON-OIL DEVELOPING COUNTRIES: CURRENT ACCOUNT FINANCING, 1973–81ᵃ (US$bn)

| | 1973 | 1974 | 1975 | 1976 | 1977 | 1978 | 1979 | 1980 | 1981 |
|---|---|---|---|---|---|---|---|---|---|
| Current account deficitᵇ | 11.5 | 36.8 | 46.5 | 32.9 | 28. | 37.5 | 57.6 | 82.1 | 97.5 |
| Financing through transactions that do not affect net debt positions | 10.4 | 12.8ᶜ | 12.0 | 11.9 | 14. | 15.3 | 21.6 | 20.6 | 23.6 |
| Net unrequited transfers received by governments of non-oil developing countries | 5.6 | 6.9ᶜ | 7.3 | 7.4 | 8. | 7.8 | 10.4 | 10.6 | 11.9 |
| SDR allocations, valuation adjustments and gold monetisation | 0.4 | 0.5 | −0.7 | −0.3 | 1. | 1.2 | 3.0 | 2.1 | 1.4 |
| Direct investment flows, net | 4.4 | 5.4 | 5.3 | 4.8 | 5. | 6.2 | 8.2 | 7.9 | 10.4 |
| Net borrowing and use of reservesᵈ | 1.1 | 24.0ᶜ | 34.6 | 21.0 | 14. | 22.2 | 36.1 | 61.5 | 73.9 |
| Reduction of reserve assets (accumulation —) | −9.7 | −2.3 | 1.8 | −13.2 | −12. | −15.2 | −11.7 | −1.9 | −1.0 |
| Net external borrowingᵉ | 10.8 | 26.2ᶜ | 32.8 | 34.3 | 26. | 37.4 | 47.8 | 63.5 | 74.9 |
| Long-term borrowing | 11.4 | 19.8ᶜ | 26.7 | 28.2 | 27. | 35.1 | 44.7 | 48.1 | 56.6 |
| From official sources | 5.7 | 9.9ᶜ | 11.7 | 10.8 | 12. | 14.3 | 14.5 | 21.0 | 24.2 |
| From private sources | 10.4 | 13.5 | 14.9 | 19.0 | 21. | 27.0 | 33.1 | 27.2 | 31.0 |
| *From financial institutions* | *9.0* | *12.3* | *13.2* | *16.1* | *17.* | *23.0* | *32.1* | *24.2* | *25.9* |
| *From other lenders* | *1.4* | *1.2* | *1.8* | *2.9* | *3.* | *4.0* | *1.0* | *3.0* | *5.1* |
| Residual flows, netᶠ | −4.7 | −3.6 | 0.1 | −1.6 | −6. | −6.1 | −2.9 | −0.1 | 1.5 |

continued on page 278

TABLE 14.1 *continued*

TABLE 14.1 BALANCE OF PAYMENTS OF NON-OIL DEVELOPING COUNTRIES: CURRENT ACCOUNT FINANCING, 1973–81 [a] (*US$bn*)

| | 1973 | 1974 | 1975 | 1976 | 1977 | 1978 | 1979 | 1980 | 1981 |
|---|---|---|---|---|---|---|---|---|---|
| Use of reserve-related credit facilities[g] | — | 1.5 | 2.3 | 3.7 | -0.6 | -0.5 | 0.2 | 3.0 | 7.5 |
| Other short-term borrowing, net | — | 5.1 | 7.8 | 4.9 | -0.5 | 2.2 | 7.6 } | 12.4 | 10.7 |
| Residual errors and omissions[h] | -0.6 | -0.3 | -4.0 | -2.5 | — | 0.5 | -4.7 | | |

[a] Excludes data for the People's Republic of China prior to 1977.

[b] Net total of balances on goods, services and private transfers, as defined for the Fund's *Balance of Payments Yearbook* purposes (with sign reversed).

[c] Excludes the effect of a revision of the terms of the disposition of economic assistance loans made by the United States to India and repayable in rupees, and of rupees already acquired by the US government in repayment of such loans. The revision has the effect of increasing government transfers by about US$2bn, with an offset in net official loans.

[d] That is, financing through changes in net debt positions (net borrowing, less net accumulation – or plus net liquidation – of official reserve assets).

[e] Includes any net use of non-reserve claims on non-residents, errors and omissions in reported balance of payments statements for individual countries, and minor deficiencies in coverage.

[f] These residual flows comprise two elements: (1) net changes in long-term external assets of non-oil developing countries and (2) residuals and discrepancies that arise from the mismatching of creditor-source data taken from debt records, with capital flow data taken from national balance of payments records.

[g] Comprises use of Fund credit and short-term borrowing by monetary authorities from other monetary authorities.

[h] Errors and omissions in reported balance of payments statements for individual countries, and minor omissions in coverage.

*Source:* International Monetary Fund; International Financial Statistics.

TABLE 14.2 NON-OIL DEVELOPING COUNTRIES: LONG-TERM
EXTERNAL DEBT, 1973–80

|      | Public debt to financial institutions[a] (US$bn) | Total debt of non-oil countries to banks, BIS series[b] (US$bn) |
|------|------|------|
| 1973 | 13   | 45   |
| 1974 | 22   | 60   |
| 1975 | 30   | 75   |
| 1976 | 39   | 96   |
| 1977 | 54   | 121  |
| 1978 | 74   | 149  |
| 1979 | 96   | 180  |
| 1980 | 113  | 235  |

[a] Owed by or guaranteed by public institutions in the borrowing country.
[b] Includes claims on the private and public sectors and short-term claims.

*Source:* International Monetary Fund, Occasional Paper No. 7, *International Capital Markets*, Appendix V, Table 33, p. 76.

TABLE 14.3 NON-OIL DEVELOPING COUNTRIES

| Overall[a] | Average[b] reserves as percentage of imports |
|------|------|
| 1952 | 36 |
| 1955 | 37 |
| 1960 | 26 |
| 1965 | 26 |
| 1970 | 28 |
| 1971 | 28 |
| 1972 | 33 |
| 1973 | 33 |
| 1974 | 24 |
| 1975 | 22 |
| 1976 | 24 |
| 1977 | 27 |
| 1978 | 29 |
| 1979 | 36 |
| 1980 | 23 |

[a] Including gold, values at SDR 35 per troy ounce.
[b] Average of December figure of preceding and listed year.

*Source: International Financial Statistics*, 1981 Year Book.

## TABLE 14.4 NOMINAL AND REAL INTEREST RATES, 1977–80

|  | 1977 (%) | 1978 (%) | 1979 (%) | 1980 (%) |
|---|---|---|---|---|
| **United States** | | | | |
| Three-month Eurodollar | | | | |
| deposit rate | 6.0 | 8.7 | 12.0 | 14.4 |
| GNP deflator | 5.8 | 7.3 | 8.5 | 9.0 |
| Real interest rate[a] | 0.2 | 1.3 | 3.2 | 5.0 |
| **Germany** | | | | |
| Three-month | | | | |
| money market rate | 4.4 | 3.7 | 6.7 | 9.5 |
| GNP deflator | 3.8 | 3.9 | 3.9 | 5.0 |
| Real interest rate[a] | 0.6 | −0.2 | 2.7 | 4.3 |
| **Japan** | | | | |
| Three-month gensaki | | | | |
| rate[b] | 5.6 | 5.1 | 5.9 | 10.7 |
| GNP deflator | 5.5 | 4.0 | 2.0 | 1.9 |
| Real interest rate[b] | 0.1 | 1.1 | 3.8 | 8.6 |

[a] If $i$ represents the nominal interest rate, $\dot{p}$ the growth of the GNP deflator, and $r$ the *ex post* real interest rate $i = r + \dot{p} - r\dot{p}$.

[b] Bond repurchase agreements.

*Source:* IMF, *International Financial Statistics*; Deutsche Bundesbank, *Monthly Report*; Bank of Japan. *Economic Statistics Monthly*.

## TABLE 14.5 DATA FOR BRAZIL

| Year | Index of relative wholesale prices[a] divided by effective exchange rate | Net capital inflow | Gross domestic capital formation | Gross domestic saving | Gross fixed capital formation |
|---|---|---|---|---|---|
| | | | As percentages of GDP (in US$) | | |
| 1970 | 116 | 2 | 23 | 22 | 22 |
| 1971 | 117 | 4 | 25 | 23 | 23 |
| 1972 | 111 | 6 | 25 | 23 | 23 |
| 1973 | 104 | 5 | 27 | 25 | 23 |
| 1974 | 102 | 6 | 31 | 25 | 24 |
| 1975 | 100 | 4 | 25[b] | 20[b] | 25 |
| 1976 | 104 | 6 | 24[b] | 20[b] | 24 |
| 1977 | 101 | 3 | 22[b] | 20[b] | 22 |
| 1978 | 96 | 4 | 22[b] | 18[b] | 22 |
| 1979 | 88 | 4 | 21[b] | 17[b] | 21 |
| 1980 | 85 | 4 | 22[b] | 17[b] | 22 |

[a] Internal availability for Brazil.

[b] Excludes inventory accumulation which, however, is normally no more than 1 or 2 per cent of GDP.

Subtotals may not sum to totals, due to rounding.

Source: Banco Central do Brazil, Departamento Económico, 13/VIII/81, page 07, and International Financial Statistics Yearbook, 1981.

NOTES

1. Including some of those analysed by Miles. Mrs Schulze wrote this analysis while a summer intern at the International Monetary Fund. The Fund, of course, bears no responsibility for the results.
2. For one country, I also tried a regression of the current account and of the capital account on various concepts of an effective real exchange rate – along with money supply, and growth of income and government expenditure. The results were not significant with reference to the effects of exchange-rate changes on capital flows.
3. Tables 22 and 23 are reproduced in Table 14.1.
4. See Table 14.2.
5. Table 14.3.
6. Federal Reserve Bank (1981) especially charts 8 and 9, p. 62 and this chapter Table 14.4.
7. See note 3 and Federal Reserve Bank (1981).
8. One should, perhaps, distinguish between real uncertainties, and confusion caused by accounting standards which produce false perceptions as well as unintended effects on taxation.
9. With respect to non-oil LDCs, this can be seen from Annex, Table 14.A1.
10. See BIS, Annual Reports: 43rd, p. 161; 65th, p. 131; 54th, p. 108.
11. A similar mechanism might be believed to affect capital inflows; but the relationship would be complicated by the very visible impact of devaluation on the cost of debt service.
12. Mrs Schulze examined the relationship between domestic saving and investment for a sample of developing countries. As one would expect, the relationship was good deal less close than that found by M. Feldstein and C. Horioka (1980) in 'Domestic Saving and International Capital Flows', *Economic Journal*, 90, June, pp. 314–29.
13. See Table 14.5.

# Annex

Testing for the Effects of Devaluation on the Current Account, the Capital Account and the Balance of Payments

MARIANNE SCHULZE

The present analysis draws heavily on Miles's work (1978, 1979) on the effects of devaluation on the trade balance and the balance of payments. While Miles provides the methodical underpinnings, this analysis differs from Miles's work in three aspects:

(i) it is concerned with a sample of developing countries only, whereas Miles's sample includes developed as well as developing countries;
(ii) its subject is the current account, the capital account and the balance of payments, with emphasis on the capital account; and,
(iii) the shift in emphasis to the capital account made it necessary not only to redefine the dependent variables of the regression equations but also – in the case of capital-account equations – to change the specification of those equations.

## I   METHOD OF ANALYSIS

Earlier studies on the effects of devaluation, by concentrating attention on 'raw' figures, failed to distinguish between the effects on the balance of payments of a change in the exchange rate and of changes in other exogenous variables, in particular policy variables. (See, for example, Miles 1978, 1979.)

Miles's work is an attempt to overcome these shortcomings by means of multiple regression analysis. In such analysis, a simple F-test can be used to test for the improvement of fit obtained from introducing a set of additional explanatory variables. For one explanatory variable, this test is formally equivalent to the standard t-test. Our first test for the effects of devaluation is therefore to regress the current account, the balance of payments, and the capital account on a set of explanatory variables, including the exchange rate. We then examine the sign and significance of the exchange-rate variable in the individual estimating equations.

When the exchange-rate variable is excluded from the estimating equations, the effects of exchange-rate changes will be reflected in the residuals. Examining the residuals from regression equations excluding the exchange-rate variable, thus provides information on how the accounts behaved in the year of devaluation and in subsequent years, as compared to the years prior to the devaluation. This is the essence of the residuals' test, employed by Fama, *et al.* (1969) in an analysis of stock prices, adapted by Miles to the analysis of the effects of devaluations. The residuals test for the exchange-rate variable, unlike the direct significance test, gives detailed information on the reaction pattern of the different accounts around the year of devaluation. In contrast to direct examination of 'raw' balance-of-payments figures, however, it ensures that the figures examined are purged of the effects of the variables accounted for in the regression equation.

## II   SPECIFICATION OF EQUATIONS

Our specification of the current-account and the balance-of-payments equations follows Miles. Miles's equation for the trade balance is:

$$\Delta\left(\frac{TB}{Y}\right)_i = a_o + \overset{(-)}{a_1}\Delta(\dot{Y}_i - \dot{Y}_{ROW})$$

$$+\overset{(-)}{a_2}\Delta\left\{\left(\frac{MB}{Y}\right)_i - \left(\frac{MB}{Y}\right)_{ROW}\right\} \tag{1}$$

$$+\overset{(-)}{a_3}\Delta\left\{\left(\frac{GE}{Y}\right)_i - \left(\frac{GE}{Y}\right)_{ROW}\right\} + \overset{(\pm)}{a_4}\Delta\frac{E_i}{E_{ROW}},$$

and for the balance of payments

$$\Delta\left(\frac{BP}{Y}\right)_i = b_o + \overset{(+)}{b_1}\Delta(\dot{Y}_i - \dot{Y}_{ROW}) \tag{2}$$

$$+\overset{(-)}{b_2}\Delta\left\{\left(\frac{MB}{Y}\right)_i - \left(\frac{MB}{Y}\right)_{ROW}\right\} + \overset{(+)}{b_3}\Delta\frac{E_i}{E_{ROW}}.$$

Here, a dot above a variable indicates its rate of growth; $i$ refers to the country analysed; $ROW$ to the rest of the world; $TB$ is the trade balance; $BP$ the balance of payments; $Y$ nominal GNP; $MB$ the domestic source of the monetary base; and $GE$ government expenditure.[1]

Miles's reasoning (summarised in 1979) regarding the included explanatory variables and the expected signs (here indicated above the coefficients) is mainly in terms of the monetary approach to balance-of-payments theory. Nevertheless, his equations should not be confused with a formal test of this approach.[2] His specifications are derived in a rather *ad hoc* fashion and were accepted as such, since our objective is not to test certain hypotheses of balance-of-payments theory, but rather to examine the effects of devaluation on different foreign accounts. Equations (1) and (2) were both estimated with the current account and the balance of payments as dependent variables.

As a direct application of Miles's specifications to the capital account yielded very unsatisfactory results, an alternative specification was chosen for the capital-account equation. This specification is based on the reduced form of a simple three asset portfolio model, as was discussed by Kouri and Porter (1974, pp. 443–67). The model includes domestic money and domestic and foreign interest-bearing assets. The asset demand functions follow the conventional approach, including wealth, income and domestic and foreign interest rates as arguments. Capital inflows result from a decrease in the net demand for foreign assets. We solve the money market equilibrium condition for the domestic interest rate; replace the endogenous domestic interest rate by the expression thus derived; drop the wealth variables for which data are lacking and, finally, take first differences. We thus arrive at the following capital flow equation:

$$\Delta CAP_i = c_o + \overset{(+)}{c_1}\Delta^2 Y_i + \overset{(+)}{c_2}\Delta^2 Y_{ROW} \tag{3}$$

$$+ \overset{(-)}{c_3}\Delta^2 I_{US} + \overset{(-)}{c_4}\Delta^2 MB_i + \overset{(-)}{c_5}\Delta CA_i + \overset{(+)}{c_6}\Delta^2 \frac{E_i}{E_{ROW}}.$$

$CAP$ denotes net capital inflows, $I_{US}$ the foreign interest rate, represented by the three-months US treasury bill rate. All other variables are defined as before. $CA$, the current account enters the equation as part of the foreign source of the money supply and is expected to have a negative coefficient, like $MB$, the domestic source of the money supply. An increase in domestic income increases the demand for money and *ceteris paribus* the domestic interest rate, or including capital imports. An increase in income abroad reduces foreign demand for interest-bearing assets, foreign as well as domestic. (See Kouri and Porter (1974) for a more detailed discussion of the model and of the expected signs of the coefficients.) The current exchange rate is a determinant of the expected exchange-rate change, which in turn is part of the expected return on foreign assets. The unobservable expected exchange rate itself was dropped.

## III  THE SAMPLE, DEFINITION OF VARIABLES, DATA SOURCE

The selection of an appropriate sample of devaluations was considerably constrained by the worldwide move towards greater exchange-rate flexibility in the second half of the 1970s. This made it virtually impossible to find relatively recent, once-and-for-all devaluations during the seven-year period required for carrying out the residuals test. The sample size was also limited by the lack of sufficiently long time series for many developing countries. A sample of fourteen devaluations in ten countries was analysed;

| Country[a] | Year of Devaluation | Estimation Period |
|---|---|---|
| Bolivia (BOL) | 1972 | 1979–79 |
| Costa Rica (CRA) | 1974, 1961 | 1958–79 |
| Ecuador (EC) | 1970, 1961 | 1958–79 |
| Jamaica (JAM) | 1968 | 1962–78 |
| Peru (PER) | 1967 | 1958–79 |
| Guyana (GUY) | 1972 | 1966–77 |
| Israel (ISR) | 1967, 1962 | 1958–79 |
| Philippines (PHI) | 1970, 1962 | 1958–79 |
| Sri Lanka (SLA) | 1967 | 1958–79 |
| Yugoslavia (YU) | 1971 | 1963–78 |

[a] Abbreviations in brackets used subsequently.

Sources
All data are annual data from IFS data files. The variables are defined as follows:

(i) current account ($CA$): trade balance (*fob*); plus other goods, services, and income (*net*); plus official unrequited transfers (*net*),

   (ii) capital account (*CAP*): total capital other than reserves (*net*); plus errors and omissions (*net*),
  (iii) balance of payments (*BP*): *CA* plus *CAP*,
  (iv) growth rate of nominal GNP (*Y*): GNP  − GNP( −1),
   (v) average domestic source of monetary base (*MB*): currency plus bank reserves, taken as an average of end of period and beginning of period stocks, minus current change in reserves (*BP*),
  (vi) government expenditure (*GE*); government consumption from IFS national accounts data,
 (vii) exchange rate (*E*): end of period value of national currency prices of 1 US$.

Series in foreign currency were converted into domestic currency, using the period average exchange rate.

In equations (1) and (2), *CA*, *CAP*, *BP*, *GE* and *MB* are expressed as a fraction of nominal GNP. In all three equations, *E* is expressed as a fraction of an index of exchange rates of the rest of the world, thus allowing for any possible effects of contemporaneous changes in other countries' dollar exchange rates.

The variables representing the rest of the world (*ROW*) are weighted averages for fourteen industrialized countries: Austria, Canada, Denmark, Finland, France, Germany, Italy, Japan, Netherlands, Spain, Sweden, Switzerland, United Kingdom, United States, the weights being each country's share in aggregate GNP (1978 basis).

As the residuals test focuses on changes in the different foreign accounts rather than their levels, all equations were estimated in first-difference form.[3]

## IV   RESULTS

### 1 SIGNIFICANCE OF EXCHANGE RATE VARIABLES

In Tables 14.A1 to 14.A3 OLS estimation results for the current account, the balance of payment and the capital equations are reported. The results for the current account are based on equation (1), for the balance of payments on equation (2), and for the capital account on equation (3).

The exchange-rate variable in the current-account equation is insignificant at the 5 per cent level throughout the sample; in the balance-of-payments equation it is significant at the 5 per cent level in four

TABLE 14.A1   THE CURRENT ACCOUNT EQUATION

$$\Delta\left(\frac{CA}{Y}\right)_i = a_o + a_1\,\Delta(\dot{Y}_i - \dot{Y}_{ROW}) + a_2\Delta\left\{\left(\frac{MB}{Y}\right)_i - \left(\frac{MB}{Y}\right)_{ROW}\right\} + a_3\Delta\left\{\left(\frac{GE}{Y}\right)_i - \left(\frac{GE}{Y}\right)_{ROW}\right\} + a_4\Delta\,\frac{E_i}{E_{ROW}} + u$$

| Country | $a_o$ | $a_1$ | $a_2$ | $a_3$ | $a_4$ | $\bar{R}^{2b}$ | $DW^c$ |
|---|---|---|---|---|---|---|---|
| BOL | .0023 (.19)[a] | -.22 (.14) | -1.44 (2.92) | .66 (.50) | -.094 (.19) | .32 | 1.88 |
| CRA | .0043 (.56) | -.28 (1.62) | -.61 (2.16) | -1.39 (1.01) | -1.83 (1.67) | .31 | 2.86 |
| EC | -.00065 (.19) | .038 (1.65) | -1.14 (5.78) | .073 (.25) | -.17 (1.02) | .74 | 2.15 |
| JAM | .0021 (.21) | .22 (1.42) | -.63 (2.44) | .47 (.55) | -.68 (1.34) | .36 | 2.02 |
| PER | -.00.4 (.67) | .21 (1.86) | -.43 (2.20) | .68 (1.25) | .023 (1.04) | .44 | 1.08 |
| GUY | .0029 (.19) | -.35 (1.29) | -1.14 (2.40) | -.28 (.21) | -9.56 (1.25) | .90 | 2.39 |
| ISR | .0063 (.70) | -.34 (2.54) | -.24 (1.40) | -.69 (3.07) | 1.29 (.55) | .33 | 2.23 |
| PHI | -.0034 (.74) | -.005 (.049) | -.87 (2.47) | -.31 (.33) | .06 (.094) | .31 | 2.36 |
| SLA | -.0031 (.59) | -.13 (1.55) | -.94 (3.01) | .57 (1.11) | .44 (1.57) | .33 | 2.46 |
| YU | -.00091 (.14) | -.16 (1.41) | -.72 (3.16) | .38 (.30) | .33 (.97) | .39 | 1.97 |

[a] In brackets t-values     [b] $\bar{R}^2$ adjusted for degrees of freedom     [c] Durbin-Watson Statistic

TABLE 14.A2   THE BALANCE OF PAYMENTS EQUATION[a]

$$\Delta\left(\frac{BP}{Y}\right)_i = b_o + b_1\Delta(\dot{Y}_i - \dot{Y}_{ROW}) + b_2\Delta\left(\frac{MB}{Y}\right)_i - \left(\frac{MB}{Y}\right)_{ROW} + a_3\,\Delta\frac{E_i}{E_{ROW}} + v$$

| Country | $b_o$ | $b_1$ | $b_2$ | $b_3$ | $\bar{R}2$ | DW |
|---|---|---|---|---|---|---|
| BOL | .0023 (1.28) | .0028 (.09) | .79 (10.9) | -.4 (1.84) | .91 | 1.38 |
| CRA | .0032 (2.54) | -.06 (2.35) | -.97 (18.9) | -.63 (3.03) | .95 | 1.46 |
| EC | .00037 (.28) | -.033 (1.53) | -.96 (13.89) | -.1 (1.89) | .91 | 1.74 |
| JAM | .0032 (2.24) | -.071 (3.40) | -1.02 (23.73) | -.1 (.39) | .97 | 1.76 |
| PER | .0013 (.72) | -.0008 (.02) | -.93 (15.46) | -.0048 (.70) | .93 | 1.47 |
| GUY | .0043 (.99) | -.16 (1.75) | -1.08 (10.64) | -.1 (.35) | .99 | 1.08 |
| ISR | .0043 (.14) | -.049 (1.06) | -.99 (16.76) | -.14 (1.26) | .93 | 1.65 |
| PHI | -.0008 (.57) | -.042 (1.96) | -1.00 (13.09) | .13 (.90) | .92 | 1.22 |
| SLA | -.00069 (.48) | -.041 (1.73) | -.92 (10.65) | .22 (2.88) | .87 | 1.23 |
| YU | .0024 (.51) | -.12 (1.7) | -.59 (3.61) | .25 (.13) | .48 | 1.63 |

[a] See notes to Table 14.A1.

290

TABLE 14.A3   THE CAPITAL ACCOUNT EQUATION[a]

$$\Delta CAP_i = c_o + c_1\Delta^2 Y_i + c_2\Delta^2 Y_{ROW} + c_3\Delta^2 IUS + c_4\Delta^2 MB_i + c_5\Delta CA_i + c_6\Delta^2 \frac{E_i}{E_{ROW}} + w$$

| Country | $c_o$ | $c_1$ | $c_2$ | $c_3$ | $c_4$ | $c_5$ | $c_6$ | $\bar{R}2$ | DW |
|---|---|---|---|---|---|---|---|---|---|
| BOL | .271 (.032) | .054 (1.96) | -.199 (.18) | -1.57 (.32) | -.214 (2.12) | -.71 (8.00) | -41.03 (.26) | .80 | 1.27 |
| CRA | -.98 (.26) | .155 (4.52) | 1.11 (2.56) | -5.108 (1.83) | -.297 (3.37) | -.607 (10.28) | 1306.33 (3.72) | .86 | 2.75 |
| EC | -7.81 (.78) | .093 (2.33) | 2.40 (1.76) | -7.74 (.98) | -.192 (1.81) | -.65 (5.98) | 886.85 (2.79) | .84 | 1.82 |
| JAM | 7.27 (1.05) | .116 (3.51) | -2.11 (2.46) | .065 (.012) | -.203 (1.42) | -.67 (4.88) | 24514.2 (4.23) | .82 | 2.73 |
| PER | 18.28 (.65) | .216 (7.18) | -6.24 (1.83) | 13.30 (.64) | -.446 (7.59) | -.70 (8.51) | 640.35 (3.57) | .87 | 2.66 |
| GUY | 6.53 (1.33) | .167 (1.07) | -.533 (.91) | 2.41 (.71) | -.076 (.87) | -.286 (1.28) | 2390.77 (1.87) | .42 | 1.82 |
| ISR | -31.54 (.64) | .110 (1.64) | 14.68 (2.31) | -19.30 (.52) | -.572 (6.16) | -.60 (6.30) | -20259.2 (1.05) | .86 | 1.78 |
| PHI | 12.24 (.26) | .112 (2.91) | -1.20 (.20) | 27.67 (.75) | -.494 (4.57) | -1.09 (7.04) | 9042.9 (1.44) | .72 | 1.49 |
| SLA | .572 (.12) | .038 (4.56) | .90 (1.47) | 1.96 (.54) | -.300 (3.20) | -.74 (7.39) | 777.38 (2.71) | .89 | 2.33 |
| YU | -7.7 (.70) | -.0034 (.10) | 30.98 (2.53) | -94.5 (1.13) | 060 (.44) | -.345 (1.72) | -1060.07 (.28) | .45 | 2.02 |

[a] See notes to Table 14.A1.

out of ten cases but only in two cases is the coefficient positive. Speci-fying the current-account equation according to equation (2) and the balance-of-payment equation according to equation (1) leaves this basic conclusion unchanged. Employing a dummy variable instead of the actual exchange-rate variable, should bring out more clearly the 'one shot' character of discrete exchange-rate changes. However, when this was done, the number of significant 'devaluation' variables in the balance-of-payments equation was reduced to two neither of which had a positive sign.

In the capital-account equation, the exchange-rate variable is significant at the 1 per cent level in five out of ten cases and has the expected positive sign in all five cases. The fact that, in contrast to the capital-account equation, in the balance-of-payments equation the exchange-rate variable is positive and significant only in two cases, might indicate that in the remaining cases opposite exchange-rate effects on the current account and the capital account cancel each other out. Indeed, in two of these remaining cases the exchange-rate coefficient in the current-account equation is negative and significant at the 10 per cent level.

Finally, one should note that the t-tests discussed here refer only to contemporaneous exchange-rate effects. In order to capture possible lagged effects of a devaluation, lagged values of the respective exchange-rate variables would have to be included in the estimating equations.[4]

## 2 THE RESIDUALS TEST

Equations (1) to (3) were estimated, excluding the exchange-rate variable. Equations (1) and (2) were estimated, each with the current account as well as the balance of payments as dependent variables. The residuals for the year of devaluation, and for the three preceed-ing and the three following years, were taken from each set of regressions. To prevent countries with large variance in the residuals from dominating the sample, all residuals were divided by their re-spective standard errors. Finally, the residuals were averaged across the sample. The residuals thus obtained can be regarded as a sample weighted average of 'purged' balance-of-payments figures, purged of the effects of the variables included in the regression equations. These average residuals are summarised in Table 14.A4. The number following the dependent variable indicates on which equation the speci-fication of the respective set of equations is based; (1) therefore means

TABLE 14.A4   RESIDUALS TEST

| Dependent variable | Year | $t-3$ | $t-2$ | $t-1$ | $t$ | $t+1$ | $t+2$ | $t+3$ |
|---|---|---|---|---|---|---|---|---|
| Current account | (1) | −0.237 | 0.078 | 0.266 | −0.383 | 0.278 | −0.324 | 0.233 |
| Current account | (2) | −0.130 | 0.065 | 0.226 | −0.420 | 0.274 | −0.337 | 0.154 |
| Balance of payments | (1) | 0.228 | 0.206 | −0.056 | −0.147 | 0.005 | −0.423 | −0.146 |
| Balance of payments | (2) | 0.050 | 0.259 | −0.098 | −0.108 | −0.036 | −0.432 | −0.112 |
| Capital account | (3) | −0.101 | −0.196 | −0.320 | 0.516 | −0.072 | −0.182 | 0.333 |

the inclusion of the government expenditure variable; (2) that this variable was excluded; it indicates the year of devaluation.

## V QUALIFICATIONS

The results obtained here are not independent of the specification of the estimating equations[5] To the extent that our equations neglect relevant explanatory variables, and that these variables are correlated with the variables included, the coefficients of the included variables will be biased. Moreover, since the residuals capture the effects of omitted variables, the exclusion of relevant explanatory variables leads to upward biased variance estimates and thus to conservative t-tests for the remaining variables, including the exchange-rate variable.[6]

In the residuals test, the residuals are assumed to reflect the effects of the dropped exchange-rate variable. However, they also reflect the effects of other omitted variables,[7] so that the results of the residuals test also depend on the specification of the estimating equations. Further research into the consequences of alternative specifications seems necessary.

NOTES

1. For a more detailed description of variables see Section III.
2. Miles's equations lack the more rigorous treatment of the determinants of money supply and demand common to empirical tests of the monetary approach to balance-of-payments theory. (See, for example, S. P. Magee (1976) 'The Empirical Evidence on the Monetary Approach to the Balance of Payments and Exchange Rate', *American Economic Review*, 66, pp. 163–9 and B. B. Aghevli and M. S. Khan (1977) 'The Monetary Approach to Balance of Payments Determination: An Empirical Test', in *The Monetary Approach to the Balance of Payments*, Washington DC: IMF, pp. 275–90). In particular, changes in the balance-of-payments accounting for adjustment of money supply to money demand should be related to the second, not the first, difference in the domestic source of money supply.
3. In the case of the capital-flow equation, this implies taking second differences of the explanatory variables, since the level of the capital account is already related to the first differences of these variables.
4. However, regarding the very limited number of observations available for the countries analysed, including further explanatory variables would impair the efficiency of our estimates.
5. Miles, however, seems to regard these effects as negligible.

6. Note that, on average, in the current-account equation only slightly more than one-third of total variation of the dependent variable is explained.
7. Rather than examining the residuals from equations excluding the exchange-rate variable, one should therefore compare the residuals from regressions including the exchange-rate variable with the residuals from regressions excluding the exchange rate.

REFERENCES

Fama, E.F., Fisher, L., Jensen, M.C. and Roll, R. (1969) 'The Adjustment of Stock Prices to New Information', *International Economic Review*, 10.
Helleiner, A.K. (1981) *The Impact of the Exchange Rate System on the Developing Countries: A Repair to the Group of 24* (Washington DC: International Monetary Fund).
International Monetary Fund (1981) *World Economic Outlook* occasional Paper No. 4 (Washington DC: IMF).
Kouri, P.J. and Porter, M.C. (1974) 'International Capital Flow and Portfolio Equilibrium', *Journal of Political Economy*, 82, May/June.
Makin, John (1974) *Capital Flows and Exchange Rate Flexibility*, Princeton Essays in International Finance, No. 103 (New Haven, Conn: Yale University Press)
Miles, Marc A. (1978) *Devaluation and the Trade Balance* (New York: Marcel Dekker).
Miles, Marc A. (1979) 'The Effects of Devaluation on the Balance of Payments: Some Results', *Journal of Political Economy*, 87, no. 3, June.
Viner, Jacob (1924) *Canada's Balance of International Indebtedness, 1880 to 1913*. (Cambridge, Mass: Harvard University Press).

# Part Four
# North and South

# 15 New Approaches to Development Finance: A Critical Look at the Brandt Proposals

**Niels Thygesen**

UNIVERSITY OF COPENHAGEN, DENMARK

## I INTRODUCTION

In December 1979 the International Commission on International Development Issues completed a document – *North–South: A Programme for Survival* – generally known as The Brandt Report (BR). This exceptionally comprehensive report surveys the record of development in the 1970s and looks at a large number of proposals for modifications of international trade, aid and financial arrangements. Some were novel, but most are familiar to those acquainted with the North–South negotiations 1975–7 in the framework of the Conference on International Economic Co-operation (CIEC) and with subsequent debates in the main international organisations. BR, understandably in view of its purpose, aimed at a very wide audience and opted for brevity. A companion volume of papers discussed by the Commission as a background to producing BR has subsequently been published and is helpful in clarifying the nature of some of the proposals (see Brandt Commission, 1981).

The purpose of this paper is to look briefly, in the light of developments in 1980–1 and of the international economic prospects for the

1980s, at those recommendations of BR that take up subjects central to this conference. Hence most of the vast range of subjects covered in BR will have to be left out. This includes arguably the most fundamental of them such as policies for food, trade in manufactures and transfer of technology. So will any discussion of domestic policies in the countries of the South. Incidentally, that is a subject also largely omitted from BR itself – an omission which has attracted much criticism (see Bauer and Yamey, 1981).

The main BR proposals relating to the external financing of development may conveniently be summarised thus:[1]

A   Proposals to modify the international monetary system and the IMF:
- more stable exchange rates between major currencies;
- new issues of improved SDRs through both allocations and a substitution account;
- linkage of SDR issues to development assistance;
- further demonetisation of gold;
- removal of contractionist pressures due to traditional IMF conditionality;
- enlargement of IMF facilities;
- greater share for LDCs in the staffing, management and decision-making of the IMF.

B   Proposals to enlarge and improve the transfer of longer-term resources:
- larger resource transfers to LDCs with more emphasis on lending to increase food production, develop energy resources and stabilise commodity prices;
- improvement of the predictability and distribution of donor country efforts through international taxation linked to national income;
- enlargement of the lending capacity of the World Bank and the Regional Development Banks;
- creation of a new international financial institution – a World Development Fund – to satisfy unmet needs in the financing structure;
- enlargement of lending to LDCs through private international credit and capital markets, with longer-maturities for loans to middle-income countries and easier access for poorer LDCs;

- co-financing between private and official sources, the latter covering notably the World Bank, including provision of guarantees, arrangements for risk assessment and other efforts to improve lending terms.

## II REFORMS OF THE INTERNATIONAL MONETARY SYSTEM AND THE IMF

This section considers the issues listed in A above. The international monetary system has not been moving in the direction of the BR proposals over the past two years, nor does it seem likely to do so in the foreseeable future. The major currencies fluctuated more sharply in 1980–1 than during the previous eight years of floating; allocations of SDRs appear to be petering out with the end of the present triennial allocation period and the idea of a substitution account has been shelved. To the extent that the role of gold as an international reserve asset is discussed, it is mainly in the context of proposals to restore to it a larger role. IMF conditionality has continued to draw criticism from spokesmen of the South; and the changes in the distribution of quotas, staffing and improvements in other fields of potential influence have been minimal. The only area in which developments could be said to have corresponded at least partly to the BR proposals is in the size of IMF facilities. On closer examination, however, the record seems less disappointing than this enumeration would suggest.

Let us briefly re-examine what the developments during the past two years in the international monetary system imply for the ability of the countries of the South to cope with continuing severe external constraints.

## III EXCHANGE RATES

The sharp changes in the dollar exchange rates of other major currencies have had three important implications for the non-oil developing countries: (i) to increase the short-run variability of their effective exchange rates; (ii) to influence in the short-to-medium-period the terms-of-trade of individual countries to an extent depending upon the precise nature of their exchange-rate regime; and (iii) to influence the real value of their net debts and debt servicing costs.

TABLE 15.1   AVERAGE MONTHLY VARIABILITY OF EFFECTIVE
EXCHANGE RATES, JAN. 1974–1980[a]

|                          | 1974–71 | 1978 | 1979 | 1980 |
|--------------------------|---------|------|------|------|
| Industrial countries     | 1.28    | 1.44 | 0.96 | 1.03 |
| All developing countries | 1.41    | 1.66 | 1.47 | 1.45 |
|   pegged to US$ | 1.05    | 1.55 | 1.51 | 1.24 |
|   pegged to SDR | 1.66    | 1.99 | 2.58 | 1.97 |
|   pegged to FF  | 0.66    | 0.70 | 0.37 | 0.46 |
|   others        | 1.87    | 1.96 | 1.52 | 1.81 |

[a] Variability defined as the standard deviation of monthly percentage changes; for groups of countries unweighted averages. Import-weighted indices based on 1977 are used; countries are classified according to their exchange arrangements on 31 January 1981.

Source: *IMF Annual Report* (1981) p. 42.

As regards the short-term variability of their effective exchange rates, Table 15.1 suggests that there has been no clear trend since the transition to floating around 1973. Regardless of the particular exchange-rate regime, the monthly variability of effective rates remained roughly the same until the end of 1980 and was typically somewhat higher than for most of the industrial countries. But short-term variability did increase in 1981 when the amplitude of changes in several individually floating currencies (dollar, sterling, yen) widened.

It is not clear how far this degree of variability directly entails real costs. Perhaps surprisingly, it has not been possible to find conclusive evidence that trade and investment flows among industrial countries have been significantly hampered by short-run exchange-rate variability. Yet greater short-run departures from purchasing power parity – that is, from a constant real effective exchange rate – must entail real costs. And this is what the gyrations in nominal rates introduce. In the case of many developing countries such departures are, however, likely to be small compared to those caused by the divergence of its national inflation rate from that of the country (or composite of countries in the case of SDR) to whose currency the developing country is pegging its currency.[2]

There are indirect effects from currency instability upon the balance-of-payments problems of the LDCs, via the impact of greater exchange-rate variability on the income and imports of the industrial countries from the LDCs. These are potentially greater, but can hardly be quantified.

As regards the impact of the strengthening of the dollar *vis-à-vis* other major currencies over the three years since the tightening of US monetary policy in November 1978, it is necessary to distinguish between LDC currencies pegged to the dollar and others. For the former group, linkage to the dollar has temporarily implied a tendency towards real appreciation. Whether the benefits consequential on a temporary terms-of-trade improvement and on lower imported inflation have outweighed the costs of a squeeze on earnings in export industries, cannot be discussed in general terms. It requires a careful country-by-country appraisal. The currencies of other LDCs have been pegged to the SDR, to some other composite, or – in the case of the French-speaking African countries – to the French franc. Here, the impact on their terms of trade and on other strategic macroeconomic variables from the cyclically strong dollar has been in the opposite direction. On the whole that effect has been far smaller. No doubt, at times, it has been perceived as inconvenient, notably because of the terms-of-trade losses arising from higher real costs of imported energy.

The most that can be said in general terms is that the cyclical strength of the dollar, in terms of other major currencies, has marginally complicated economic management both for dollar-pegging countries and others, though primarily for the former. If the complications had been seen as important, there would no doubt have been a more pronounced move away from the dollar as a peg than has actually been observed. By mid-1981, thirty eight LDCs were pegging their currencies to the dollar, only two less than a year before. The choice of an exchange-rate regime is made on the basis of a number of factors in addition to the ease with which the terms of trade may be stabilised. Even so, had there been serious inconveniences in pegging to the dollar (or any other individually floating currency) that would no doubt have prompted a stronger move away from such a practice and towards pegging to the SDR or some individual basket of currencies.

The third kind of impact which exchange-market instability has in the short and medium term affects a country's net financial position. No currency by currency breakdown of the outstanding net debt of the LDCs is available. It totals about $600bn and there are also official holdings of foreign exchange, equal to about one-fifth of the outstanding debt. The bulk of the debt is denominated in dollars. An appreciation of the dollar *vis-à-vis* other currencies therefore adds significantly to the value of net external debt of LDCs, when that is expressed in units which reflect both the productive and the debt-servicing capacity of LDC borrowers.

In recent years, any such effects have, however, been swamped by the far larger impact of moves towards significantly higher real interest rates on a substantial part of outstanding LDC external debt. Since most LDC borrowing in recent years has been subject to floating interest rates, this movement has been swift. The interest cost of most Euro-currency credits has become linked to the London interbank offer rate (LIBOR) for dollar deposits of six months' maturity. Measured by this, the increase has been as much as 8–9 percentage points over the past three years (from an average of 9 per cent in 1978 to nearly twice that in 1981). Though some of that unprecedented jump reflects both higher inflationary expectations and actual inflation, several percentage points have temporarily been added to the real interest rate. Tighter monetary policies in the United States have affected both the exchange value of the dollar and international bank lending rates. The net result has been to impose higher debt-servicing costs on LDC international debtors and an underlining of the risks inherent in mobilising external resources for economic development. (For a detailed analysis of the interaction of exchange-rate fluctuations and higher interest rates in producing higher real debt-servicing costs, one should see IMF, 1981b).

In summary, the experiences of the past few years have added a new twist to the emphasis given in BR to the need for more stable exchange rates between major currencies. If the arguments in favour of such stability had to rest solely on the effects on trade flows and terms of trade in the short to medium term, it is not clear that they should be regarded as important. For most LDCs such effects are likely to be of a secondary order of magnitude. But the implications for external development financing of exchange-rate instability (and of the monetary divergences that have helped to produce it) add urgency to some criticisms made by industrial countries outside North America. These relate to the choice of monetary techniques and of the policy-mix – particularly the adoption of a strongly non-interventionist attitude in the exchange market – by the US authorities.[3]

A three-year *allocation period for SDRs* is coming to an end and no decisions on further allocations have proved feasible. Agreement at the 1981 Annual Meeting was limited to a request to the IMF Executive Board to keep the matter, including the possibility of extending the present allocation period, under consideration.

The annual allocations in 1979–81 of SDR 4 billion, out of which SDR 1 billion went to the non-oil LDCs, were modest and it is difficult to defend the view that to have continued at this rate would have been inflationary. That argument becomes more credible in the light of the plan, advocated in BR and often elsewhere, to link new allocations to development assistance. This could have been done either by giving non-oil LDCs larger allocations than their IMF quotas would imply, or by making some allocations through longer-term development institutions. (A condensed version of the main pros and cons of the scheme and of its main variants may be found in Committee of Twenty (1974), pp. 95 ff.)

Still, it is difficult to avoid the impression that the SDR/Aid Link proposal has been given more attention than its potential quantitative importance justifies. The conceivable size of allocations would not be large enough to warrant either serious fears of inflation or hopes of any significant net increase in the external resources available to non-oil LDCs. In addition, the costs of being a net user of SDRs have increased as interest rates charged and paid have moved closer to market levels, making it likely that part of the SDRs allocated to non-oil LDCs would remain unspent. Using SDRs would still be cheaper than borrowing in international financial markets, to an extent depending on the credit rating of the borrowing LDC, as reflected in the interest-rate spread; but some LDCs will not be tempted to use their SDRs in order to improve their credit rating.

The main reason why the SDR/Aid Link Proposal remains on the agenda of the North–South negotiations is hardly an economic one; the amounts and the maximum possible benefits to be derived are too modest for that. Its significance is rather that it has come to epitomise the efforts of the LDCs to modify the distribution of quotas in the IMF.

Of much greater immediate significance is the very major *enlargement of the total lending resources potentially available through the IMF*. The Seventh quota increase, agreed upon in 1979 and finally implemented in late 1980, has augmented the combination of facilities available, many of them unconditional, which permit members to draw up to $4\frac{1}{2}$ times the size of their quotas. Together, these moves restored the lending capacity of the IMF to approximately the same level relative to current imports as was found suitable in the 1950s and early 1960s. The present aggregate of quotas is close to SDR 60bn, of which the share of the non-oil LDCs is about one-fourth. Multiplying this by the enlarged gearing ratio, one arrives at a hypothetical maximum of close to SDR 70bn for the total borrowing capacity of non-oil LDCs, through the IMF, or about the order of magnitude of their collective annual current account deficit in 1980 or 1981.

Such a figure is hypothetical in double sense: (i) not all non-oil LDCs wish to borrow from the IMF – or could meet the conditionality tests if they did – and (ii) if they did, the IMF would soon be constrained by the availability of the convertible currencies required. Calculations made by IMF staff in 1981 suggest that net lending, i.e. net of repayments, by the IMF might amount to SDR 14bn annually in the financial years 1981–2, 1982–3 and 1983–4: and a (minor) part of that lending would presumably go to industrial countries. To meet a demand of this magnitude, the IMF would have – prior to the eighth quota increase, which will become operative only around 1984 – to supplement its resources by borrowing SDR 7–8bn annually from governments or in the private markets. A very promising beginning has been made with the loan extended by the Saudi Arabian Monetary Authority (SAMA) to the IMF, which covers about half of this borrowing requirement for 1981–2 and 1982–3. The problems of covering the remainder of the IMF's borrowing needs – and particularly determining whether some of that borrowing should take the form of market-issues of IMF debt – will continue to preoccupy the decision-making bodies of the IMF. There is, however, no doubt that the IMF will, over the next few years, be far better prepared than ever to play an active and major role in providing external finance to the non-oil LDCs.

This enlarged scope for IMF participation in the recycling process has long been sought by spokesmen of the LDCs and was an important element in BR.[4] In the way it is now coming about, it also helps to achieve another main objective, namely, to make the SDR the central reserve asset of the international monetary system. Proposals to achieve this objective have traditionally centred on larger allocations of SDRs and on the substitution of national currency assets for SDRs. The scheme for an IMF Substitution Account, in which official holders of dollars and other national currencies could swap these for SDR-denominated claims on the IMF, would have been a reform well designed to dampen the exchange-market instability that results from large-scale currency diversification. As such, it was advocated by LDCs and BR. We are now seeing the beginning of an organised diversification of reserves, in the form of the acquisition by some surplus countries of medium-term, SDR-denominated claims on the IMF. This is on a smaller scale than the SDR 50bn planned for the defunct Substitution Account, but it could have similarly desirable effects when continued and enlarged over a period of several years.

Both because of its direct and indirect effects, one would expect the enlarged IMF role in recycling also to have been acclaimed more widely by the non-oil LDCs as a major step towards a more stable international monetary framework. It has not, because the prevailing view of IMF lending among LDC spokesmen and economists continues to be highly critical. *IMF conditionality* is seen as too harsh a medicine, requiring balance-of-payments adjustments within a time frame that is too short to deal with the problems faced by most of the LDCs that are among the IMFs potential clients.

It is obvious that the term 'adjustment' is being used in two rather different ways. In traditional IMF terminology, it relates to the need to adjust unduly expansionary fiscal or monetary policies or to restore competitiveness through devaluation. In other words, it refers to correct policies that would, even in a benign external environment, have led to major external imbalance. There are no doubt many such examples of policies in need of adjustment, to which traditional prescriptions apply; and the IMF is well justified to devote attention to them. But over the next decade 'adjustment' in a large number of non-oil LDCs signifies the need to make more fundamental changes in their policies in order to cope with a span of years of sharply worsened terms of trade and of slow growth in their main export markets in the industrial economies. The means of adjustment are summarised under headings such as energy conservation and industrial adaptation, all with some emphasis on supply-side measures rather than pure demand-management policies. Both the policy instruments required and the time-horizon within which results may be expected are different from those associated with the implementation of traditional stabilisation programmes.

There is a wide range of experience of the typical effects of such programmes, even if one disregards these implemented prior to the first oil-price increase and the subsequent prolonged recession in the industrial countries.[5] More recent developments in IMF practices are reviewed in surveys by Khan and Knight (1981) and Williamson (1980). On the basis of these interpretations of the evidence, some of the criticisms levelled by *inter alia* BR[6] at traditional stabilisation programmes appear excessive. In particular, the accusation that there is an element of dogmatic adherence to the monetary approach to the balance of payments, in the prescriptions typically made by IMF missions, would be difficult to substantiate. A careful reading of the record would suggest that the IMF recommendations have invariably included a wide range of policies in addition to monetary restraint. With respect to these fiscal and other policies, borrowing countries have been given the benefit of any reasonable doubts in the interpretation of performance criteria expressed in terms of public-sector deficits.

There has been, as argued in BR and elsewhere, an obvious need for the IMF to modify its lending practices relative to those in the pre-1974 period. But the modifications already introduced go a long way towards meeting that need. In addition to the sheer size of the present facilities, one may point to the extension of the typical time-horizon of stabilisation programmes to three years and to the lengthening of credit under the Extended Facility towards ten years. These changes fit well into the pattern required for the 1980s. It is not a sign of their inadequacy, as is sometimes argued, that relatively few among the middle- or low-income countries have so far made use of the IMF for balance-of-payments financing and adjustment. If other mechanisms for transferring resources operated smoothly there would be a very limited role for the IMF in the process. There would be little point in having the IMF take over financing which could be organised through international capital markets, even though costs to borrowers would be marginally reduced. The special role for the IMF is to bridge, through its conditional lending, the time gap between the introduction of an adjustment programme and the time where credit-worthiness has been sufficiently restored. This is the point where private international markets can take over further financing, while permitting liberal trading practices to survive in this interim period. Ideally, that role will involve some measure of co-financing with private lenders, as discussed in Section III. It is difficult to understand how conditionality – in roughly the form practised in the most recent period, and relying on some quantifiable performance criteria – could be dispensed with. Borrowing countries will obviously want to pursue broader policy aims than those that can be specified in a standby agreement with the IMF: but objectives of political and social stability hardly lend themselves to monitoring – and even less if the judgements are to be made by international institutions.

We have noted the enlargement of potential access to the IMF and the smoothness with which the IMF's normal resources seem likely to be supplemented by borrowing from national monetary authorities or, if necessary to gain additional flexibility, international capital markets. This offers some hope that real progress is being made, though not entirely in the direction proposed in BR. But the larger role of the IMF is one that will benefit primarily those countries whose creditworthiness is capable of restoration, i.e. most of the middle-income LDCs. It will be less adequate for the needs of the low-income LDCs. Those countries can hardly be brought to the point of gaining access to private capital markets within any manageable time-horizon. Yet the cost of financing their external deficits through standby arrangements with the IMF appears far higher than is justified by their development prospects and their projected debt-servicing capacity. In this perspective, it is disappointing that the subsidisation of borrowing costs made possible by transferring part of the profits of gold sales by the IMF to the Trust Fund has not been continued and on a larger scale. A strong case remains that an extension of the gold sales would have been a constructive way of (i) appropriating these profits to a genuinely international reserve and in favour of international development,[1] and (ii) underlining a determination to diminish the role of gold in the international monetary system.

In short, we must reassess BR's proposals on reform of the international monetary system and the IMF in the light of the record of 1980–1 and of the prospects for the nearer-term future. This suggests that some progress has been made, notably on the important issue of the size of resources potentially available through the IMF. The main immediate problem is the rise in the level of real interest rates in the international markets. This has aggravated the debt-servicing problems of most LDCs in a way that was not – understandably in the light of the policy environment in 1975–80 – foreseen in BR.

The remainder of BR's proposals are generally of a far more limited quantitative significance, or could indeed prove counterproductive, in achieving the overall aims of the proponents themselves. That is certainly the case with the proposal to remove traditional conditionality more systematically; and it is probable that pressures to implement shifts in favour of the LDCs in the decision-making and management of the IMF will block progress in more substantive areas. Quota revision is an extremely difficult process, as we may soon witness in the eighth revision. If the LDCs push their demands for enlarging their share of quotas – and they are already well above what strict application of the formal criteria would imply – that may jeopardise the prospects for getting an overall increase of the size required. In that sense, there is a trade-off between the political and the financial elements in the BR proposals.

With international trade and investment, including the transfer of technology, there is little agreement on the best theoretical framework for evaluating current arrangements. The general principles underlying the design of a well-functioning international monetary system are, however, much more widely accepted. (See the editor's illuminating introductory chapter in Helleiner (ed.) 1981.) It is disappointing that this wider acceptability was not reflected more fully in the proposals of BR.

## IV   ENLARGEMENT AND IMPROVEMENT OF TRANSFERS OF LONGER-TERM RESOURCES

The range of issues considered by BR under this heading is so vast that it is necessary to concentrate here on two sets of issues: (i) the idea of an international development tax to improve the predictability and distribution of official development assistance (ODA): and (ii) methods for enlarging and stabilising the flow of resources available to LDC borrowers through international capital markets.

Among the proposals of BR, none has attracted greater attention than the idea of *enlarging ODA and making it more automatic through separate, internationally co-ordinated, taxation*. BR argues that it would be highly desirable to take aid appropriations out of annual budgetary debates in the industrial countries. BR advocates a move towards an internationalisation of the domestic situation in a welfare state where 'taxes are progressive in incidence, social expenditures are redistributive and the links between taxpayers and beneficiaries are indirect'.[9] Some more specific proposals for the design of such taxes are then reviewed, the one favoured being a flat rate levy on international trade.

In principle, existing procedures in the industrial countries are already designed to achieve continuity and growth in ODA. With the exceptions of the USA and Switzerland, the OECD member countries have publicly subscribed to the principle of providing 0.7 per cent of their GNP in ODA; and they are asked in the OECD's Development Assistance Committee to explain shortfalls. In those – relatively few – industrial countries that have reached the ODA target, implementation of the BR proposal might not be very controversial; nor would it be likely to make more resources available. In countries that fall far short of the target, the proposal would be most unlikely to be implemented. In all OECD countries, legislators and the public would be reluctant to remove the possibility of revising commitments in the light of actual achievements; there is a recurrent need for demonstrating that aid is being used effectively, if political support is to be maintained. Indeed, such an attitude is being applied even to domestic expenditure programmes, which were until recently considered an integral part of the welfare state. Given the sharpening of a critical attitude to domestic transfer payments, the scope for moving to a high degree of automaticity in international transfers has become more difficult to make. Though a higher degree of continuity and predictability of ODA is certainly desirable, more pedestrian methods of achieving this will have to be used to facilitate success.

*Non-concessional capital flows* are at the other end of the wide spectrum of types of resource transfer. They have, on the average in recent years, been twice as large as ODA flows. It is therefore of the greatest significance how well the LDCs (and particularly the middle-income LDCs for whom this source of external financing is completely dominant) manage to maintain and improve their access to the international capital markets.

BR reiterates the need for enlarging the lending capacity of the World Bank – through a mixture of increased capital and higher gearing – and of the regional development banks. It also discusses a number of ways in which the flow of private lending could be enlarged and stabilised. Underlying these proposals is the concern that such lending is not only unduly costly to the LDC borrowers, it is also unpredictable in volume because of the prospect of sudden shifts in perceptions of risk, in national regulations in the home countries and in other imponderables. Unfortunately, the discussion in BR suffers from excessive optimism, as subsequent contributions have made clear; it is in fact very difficult to outline methods for increasing the net flow of private capital which do not produce undesired side effects.

One proposal often made, and partly implemented, is for more *co-financing* for private lenders teaming up with the World Bank in particular. The potential advantages are clear enough; private lenders may share the results of the detailed project analysis made by the Bank, while the bargaining position of lenders may be mutually reinforced by 'cross-default' clauses. Here the World Bank retains the option (but is not obliged) to suspend disbursements if a borrowing country defaults *vis-à-vis* one or more of the private lenders. To the borrowing country, the advantage of co-financing is that private lenders are attracted who might not have lent on their own.

If one looks at the record of the co-financing arrangements in which the World Bank has been involved since the first agreement (in 1975), it is striking that the projects financed have been heavily concentrated in the more developed countries in Latin America, which are already very familiar to the major international banks. There are very few examples of a co-financed project opening up a new area to international bank lending. Furthermore, 'cross-default clauses' have proved less applicable than may initially have been expected, and accordingly less attractive to private lenders. Tightening these clauses might, on the other hand, create difficulties with borrowers. In these circumstances, the growth of co-financing arrangements is likely to continue to be slow and they may contribute less extra finance than is often implied by their proponents.

Another possible method for increasing the flow of private bank lending is through *guarantees extended by the World Bank* or another multilateral agency (not the IMF which is not permitted to guarantee debt). Again, the question is whether such a procedure would lead to a net enlargement of the resources available to non-oil LDCs. That would not appear to be the case, under the reasonable assumption that the guarantor has to backup his commitment with his capital; in that case, the guaranteed private loan is essentially a substitute for a loan directly from the guarantor. There may be larger scope for increasing the net capital flow to LDCs through government guarantees in individual industrial countries. Indeed, such schemes already abound in the field of export credits, where the main aim of national policy is to promote exports, subject to the constraint imposed by international agreement to set a limit to this form of competition.

Easier access for LDC bond issues in the *Euro-bond and foreign bond markets* is another possible way of increasing resource availability. It has been a remarkable feature of LDC borrowing throughout the period of massive external deficits since 1973, that it has relied almost entirely on medium- and long-term syndicated bank credits. On average, bond-financing has amounted to only about 10 per cent of the gross amounts raised. This situation hardly corresponds to the preferences of the LDCs, for whom access to the longer-term funds of the bond markets at predictable interest rates would be a useful supplement to borrowing through the market for syndicated bank credit.

Better access to international and foreign bond markets would be useful, making it possible for longer-term institutional investors, such as pension funds and insurance companies in the industrial countries, to invest in LDC debt. Even so, in a number of countries the scope for making such placements on a very substantial scale would remain constrained, because of statutory regulations limiting foreign-security holdings to a small percentage of total assets. In any case, substantial marketing efforts would be required before significant amounts of LDC debt could be sold, and assistance from one or more of the international institutions in organising the market would be helpful. If the possibility of partial guarantees by regional develoment banks or the World Bank has to be discarded (for the reasons given above), some help from these sources in developing a secondary market in LDC bonds could provide the best method for improving access to this source of external financing. Such a proposal was put forward in an official report some years ago (World Bank and the IMF, 1978).

The central issue in the evaluation of the scope for continuing and large flows of bank credits to the LDCs is that of keeping perceived and actual risk in lending within manageable bounds. Has the indebtedness to the major commercial banks reached such proportions that continued lending is running into self-imposed limits, or prudential regulations, imposed by the national monetary authorities of the industrial countries? Are the sanctions in the present system, against sovereign borrowers who default and request rescheduling, sufficiently clear to encourage lenders to continue extending their commitments? It is surprising how little BR had to say on this set of interrelated issues, in view of its importance to the prospects for economic development over the next decade.[10] The report, as a radical document, focuses instead on gaps in financing and on the creation of a new institution, a World Development Fund. It thereby takes a much longer time-horizon than that of the next few years. Yet the lack of more pragmatic contributions on how the present system could be improved and stabilised is a major omission, to say the least.

Some prominent private bankers have put forward ideas on how the main international banks could themselves contribute to a strengthening of confidence through establishing, by analogy with the swap network among the major central banks, *a net of reciprocal credit facilities*. Most observers have agreed, however, that such arrangements, while they might be helpful in minor crises, are not adequate to the task in a situation where confidence has been sharply reduced. Only the central banks, acting in close co-operation within their respective jurisdictions as lenders of last resort in accordance with the principles that are announced from time to time following the so-called Basle Concordat of 1975, can avert any serious consequences. There continues to be doubt, though, about how operational is the comprehensive reporting system on maturity transformation, capital adequacy and risk exposure. The Governors of the central banks in the Group of Ten countries plus Switzerland announced in April 1981 that this was being put into place at the Bank for International Settlements.[11] The delay of six years, between the adoption of the Concordat and the implementation of the reporting system which was to underpin it, is surprising and does create doubts whether central bank co-operation is adequate to the task.

A crucial factor in assessing the future viability of the system is how it copes with the recurrent instances of *debt rescheduling*. If the system is seen to be handling the repudiation of sovereign debt very leniently, that is bound to have a major impact on the readiness of the major banks to continue to extend credit. Careful analysis of these issues and of the recent experience has been provided recently in Eaton and Gersovitz (1981) and IMF (1981a).

Eaton and Gersovitz argue persuasively that the inability to impose credible sanctions on defaulting borrowers is the main impediment to additional private bank lending to LDCs. Proposals to improve co-ordination between private lenders and to involve the IMF more directly in debt rescheduling, including that of banking debt, are made. Resistance to such arrangements and regular demands by UNCTAD, the G 24 or other groupings in which the LDCs have a decisive influence for massive collective debt reschedulings are more likely to lower existing country limits than to make more external finance available. Significantly, the largest LDC borrowers have typically not endorsed these positions.

In its study of recent trends of LDC external indebtedness the IMF staff reviews the experience with rescheduling of debt for eleven developing countries which engaged in a total of eighteen rounds of multilateral debt renegotiations in the 1975–80 period. The IMF has participated actively and has provided analytical background ma-terial for the negotiations in the framework of the informal Paris Club of creditor countries and there appears to be little need for modifying these procedures. What might usefully be considered is a closer involvement of the IMF at an early stage of debt renegotiations with private creditors. Six such cases of rescheduling of private debt in the 1970s are reviewed; since the creditors in most cases urged the borrowing country to seek IMF credit in the upper tranches, the IMF was brought in at a later stage.

There is understandable reluctance on the part of the IMF to become heavily engaged in such private debt reschedulings. The case studies referred to above suggested that there had, in nearly all cases, been temporarily very high inflows of market financing in the years prior to rescheduling. It is not a natural task for the IMF to bail out

TABLE 15.2 BANKING GROUP LDC EXPOSURE
(*end 1980*)

|  | Total foreign assets ($USbn) | Per cent of all foreign assets | | |
|---|---|---|---|---|
|  |  | All LDCs | Non-OPEC | OPEC |
| US banks | 352 | 28.3 | 22.0 | 6.3 |
| French banks | 143 | 22.7 | 17.2 | 5.5 |
| UK banks | 106 | 23.4 | 16.9 | 6.5 |
| Luxembourg banks | 89 | 15.8 | 14.8 | 1.0 |
| German banks | 73 | 20.5 | 13.8 | 6.7 |
| Dutch banks | 62 | 9.1 | 7.8 | 1.3 |
| Other | 498 | 14.8 | 9.6 | 5.1 |
| Total Euro market | 1000 | 20.0 | 14.7 | 5.3 |

*Source: The Amex Bank Review*, September 1981, p. 3.

commercial banks who have overextended their lending in a period during which neither the national monetary authorities of the lenders nor the IMF have had any means of reliably monitoring the evolution of market financing. That is why the tighter reporting system now being put into place is a prerequisite for heavier IMF and other official involvement in debt renegotiations.

How this balance is struck seems more important than any feasible proposal to modify existing international financial arrangements. It will determine, more specifically, whether the US banks that are clearly the most exposed with an LDC share of their total foreign assets of 28 per cent can edge up higher, and whether the European banks are prepared to move from their much lower share towards the US exposure level (see Table 15.2). If the answer to both questions is affirmative, the aggregate size of the projectd LDC requirements for private financing in the next few years does not look unmanageable.

This brief review of possible new advances in development finance has, apart from some sceptical comments on automatic transfers through an international development tax, focused on issues within a shorter time perspective than those raised in the BR. In its keenness to bring across the message that a radical reform of international financial mechanisms, involving the launching of a new institution, the World Development Fund, the BR passed very quickly over the many smaller steps which could become feasible and which in combi-nation might enable the financial flows to the middle-income LDCs to be sustained during the prolonged period in which the massive balance-of-payments deficits of this group must persist. For the low-income LDCs to whom market financing is unlikely to become feasible on any important scale, ODA will have to continue to supply the bulk of external financing; the prospects for that happening on a satisfactory scale in the present political climate in several of the important industrial countries are distinctly less promising.

## Conclusions

The present paper has looked at the concerns voiced in the BR with respect to the international monetary system and resource transfers to LDCs and at some of the reform proposals made.

As regards the international monetary system developments in 1980–1, contrary to what may be inferred from the concerns of the BR, have not been entirely unfavourable to the LDCs. The enlargement of IMF resources and a more flexible attitude in the application of conditionality have been positive elements. It is difficult to find evidence that observed exchange-rate changes have been, on balance, harmful. The failure to continue SDR allocations is regrettable, but its importance is secondary only. The movement in the course of 1980–1 to a significantly positive real rate of interest in the United States and thereby in international capital markets is the major cause for complaint by the LDCs. A move to a different policy-mix in the industrial countries would be the single most helpful step to ease the burden of external financing.

On resource transfers it appears that the recommendations of the BR are not particularly helpful. The suggested move towards a development tax, apart from being beyond the range of feasibility for some time to come, fails to emphasise the domestic policy requirements in the LDCs. The BR seems to take an overly negative view of the functioning of international financial markets and its recommendations seem unlikely, if implemented, to lead to any major increase in the resources available to LDC borrowers.

It is, obviously, too early to judge the impact of the BR, and possibly unfair to confront its long-term solutions with the short-term concerns which form the substance of ongoing negotiations. Yet it is difficult to avoid the impression that the proposals, by their very ambition and by the overly sharp criticism of current arrangements on which they are based, will not be of much help in the design of changes in the international monetary system or in the ways in which resources are transferred to LDCs.

NOTES

1. For a fuller text see the summary of the proposals in BR, pp. 289–92.
2. A careful empirical study of the experiences of four Latin American countries prior to 1979 support the conclusion that the impact of the floating of the dollar (to which the four currencies were pegged) was minor (see Bacha, 1981).
3. This critical attitude is shared by many US observers. For a cogent criticism of non-intervention, see e.g. Kenen (1981).
4. See BR, pp. 211–12, and the elaboration of the argument in *Brandt Commission Papers*, pp. 587–8.
5. A summary of such early experiences is presented by Reichmann and Stillson (1978) for 1963–72. More general comments on stabilisation policies in developing countries may be found in Dell and Lawrence (1980); Clie and Weintraub (1981) and Croekett (1981); Johnson and Salop (1980) address the distributional impact of IMF programmes.
6. Notably BR (1980) pp. 215–17, and *Brandt Commission Paper* (1981), pp. 580–4.
7. IMF gold holdings are almost on a par with minerals in the sea-bed of the oceans, also suggested in BR as a natural vehicle for effective transfers to LDCs in being removed from national ownership.
8. See notably BR, pp. 244–7.
9. BR, p. 244.
10. Remarks directly relevant to the issues mentioned are limited to a few scattered paragraphs, notably BR, pp. 229 and 256, while the *Brandt Commission Papers* contain only a passing reference to debt reorganisation (pp. 622–4) and hardly any mention of commercial bank lending.
11. The full text of the Concordat has not been published, but a recent article offers a summary of the main considerations (see Cooke, 1981).


REFERENCES

Bacha, E. (1981) 'The Impact of the Float on LDCs: Latin American Experience in the 1979s', in J. Williamson (ed.) *Exchange-Rate Rules* (London: Macmillan).
Bauer, P.T. and Yamey, B.S. (1981) 'The Political Economy of Foreign Aid', *Lloyds Bank Review*, October.
Brandt Commission (1980) *North–South: A Programme for Survival* (Brandt Report), The Report of the Independent Commission on International Development Issues (London).
Brandt Commission (1981) *The Brandt Commission Papers: Selected Background Papers*, Independent Bureau for International Development Issues (Geneva and The Hague).
Clive, W.R. and Weintraub, S. (eds) (1980) *Economic Stabilization in Developing Countries (New York)*.
Committee of Twenty (1974) *International Monetary Reform* (Washington DC: IMF).
Cooke, W.P. (1981) 'Developments in Co-operation Among Bank Supervisory Authorities,' *Bank of England Quarterly Bulletin*, June.

Crockett, A. (1981) 'Stabilization Policies in Developing Countries: Same Policy Considerations', *IMF Staff Papers*, March.

Dell, S. and Lawrence, R. (1980) *The Balance of Payments Adjustment Process in Developing Countries* (New York: United Nations and Pergamon Press).

Eaton, J. and Gersovitz, M. (1981) *Poor-Country Borrowing in Private Financial Markets and the Repudiation Issue*, Princeton Studies in International Finance, No. 47, June.

Helleiner, G.K. (ed.) (1981) *For Good or Evil: Economic Theory and North-South Negotiations* (Oslo).

International Monetary Fund (1981a) Annual Report (Washington DC: IMF).

International Monetary Fund (1981b) *External Indebtedness of Developing Countries*, Occasional Paper, No. 3, May.

Johnson, O. and Salop, J. (1980) 'Distributional Aspects of Stabilization Programs in Developing Countries, *IMF Staff Papers*, March.

Kenen, P.B. (1981) 'Monetary Relations Between the USA and Europe – The American Point of View', in Abraham, J.P. and Vanden Abeele (eds.) *European Monetary System and International Monetary Reform* (Brussels).

Khan, M.S. and Knight, M.D. (1981) 'Stabilisation Programs in Developing Countries: A Formal Framework', *IMF Staff Papers*, March.

Reichman, T.M. and Stillson, R.T. (1978) 'Experience with Balance of Payments Adjustment: Stand-By Arrangements in the Higher Credit Tranches 1963–72'.

Williamson, J. (1980) 'Economic Theories and International Monetary Fund Policies', in *Monetary Institutions and the Policy Process*, K. Brunner and Meltzer, A.H. (eds). Supplement to the *Journal of Monetary Economics*; Amsterdam.

World Bank and International Monetary Fund (1979) *Developing Country Access to Capital Markets*, Report by the Joint Ministerial Committee of the two Institutions on the Transfer of Real Resources to Developing Countries (Washington DC: World Bank).

# Part Five
# The Discussions

# 16 Points from the Discussions

**A.A. Arnaudo***

## 1 Capital Requirements in Economic Development – Colaço

*Professor Teng* showed great optimism over the effect that the recovery of the American economy would have on all other economies, in particular the less-developed ones. The main problem would always be, nevertheless, how to increase capital flows towards the underdeveloped world and to ensure that the capital actually was used for their industrialisation and growth.

The assumptions made in the paper about the future evolution of oil prices were constantly questioned. It was likely that its real price would not increase in the next few years, or that it would do so to a lesser extent than was thought, because energy substitutes took time to develop and to bring into use. This substitution required heavy investment, which would mature only after several years. It must also be clearly established whether the oil-price increase led to a recession in the industrialised countries, and if so, how long it would take before these countries adapted to the new price level.

* The summary of the discussions was made originally in Spanish, in July 1983, by Professor Aldo A. Arnaudo, and later translated into English by Miss Florence Chaudet, Lecturer in the English Department of the School of Languages of the National University of Córdoba, Argentina. As special circumstances made it necessary· to base this summary on notes taken during the conference, only the discussants officially appointed have been identified. The main points that aroused the interest and attention of participants have been summarised. Not every intervention has been registered, for which an apology is therefore due; and some matters discussed have had to be omitted. Finally, the points attributed to the discussant, as well as the answers of the author, have not been submitted for the approval of those concerned. Any omissions and incorrect interpretations are exclusively the responsibility of the writer of the summary.

319

The impact of the recession and the increase of interest rates occurring in the industrialised countries was very important for the developing world. This was because the difference between imports and GNP had to be reduced as much as possible, especially when an import substitution strategy was followed. Hence, the financing of balance-of-payments deficits should not be confused with the financing of the growth process. Capital flows, in the past, had been subject to two limitations: (i) the capacity of developing countries to absorb real investment, and (ii) the availability of international finance; however, the different scenarios presented by the author supposed only that the second restriction was present. It could be anticipated that most international finance would be used to pay for imports of oil and of other goods necessary to satisfy basic needs. Thus only a very small part would be used in productive investment. In practice, and whether countries fell into one category or the other, there was the additional factor of a deterioration in the price of their export goods relative to that of imported equipment.

Recession in industrialised countries was not necessarily due to the oil-price increase but, more generally, to a fall in capital productivity accompanied by real wage increases: and to higher prices of imports from developing countries. This decline in returns on capital had reduced savings and the potential growth of the economy. Although savings had increased in oil exporting countries, the needs arising from other countries' balance-of-payment deficits seemed to have done so even more. Recession had been accompanied by a persistence of high interest rates, which had contributed to worsening it even more. To forecast whether this phenomenon of high interest rates was transitory or not became a central problem.

The role of domestic policies in making adjustments was of marginal importance: nevertheless, it was necessary to evaluate the policies which proved successful, so that they could be considered by developing countries.

Doctor Colaço's view was that the experience of the 1970s showed that some countries had a satisfactory rate of growth, and that some did not. The oil-price increase had affected them, but on top of its effects one should add international inflation, a worsening of the terms of trade, recession, high interest rates, etc. Developing countries were not passive recipients of external shocks; they also experienced the effects of their own domestic policies. The scenarios considered were not forecasts of future world economic behaviour; they were only terms of reference by which to assess economic policies aimed at facing them. To create the scenarios, energy prices (estimated in several studies) and a real interest rate of between 2 and 3 per cent – even when at present it might be around 5 or 6 per cent – were taken into account.

## 2 The Role of Domestic Financing in the Process of Economic Development – Kemenes

*Professor Petrei* pointed out first that the mere existence of a surplus in the agricultural sector – which could be transformed into real investment and might increase the rate of economic growth – did not ensure that this was always achieved automatically. The transfer of this potential surplus might contribute to a better use of resources or to greater efficiency in public expenditure, but there were many examples of the contrary having occurred, so that such a measure turned out to be self-defeating. The existence of an agricultural surplus might contribute to the determination of relative prices and so fulfil an important function in the allocation of resources: a tax intended to expropriate it totally or, in some cases, partially, might become inefficient. Likewise, no principle could ensure a better functioning of public enterprises relative to alternative forms of management or ownership. Finally, economies that depended essentially on foreign capital to mobilise their internal resources might be faced with serious difficulties if they tried to replace it by domestic finance.

In spite of the general agreement to favour a land-value tax as an instrument to raise funds from the agricultural sector, some drawbacks were pointed out. First, the tax base was the total agricultural surplus, derived as much from the part which could be devoted to consumption as by the part to be allocated to productive investment in the same sector. If the land tax discouraged investment without decreasing consumption, the effect would be the opposite of the one sought for, because the sector would be prevented from having greater capitalisation. It might happen that in a second stage of development the transfer would be from the non-agricultural sectors to agricultural investment. In the first stage of development, one must suppose that investment financed by the tax always had a higher social rate of return than any other alternative in the agricultural sector. Second, the land tax was relatively sophisticated and not very suitable for poorer countries by comparison with any other indirect tax. The alternative of a compulsory levy on the agricultural surplus through control of the exchange rate had very bad effects in practice. Third, the exemption of certain groups of farmers from paying taxes (contrary to what Kemenes said in his paper, the éjidos in Mexico were not taxed) might create an important distributive problem. In the second stage of development a subsidy to the agricultural sector might actually be a subsidy to the urban population.

The efficiency with which other sectors used the resources coming from the agricultural surplus could be measured through the operation of a relatively free financial system; the latter would make it possible to contrast the market rate of interest with the profits earned from different investments. Such would seem to have been the case of Japan in the first stage of its development, when action taken by the government to extract the agricultural surplus was accompanied by the growth, and great influence, of the banking sector. Using the financial sector implied paying intermediaries, whose cost had to be compared with the cost of transfers through any public mechanism. Nothing ensured that the latter would be smaller than the former more than if one took into account the losses, delays and bad allocations imposed by government bureaucracy.

Confidence in the contribution of domestic finance through using the agricultural surplus seemed to be based on the Hungarian experience, so that general conclusions applicable to all political systems could not be drawn. Some countries, like Switzerland, were counterexamples of this pattern. Furthermore, it was not clear whether England and Japan did, or did not, absorb foreign finance in the initial periods of their development. When Russian socialist development started, accumulation of capital took the form of an allocation of real resources. Even today, the implications which tax payments made by the agricultural sector had for the allocation of resources and the distribution of income was the subject of debate in socialist countries.

*Professor Kemenes* stated that, especially after the technological innovations introduced in Europe in the seventeenth century, the agricultural sector was crucial in the development that took place later, although this stylised process should be adjusted to allow for other facts and experiences. This sector, with backward conditions, did not respond to price incentives, so making it essential to tax the great mass of the population in an indirect and little felt way. The role of the government in countries that were in the first stage of development was basic: the banks should also be in public hands so as to inspire greater confidence in them among the population. Although domestic finance did not exclude foreign finance, only nations in the second stage of development were in a condition to choose between them.

## 3 The Financial Sector in the Planning of Economic Development – Backus, Blanco and Levine*

The adoption of financial programming as a key tool for managing a development process was debatable and had little chance of being applied in practice, although some countries, like Hungary, claimed that they had done so successfully. In a process of rapid growth, input–output techniques might lead to results far from the specified values because the assumption of constant relationships and coefficients conflicted with the large variability observed in the real world. A general equilibrium model might be useful if it contained two or three sectors; if this number were exceeded, the use of a partial equilibrium analysis would be preferable. Finally, development economics should not be content if it can provide only exercises in positive economies, but should also establish principles to improve policy-makers' decisions.

The model for the Mexican economy was also applicable to any developed country. That was why the assumptions made were not sufficiently clear and why it was impossible to determine their meaning in terms of the underlying economic behaviour. The statistical requirements were too demanding to be satisfied by a developing country.

*Professor Backus* stated that the relatively important conclusions drawn from simple models could be disproved by other equally simple ones, for which reason general equilibrium models represented a sort of balance between antagonistic positions. A financial plan could be formulated either in terms of objectives (of economic growth in this case) or in terms of instruments. If taken in this last sense, the model contained all the instruments of economic and financial character. Nevertheless, it was difficult to assess the effects of these instruments on employment, wages, distribution of income, and so on.

## 4 Savings Generation and Financial Programming in a Basic Needs Constrained Economy – Borpujari

*Professor Massad* was unfortunately unable to attend the conference, although his comments were made known in writing. He stressed the

---

*The paper did not have a specially appointed discussant.

fact that the model here developed was applied only to economies with the lowest income per capita, where disequilibria in the real sector were more important than disequilibria arising from the transfer of funds for the capitalisation process. If the discontinuity in the consumption function created by the existence of basic needs were not to appear in real life, the price system would become essential to the allocation resources; thus the dichotomy between the real sector and the financial sector would lose its precision. Since the model seemed to be based on a transformation function with international prices, rather than on individual indifference curves, the external sector of the economy should be included from the outset. The author maintained that his model was applicable to economies regardless of their political framework, be they market or centrally planned economies. That happened because he worked without price elasticities and took the technical coefficients in production and consumption as fixed, but in the long run this was no longer true, and the distinction between basic needs and the remaining needs became unnecessary.

Considerable argument took place over the very concept of 'basic need'. One point of view assumed that the nature of basic needs corresponded not to a technical but to a social concept. Even if one accepted this opinion, there must be a quantitative method of measuring it. Another position held that if this purely humanitarian principle were to be followed, any operational definition of basic needs would lead, in many cases, to an amount several times larger than the country's GNP.

Private saving constituted a voluntary activity to which the precepts of a social burden might not be applied. The financial problem consisted in channelling the domestic resources derived from that saving into productive investment, or in obtaining funds from rich countries where the productivity of capital was low. Should a financial market not fulfilling that goal not exist, the immediate implication of the analysis would be the need for a balance between departments 1 and 2, which must exist in a centrally planned economy. One could then speak of forced saving in the USSR, for example; but in developing countries, forced dissaving by the government would appear because it did not finance the whole of its military and welfare expenditures with taxes, but left the remainder to be financed by the capital market. In short, a reconciliation between resource mobilisation and resource allocation did not seem to take place satisfactorily in the model of basic needs.

Imbalances appeared in different sectors when the pattern of production was different from that of consumption, and these would not be eliminated because there was no price mechanism. It was true that the operation of the market was not instantaneous, but in the long run the economic authorities would have to permit changes in relative prices in order to tackle those maladjustments. The same would happen with time preferences in establishing interest rates, when the preferences of individuals and of the government differed, even when the representatives of the latter were democratically elected. In any case, one could question the real meaning of capital in a stationary economy that only produced enough to satisfy basic needs.

Doctor Borpujari insisted that it made no sense to speak of sophisticated financial problems in an economy that had not satisfactorily solved its real problems; for instance, when the average propensity to consume was close to one, the rate of interest might be of no importance. Even if the concept of basic need contained a good portion of humanitarianism, consumption elasticities in different income groups were very dissimilar. The proposed statistical method for evaluating aggregate consumption was an empirical attempt to arrive at the concept of basic needs. In any case, it corresponded to the concept of wage goods, in the terminology of classical economists. The existence of a minimum price (relative to the other goods) which must be achieved if the manufacturing sector were to be self-sustainable, and below which it would not produce, made the price mechanism a very doubtful instrument to use in tackling imbalances.

## 5 The Role of Financial Institutions in Economic Development – Kapur

*Professor Spaventa's* view was that there were no theoretical inconsistencies in the model. Hence the question of its practical importance for policy discussions should be based, first, on the implicit hypothesis that characterised the economy Professor Kapur had sketched; and, second, on the sensitivity of the results when those assumptions were changed. The results would not hold if individual behaviour were affected by uncertainty.

It was not clear why entrepreneurs should hold money assets whose interest rate would be lower than the rate of return on investment in the same sector. The distinction between people who saved and those who invested seemed to be more relevant to this problem; moreover, it was the natural way to introduce financial intermediation. If one did so, the present results would not follow, since a crucial assumption concerned the way businessmen saved and obtained funds through the ownership of money assets. An increase in the preferential interest rate allowed to the industrial sector would lead to an immediate increase in the return on money assets, while at the same time entrepreneurs' propensity to save would remain constant. Inspection of the equations showed that the rate of balanced growth would not be affected by the degree of intermediation, when the latter was understood as the share of investment financed by bank credit relative to that coming from the business's own savings. The inclusion of an external sector, which would apparently add realism to the model, did not seem necessary in order to arrive at the conclusions. The effect which a decrease in the rate of money creation would have on production in the different sectors, especially agriculture, was not considered.

The assumption of a wage rate fixed in terms of the agricultural good, which corresponded to development with unlimited supply of labour, was too strong in some cases. This was especially so when wage differentials were the rule. A more complete model should include human capital specifically.

Even when the hypothesis referring to savings and to price fixing according to a constant mark-up might be reasonable, the same was not true with some other assumptions. As regards production, the function selected was linearly homogeneous and had returns which were the opposite of those which one would expect in the agricultural and the manufacturing sectors. The method of analysing steady-state equilibria was essentially static, since it did not include time with an historical perspective. Finally, the model did not fit very well into a financially repressed economy.

To enable one to draw up policy recommendations, a model must be as realistic as possible. Two prices for the same commodity, such as two different interest rates, could not exist permanently, not even in a centrally planned economy. The limits that were imposed on firms seeking to obtain subsidised funds at low interest rates were not well defined. The subsidy to manufacturing would lead to savings in this sector being employed for investment in agriculture or in foreign markets. An increase in the interest rate for the industrial sector, a policy generally advocated, would affect the existing capital–labour ratio. Consequently, the distribution of income would not be the same and the assumption of a constant propensity to save would no longer hold.

Professor Kapur believed that by the analysis of alternative steady-state growth paths one could reach significant qualitative conclusions and that more specific results required policy simulations. Wage differentials did not exist in many countries – in any case they would introduce an additional distortion – and a fixed wage in terms of the agricultural commodity eliminated the need to consider income distribution problems. The Green Revolution had cast doubts on the traditional view of decreasing productivity in the agricultural sector. It had not been statistically proved, either, that the manufacturing sector consistently enjoyed returns to scale. Arbitrage between subsidised and non-subsidised funds would disappear with the elimination of market fragmentation – something the monetary authorities could obtain by using an adequate bank reserve policy. Greater intermediation would increase the interest rate paid on monetary assets and charged on bank loans, and so would contribute to the reallocation of funds from the industrial to the agricultural sector. The general recommendation that there should be more extensive intermediation must be directed towards improving the domestic market potential rather than towards making that market open to international capital. An increase in interest rates, linked to financial liberalisation, would influence not only the saving–investment gap but also the external sector, in the well-known model of two gaps. This would make it possible to face phenomena like the increase of oil prices.

## 6 The Role of the Public Sector in Mobilisation and Allocation of Financial Resources – Newlyn

*Professor Urquidi* first pointed out that the duty of the government of a low-income country was to develop the economy and society before it could redistribute income; a role that, unfortunately, had not been understood by most foreign creditors. The operational deficit of some public enterprises concerned with the provision of goods and services was often due to a price policy which had distributive purposes in mind. This also occurred with social security systems, which in most cases did not imply a net tax but a subsidy to the beneficiaries. The consumption of luxuries by social classes which were in the upper income bracket was usually classified as a potential source of funds for development whereas, in practice, it could be taxed only with rather narrow limits. Thus, one must rely on savings made by enterprises. Easily obtained external funds decreased the fiscal effort that the domestic economy needed to make, so that the analysis of government expenditures and of social productivity became crucial.

Maximising the proportion of financial resources transferred through the use of government operations could make sense only in the preliminary stages of the development process; later it was competition between public and private funds that must prevail. Since the facts taught that governments spent rather inefficiently, the appropriate rule might turn out to be the opposite one: to minimise the proportion of funds available for public investment. Consequently, the suggestion of an increase in public savings could not be thought of independently of the criteria for investment. Nevertheless, since a look at the general pattern of public consumption in less-developed nations indicated that it was more restricted than in industrialised countries, the recommendation to transfer savings through government intervention sounded logical. This could be done directly through government investment or by building up a public financial system and raising the confidence of the society in its functioning.

The statistical inference that higher taxation, measured as the proportion of taxation to GNP, had a positive effect on investment was based on an incorrectly specified relation. In general, studies in this area turned out to be somewhat unsatisfactory. Also, the proposition that inflation of the order of 30 per cent per annum fostered investment must be taken rather sceptically. Because of fiscal lags, it was doubtful whether a stable rate of inflation could exist; on the contrary, acceleration would most probably take place. To promote an inflationary process, even by undertaking such a worth-while purpose as creating higher investment, was a very dangerous action; for it was almost certain that it would not be possible to stop it.

The partial or total substitution of domestic savings by international capital might not be postulated in a general way. There were certain forms of foreign capital, such as direct investment, where such a substitution did not operate. It was not very logical to assume that foreign funds would be available if it was certain that they would be used for consumption – a fact which lowered the probability of repayment. However, private foreign financial institutions did not seem to bother much about the intended use for the funds they loaned, whether for consumption, for the acquisition of consumer durable goods or for truly productive investment. This lack of interest did not even imply a greater risk if the borrower was a government or a public agency since these generally did not go bankrupt.

*Professor Newlyn* stated that the concept of maximising the flow of funds did not mean that investment should not be judged according to its marginal value. A welfare function must require that the cost of taxation should be smaller than the benefits of the investment carried out with the proceeds. The correct size of government investment must also be deduced from that rule. Subsidies granted by the government could be used to satisfy basic needs: the distribution between basic needs and capital formation might be, in essence, a political question. Even if statistical analysis did not fully support it, there seemed to be a positive correlation between the scale of the tax effort and growth. On the other hand, this correlation did not appear with inflation, for the so-called inflationary tax did not lead to more rapid growth. Finally, statistical evidence would suggest a ratio of less than one between foreign funds and investment; hence the conclusion that approximately half of the former went into consumption.

## 7  Inflation and the Financing of Alternative Development Strategies – Canavese and Montuschi

*Professor Maynard* pointed out that the paper referred to Argentina, which was not an underdeveloped but a developed country, though badly developed; this might be due to the failure of the import-substituting industrialisation strategy. Inflation as a means of financing Argentinian industrialisation had behaved differently in the two periods. Up to 1945 it had increased savings; after 1945 it had destroyed them. More recently, it had become associated with recession, since it served to correct relative prices, and in particular incomes from agricultural and cattle-raising activities. The unsatisfactory situation arising from the import-substitution strategy and from financial repression might have been overcome by adopting four policies: (i) a financial reform to monetise the economy; (ii) a tax reform to eliminate the fiscal deficit and favour the agricultural and cattle-raising sectors; (iii) a liberalisation of international trade to promote productive efficiency and, eventually, to reduce inflation; (iv) the elimination of exchange-rate controls. Since these policies did not seem to have had their expected results promptly, one could ask whether financial repression should not be maintained, since there was an inconsistency between the short- and medium-term objectives. Finally, an import-substitution strategy was not bad in itself if it moved the economy closer to international productivity patterns.

The cause of inflation might not have been the need to increase savings; productivity differentials between sectors or a distributive struggle might have taken its place. The aggregate relationship between added value in manufacturing and GNP was usually determined by Engels' Law: When the price relationships aiming for a given income distribution did not help to achieve it, inconsistent demands appeared. Likewise, enough emphasis should be put on fiscal deficits and the losses of government-controlled enterprises as the main source of increases in the monetary base.

An import-substitution strategy did not necessarily lead to financial repression, so one should look independently for the causes of the former. Financial repression did not even lead to lower savings rates, which were due to a different phenomenon – inflation. Inflation led to a decrease in the value of financial (*vis-à-vis* real) assets, bringing about a consequent increase in the demand for real assets and fostering an increase in the price level. But one should not misinterpret the fact that financial repression was not the result of an import-substitution strategy. It was not unreasonable to postulate that its mere existence, or that of bad financial management, made it impossible to attain the financial requirements for such a strategy. As could be seen, one might find arguments in favour of each position, and this would seem to give rise to a vicious circle; slow economic growth due to a shortage of savings led to a fragmentation of the financial market; and that fragmentation was frequently considered the origin of meagre economic growth.

The existence of an acute inflationary process generally implied negative real interest rates and a subsidy to the borrower. Hence it might be concluded that investment and the capitalisation of the economy would increase. This did not seem to have happened in the Argentinian case, so it was not irrelevant to analyse the behaviour of investment in the presence of positive real interest rates. The indexation of financial assets and wages in economies with such significant disequilibria could lead to tremendous lack of stability. The random redistributive effects of inflation completed the picture.

Opening up the economy to foreign trade and capital, financial reform and a programme of price stabilisation were usually treated as a combined whole. Nevertheless, stabilisation had nothing to do with the opening up of the economy; neither was financial reform a crucial element in it. Argentinian experience showed that the social cost of using the three instruments simultaneously was enormous. The failure of exchange-rate and interest-rate liberalisation to stabilise prices called for the conclusion that financial repression was not the structural cause of inflation.

*Professors Canavese and Montuschi* analysed some of these comments. In Argentina, inflation was not sought as a way to increase savings but was the outcome of the import-substitution strategy. This strategy demanded periodic correction of sectoral disequilbria and so introduced a 'stop–go' sequence. These phenomena were accentuated by an essentially oligopolistic manufacturing sector, and the structural theory of inflation underlying their analysis was not much different from the Scandinavian model for developed countries. The paradox of a high savings ratio that did not seem consistent with slow economic growth was due to the high cost of investment goods, as had been shown by several economists. Argentina went a very long way in her substitution strategy, so that the costs of abandoning it were also bound to be high. Whether the liberalisation measures led to failure because they were introduced too rapidly or because the sequence was badly arranged was a question not easy to answer. In the end, one had to conclude that the blame must be put on both. Finally, Argentinian economic history showed that indexed assets had been well received by the public and that the ultimate beneficiaries of inflation could not be clearly established.

## 8  The Flow of Public and Private Financial Resources to Developing Countries – Führer*

The conclusions reached in the paper were supported by statistical information whose reliability might be questioned, in so far as it was not possible to reconcile it with information from other sources. For instance, the method of deflating the series of nominal figures was important since it determined the apparent effect of inflation on the level and the rate of growth of real GNP in each country; on the magnitude of external deficits; and on the inflow of foreign capitals. The results might also vary if the classification of countries were different, especially when some of them were regarded as developed, and if alternative criteria were used to measure per capita GNP.

The persistence in recent years of high interest rates, even though they may have affected developed and developing countries equally, had been harmful for the latter as a whole. They were net debtors and consequently not in a position to achieve a redistribution of

---

* The text of the introductory comments was not available.

income among themselves in the way that nations in the first category could. High interest payments were the source of a large proportion of the external deficits of the developing nations and of their need to devote most of their trade surpluses to meeting them. The situation was made even worse by two additional causes: first, the tendency to use fewer concessionary funds, as a proportion of total foreign financing, made the average interest rate rise for debtor countries; second; the developing countries could not reduce their imports of capital goods because these represented the way in which they obtained new technology. These short-term constraints could not be offset by an increase in American or European aid, especially since the present US administration was rather reluctant to grant this kind of support.

The complaints which the developing countries made on account of the inadequacy of the inflow of international funds had been directed towards the developed world, though the balance had been modified just a little by direct agreements between some oil-exporting countries and those lacking energy resources.

*Doctor Führer* did not find the use of statistics entirely satisfactory either, but he had not observed any methodological effort on the part of most international bureaucrats to unify the series for GNP, inflation, the economic characteristics of the countries, etc. In general, it could be said that the rate of increase of foreign debt in developing countries closely paralled their rate of economic growth. International financial turbulence had provoked a rapid reaction in recent years that had caused certain countries to overborrow. Nevertheless, the authorities in the International Monetary Fund and World Bank considered that these external deficits could no longer be sustained and that some sort of domestic adjustment was necessary. For its part, the oil-price rise had provoked an increase in world savings and their transfer to less-developed countries. Pessimism about the proposals for an increase in aid, as well as for greater American co-operation was shared by Dr. Führer. It was essential to put greater weight in future on support from multilateral financial institutions whose help was not tied (that is, did not have to be spent on the products of the lending country).

## 9   The Role of International Financial Markets – Rybczynski

*Doctor Scharrer* started by pointing out that the concept of a structural external deficit was too imprecise for practical application. First, in contrast to the cyclical deficit due to fluctuations in economic activity, it was not clear whether the oil-price increases led to a permanent deterioration of the balance of payments. Second, it was doubtful whether the systematic growth of the external deficit of certain countries (after the first and second oil crises) indicated a greater opportunity for investment. Third, international banks believed, or at least wished, that this situation would not persist, while the concept of structural deficit did. The existence of an external deficit must necessarily be connected with an increase in the investment GNP ratio and in the level of productivity, since these were the elements which constituted the difference between developed and developing countries. Otherwise, the latter were condemned to mere survival or to relying on official aid for their development. The flow of external loans had been concentrated on a few middle-income developing countries. In general, these had been the newly industrialising countries, like Brazil and Argentina, which had experienced a rapid increase in their rates of economic growth, to the detriment of other less-developed nations. Determining whether one had enough confidence in a country to grant it credit had been evaluated in the past by looking at the relationship between the cost of debt services and the level of exports. In so far as the balance on current account of debtor countries became negative, what should be looked at first was its ability to generate a greater production rather than the amount of its foreign exchange holdings. In parenthesis, it must be emphasised that the community of developed countries must be ready to accept a greater inflow of exports from developing countries.

Since the oil crisis, international banks had shown a trend towards providing funds without paying too much attention to whether productivity was growing and to the ability of their money to turn into domestic, reproducible capital. The gap between domestic saving and investment, which corresponded to the gap between imports and exports, was the result of an *ex post* identity and not of an *ex ante* relation reflecting the behaviour of economic agents. An attempt to increase savings in order to increase exports or to decrease imports might end up either by modifying neither, or by lowering the level of national income. The transformation of savings into exports would be made even more difficult if a country had an overvalued currency.

Foreign capital inflows had been accompanied by an increase in the receiving country's international reserves, without there being much economic reason for this. It was based, more than anything, on the desire to create a good image for future borrowing. This point of view could not hold universally, since the aggregate percentage of reserves relative to international trade did not seem to have changed much in recent years; and it might even have decreased.

The refinancing of foreign debts was one of the most important questions, both for developing countries and for international banking. The rich lending nations were not very ready to permit rescheduling since this meant that they would lose command over their assets, even though a delay in the repayment of principal did not imply disaster; much less the bankruptcy of a nation. Moreover, banks usually assumed that the government of their home country would, in the last resort, come to their rescue. The need for international banking institutions to evaluate countries afresh had to be confronted with the concept of structural deficits. Even when countries regarded loans from the International Monetary Fund as giving them an excuse to postpone certain necessary adjustments, the bankers' judgement did not seem very satisfactory. This made it essential to establish new patterns for supervising the international operations of banks. It was also essential to consider the proposal to create an intermediary agency between debtor countries and the international banks.

*Doctor Rybczynski* emphasised that the question dealt with in his paper was not whether there were a need for external financing of the developing countries; it concerned the degree of availability of funds in the international banking system. According to this point of view, what should be stressed was: (i) international banks were not altruistic institutions that could administer their resources without any efficiency criterion. This was all the more true when they managed private savings and had moved away from direct financing (which existed up to the 1930s), and where the effects of borrowers' insolvency fell upon investors; (ii) this transference of risk from individuals to financial institutions had created the danger of a loss of confidence and the possibility of an international financial collapse; (iii) the need to grant any kind of refinancing constituted a penalty for the institution involved. Financial problems could be attributed to the high volatility of present interest rates in developed countries; but that was not necessarily bad if it was the result of a restructuring of the world economy.

## 10   How to Manage a Repressed Economy – McKinnon*

Some implicit or explicit assumptions in a paper like this might be criticised because they lacked realism. First, an economy having the controls that it advocated required for such a task a quantity of productive resources, and especially a work-force, whose cost was, in most cases, greater than the resulting benefit, with a resultant net loss of welfare. Second, private sector financial assets might escape the inflationary tax through financial innovations, in whose invention the ingenuity of economic agents had been so fertile in recent times. Third, a pre-announced devaluation rate, fixed in accordance with the price of tradeables, could not prevent the feedback effect. Fourth, the substitution of direct government subsidies for credit subsidies in the form of reduced interest rates, although desirable, seldom occurred in practice. Fifth, the optimal reserve coefficient for bank deposits was not easy to determine in real-world situations. Sixth, the potential seignorage which a government could extract was very small compared with the rates of price increase in an inflationary economy. Even so, there seemed to be a question over the relative sizes of budget deficits and GNP. The connection between increases in the monetary base used to raise the reserves of the banking system and those which corresponded to loans used to finance budget deficits was not clear either. Finally, if the budget deficit was taken as a constant proportion of GNP, this seemed to imply that its very existence was undesirable. In fact, what was to be considered undesirable was the way in which it was financed.

Argentinian experience was that the elimination of the market for primary financial assets was the result of the inflationary process and of financial repression. The negative impact of inflation on financial assets could be overcome through the issue of indexed securities by the government, and this would help to avoid a complete substitution for private loans. In any case, the time-path of nominal interest rates, when they were liberalised, and the eventual occurrence of abnormally high real interest rates, was of fundamental importance: in such a situation, domestic borrowers would tend to resort to foreign credits.

The advice that one should deny domestic agents access to the foreign credit market is debatable. It seemed to stem from the reasoning that any foreign loan increased the international reserves

---

* The official discussant's text was not available.

of the monetary authorities, diminished the amount of money, increased income velocity and unleashed inflationary pressures. However this causal chain would depend essentially on the exchange-rate system. The restrictions on foreign capital inflows were due rather to the loss of control over the domestic economy.

No qualification was made in the paper about possible substitution between inflation and a higher growth of GNP. This was so even after the admission that holdings of real balances were reduced to a minimum and that the reserve coefficient on deposits was set at a level where price increases were minimised. If that substitution were to exist, inflation would depend not only on the quantity of monetary assets, but also on the distribution of credit between the private and the public sectors. It was likely that any decrease in the former's participation would result in a GNP reduction.

*Professor McKinnon* saw it as ironic that, having been a supporter of capital market freedom, he now had to recommend restrictions on the entry of international capital. This change of attitude was a consequence of having found that, in developing countries, the government had negative savings and did not have a market for its primary financial instruments. To finance its operations, such a government resorted to an inflationary tax under the guise of compulsory reserves for deposits in the financial system. The problem was then to find the reserve coefficient corresponding to the lowest inflation rate. By contrast with the Chicago economists, Professor McKinnon was not interested in determining the rate of inflation that might maximise fiscal revenue, but in the reserve coefficient for deposits – a species of taxation on the financial system – which would minimise the inflation rate for a given government deficit. As demand deposits were (almost) perfect substitutes for currency, a 100 per cent reserve coefficient would prevent the banks paying any interest at all; a reserve coefficient consistent with interest rates on term deposits and on lending was the result of a later optimisation process. The inflation rate and the differential between the interest rate paid to depositors and that charged to borrowers moved in the same direction. The call for the liberalisation of the entry of foreign capital was based on the need to avoid high interest rate differentials. Here the argument ran in the opposite direction: foreign capital inflows must be prohibited if there were to be an adequate base for higher taxation and to prevent any attempt to evade the domestic interest rate differential; otherwise that differential would be even bigger. Substitution between inflation and GNP was not considered in the analysis because at present there was a great deal of scepticism about it. Nevertheless, more rapid inflation would lead to a smaller quantity of sight deposits and probably a fall in GNP, so that the relation would be the converse of that postulated by the Phillips curve. Whether seignorage was great or small, whether a budget deficit was good or bad, it would always be advantageous to aim at the smallest possible inflation rate.

## 11 Oil Surplus Funds – El Beblawi

*Professor Kafka* expressed complete sympathy with the widespread fear that the funds coming from the oil-exporting countries might not match a greater need for investment in the less-developed economies. Nevertheless, Scenario III (financial investment) did not seem to differ from that with redistribution of income. This was because, in practice, it was difficult to determine whether an external deficit was due to a worsening of the terms of trade or to an increase in domestic investment. A deterioration in the terms of trade, and the institution of methods devised to cope with the corresponding external deficit, did not in any way mean a transfer of resources to be used in the investment process. The International Monetary Fund's oil facility, created to mitigate the effects of the price increase that took place in 1973, was aimed toward the developed European countries rather than the developing world. Even though concern over the way that the funds of the oil-exporting countries were converted into investment in the developing nations was commendable, the analysis in the paper was ambiguous about the way it took place in practice. On the one hand, the oil producers were in the embarrassing situation of being forced to sell oil against their wishes and to receive in exchange financial assets of uncertain future value. On the other hand, the underdeveloped world aspired to satisfy its basic needs as best it could. These two requirements might complement each other: this could be done by drawing on the enormous ability of the developed countries to produce basic goods, on their need for oil imports and on their corresponding ability to set free resources for development. It was unfortunate that the scenarios discussed did not provide a great deal of help for those drawing up plans to face such a challenge.

The additional savings originating in the surplus of the oil-exporting countries was not offset, at least not wholly, by an increase in investment. This gave rise to a Keynesian downward drift in world

GNP, which was a possible explanation for the international recession observed in recent years. The monetary policies followed by
most countries, and the accompanying high real interest rates, did
not help to stimulate investment. Despite the temporary fall in
interest rates immediately after the oil-price rise, the expected return
from investment seemed to have decreased even more, because of a
greater availability of funds and because of the recession in developed countries. The increase in the price of manufactured goods
which paralleled that of oil, favoured the developed world to the
detriment of the less-developed countries.

Assuming that a transfer of funds from the oil-exporting to the
less-developed nations were possible, everyone should be willing to
accept the deterioration in the terms of trade produced by the
increased prices, a point on which a general agreement had not yet
been reached. What had actually happened was that trade unions in
advanced economies had proved reluctant to accept changes in
relative prices that went against their interests; hence, the economic
authorities were put in the unenviable situation of having to choose
between unemployment or inflation (since nominal prices were in-
flexible downwards) and of having to permit an increase of the
capital/GNP ratio.

There was at least one alternative to a process whereby the oil
exporters could channel funds to these less-developed countries
which suffered from unfavourable terms of trade and high international interest rates. This would be increased investment in the
developed nations. In this way they could help to offset the secular
decline in productivity in the advanced economies.

*Professor Fahmi*, answering the comments on behalf of Professor
El Beblawi, pointed out that he was in a less favourable position to
reply than the author would have been. Nevertheless, he reiterated
that the paper was intended to consider the macroeconomic variables
involved in any consideration of the oil-price increases from the point
of view of those oil-exporting countries which were not able to use all
their additional revenue in importing goods and services. For them
oil, being a non-reproducible commodity, was an asset – hence their
interest in turning it into investment in developing countries. The
equality between savings and investment would always hold, despite
the redistributive income shifts imposed by the oil crisis. The restoration of this equality in *ex ante* terms required either an increase in
investment or net dissaving. A third possibility, a purely financial
reallocation, must be ruled out because of its inflationary effects.

## 12 External Financing and the Level of Development – Aliber

*Professor Borner* felt that his observations could be summarised under three main points. (i) There was the role played by multi-national corporations in the international financial framework. The risk associated with projects, and more specifically with countries, in effect was insured internally by multinational corporations. Their decisions did not depend purely on rates of return on capital, but also on their having the newest technology and also better abilities in economic management, both elements going hand-in-hand with their foreign investment. In any case, if the solution were insurance against the risks of international investment, the practice of insurance against import risks already existed. (ii) The different stages of financial development considered in the paper did not reflect what had really happened in less-developed countries. (iii) The underlying concept of static equilibrium (implied in the whole analysis) did not seem to be the most satisfactory way to deal with the issue.

Some of the participants took the view that the discussion was carried out substantially from the point of view of the foreign saver, the interest of the recipient country being scarcely taken into account. The benefits obtained through the inflow of foreign capital led, in practice, to an unequal distribution of income because they benefited a small minority of privileged people. An alternative typology of the developing countries would consider not only the traditional growth indicators, but also the institutions in which this growth took place. The institutional environment would also lead to better appraisal of the relationship between a country's external deficits and the way they were financed.

Country risk implied a cost to be added to the international interest rate. In so far as this risk was a function of the growth rate and the political stability of the country, it was not at all easy to determine. Until quite recently it was considered that countries could not go bankrupt and that the risk on that account was zero. The role played nowadays by the International Monetary Fund, a lender of last resort which was committed to provide funds to avoid problems in countries' balances of payments, had introduced distortion into the previous scheme. A growing aversion to country risk was reflected by the behaviour of both traditional international lenders, who had shown their trust in a small number of countries in the past, and that of the newly created financial institutions which had been added to them. This was also perceivable in the sensitivity of national agencies as they controlled banks that made foreign loans. The economic authorities of the borrowing countries worried more about the effect of country risk and the additional cost of their international loans than about the reduction of that risk itself. The latter might be achieved through substituting a fixed for a flexible exchange rate.

The financial attitude of the multinational corporations (MNCs) was the subject matter of a great deal of debate. In relation to their aggregate financing, one of two policies was present; either MNCs collected funds from various places at different costs, obtained a single interest rate and compared this with the rate of return from investment they might make in each country; or else they took into account domestic investment returns and the cost of local financing. In the first case, a tendency towards the internalisation of financial markets would be sufficient because the MNCs would distribute risk geographically, taking resources from developed to developing countries. In practice, in general multinationals followed the second path in order to take advantage of the local credit markets, usually subsidised, and also to provide a small amount of their own funds. The ultimate outcome of this action was to cause keen competition with, and a smaller availability of funds for, local enterprises. Foreign investment accompanied by transfers of technology, a desirable aim in itself, was not easily achieved.

It was pointed out, incidentally, that the productivity of the financial sector in developing countries was very low.

*Professor Aliber* himself emphasised that his paper did not imply any kind of value judgement and that it was not written with the interests of foreign investors in mind. He also reminded the conference that a few years ago the free flow of capital among nations was considered harmful by the American trade unions, and that Keynes himself expressed strong reservations against the foreign capital that contributed to the building of New York's underground railway system and ended up losing the savings of British investors. In contrast with the thesis that makes the financial development of a country depend upon the degree of its economic development, it was postulated here that the former depended upon the lowering of the cost of indirect finance. This cost was reduced as economic development proceeded because that development provided a better basis for evaluating risks and establishing their price. The development of the international financial structure was similar to that of the domestic market, starting with a first stage when external deficits were financed by official aid from the richer countries. This was followed by a stage of direct investment by foreign firms, and ended up with a stage where there was free movement of international capital.

Professor Aliber agreed with the observation that the cost of the financial sector in developing countries was very high, and that it led to large differentials between interest rates on loans and on deposits. Finally, country risk could not be actuarially insurable, except in a limited way.

## 13  Foreign Indebtedness and Economic Growth – Gutowski

*Doctor Hardy* emphasised that capital importing countries should not consider the rate of return on specific projects financed with foreign funds, but the average rate of return in the whole economy. To do so could lead creditors to wrong decisions. The unrestricted application of neoclassical theory to investment decisions in less-developed countries had several weaknesses. (i) The borrowing countries were not faced with a perfectly competitive international capital market which could provide as much credit as they wanted. (ii) Neoclassical rules were not applicable to such important commodity price changes as those which had resulted from the oil crisis. (iii) Creditors took into account the flow of funds (or liquidity) on external accounts; that is to say, they looked at the debtors' capacity to pay and not at the long-term economic outlook of the country. In the past, for example, the countries borrowing capital were able to count on loans with maturities from fifty to a hundred years. (iv) Countries were not private businesses, and creditors might attribute a high risk to them – which led to the penalty of not being granted credit. The present relationships, based on ability to service debt, were not satisfactory. Nevertheless, it was desirable for debtor countries to improve their administration of external funds, to abstain from projects whose only aim was prestige, to try to increase returns on their investment and to encourage their domestic capacity to save.

The principle that investments made with foreign funds must have a marginal productivity not lower than the international interest rate might be accepted if it could be reconciled with the traditional view that savings needs were a function of the growth rate. In this way, objections to the static connotations of the former view would be overcome by the dynamic aspects of the latter. Likewise, it was doubtful whether that relationship should refer to the marginal productivity of capital or to the time preference of the society in question. The equalisation of marginal productivities on projects financed with foreign funds and those financed by domestic resources gave a rational rule for evaluating how far a country needed to resort to foreign investment at different stages of its development. Unfortunately, this seemed far removed from practical applications. The difficulties would be even greater if it were accepted that complementing domestic with international capital was a necessary pre-condition for development, or at least that it would be convenient if it occurred.

From the foregoing analysis one had to infer that measuring the marginal productivity of capital became essential. If this had to be done, it should always be done *ex post*; and *ex ante* evaluation should be based on expectations, which did not always record the true productivity of investment. When there were no market forces to help in evaluating productivity, the policy-maker had to resort to other criteria (for example, supposing productivity constant over time) and these could turn out to be wrong. The most important problem, however, was to decide whether the marginal productivity of capital (or the rate of return on a specific project) was to be taken into account from an individual, or from a social point of view. If one accepted this last concept, one was immediately led to the problem of investing in the social and economic infrastructure and the problem of how to evaluate them. Investment in the infrastructure was generally a necessary condition for obtaining positive productivity in other sectors.

A rationalisation was made in the paper about foreign debt incurred for the purpose of paying interest on already outstanding debt. This was a new principle which had to be considered by nations in such a situation. This was in contrast to the conventional wisdom (adopted by international banking institutions) which considered flows of capital linked to monetary rather than physical phenomena. The need for new principles which could govern international investment decisions was today a consequence of the situation brought about by the oil crisis and by the fall in the rate of growth of the developing countries. The shaping of such principles would be assisted by economists when they proposed new criteria; the attitudes of the international banks might have rested on the old principles because they lacked new ones, even though it was true that the former principle had been to their own benefit.

*Professor Gutowski* pointed out that foreign creditors could base themselves on incorrect theoretical concepts, such as those which considered only the liquidity of their assets or led them to pay too little attention to investment in the infrastructure which required time to bear fruit. Foreign lenders granted credits to countries which they deemed trustworthy, leaving aside any other consideration. This tendency became even stronger when the risk of default was increased by unwise policies on the part of the debtor. One could not expect countries to implement policies that would bring about rapid increases in their exports or big reductions in their imports when they faced deficits in their balance of payments. The existence of national frontiers imposed additional constraints. For instance, Saudi Arabia's behaviour, even when it was concerned with the finance of foreign lending to other countries, would be different from that of a German 'Land' which must invest elsewhere in Germany. One could not accept the principle that one should devote national savings to the finance of investment in domestically produced goods and foreign savings to those of foreign origin. China might find herself forced to finance imports of food when the labour force engaged in her national production was set free to work on developing the economic or social infrastructure. Finally, the equalisation of the marginal productivities derived from the investment of foreign and domestic resources, and of these with the international interest rate, did not imply the acceptance of situations that lay within the production possibility frontier. The marginal efficiency of investment in less-developed countries was very small and generally below the international interest rate. Nevertheless, such a situation could be overcome only by an improvement in the quality of factors of production over time.

## 14 Exchange-Rate Policy, International Capital Movements and the Financing of Development – Kafka

*Doctor de la Dehesa* believed that sophisticated models should lead only to simple conclusions, given that part of the behaviour of economic agents in less-developed countries which aimed at avoiding complex and restrictive foreign exchange regulations. The apparent causal relationship between devaluation and a succeeding inflow of foreign capital was due to the fact that devaluation was always delayed because of the political costs involved; lags in export operations, leads in import payments, etc. which were carried out in view of an expected devaluation were accounted as inflows of capital. This required the formulation of a better definition of foreign capital flows, so as to establish whether these reacted to an exchange-rate variation (like a devaluation) or to a more permanent condition, when the domestic currency was undervalued (the level of the exchange rate was involved in such a case). In this last situation, causality might run from an overvaluation of foreign currencies to an inflow of capital. This was so even where the inflow of capital later produced a revaluation of the domestic currency, as seemed to have happened in some countries after 1973. All undervaluation of currencies, by reducing the real value of monetary assets, reduced domestic savings and induced foreign savings; nevertheless, the conclusions might be reversed when a devaluation was expected. Restrictions on foreign trade represented a road to the overvaluation of the domestic currency. Therefore they usually facilitated either the inflow of capital goods from other countries, or local production with cheap imported inputs. Finally, the assertion that foreign saving did not substitute for domestic saving could not be reconciled with the finding stated by Newlyn that half of foreign funds went to consumption; in any case, foreign capital flows reduced interest rates, and as a result reduced potential domestic saving and credit.

The very concept of the overvaluation of a currency was quite imprecise. This was because it might refer either to an exchange rate that established equilibrium in the trade balance or in payments on current account, or to some version of purchasing power parity theory. In any case, the existence of some kind of equilibrium situation seemed essential if one were to carry out any meaningful comparison. The behaviour of the central bank became an insufficient criterion by which to judge whether a given exchange rate was over- or undervalued. An exchange rate could be maintained out of equilibrium for a considerable time, as with West Germany, where a kind of confidence bonus allowed international capital to move freely either in or out according to the risks assumed by the economic agents.

An explanation of the overvaluation of the domestic currency found at present in some developing countries held that this was a temporary phenomenon, attributable to the oil-price increase. This brought about a fall in their real production so that they had to resort to foreign borrowing if they were unwilling to reduce their consumption. When the growth process was renewed, any possible overvaluation would disappear. This overvaluation also served to increase the price of capital goods sold by developed countries, so that the terms of trade of the developing countries deteriorated even more.

Those situations where capital inflows occurred side by side with overvaluation seemed to be a phenomenon of developed countries caused by cyclical changes that took place every two or four years, with shifts to positions above or below the equilibrium exchange rate.

The respective advantages of fixed or floating parities for the exchange rate did not run in only one direction. The short-term changes implicit in moving to a floating rate could not help to make investment decisions simple, but they could have the right effect on the price of the exports of those countries that were reluctant to devalue. A floating rate system would also increase the cost of servicing foreign debt if the currency in which the debt was denominated enjoyed an appreciation.

*Professor Kafka* pointed out that there was a widespread scepticism about the significance of certain economic variables, for example, the international interest rate in an environment which was full of restrictions, like the exchange market in a developing country. The same sentiment applied when behaviour in developed nations was extrapolated to developing countries, even though the presence of multinational corporations should justify it. Overvaluation of the exchange rate, whether sustainable or not, was a disequilibrium concept, and did not refer to a specific earlier period. Its identification rested on the perceptions of the international community, on the relationship between reserves and imports, etc. The non-substitutability of domestic and foreign savings was based on Brazilian experience, where devaluation stimulated imports of capital goods. The advantages of systems with fixed or floating parities were very similar but, whichever system a developing country chose, this had a kind of negative confidence bonus for the developed world.

## 15 New Approaches to Development Finance – Thygesen

*Doctor Rweyemamu* began his comments with three proposals of the Brandt Report which concerned the International Monetary Fund and international monetary reform. The prospect of greater use of Special Drawing Rights was a rather gloomy one, although at present these SDRs gave a competitive interest rate. This was not only for political reasons, but also because the fact that there were few strictly economic advantages in respect of international currencies (basically, the dollar) conspired against their general use. This was, first, because the seignorage earned by a few rich nations – measured as the interest-rate differential between that charged by the international banks for their loans and that on the Special Drawing Rights

– disappeared; second, because SDRs represented unconditional liquidity. The enlargement of the IMF's lending capacity gave rise to conditional aid; only with certain limitations could this not be equally applicable to compensatory financing. Neither had this increase in the IMF's resources restored it to the proportion of international transactions it had in the 1950s and 1960s. Recent experience showed that this enlargement did not seem to have been flexible enough, or without problems for the less-developed countries. As for the proposals to enlarge the transfer of resources from developed to developing countries, taxation of the income of the former did not appear to be practicable, though it was certainly possible to expand the inflow of concessional funds and to increase the less-developed countries' capacity to obtain loans. Two principles discussed in the paper might be interpreted as giving rules for a new approach to the financing of development. On the one hand, there was the need to restore the confidence of creditors' participation in developing countries by means of reports, IMF, etc. especially for the developing countries which needed credit refinancing programmes. On the other hand, greater stability in international financial relations (subsequent to a stronger presence of the Fund) and the adoption of the Special Drawing Right was necessary as the preponderant asset in future international transactions.

Making a distinction between problems associated with the long-term financing of development and those resulting from current deficits in balances of payments, and then assigning the task of solving the former to the World Bank and of the latter to the International Monetary Fund, became rather artificial in practice. The climate of financial restrictions had been improved by increasing the potential assets of the Fund and by giving it the ability to grant loans with longer maturities. This change had turned out to be hardly adequate for enabling the less-developed countries to face the additional burden imposed by floating exchange rates – a system which they found themselves ill prepared to manage in a satisfactory way.

As had been explained, an international tax that would allow the transfer of a fixed proportion of the developed countries' income to the less-developed world, though desirable, had little chance of being introduced: the developed nations had to solve their own problems and to endure their own domestic pressures. If a tax were introduced on their GNP, one would have to expect that other kinds of concessional aid would be reduced so as to maintain the same aggregate burden on the developed countries as in the past. Incidentally, although the advanced capitalist countries often argued in favour of a great reliance on the market (and belief in it) they did not often follow this principle themselves (as happened with the agricultural policy of the European Economic Community).

An alternative repeatedly recommended was to assign Special Drawing Rights exclusively to the developing countries, their total amount being determined by the developed nations in such a way as to avoid inflationary pressures. Leaving aside the fact that these inflationary effects had been over-emphasised, the benefits of such an arrangement aroused a great scepticism. This was becuse the recipient debtor countries would gain only from the interest differential (between the market rate and the interest rate on Special Drawing Rights) and this was not very different from the risk premium assigned to each country. These considerations might well be more appropriate to discussions of a more general framework for a new system of international finance and monetary structure. The Brandt Report did not question the arrangements which resulted from the Bretton Woods agreements, but accepted the logic of the system exactly as it was.

*Professor Thygesen* replied that the Brandt Report clearly had a praiseworthy purpose, but that its reception in academic and official circles (inclined towards a greater international equity) was not very enthusiastic. That was because automatic or unconditional income transfers were much criticised in their own countries. The Report did not put enough emphasis on domestic policies and was too critical of existing institutions. However, the aggregate credit capacity of the World Bank and of the International Monetary Fund had shown a dramatic increase in recent years, with more effective results than would come from many of the proposals contained in the Report. In particular, the Report was too optimistic about issues which could have only a marginal impact. For instance, the rescheduling of certain developing countries' foreign debt must always be an exceptional event, and subject to some ordered arrangement. Finally, if the allocation of Special Drawing Rights exclusively among developing countries were to be accepted, the no less important problem of establishing the criteria for assigning them would still remain.

# Index

349